D1358105

# BIOGRAPHIES

OF

# DISTINGUISHED SCIENTIFIC MEN.

# BIOGRAPHIES

OF

## DISTINGUISHED SCIENTIFIC MEN.

BY FRANÇOIS ARAGO

TRANSLATED BY

ADMIRAL W. H. SMYTH

THE REV. BADEN POWELL

AND

ROBERT GRANT

FIRST SERIES

*Essay Index Reprint Series*

BOOKS FOR LIBRARIES PRESS

FREEPORT, NEW YORK

First Published 1859
Reprinted 1972

Library of Congress Cataloging in Publication Data

Arago, Dominique François Jean, 1786-1853.
    Biographies of distinguished scientific men.

    (Essay index reprint series)
    Reprint of the 1859 ed.
    CONTENTS: 1st ser. The history of my youth.
--Bailly.--Herschel. [etc.]
    1. Scientists--Biographies. I. Title.
Q141.A65  1972        509'.22 [B]        72-39662
ISBN 0-8369-2737-0

PRINTED IN THE UNITED STATES OF AMERICA
BY
NEW WORLD BOOK MANUFACTURING CO., INC.
HALLANDALE, FLORIDA 33009

# TRANSLATORS' PREFACE.

THE present volume of the series of English translations of M. Arago's works consists of his own autobiography and a selection of some of his memoirs of eminent scientific men, both continental and British.

It does not distinctly appear at what period of his life Arago composed the autobiography, but it bears throughout the characteristic stamp of his ardent and energetic disposition. The reader will, perhaps, hardly suppress a smile at the indications of self-satisfaction with which several of the incidents are brought forward, while the air of romance which invests some of the adventures may possibly give rise to some suspicion of occasional embellishment; on these points, however, we leave each reader to judge for himself. In relation to the history of science, this memoir gives some interesting par-

ticulars, which disclose to us much of the interior spirit of the Academy of Sciences, not
always of a kind the most creditable to some
of Arago's former contemporaries.

But a far higher interest will be found to
belong to those eloquent memoirs, or éloges of
eminent departed men of science, who had attained the distinction of being members of the
Academy.

In these the reader will find a luminous,
eminently simple, and popular account of the
discoveries of each of those distinguished individuals, of a kind constituting in fact a brief
history of the particular branch of science to
which he was devoted. And in the selection
included in the present volume, which constitutes but a portion of the entire series, we have
comprised the accounts of men of such varied
pursuits as to convey no inadequate impression
of the progress of discovery throughout a considerable range of the whole field of the physical sciences within the last half century.

The account given by the author, of the principal discoveries made by the illustrious subjects
of his memoirs, is in general very luminous,
but at the same time presupposes a familiarity
with some parts of science which may not
really be possessed by all readers. For the

sake of a considerable class, then, we have
taken occasion, wherever the use of new technical terms or other like circumstances seemed
to require it, to introduce original notes and
commentaries, sometimes of considerable extent,
by the aid of which we trust the scientific principles adverted to in the text will be rendered
easily intelligible to the general reader.

In some few instances also we have found
ourselves called upon to adopt a more critical
tone; where we were disposed to dissent from
the view taken by the author on particular
questions of a controversial kind, or when he
is arguing in support, or in refutation, of opposing theories on some points of science not
yet satisfactorily cleared up.

We could have wished that our duty as
translators and editors had not extended beyond such mere occasional scientific or literary
criticism. But there unfortunately seemed to
be one or two points where, in pronouncing on
the claims of distinguished individuals, or criti-
cizing their inventions, a doubt could not but
be felt as to the perfect *fairness* of Arago's
judgment, and in which we were constrained
to express an unfavourable opinion on the manner in which the relative pretensions of men of
the highest eminence seemed to be decided, in-

volving what might sometimes be fairly regarded as undue prejudice, or possibly a feeling
of personal or even national jealousy. Much
as we should deprecate the excitement of any
feeling of hostility of this kind, yet we could
not, in our editorial capacity, shrink from the
plain duty of endeavouring to advocate what
appeared to us right and true; and we trust
that whatever opinion may be entertained as
to the *conclusions* to which we have come on
such points, we shall not have given ground
for any complaint that we have violated any
due courtesy or propriety in our *mode* of expressing those conclusions, or the reasons on
which they are founded.

# CONTENTS.

## THE HISTORY OF MY YOUTH.

## HERSCHEL.

# LIVES

OF

# DISTINGUISHED SCIENTIFIC MEN.

---

## THE HISTORY OF MY YOUTH:

### AN AUTOBIOGRAPHY OF FRANCIS ARAGO.

I HAVE not the foolish vanity to imagine that any one, even a short time hence, will have the curiosity to find out how my first education was given, and how my mind was developed ; but some biographers, writing off hand and without authority, having given details on this subject utterly incorrect, and of a nature to imply negligence on the part of my parents, I consider myself bound to put them right.

I was born on the 26th of February, 1786, in the commune of Estagel, an ancient province of Roussillon (department of the Eastern Pyrenees). My father, a licentiate in law, had some little property in arable land, in vineyards, and in plantations of olive-trees, the income from which supported his numerous family.

I was thus three years old in 1789, four years old in 1790, five years in 1791, six years in 1792, and seven years old in 1793, &c.

The reader has now himself the means of judging
whether, as has been said, and even stated in print, I had
a hand in the excesses of our first revolution.

My parents sent me to the primary school in Estagel,
where I learnt the rudiments of reading and writing    I
received, besides, in my father's house, some private lessons in vocal music.   I was not otherwise either more or
less advanced than other children of my age.   I enter
into these details merely to show how much mistaken are
those who have printed that at the age of fourteen or fifteen years I had not yet learnt to read.

Estagel was a halting-place for a portion of the troops
who, coming from the interior, either went on to Perpignan, or repaired direct to the army of the Pyrenees.
My parents' house was therefore constantly full of officers and soldiers.   This, joined to the lively excitement
which the Spanish invasion had produced within me, inspired me with such decided military tastes, that my
family was obliged to have me narrowly watched to prevent my joining by stealth the soldiers who left Estagel.
It often happened that they caught me at a league's distance from the village, already on my way with the
troops.

On one occasion these warlike tastes had nearly cost
me dear.   It was the night of the battle of Peires-Tortes.
The Spanish troops in their retreat had partly mistaken
their road.   I was in the square of the village before
daybreak ; I saw a brigadier and five troopers come up,
who, at the sight of the tree of liberty, called out, " *So-
mos perdidos !* "   I ran immediately to the house to arm
myself with a lance which had been left there by a soldier of the *levée en masse*, and placing myself in ambush
at the corner of a street, I struck with a blow of this

weapon the brigadier placed at the head of the party. The wound was not dangerous; a cut of the sabre, however, was descending to punish my hardihood, when some countrymen came to my aid, and, armed with forks, overturned the five cavaliers from their saddles, and made them prisoners. I was then seven years old.*

My father having gone to reside at Perpignan, as treasurer of the mint, all the family quitted Estagel to follow him there. I was then placed as an out-door pupil at the municipal college of the town, where I occupied myself almost exclusively with my literary studies. Our classic authors had become the objects of my favourite reading. But the direction of my ideas became changed all at once by a singular circumstance which I will relate.

Walking one day on the ramparts of the town, I saw an officer of engineers who was directing the execution of the repairs. This officer, M. Cressac, was very young; I had the hardihood to approach him, and to ask him how he had succeeded in so soon wearing an epaulette. "I come from the Polytechnic School," he answered. "What school is that?" "It is a school which one enters by an examination." "Is much expected of the candidates?" "You will see it in the programme which the Government sends every year to the departmental administration; you will find it moreover in the numbers of the journal of the school, which are in the library of the central school."

I ran at once to the library, and there, for the first time, I read the programme of the knowledge required in the candidates.

---

* With such precocious heroism it is by no means so clear that the author might not have had a hand in the revolution, from which he endeavours above to exculpate himself.

From this moment I abandoned the classes of the central school, where I was taught to admire Corneille, Racine, La Fontaine, Molière, and attended only the mathematical course. This course was entrusted to a retired ecclesiastic, the Abbé Verdier, a very respectable man, but whose knowledge went no further than the elementary course of La Caille. I saw at a glance that M. Verdier's lessons would not be sufficient to secure my admission to the Polytechnic School; I therefore decided on studying by myself the newest works, which I sent for from Paris. These were those of Legendre, Lacroix, and Garnier. In going through these works I often met with difficulties which exceeded my powers; happily, strange though it be, and perhaps without example in all the rest of France, there was a proprietor at Estagel, M. Raynal, who made the study of the higher mathematics his recreation. It was in his kitchen, whilst giving orders to numerous domestics for the labours of the next day, that M. Raynal read with advantage the "Hydraulic Architecture" of Prony, the "Mécanique Analytique," and the "Mécanique Céleste." This excellent man often gave me useful advice; but I must say that I found my real master in the cover of M. Garnier's "Treatise on Algebra." This cover consisted of a printed leaf, on the outside of which blue paper was pasted. The reading of the page not covered made me desirous to know what the blue paper hid from me. I took off this paper carefully, having first damped it, and was able to read underneath it the advice given by d'Alembert to a young man who communicated to him the difficulties which he met with in his studies: "Go on, sir, go on, and conviction will come to you."

This gave me a gleam of light; instead of persisting

in attempts to comprehend at first sight the propositions before me, I admitted their truth provisionally ; I went on further, and was quite surprised, on the morrow, that I comprehended perfectly what overnight appeared to me to be encompassed with thick clouds.

I thus made myself master, in a year and a half, of all the subjects contained in the programme for admission, and I went to Montpellier to undergo the examination. I was then sixteen years of age. M. Monge, junior, the examiner, was detained at Toulouse by indisposition, and wrote to the candidates assembled at Montpellier that he would examine them in Paris. I was myself too unwell to undertake so long a journey, and I returned to Perpignan.

There I listened for a moment to the solicitations of my family, who pressed me to renounce the prospects which the Polytechnic School opened. But my taste for mathematical studies soon carried the day ; I increased my library with Euler's " Introduction à l'Analyse Infinitésimale," with the " Résolution des Equations Numériques," with Lagrange's " Théorie des Fonctions Analytiques," and " Mécanique Analytique," and finally with Laplace's " Mécanique Céleste." I gave myself up with great ardour to the study of these books. From the journal of the Polytechnic School containing such investigations as those of M. Poisson on Elimination, I imagined that all the pupils were as much advanced as this geometer, and that it would be necessary to rise to this height to succeed.

From this moment, I prepared myself for the artillery service,—the aim of my ambition; and as I had heard that an officer ought to understand music, fencing, and dancing, I devoted the first hours of each day to the cultivation of these accomplishments.

The rest of the time I was seen walking in the moats of the citadel of Perpignan, seeking by more or less forced transitions to pass from one question to another, so as to be sure of being able to show the examiner how far my studies had been carried.*

At last the moment of examination arrived, and I went to Toulouse in company with a candidate who had studied at the public college. It was the first time that pupils from Perpignan had appeared at the competition. My intimidated comrade was completely discomfited. When I repaired after him to the board, a very singular

---

* Méchain, member of the Academy of Sciences and of the Institute, was charged in 1792 with the prolongation of the measure of the arc of the meridian in Spain as far as Bärcelona.

During his operations in the Pyrenees, in 1794, he had known my father, who was one of the administrators of the department of the Eastern Pyrenees. Later, in 1803, when the question was agitated as to the continuation of the measure of the meridian line as far as the Balearic Islands, M. Méchain went again to Perpignan, and came to pay my father a visit. As I was about setting off to undergo the examination for admission at the Polytechnic School, my father ventured to ask him whether he could not recommend me to M. Monge. " Willingly," answered he; " but, with the frankness which is my characteristic, I ought not to leave you unaware that it appears to me improbable that your son, left to himself, can have rendered himself completely master of the subjects of which the programme consists. If, however, he be admitted, let him be destined for the artillery, or for the engineers; the career of the sciences, of which you have talked to me, is really too difficult to go through, and unless he had a special calling for it, your son would only find it deceptive." Anticipating a little the order of dates, let us compare this advice with what occurred: I went to Toulouse, underwent the examination, and was admitted; one year and a half afterwards I filled the situation of secretary at the Observatory, which had become vacant by the resignation of M. Méchain's son; one year and a half later, that is to say, four years after the Perpignan " horoscope," associated with M. Biot, I filled the place, in Spain, of the celebrated academician who had died there, a victim to his labours.

conversation took place between M. Monge (the examiner) and me.

"If you are going to answer like your comrade, it is useless for me to question you."

"Sir, my comrade knows much more than he has shown; I hope I shall be more fortunate than he; but what you have just said to me might well intimidate me and deprive me of all my powers."

"Timidity is always the excuse of the ignorant; it is to save you from the shame of a defeat that I make you the proposal of not examining you."

"I know of no greater shame than that which you now inflict upon me. Will you be so good as to question me? it is your duty."

"You carry yourself very high, sir! We shall see presently whether this be a legitimate pride."

"Proceed, sir; I wait for you."

M. Monge then put to me a geometrical question, which I answered in such a way as to diminish his prejudices. From this he passed on to a question in algebra, to the resolution of a numerical equation. I had the work of Lagrange at my fingers' ends; I analyzed all the known methods, pointing out their advantages and defects; Newton's method, the method of recurring series, the method of depression, the method of continued fractions,—all were passed in review; the answer had lasted an entire hour. Monge, brought over now to feelings of great kindness, said to me, "I could, from this moment, consider the examination at an end. I will, however, for my own pleasure, ask you two more questions. What are the relations of a curved line to the straight line which is a tangent to it?" I looked upon this question as a particular case of the theory of osculations which I

had studied in Legrange's " Fonctions Analytiques."
" Finally," said the examiner to me, " how do you determine the tension of the various cords of which a
funicular machine is composed ? " I treated this problem according to the method expounded in the " Mécanique Analytique." It was clear that Lagrange had
supplied all the resources of my examination.

I had been two hours and a quarter at the board.
M. Monge, going from one extreme to the other, got up,
came and embraced me, and solemnly declared that I
should occupy the first place on his list.   Shall I confess
it ?   During the examination of my comrade I had heard
the Toulousian candidates uttering not very favourable
sarcasms on the pupils from Perpignan ; and it was
principally for the sake of reparation to my native town
that M. Monge's behaviour and declaration transported
me with joy.

Having entered the Polytechnic School, at the end of
1803, I was placed in the excessively boisterous brigade
of the Gascons and Britons.   I should have much liked
to study thoroughly physics and chemistry, of which I
did not even know the first rudiments ; but the behaviour
of my companions rarely left me any time for it.   As
for analysis, I had already, before entering the Polytechnic School, learnt much more than was required for
leaving it.

I have just related the strange words which M. Monge,
junior, addressed to me at Toulouse in commencing my
examination for admission.   Something analogous occurred at the opening of my examination in mathematics
for passing from one division of the school to another.
The examiner, this time, was the illustrious geometer
Legendre, of whom, a few years after, I had the honour
of becoming the colleague and the friend.

I entered his study at the moment when M. T——,
who was to undergo his examination before me, having
fainted away, was being carried out in the arms of two
servants. I thought that this circumstance would have
moved and softened M. Legendre; but it had no such
effect. " What is your name," he said to me sharply.
"Arago," I answered. " You are not French then?"
" If I was not French I should not be before you; for I
have never heard of any one being admitted into the
school unless his nationality had been proved." " I
maintain that he is not French whose name is Arago."
" I maintain, on my side, that I am French, and a very
good Frenchman too, however strange my name may
appear to you." " Very well; we will not discuss the
point farther; go to the board."

I had scarcely taken up the chalk, when M. Legendre,
returning to the first subject of his preoccupations, said
to me: " You were born in one of the departments recently united to France?" " No, sir; I was born in the
department of the Eastern Pyrenees, at the foot of the
Pyrenees." "Oh! why did you not tell me that at once?
all is now explained. You are of Spanish origin, are
you not?" " Possibly; but in my humble family there
are no authentic documents preserved which could enable
me to trace back the civil position of my ancestors; each
one there is the child of his own deeds. I declare to you
again that I am French, and that ought to be sufficient
for you."

The vivacity of this last answer had not disposed M.
Legendre in my favour. I saw this very soon; for, having put a question to me which required the use of
double integrals, he stopped me, saying: " The method
which you are following was not given to you by the

1*

professor. Whence did you get it?" "From one of
your papers." "Why did you choose it? was it to bribe
me?" "No; nothing was farther from my thoughts.
I only adopted it because it appeared to me preferable."
"If you are unable to explain to me the reasons for your
preference, I declare to you that you shall receive a bad
mark, at least as to character."

I then entered upon the details which established, as I
thought, that the method of double integrals was in all
points more clear and more rational than that which
Lacroix had expounded to us in the amphitheatre.
From this moment Legendre appeared to me to be satisfied, and to relent.

Afterwards, he asked me to determine the centre of
gravity of a spherical sector. "The question is easy,"
I said to him. "Very well; since you find it easy, I
will complicate it: instead of supposing the density constant, I will suppose that it varies from the centre to the
surface according to a determined function." I got
through this calculation very happily; and from this
moment I had entirely gained the favour of the examiner. Indeed, on my retiring, he addressed to me
these words, which, coming from him, appeared to my
comrades as a very favourable augury for my chance of
promotion: "I see that you have employed your time
well; go on in the same way the second year, and we
shall part very good friends."

In the mode of examination adopted at the Polytechnic
School in 1804, which is always cited as being better
than the present organization, room was allowed for the
exercise of some unjustifiable caprices. Would it be
believed, for example, that the old M. Barruel examined
two pupils at a time in physics, and gave them, it is said,

the same mark, which was the mean between the actual
merits of the two? For my part, I was associated with
a comrade full of intelligence, but who had not studied
this branch of the course. We agreed that he should
leave the answering to me, and we found the arrangement advantageous to both.

As I have been led to speak of the school as it was in
1804, I will say that its faults were less those of organization than those of personal management; for many of
the professors were much below their office, a fact which
gave rise to somewhat ridiculous scenes. The pupils, for
instance, having observed the insufficiency of M. Hassenfratz, made a demonstration of the dimensions of the
rainbow, full of errors of calculation, but in which the
one compensated the other so that the final result was
true. The professor, who had only this result whereby
to judge of the goodness of the answer, when he saw it
appear on the board, did not hesitate to call out, " Good,
good, perfectly good! " which excited shouts of laughter
on all the benches of the amphitheatre.

When a professor has lost consideration, without which
it is impossible for him to do well, they allow themselves
to insult him to an incredible extent. Of this I will cite
a single specimen.

A pupil, M. Leboullenger, met one evening in company this same M. Hassenfratz, and had a discussion
with him. When he reëntered the school in the morning, he mentioned this circumstance to us. " Be on your
guard," said one of our comrades to him; " you will be
interrogated this evening. Play with caution, for the
professor has certainly prepared some great difficulties
so as to cause laughter at your expense."

Our anticipations were not mistaken. Scarcely had

the pupils arrived in the amphitheatre, when M. Hassenfratz called to M. Leboullenger, who came to the board.

" M. Leboullenger," said the professor to him, " you
have seen the moon ? " " No, sir." " How, sir ! you
say that you have never seen the moon ? " ·" I can only
repeat my answer—no, sir." Beside himself, and seeing
his prey escape him, by means of this unexpected answer,
M. Hassenfratz addressed himself to the inspector charged
with the observance of order that day, and said to him,
" Sir, there is M. Leboullenger, who pretends never to
have seen the moon." " What would you wish me to
do ? " stoically replied M. Le Brun. Repulsed on this
side, the professor turned once more towards M. Leboullenger, who remained calm and earnest in the midst of
the unspeakable amusement of the whole amphitheatre,
and cried out with undisguised anger, " You persist in
maintaining that you have never seen the moon ? "
" Sir," returned the pupil, " I should deceive you if I
told you that I had not heard it spoken of, but I have
never seen it." " Sir, return to your place."

After this scene, M. Hassenfratz was but a professor
in name ; his teaching could no longer be of any use.

At the commencement of the second year, I was appointed "*chef de brigade.*" Hatchette had been professor
of hydrography at Collioure ; his friends from Roussillon
recommended me to him. He received me with great
kindness, and even gave me a room in his lodgings. It
was there that I had the pleasure of making Poisson's
acquaintance, who lived next to us. Every evening the
great geometer entered my room, and we passed entire
hours in conversing on politics and mathematics, which
is certainly not quite the same thing.

In the course of 1804, the school was a prey to politi-

cal passions, and that through the fault of the government.

They wished forthwith to oblige the pupils to sign an
address of congratulation on the discovery of the conspir-
acy in which Moreau was implicated.  They refused to
do so on the ground that it was not for them to pronounce
on a cause which had been in the hands of justice.  It
must, however, be remarked, that Moreau had not yet
dishonoured himself by taking service in the Russian
army, which had come to attack the French under the
walls of Dresden.

The pupils were invited to make a manifestation in
favour of the institution of the Legion of Honour.  This
again they refused.  They knew well that the cross,
given without inquiry and without control, would be, in
most cases, the recompense of charlatanism, and not of
true merit.

The transformation of the Consular into the Imperial
Government gave rise to very animated discussions in
the interior of the school.

Many pupils refused to add their felicitations to the
mean adulations of the constituted bodies.

General Lacuée, who was appointed governor of the
school, reported this opposition to the Emperor.

" M. Lacuée," cried Napoleon, in the midst of a group
of courtiers, who applauded with speech and gesture,
" you cannot retain at the school those pupils who have
shown such ardent Republicanism ; you will send them
away."  Then, collecting himself, he added, " I will first
know their names and their stages of promotion."  Seeing the list the next day, he did not proceed further than
the first name, which was the first in the artillery.  " I
will not drive away the first men in advancement," said

he. " Ah! if they had been at the bottom of the list!
M. Lacuée, leave them alone."

Nothing was more curious than the *séance* to which
General Lacuée came to receive the oath of obedience
from the pupils. In the vast amphitheatre which contained them, one could not discern a trace of the gravity
which such a ceremony should inspire. The greater
part, instead of answering, at the call of their names, " I
swear it," cried out, " Present."

All at once the monotony of this scene was interrupted
by a pupil, son of the Conventionalist Brissot, who called
out in a stentorian voice, " I will not take the oath of
obedience to the Emperor." Lacuée, pale and with little
presence of mind, ordered a detachment of armed pupils
placed behind him to go and arrest the recusant. The
detachment, of which I was at the head, refused to obey.
Brissot, addressing himself to the General, with the
greatest calmness said to him, " Point out the place to
which you wish me to go ; do not force the pupils to dis-
honour themselves by laying hands on a comrade who
has no desire to resist."

The next morning Brissot was expelled.

About this time, M. Méchain, who had been sent to
Spain to prolong the meridional line as far as Formentera, died at Castellon de la Plana. His son, Secretary
at the Observatory, immediately gave in his resignation.
Poisson offered me the situation. I declined his first
proposal. I did not wish to renounce the military career,
—the object of all my predilections, and in which, moreover, I was assured of the protection of Marshal Lannes,
—a friend of my father's. Nevertheless I accepted, on
trial, the position offered me in the Observatory, after a
visit which I made to M. de Laplace in company with

M. Poisson, under the express condition that I could re-enter the Artillery if that should suit me. It was from this cause that my name remained inscribed on the list of the pupils of the school. I was only detached to the Observatory on a special service.

I entered this establishment, then, on the nomination of Poisson, my friend, and through the intervention of Laplace. The latter loaded me with civilities. I was happy and proud when I dined in the Rue de Tournon with the great geometer. My mind and my heart were much disposed to admire all, to respect all, that was connected with him who had discovered the cause of the secular equation of the moon, had found in the movement of this planet the means of calculating the ellipticity of the earth, had traced to the laws of attraction the long inequalities of Jupiter and of Saturn, &c. &c. But what was my disenchantment, when one day I heard Madame de Laplace, approaching her husband, say to him, " Will you entrust to me the key of the sugar ? "

Some days afterwards, a second incident affected me still more vividly. M. de Laplace's son was preparing for the examinations of the Polytechnic School. He came sometimes to see me at the Observatory. In one of his visits I explained to him the method of continued fractions, by help of which Lagrange obtains the roots of numerical equations. The young man spoke of it to his father with admiration. I shall never forget the rage which followed the words of Emile de Laplace, and the severity of the reproaches which were addressed to me, for having patronized a mode of proceeding which may be very long in theory, but which evidently can in no way be found fault with on the score of its elegance and precision. Never had a jealous prejudice shown itself more openly, or under a more bitter form. "Ah!" said I to myself, "how true was the inspiration of the ancients when they attributed weaknesses to him who nevertheless made Olympus tremble by a frown!"

Here I should mention, in order of time, a circumstance which might have produced the most fatal consequences for me. The fact was this: —

I have described above, the scene which caused the expulsion of Brissot's son from the Polytechnic School. I had entirely lost sight of him for several months, when he came to pay me a visit at the Observatory, and placed me in the most delicate, the most terrible, position that an honest man ever found himself in.

"I have not seen you," he said to me, "because since leaving the school I have practised daily firing with a pistol; I have now acquired a skill beyond the common, and I am about to employ it in ridding France of the tyrant who has confiscated all her liberties. My measures are taken: I have hired a small room on the Carrousel, close to the place by which Napoleon, on coming out from the court, will pass to review the cavalry; from the humble window of my apartment will the ball be fired which will go through his head."

I leave it to be imagined with what despair I received this confidence. I made every imaginable effort to deter Brissot from his sinister project; I remarked how all those wno had rushed on enterprises of this nature had been branded in history by the odious title of assassin. Nothing succeeded in shaking his fatal resolution; I only obtained from him a promise on his honour that the execution of it should be postponed for a time, and I put myself in quest of means for rendering it abortive.

The idea of announcing Brissot's project to the author-

ities did not even enter my thoughts.  It seemed a fatality which came to smite me, and of which I must undergo
the consequences, however serious they might be.

I counted much on the solicitations of Brissot's mother,
already so cruelly tried during the revolution.  I went to
her home, in the Rue de Condé, and implored her earnestly to coöperate with me in preventing her son from
carrying out his sanguinary resolution.  "Ah, sir," replied this lady, who was naturally a model of gentleness,
"if Silvain" (this was the name of her son) "believes
that he is accomplishing a patriotic duty, I have neither
the intention nor the desire to turn him from his project."

It was from myself that I must henceforth draw all my
resources.  I had remarked that Brissot was addicted to
the composition of romances and pieces of poetry.  I
encouraged this passion, and every Sunday, above all,
when I knew that there would be a review, I went to
fetch him, and drew him into the country, in the environs
of Paris.  I listened then complacently to the reading
of those chapters of his romance which he had composed
during the week.

The first excursions frightened me a little, for armed
with his pistols, Brissot seized every occasion of showing
his great skill; and I reflected that this circumstance
would lead to my being considered as his accomplice, if
he ever carried out his project.  At last, his pretensions
to literary fame, which I flattered to the utmost, the
hopes (though I had none myself) which I led him to
conceive of the success of an attachment of which he
had confided the secret to me, made him receive with attention the reflections which I constantly made to him on
his enterprise.  He determined on making a journey be-

yond the seas, and thus relieved me from the most serious anxiety which I have experienced in all my life.

Brissot died after having covered the walls of Paris with printed handbills in favour of the Bourbon restoration.

I had scarcely entered the Observatory, when I became the fellow-labourer of Biot in researches on the refraction of gases, already commenced by Borda.

While engaged in this work the celebrated academician and I often conversed on the interest there would be in resuming in Spain the measurement interrupted by the death of Méchain. We submitted our project to Laplace, who received it with ardour, procured the necessary funds, and the Government confided to us two this important mission.

M. Biot, I, and the Spanish commissary Rodriguez departed from Paris in the commencement of 1806. We visited, on our way, the stations indicated by Méchain; we made some important modifications in the projected triangulation, and at once commenced operations.

An inaccurate direction given to the reflectors established at Iviza, on the mountain Campvey, rendered the observations made on the continent extremely difficult. The light of the signal of Campvey was very rarely seen, and I was, during six months, in the *Desierto de las Palmas*, without being able to see it, whilst at a later period the light established at the Desierto, but well directed, was seen every evening from Campvey. It will easily be imagined what must be the *ennui* experienced by a young and active astronomer, confined to an elevated peak, having for his walk only a space of twenty square metres, and for diversion only the conversation of two Carthusians, whose convent was situated at the foot of the mountain, and who came in secret, infringing the rule of their order.

At the time when I write these lines, old and infirm, my legs scarcely able to sustain me, my thoughts revert involuntarily to that epoch of my life when, young and vigorous, I bore the greatest fatigues, and walked day and night, in the mountainous countries which separate the kingdoms of Valencia and Catalonia from the kingdom of Aragon, in order to reëstablish our geodesic signals which the storms had overset.

I was at Valencia towards the middle of October, 1806. One morning early the French consul entered my room quite alarmed : " Here is sad news," said M. Lanusse to me ; " make preparations for your departure ; the whole town is in agitation ; a declaration of war against France has just been published ; it appears that we have experienced a great disaster in Prussia. The Queen, we are assured, has put herself at the head of the cavalry and of the royal guard ; a part of the French army has been cut to pieces ; the rest is completely routed. Our lives would not be in safety if we remained here ; the French ambassador at Madrid will inform me as soon as an American vessel now at anchor in the ' Grao ' of Valencia can take us on board, and I will let you know as soon as the moment is come." This moment never came ; for a few days afterwards the false news, which one must suppose had dictated the proclamation of the Prince of the Peace, was replaced by the bulletin of the battle of Jéna. People who at first played the braggart and threatened to root us out, suddenly became disgracefully cast down ; we could walk in the town, holding up our heads, without fear henceforth of being insulted.

This proclamation, in which they spoke of the critical

circumstances in which the Spanish nation was placed; of the difficulties which encompassed this people; of the safety of their native country; of laurels, and of the god of victory; of enemies with whom they ought to fight;— did not contain the name of France. They availed themselves of this omission (will it be believed?) to maintain that it was directed against Portugal.

Napoleon pretended to believe in this absurd interpretation; but from this moment it became evident that Spain would sooner or later be obliged to render a strict account of the warlike intentions which she had suddenly evinced in 1806; this, without justifying the events of Bayonne, explains them in a very natural way.

I was expecting M. Biot at Valencia, he having undertaken to bring some new instruments with which we were to measure the latitude of Formentera. I shall take advantage of these short intervals of repose to insert here some details of manners, which may, perhaps, be read with interest.

I will recount, in the first instance, an adventure which nearly cost me my life under somewhat singular circumstances.

One day, as a recreation, I thought I could go, with a fellow-countryman, to the fair at Murviedro, the ancient Saguntum, which they told me was very curious. I met in the town the daughter of a Frenchman resident at Valencia, Madlle. B——. All the hotels were crowded; Madlle. B—— invited us to take some refreshments at her grandmother's; we accepted; but on leaving the house she informed us that our visit had not been to the taste of her betrothed, and that we must be prepared for some sort of attack on his part; we went directly to an armourer's, bought some pistols, and commenced our return to Valencia.

On our way I said to the calezero (driver), a man whom I had employed for a long time, and who was much devoted to me : —

" Isidro, I have some reason to believe that we shall be stopped ; I warn you of it, so that you may not be surprised at the shots which will be fired from the caleza (vehicle)."

Isidro, seated on the shaft, according to the custom of the country, answered :—

" Your pistols are completely useless, gentlemen ; leave me to act ; one cry will be enough ; my mule will rid us of two, three, or even four men."

Scarcely one minute had elapsed after the calezero had uttered these words, when two men presented themselves before the mule and seized her by the nostrils. At the same instant a formidable cry, which will never be effaced from my remembrance,—the cry of *Capitana!*—was uttered by Isidro. The mule reared up almost vertically, raising up one of the men, came down again, and set off at a rapid gallop. The jolt which the carriage made led us to understand too well what had just occurred. A long silence succeeded this incident ; it was only interrupted by these words of the calezero, " Do you not think, gentlemen, that my mule is worth more than any pistols ? "

The next day the captain-general, Don Domingo Izquierdo, related to me that a man had been found crushed on the road to Murviedro. I gave him an account of the prowess of Isidro's mule, and no more was said.

One anecdote, taken from among a thousand, will show what an adventurous life was led by the delegate of the *Bureau of Longitude.*

During my stay on a mountain near Cullera, to the

north of the mouth of the river Xucar, and to the south
of the Albuféra, I once conceived the project of establishing a station on the high mountains which are in front of
it. I went to see them. The alcaid of one of the neighbouring villages warned me of the danger to which I was
about to expose myself. " These mountains," said he to
me, " form the resort of a band of highway robbers." I
asked for the national guard, as I had the power to do so.
My escort was supposed by the robbers to be an expedition directed against them, and they dispersed themselves
at once over the rich plain which is watered by the Xucar. On my return I found them engaged in combat
with the authorities of Cullera. Wounds had been given
on both sides, and, if I recollect right, one alguazil was
left dead on the plain.

The next morning I regained my station. The following night was a horrible one ; the rain fell in a deluge.
Towards night, there was knocking at my cabin door.
To the question " Who is there? " the answer was, " A
custom-house guard, who asks of you a shelter for some
hours." My servant having opened the door to him, I
saw a magnificent man enter, armed to the teeth. He
laid himself down on the earth, and went to sleep. In
the morning, as I was chatting with him at the door of
my cabin, his eyes flashed on seeing two persons on the
slope of the mountain, the alcaid of Cullera and his principal alguazil, who were coming to pay me a visit. " Sir,"
cried he, " nothing less than the gratitude which I owe to
you, on account of the service which you have rendered
to me this night, could prevent my seizing this occasion
for ridding myself, by one shot of this carabine, of my
most cruel enemy. Adieu, sir ! " And he departed,
springing from rock to rock as light as a gazelle.

On reaching the cabin, the alcaid and his alguazil recognized in the fugitive the chief of all the brigands in
the country.

Some days afterwards, the weather having again become very bad, I received a second visit from the pretended custom-house guard, who went soundly to sleep
in my cabin. I saw that my servant, an old soldier, who
had heard the recital of the deeds and behaviour of this
man, was preparing to kill him. I jumped down from my
camp bed, and, seizing my servant by the throat,—" Are
you mad ? " said I to him ; " are we to discharge the duties of police in this country? Do you not see, moreover, that this would expose us to the resentment of all
those who obey the orders of this redoubted chief? And
we should thus render it impossible for us to terminate
our operations."

Next morning, when the sun rose, I had a conversation
with my guest, which I will try to reproduce faithfully.

" Your situation is perfectly known to me ; I know that
you are not a custom-house guard ; I have learnt from
certain information that you are the chief of the robbers
of the country. Tell me whether I have any thing to
fear from your confederates ? "

" The idea of robbing you did occur to us ; but we
concluded that all your funds would be in the neighbouring towns ; that you would carry no money to the summit
of mountains, where you would not know what to do
with it, and that our expedition against you could have
no fruitful result. Moreover, we cannot pretend to be as
strong as the King of Spain. The King's troops leave
us quietly enough to exercise our industry ; but on the
day that we molested an envoy from the Emperor of the
French, they would direct against us several regiments,

and we should soon have to succumb.  Allow me to add, that the gratitude which I owe to you is your surest guarantee."

" Very well, I will trust in your words ; I shall regulate my conduct by your answer.  Tell me if I can travel at night ?  It is fatiguing to me to move from one station to another in the day under the burning influence of the sun."

" You can do so, sir ; I have already given my orders to this purpose ; they will not be infringed."

Some days afterwards, I left for Denia ; it was midnight, when some horsemen rode up to me, and addressed these words to me :—

" Stop there, señor ; times are hard ; those who have something must aid those who have nothing.  Give us the keys of your trunks ; we will only take your superfluities."

I had already obeyed their orders, when it came into my head to call out—" But I have been told, that I could travel without risk."

" What is your name, sir ? "

" Don Francisco Arago."

" *Hombre ! vaya usted con Dios* (God be with you)."

And our cavaliers, spurring away from us, rapidly lost themselves in a field of " algarrobos."

When *my friend* the robber of Cullera assured me that I had nothing to fear from his subordinates, he informed me at the same time that his authority did not extend north of Valencia.  The banditti of the northern part of the kingdom obeyed other chiefs ; one of whom, after having been taken, was condemned and hung, and his body divided into four quarters, which were fastened to posts, on four royal roads, but not without their having previously been boiled in oil, to make sure of their longer preservation.

This barbarous custom produced no effect; for scarcely was one chief destroyed before another presented himself to replace him.

Of all these brigands those had the worst reputation who carried on their depredations in the environs of Oropeza. The proprietors of the three mules, on which M. Rodriguez, I, and my servant were riding one evening in this neighbourhood, were recounting to us the "grand deeds" of these robbers, which, even in full daylight, would have made the hair of one's head stand on end, when, by the faint light of the moon, we perceived a man hiding himself behind a tree; we were six, and yet this sentry on horseback had the audacity to demand our purses or our lives: my servant at once answered him—"You must then believe us to be very cowardly; take yourself off, or I will bring you down by one shot of my carabine." "I will be off," returned the worthless fellow, "but you will soon hear news of me." Still full of fright at the remembrance of the stories which they had just been relating, the three "arieros" besought us to quit the high road and cast ourselves into a wood which was on our left. We yielded to their proposal; but we lost our way. "Dismount," said they, "the mules have been obeying the bridle and you have directed them wrongly. Let us retrace our way as far as the high road, and leave the mules to themselves, they will well know how to find their right way again." Scarcely had we effected this manœuvre, which succeeded marvellously well, when we heard a lively discussion taking place at a short distance from us. Some were saying:

" We must follow the high road, and we shall meet with them." Others maintained that they must get into the wood on the left. The barking of the dogs, by which these individuals were accompanied, added to the tumult. During this time we pursued our way silently, more dead than alive. It was two o'clock in the morning. All at once we saw a faint light in a solitary house; it was like a light-house for the mariner in the midst of the tempest, and the only means of safety which remained to us. Arrived at the door of the farm, we knocked and asked for hospitality. The inmates, very little reassured, feared that we were thieves, and did not hurry themselves to open to us.

Impatient at the delay, I cried out, as I had received authority to do so, " In the name of the King, open to us ! " They obeyed an order thus given ; we entered pell-mell, and in the greatest haste, men and mules, into the kitchen, which was on the ground-floor ; and we hurried to extinguish the lights, in order not to awaken the suspicions of the bandits who were seeking for us. Indeed, we heard them, passing and repassing near the house, vociferating with the whole force of their lungs against their unlucky fate. We did not quit this solitary house until broad day, and we continued our route for Tortosa, not without having given a suitable recompense to our hosts. I wished to know by what providential circumstance they happened to have a lamp burning at that unseasonable hour. " We had killed a pig," they told me, " in the course of the day, and we were busy preparing the black puddings." Had the pig lived one day more, or had there been no black puddings, I should certainly have been no longer in this world, and I should not have the opportunity to relate the story of the robbers of Oropeza.

Never could I better appreciate the intelligent measure by which the constituent assembly abolished the ancient division of France into provinces, and substituted its division into departments, than in traversing for my triangulation the Spanish border kingdoms of Catalonia, Valencia, and Aragon. The inhabitants of these three provinces detested each other cordially, and nothing less than the bond of a common hatred was necessary to make them act simultaneously against France. Such was their animosity in 1807 that I could scarcely make use at the same time of Catalonians, Aragons, and Valencians, when I moved with my instruments from one station to another. The Valencians, in particular, were treated by the Catalonians as a light, trifling, inconsistent people. They were in the habit of saying to me, " *En el reino de Valencia la carne es verdura, la verdura agua, los hombres mugeres, las mugeres nada;* which may be translated thus : " In the kingdom of Valencia meat is a vegetable, vegetables are water, men are women, and women nothing."

On the other hand, the Valencians, speaking of the Aragons, used to call them " *schuros.*"

Having asked of a herdsman of this province who had brought some goats near to one of my stations, what was the origin of this denomination, at which his compatriots showed themselves so offended :

" I do not know," said he, smiling cunningly at me, " whether I dare answer you." " Go on, go on," I said to him, " I can hear anything without being angry." " Well, the word *schuros* means that, to our great shame, we have sometimes been governed by French kings. The sovereign, before assuming power, was bound to promise under oath to respect our freedom and to artic-

ulate in a loud voice the solemn words *lo Juro !* As he
did not know how to pronounce the J he said *schuro.*
Are you satisfied, señor?" I answered him, "Yes, yes.
I see that vanity and pride are not dead in this country."

Since I have just spoken of a shepherd, I will say that
in Spain, the class of individuals of both sexes destined
to look after herds, appeared to me always less further
removed than in France, from the pictures which the
ancient poets have left us of the shepherds and shepherd-
esses in their pastoral poetry. The songs by which they
endeavour to while away the tedium of their monotonous
life, are more remarkable in their form and substance
than in the other European nations to which I have had
access. I never recollect without surprise, that being on
a mountain situated at the junction-point of the kingdoms
of Valencia, Aragon, and Catalonia, I was all at once
overtaken by a violent storm, which forced me to take
refuge in my tent, and to remain there squatting on the
ground. When the storm was over and I came out from
my retreat, I heard, to my great astonishment, on an
isolated peak which looked down upon my station, a
shepherdess who was singing a song of which I only
recollect these eight lines, which will give an idea of the
rest :—

\*    \*    \*    \*    \*

A los que amor no saben
Ofreces las dulzuras
Y a mi las amarguras
Que s'e lo que es amar.

Las gracias al me certé
Eran cuadro de flores
Te cantaban amores
Por hacerte callar.

Oh! how much sap there is in this Spanish nation! What a pity that they will not make it yield fruit!

In 1807, the tribunal of the Inquisition existed still at Valencia, and at times performed its functions. The reverend fathers, it is true, did not burn people, but they pronounced sentences in which the ridiculous contended with the odious. During my residence in this town, the holy office had to busy itself about a pretended sorceress; it doomed her to go through all quarters of the town astride on an ass, her face turned towards the tail, and naked down to the waist. Merely to observe the commonest rules of decency, the poor woman had been plastered with a sticky substance, partly honey, they told me, to which adhered an enormous quantity of little feathers, so that to say the truth, the victim resembled a fowl with a human head. The procession, whether attended by a crowd I leave it to be imagined, stationed itself for some time in the cathedral square, where I lived. I was told that the sorceress was struck on the back a certain number of blows with a shovel; but I do not venture to affirm this, for I was absent at the moment when this hideous procession passed before my windows.

We thus see, however, what sort of spectacles were given to the people in the commencement of the nineteenth century, in one of the principal towns of Spain, the seat of a celebrated university, and the native country of numerous citizens distinguished by their knowledge, their courage, and their virtues. Let not the friends of humanity and of civilization disunite; let them form, on the contrary, an indissoluble union, for superstition is always on the watch, and waits for the moment again to seize its prey.

I have mentioned in the course of my narrative that
two Carthusians often left their convent in the *Desierto
de las Palmas,* and came, though prohibited, to see me at
my station, situated about two hundred metres higher.
A few particulars will give an idea of what certain monks
were, in the Peninsula, in 1807.

One of them, Father Trivulce, was old; the other was
very young. The former, of French origin, had played
a part at Marseilles, in the counter-revolutionary events
of which this town was the theatre, at the commencement of our first revolution. His part had been a very
active one; one might see the proof of this in the scars
of sabre cuts which furrowed his breast. It was he who
was the first to come. When he saw his young comrade
march up, he hid himself; but as soon as the latter had
fully entered into conversation with me, Father Trivulce
showed himself all at once. His appearance had the
effect of Medusa's head. " Reassure yourself," said he
to his young compeer; " only let us not denounce each
other, for our prior is not a man to pardon us for having
come here and infringed our vow of silence, and we
should both receive a punishment, the recollection of
which would long remain." The treaty was at once
concluded, and from that day forward the two Carthusians came very often to converse with me.

The youngest of our two visitors was an Aragonian,
his family had made him a monk against his will. He
related to me one day, before M. Biot, (then returned
from Tarragon, where he had taken refuge to get cured
of his fever,) some particulars which, according to him,
proved that in Spain there was no longer more than the
ghost of religion. These details were mostly borrowed
from the secrets of confession. M. Biot manifested

sharply the displeasure which this conversation caused
him; there were even in his language some words which
led the monk to suppose that M. Biot took him for a kind
of spy. As soon as this suspicion had entered his mind,
he quitted us without saying a word, and the next morning I saw him come up early, armed with a light gun.
The French monk had preceded him, and had whispered
in my ear the danger that threatened my companion.
"Join with me," he said, "to turn the young Aragonian
monk from his murderous project." I need scarcely say
that I employed myself with ardour in this negotiation,
in which I had the happiness to succeed. There were
here, as must be seen, the materials for a chief of *gueril-
leros.* I should be much astonished if my young monk
did not play his part in the war of independence.

The anecdote which I am about to relate will amply
prove that religion was, with the Carthusian monks of
the *Desierto de las Palmas,* not the consequence of elevated sentiments, but a mere compound of superstitious
practices.

The scene with the gun, always present to my mind,
seemed to make it clear to me that the Aragon monk, if
actuated by his passions, would be capable of the most
criminal actions. Hence, I had a very disagreeable impression when one Sunday, having come down to hear
mass, I met this monk, who, without saying a word, conducted me by a series of dark corridors into a chapel
where the daylight penetrated only by a very small
window. There I found Father Trivulce, who prepared
himself to say mass for me alone. The young monk as-
sisted. All at once, an instant before the consecration,
Father Trivulce, turning towards me, said these exact
words: "We have permission to say mass with white

wine; we therefore make use of that which we gather
from our own vines: this wine is very good. Ask the
prior to let you taste it, when on leaving this you go to
breakfast with him. For the rest, you can assure yourself this instant of the truth of what I say to you." And
he presented me the goblet to drink from. I resisted
strongly, not only because I considered it indecent to
give this invitation in the middle of the mass, but because, besides, I must own I conceived the thought for
a moment that the monks wished, by poisoning me, to
revenge themselves on me for M. Biot having insulted
them. I found that I was mistaken, that my suspicions
had no foundation; for Father Trivulce went on with
the interrupted mass, drank, and drank largely, of the
white wine contained in one of the goblets. But when I
had got out of the hands of the two monks, and was able
to breathe the pure air of the country, I experienced a
lively satisfaction.

The right of asylum accorded to some churches was
one of the most obnoxious privileges among those of
which the revolution of 1789 rid France. In 1807, this
right still existed in Spain, and belonged, I believe, to all
the cathedrals. I learnt, during my stay at Barcelona,
that there was, in a little cloister contiguous to the largest
church of the town, a brigand,—a man guilty of several
assassinations, who lived quietly there, guaranteed against
all pursuit by the sanctity of the place. I wished to assure myself with my own eyes of the reality of the fact,
and I went with my friend Rodriguez into the little
cloister in question. The assassin was then eating a
meal which a woman had just brought him. He easily
guessed the object of our visit, and made immediately
such demonstrations as convinced us that, if the asylum

was safe for the robber, it would not be so long for us. We retired at once, deploring that, in a country calling itself civilized, there should still exist such crying, such monstrous abuses.

In order to succeed in our geodesic operations, to obtain the coöperation of the inhabitants of the villages near our stations, it was desirable for us to be recommended to the priests. We went, therefore,—M. Lanusse, the French Vice-Consul, M. Biot, and I,—to pay a visit to the Archbishop of Valencia, to solicit his protection. This archbishop, a man of very tall figure, was then chief of the Franciscans; his costume more than negligent, his gray robe, covered with tobacco, contrasted with the magnificence of the archiepiscopal palace. He received us with kindness, and promised us all the recommendations we desired; but, at the moment of taking leave of him, the whole affair seemed to be spoiled. M. Lanusse and M. Biot went out of the reception room without kissing the hand of his grace, although he had presented it to each of them very graciously. The archbishop indemnified himself on my poor person. A movement, which was very near breaking my teeth, a gesture which I might justly call a blow of the fist, proved to me that the chief of the Franciscans, notwithstanding his vow of humility, had taken offence at the want of ceremony in my fellow visitors. I was going to complain of the abrupt way in which he had treated me, but I had the necessities of our trigonometrical operations before my eyes, and I was silent.

Besides this, at the instant when the closed fist of the archbishop was applied to my lips, I was still thinking of the beautiful optical experiments which it would have been possible to make with the magnificent stone which

2*

ornamented his pastoral ring. This idea, I must frankly declare, had preoccupied me during the whole of the visit.

M. Biot having at last come to seek me again at Valencia, where I expected, as I have before said, some new instruments, we went on to Formentera, the southern extremity of our arc, of which place we determined the latitude. M. Biot quitted me afterwards to return to Paris, whilst I made the geodesical junction of the island of Majorca to Iviza, and to Formentera, obtaining thus, by means of one single triangle, the measure of an arc of parallel of one degree and a half.

I then went to Majorca, to measure there the latitude and the azimuth.

At this epoch, the political fermentation, engendered by the entrance of the French into Spain, began to invade the whole Peninsula and the islands dependent on it. This ferment had as yet in Majorca only reached to the ministers, the partisans, and the relations of the Prince of Peace. Each evening, I saw, drawn in triumph in the square of Palma, the capital of the island of Majorca, on carriages, the effigies in flames, sometimes of the minister Soller, another time those of the bishop, and even those of private individuals supposed to be attached to the fortunes of the favourite Godoï. I was far from suspecting then that my turn would soon arrive.

My station at Majorca, the *Clop de Galazo,* a very high mountain, was situated exactly over the port where *Don Jayme el Conquistator* disembarked when he went to deliver the Balearic Islands from the Moors. The report spread itself through the population that I had established myself there in order to favour the arrival of the French army, and that every evening I made signals

to it.  But these reports had nothing menacing until the
moment of the arrival at Palma, the 27th of May, 1808,
of an ordnance officer from Napoleon.  This officer was
M. Berthémie ; he carried to the Spanish squadron, at
Mahon, the order to go in all haste to Toulon.  A general
rising, which placed the life of this officer in danger,
followed the news of his mission.  The Captain-General
Vivés only saved his life by shutting him up in the
strong castle of Belver.  They then bethought themselves of the Frenchman established on the *Clop de
Galazo,* and formed a popular expedition to go and seize
him.

M. Damian, the owner of a small kind of vessel called
a Mistic, which the Spanish Government had placed at
my disposal, was beforehand with them, and brought me
a costume by means of which I disguised myself.  In
directing myself towards Palma, in company with this
brave seaman, we met with the rioters who were going
in search of me.  They did not recognize me, for I spoke
Majorcan perfectly.  I strongly encouraged the men of
this detachment to continue their route, and I pursued
my way towards Palma.  At night I went on board the
Mistic, commanded by Don Manuel de Vacaro, whom
the Spanish Government had placed under my orders.
I asked this officer if he would conduct me to Barcelona,
occupied by the French, promising him that if they made
any attempt to keep him there, I would at once return and
surrender myself a prisoner.

Don Manuel, who up to this time had shown extreme
obsequiousness towards me, had now no words but those
of rudeness and distrust.  There occurred on the pier
where the Mistic was moored a riotous movement, which
Vacaro assured me was directed against me.  " Do not

be uneasy," said he to me; "if they should penetrate into the vessel you can hide yourself in this trunk." I made the attempt; but the chest which he showed me was so small that my legs were entirely outside, and the cover could not be shut down. I understood perfectly what that meant, and I asked M. Vacaro to let me also be shut up in the castle of Belver. The order for incarceration having arrived from the captain-general, I got into the boat, where the sailors of the Mistic received me with emotion.

At the moment of their crossing the harbour the populace perceived me, commenced a pursuit, and it was not without much difficulty that I reached Belver safe and sound. I had only, indeed, received on my way one slight wound from a dagger in the thigh. Prisoners have often been seen to run with all speed *from* their dungeon; I am the first, perhaps, to whom it has happened to do the reverse. This took place on the 1st or 2d of June, 1808.

The governor of Belver was a very extraordinary personage. If he is still alive he may demand of me a certificate as to his priority to the modern hydropathists; the grenadier-captain maintained that pure water, suitably administered, was a means of treatment for all illnesses, even for amputations. By listening very patiently to his theories, and never interrupting him, I won his good opinion. It was at his request, and from interest in our safety, that a Swiss garrison replaced the Spanish troop which until then had been employed as the guard of Belver. It was also through him that I one day learnt that a monk had proposed to the soldiers who went to bring my food from the town, to put some poison into one of the dishes.

All my old Majorcan friends had abandoned me at the moment of my detention. I had had a very sharp correspondence with Don Manuel de Vacaro in order to obtain the restitution of the passport of safety which the English Admiralty had granted to us. M. Rodriguez alone ventured to visit me in full daylight, and bring me every consolation in his power.

The excellent M. Rodriguez, to while away the monotony of my incarceration, remitted to me from time to time the journals which were then published at different parts of the Peninsula. He often sent them to me without reading them. Once I saw in these journals the recital of the horrible massacres of which the town of Valencia—I make a mistake, the *square of the Bullfights*—had been the theatre, and in which nearly the whole of the French established in this town (more than 350) had disappeared under the pike of the bull-fighter. Another journal contained an article bearing this title : " Relacion de la ahorcadura del señor Arago e del señor Berthémie,"—literally, "Account of the execution of M. Arago and M. Berthémie." This account spoke of the two executed men in very different terms. M. Berthémie was a Huguenot ; he had been deaf to all exhortations ; he had spit in the face of the ecclesiastic who was present, and even on the image of Christ. As for me, I had conducted myself with much decency, and had allowed myself to be hung without giving rise to any scandal. The writer also expressed his regret that a young astronomer had been so weak as to associate himself with treason, coming under the disguise of science to assist the entrance of the French army into a friendly kingdom.

After reading this article I immediately made my decision: "Since they talk of my death," said I to my friend Rodriguez, "the event will not be long in coming. I should prefer being drowned to being hung. I will make my escape from this fortress; it is for you to furnish me with the means."

Rodriguez, knowing better than any one how well founded my apprehensions were, set himself at once to the work.

He went to the captain-general, and made him feel what would be the danger of his position if I should disappear in a popular riot, or even if he were forced to give me up. His observations were so much the better comprehended, as no one could then predict what might be the issue of the Spanish revolution. "I will undertake," said the captain-general Vivés to my colleague Rodriguez, "to give an order to the commander of the fortress, that when the right moment arrives, he shall allow M. Arago, and even the two or three other Frenchmen who are with him in the castle of Belver, to pass out. They will then have no need of the means of escape which they have procured; but I will take no part in the preparations which will become necessary to enable the fugitives to leave the island; I leave all that to your responsibility."

Rodriguez immediately conferred secretly with the brave commander Damian. It was agreed between them that Damian should take the command of a half-decked boat, which the wind had driven ashore; that he should equip it as if for a fishing expedition; that he should carry us to Algiers; after which his reëntrance at Palmas, with or without fish, would inspire no suspicion.

All was executed according to agreement, notwith-

standing the inquisitorial surveillance which Don Manuel de Vacaro exercised over the commander of his
" Mistic."

On the 28th July, 1808, we silently descended the hill
on which Belver is built, at the same moment that the
family of the minister Soller entered the fortress to escape the fury of the populace. Arrived at the shore,
we found there Damian, his boat, and three sailors. We
embarked at once, and set sail. Damian had taken the
precaution of bringing with us in this frail vessel the instruments of value which he had carried off from my
station at the Clop de Galazo. The sea was unfavourable; Damian thought it prudent to stop at the little
island of Cabrera, destined to become a short time afterwards so sadly celebrated by the sufferings which the
soldiers of the army of Dupont experienced after the
shameful capitulation of Baylen. There a singular incident was very near compromising all. Cabrera, tolerably near to the southern extremity of Majorca, is often
visited by fishermen coming from that part of the island.
M. Berthémie feared, justly enough, that the rumour of
our escape having spread about, they might dispatch
some boats to seize us. He looked upon our going into
harbour as inopportune; I maintained that we must
yield to the prudence of the commander. During this
discussion, the three seamen whom Damian had engaged
saw that M. Berthémie, whom I had endeavoured to pass
off as my servant, maintained his opinion against me on
a footing of equality. They then addressed themselves
in these terms to the commander :—

" We only consented to take part in this expedition
upon condition that the Emperor's aide-de-camp, shut up
at Belver, should not be of the number of those persons

whom we should help off. We only wished to aid the flight of the astronomer. Since it seems to be otherwise, you must leave this officer here, unless you would prefer to throw him into the sea."

Damian at once informed me of the imperative wishes of his boat's crew. M. Berthémie agreed with me to suffer some abuse such as could only be tolerated by a servant threatened by his master; all the suspicions disappeared.

Damian, who feared also for himself the arrival of Majorcan fishermen, hastened to set sail on the 29th of July, 1808, the first moment that was favourable, and we arrived at Algiers on the 3d of August.

Our looks were anxiously directed towards the port, to guess what reception might await us. We were reassured by the sight of the tri-coloured flag, which was flying on two or three buildings. But we were mistaken; these buildings were Dutch. Immediately upon our entrance, a Spaniard, whom, from his tone of authority, we took for a high functionary of the Regency, came up to Damian, and asked him: "What do you bring?" "I bring," answered the commander, "four Frenchmen." "You will at once take them back again. I prohibit you from disembarking." As we did not seem inclined to obey his order, our Spaniard, who was the constructing engineer of the ships of the Dey, armed himself with a pole, and commenced battering us with blows. But immediately a Genoese seaman, mounted on a neighbouring vessel, armed himself with an oar, and struck our assailant both with edge and point. During this animated combat we managed to land without any opposition. We had conceived a singular idea of the manner in which the police act on the coast of Africa.

We pursued our way to the French Consul's, M. Dubois Thainville. He was at his country house. Escorted by the janissary of the consulate, we went off towards this country house, one of the ancient residences of the Dey, situated not far from the gate of Bab-azoum. The consul and his family received us with great amity, and offered us hospitality.

Suddenly transported to a new continent, I looked forward anxiously to the rising of the sun to enjoy all that Africa might offer of interest to a European, when all at once I believed myself to be engaged in a serious adventure. By the faint light of the dawn, I saw an animal moving at the foot of my bed. I gave a kick with my foot : all movement ceased. After some time, I felt the same movement made under my legs. A sharp jerk made this cease quickly. I then heard the fits of laughter of the janissary, who lay on the couch in the same room as I did ; and I soon saw that he had simply placed on my bed a large hedgehog to amuse himself by my uneasiness.

The consul occupied himself the next day in procuring a passage for us on board a vessel of the Regency which was going to Marseilles. M. Ferrier, the Chancellor of the French Consulate, was at the same time Consul for Austria. He procured for us two false passports, which transformed us—M. Berthémie and me—into two strolling merchants, the one from *Schwekat*, in Hungary, the other from *Leoben*.

The moment of departure had arrived; the 13th of August, 1808, we were on board, but our ship's company was not complete. The captain, whose title was Raï Braham Ouled Mustapha Goja, having perceived that the Dey was on his terrace, and fearing punishment if he should delay to set sail, completed his crew at the expense of the idlers who were looking on from the pier, and of whom the greater part were not sailors. These poor people begged as a favour for permission to go and inform their families of this precipitate departure, and to get some clothes. The captain remained deaf to their remonstrances. We weighed anchor.

The vessel belonged to the Emir of Seca, Director of the Mint. The real commander was a Greek captain, named Spiro Calligero. The cargo consisted of a great number of *groups*. Amongst the passengers there were five members of the family which the Bakri had succeeded as kings of the Jews; two ostrich-feather merchants, Moroccans; Captain Krog, from Berghen in Norway, who had sold his ship at Alicant; two lions sent by the Dey to the Emperor Napoleon, and a great number of monkeys. Our voyage was prosperous. Off Sardinia we met with an American ship coming out from Cagliari. A cannon-shot (we were armed with forty pieces of small power) warned the captain to come to be recognized. He brought on board a certain number of counterparts of passports, one of which agreed perfectly with that which we carried. The captain being thus all right, was not a little astonished when I ordered him, in the name of Captain Braham, to furnish us with tea, coffee, and sugar. The American captain protested; he called us brigands, pirates, robbers. Captain Braham admitted without difficulty all these qualifications, and persisted none the less in the exaction of sugar, coffee, and tea.

The American, then driven to the last stage of exasperation, addressed himself to me, who acted as interpreter, and cried out, " Oh ! rogue of a renegade ! if ever

I meet you on holy ground I will break your head."
" Can you then suppose," I answered him, "that I am
here for my pleasure, and that, notwithstanding your
menace, I would not rather go with you, if I could?"
These words calmed him; he brought the sugar, the coffee, and the tea claimed by the Moorish chief, and we
again set sail, though without having exchanged the usual
farewell.

We had already entered the Gulf of Lyons, and were
approaching Marseilles, when on the 16th August, 1808,
we met with a Spanish corsair from Palamos, armed at
the prow with two twenty-four pounders.   We made full
sail; we hoped to escape it: but a cannon-shot, a ball
from which went through our sails, taught us that she
was a much better sailer than we were.

We obeyed an injunction thus expressed, and awaited
the great boat from the corsair.   The captain declared
that he made us prisoners, although Spain was at peace
with Barbary, under the pretext that we were violating
the blockade which had been lately raised on all the
coasts of France: he added, that he intended to take us
to Rosas, and that there the authorities would decide on
our fate.

I was in the cabin of the vessel; I had the curiosity
to look furtively at the crew of the boat, and there I perceived, with a dissatisfaction which may easily be imagined, one of the sailors of the " Mistic," commanded by
Don Manuel de Vacaro, of the name of Pablo Blanco, of
Palamos, who had often acted as my servant during my
geodesic operations.   My false passport would become
from this moment useless, if Pablo should recognize me :
I went to bed at once, covered my head with the counter-
pane, and lay as still as a statue.

During the two days which elapsed between our capture and our entrance into the roads of Rosas, Pablo, whose curiosity often brought him into the room, used to exclaim, "There is one passenger whom I have not yet managed to get a sight of."

When we arrived at Rosas it was decided that we should be placed in quarantine in a dismantled windmill, situated on the road leading to Figueras. I was careful to disembark in a boat to which Pablo did not belong. The corsair departed for a new cruise, and I was for a moment freed from the harassing thoughts which my old servant had caused me.

Our ship was richly laden; the Spanish authorities were immediately desirous to declare it a lawful prize. They pretended to believe that I was the proprietor of it, and wished, in order to hasten things, to interrogate me, even without awaiting the completion of the quarantine. They stretched two cords between the mill and the shore, and a judge placed himself in front of me. As the interrogatories were made from a good distance, the numerous audience which encircled us took a direct part in the questions and answers. I will endeavour to reproduce this dialogue with all possible fidelity :—

"Who are you?"

"A poor roving merchant."

"Whence do you come?"

"From a country where you certainly never were."

"In a word, what country is it?"

I was afraid to answer, for the passports, steeped in vinegar, were in the hands of the judge-instructor, and I had forgotten whether I was from Schwekat or from Leoben. Finally I answered at all hazards :—

"I come from Schwekat."

And this information happily was found to agree with that of the passport.

" You are as much from Schwekat as I am," answered the judge. " You are Spanish, and, moreover, a Spaniard from the kingdom of Valencia, as I perceive by your accent."

" Would you punish me, sir, because nature has endowed me with the gift of languages? I learn with facility the dialects of those countries through which I pass in the exercise of my trade; I have learnt, for example, the dialect of Iviza."

" Very well, you shall be taken at your word. I see here a soldier from Iviza; you shall hold a conversation with him."

" I consent; I will even sing the goat song."

Each of the verses of this song (if verses they be) terminates by an imitation of the bleating of the goat.

I commenced at once, with an audacity at which I really feel astonished, to chant this air, which is sung by all the shepherds of the island.

> Ah graciada señora
> Una canzo bouil canta
> Bè, bè, bè, bè.
>
> No sera gaira pulida
> Nosé si vos agradara
> Bè, bè, bè, bè.

At once my Ivizacan, upon whom this air had the effect of the *ranz des vaches* on the Swiss, declared, all in tears, that I was a native of Iviza.

I then said to the judge that if he would put me in communication with a person knowing the French language, he would arrive at just as embarrassing a result.

An *émigré* officer of the Bourbon regiment offered at once to make the experiment, and, after some phrases interchanged between us, affirmed without hesitation that I was French.

The judge, rendered impatient, exclaimed, "Let us put an end to these trials which decide nothing. I summon you, sir, to tell me who you are. I promise that your life will be safe if you answer me with sincerity.

"My greatest wish would be to give an answer to your satisfaction. I will, then, try to do so; but I warn you that I am not going to tell you the truth. I am son of the innkeeper at Mataro." "I know that innkeeper; you are not his son." "You are right. I announced to you that I should vary my answers until one of them should suit you. I retract then, and tell you that I am a *titiretero*, (player of marionettes,) and that I practised at Lerida."

A loud shout of laughter from the multitude encircling us greeted this answer, and put an end to the questions.

"I swear by the d——l," exclaimed the judge, "that I will discover sooner or later who you are!"

And he retired.

The Arabs, the Moroccans, the Jews, who witnessed this interrogatory, understood nothing of it; they had only seen that I had not allowed myself to be intimidated. At the close of the interview they came to kiss my hand, and gave me, from this moment, their entire confidence.

I became their secretary for all the individual or collective remonstrances which they thought they had a right to address to the Spanish Government; and this right was incontestable. Every day I was occupied in drawing up petitions, especially in the name of the two ostrich-feather merchants, one of whom called himself a tolerably near relation of the Emperor of Morocco. Astonished at the rapidity with which I filled a page of my writing, they imagined, doubtless, that I should write as fast in Arabic characters, when it should be requisite to transcribe passages from the Koran; and that this would form both for me and for them the source of a brilliant fortune, and they besought me, in the most earnest way, to become a Mahometan.

Very little reassured by the last words of the judge, I sought means of safety from another quarter.

I was the possessor of a safe-conduct from the English Admiralty; I therefore wrote a confidential letter to the captain of an English vessel, The Eagle, I think, which had cast anchor some days before in the roads at Rosas. I explained to him my position. "You can," I said to him, "claim me, because I have an English passport. If this proceeding should cost you too much, have the goodness at least to take my manuscripts and to send them to the Royal Society in London."

One of the soldiers who guarded us, and in whom I had fortunately inspired some interest, undertook to deliver my letter. The English captain came to see me; his name was, if my memory is right, George Eyre. We had a private conversation on the shore. George Eyre thought, perhaps, that the manuscripts of my observations were contained in a register bound in morocco, and with gilt edges to the leaves. When he saw that these manuscripts were composed of single leaves, covered with figures, which I had hidden under my shirt, disdain succeeded to interest, and he quitted me hastily. Having returned on board, he wrote me a letter which I could find if needful, in which he said to me,—" I cannot mix myself up in your affairs; address yourself to the Spanish

Government; I am persuaded that it will do justice to your remonstrance, and will not molest you." As I had not the same persuasion as Captain George Eyre, I chose to take no notice of his advice.

I ought to mention that some time after having related these particulars in England, at Sir Joseph Banks's, the conduct of George Eyre was severely blamed; but when a man breakfasts and dines to the sound of harmonious music, can he accord his interest to a poor devil sleeping on straw and nibbled by vermin, even though he have manuscripts under his shirt? I may add that I (unfortunately for me) had to do with a captain of an unusual character. For, som edays later, a new vessel, The Colossus, having arrived in the roads, the Norwegian, Captain Krog, although he had not, like me, an Admiralty passport, made an application to the commander of this new ship; he was immediately claimed, and relieved from captivity.

The report that I was a Spanish deserter, and proprietor of the vessel, acquiring more and more credit, and this position being the most dangerous of all, I resolved to get out of it. I begged the commandant of the place, M. Alloy, to come to receive my declaration, and I announced to him that I was French. To prove to him the truth of my words, I invited him to send for Pablo Blanco, the sailor in the service of the corsair who took us, and who had returned from his cruise a short time before. This was done as I wished. In disembarking, Pablo Blanco, who had not been warned, exclaimed with surprise: "What! you, Don Francisco, mixed up with all these miscreants!" The sailor gave the Governor circumstantial evidence as to the mission which I fulfilled with two Spanish commissaries. My nationality thus became proved.

That same day Alloy was replaced in the command of the fortress by the Irish Colonel of the Ultonian regiment; the corsair left for a fresh cruise, taking away Pablo Blanco; and I became once more the roving merchant from Schwekat.

From the windmill, where we underwent our quarantine, I could see the tricoloured flag flying on the fortress of Figueras. The reconnoitring parties of the cavalry came sometimes within five or six hundred metres; it would not then have been difficult for me to escape. However, as the regulations against those who violate the sanitary laws are very rigorous in Spain, as they pronounce the penalty of death against him who infringes them, I only determined to make my escape on the eve of our admission to pratique.

The night being come I crept on all-fours along the briars, and I should soon have got beyond the line of sentinels who guarded us. A noisy uproar which I heard among the Moors made me determine to reënter, and I found these poor people in an unspeakable state of uneasiness, thinking themselves lost if I left; I therefore remained.

The next day a strong picquet of troops presented itself before the mill. The manœuvres made by it inspired all of us with anxiety, but especially Captain Krog.* " What will they do with us?" he exclaimed. "Alas! you will see only too soon," replied the Spanish officer. This answer made every one believe that they were going to shoot us. What might have strengthened me in this idea was the obstinacy with which Captain Krog and two other individuals of small size hid them-

* This appears to be an oversight, as in a preceding page M. Arago described the fortunate release of Captain Krog from this captivity.

selves behind me. A handling of arms made us think
that we had but a few seconds to live.

In analyzing the feelings which I experienced on this
solemn occasion, I have come to the conclusion that the
man who is led to death is not as unhappy as the public
imagines him to be. Fifty ideas presented themselves
nearly simultaneously to my mind, and I did not rack my
brain for any of them; I only recollect the two following,
which have remained engraved on my memory. On
turning my head to the right, I saw the national flag
flying on the bastions of Figueras, and I said to myself,
"If I were to move a few hundred metres, I should be
surrounded by comrades, by friends, by fellow citizens,
who would receive me affectionately. Here, without
their being able to impute any crime to me, I am going
to suffer death at twenty-two years of age." But what
agitated me more deeply was this: looking towards the
Pyrenees, I could distinctly see their peaks, and I reflected that my mother, on the other side of the chain,
might at this awful moment be looking peaceably at them.

The Spanish authorities, finding that to redeem my
life I would not declare myself the owner of the vessel,
had us conducted without farther molestation to the fortress of Rosas. Having to file through nearly all the
inhabitants of the town, I had wished at first, through a
false feeling of shame, to leave in the mill the remains
of our week's meals. But M. Berthémie, more prudent
than I, carried over his shoulder a great quantity of
pieces of black bread, tied up with packthread. I imitated him. I furnished myself famously from our old
stock, set it on my shoulder, and it was with this ac-
coutrement that I made my entrance into the famous
fortress.

They placed us in a casemate, where we had barely the space necessary for lying down. In the windmill, they used to bring us, from time to time, some provisions, which came from our boat. Here, the Spanish government purveyed our food. We received every day some bread and a ration of rice ; but as we had no means of dressing food, we were in reality reduced to dry bread.

Dry bread was very unsubstantial food for one who could see from his casemate, at the door of his prison, a sutler selling grapes at two farthings a pound, and cooking, under the shelter of half a cask, bacon and herrings ; but we had no money to bring us into connection with this merchant. I then decided, though with very great regret, to sell a watch which my father had given me. I was only offered about a quarter of its value; but I might well accept it, since there were no competitors for it.

As possessors of sixty francs, M. Berthémie and I could now appease the hunger from which we had long suffered ; but we did not like this return of fortune to be profitable to ourselves alone, and we made some presents, which were very well received by our companions in captivity. Though this sale of my watch brought some comfort to us, it was doomed at a later period to plunge a family into sorrow.

The town of Rosas fell into the power of the French after a courageous resistance. The prisoners of the garrison were sent to France, and naturally passed through Perpignan. My father went in quest of news wherever Spaniards were to be found. He entered a café at the moment when a prisoner officer drew from his fob the watch which I had sold at Rosas. My good father saw in this act the proof of my death, and fell into a swoon.

The officer had got the watch from a third party, and could give no account of the fate of the person to whom it had originally belonged.

The casemate having become necessary to the defenders of the fortress, we were taken to a little chapel, where they deposited for twenty-four hours those who had died in the hospital. There we were guarded by peasants who had come across the mountain, from various villages, and particularly from Cadaquès. These peasants, eager to recount all that they had seen of interest during their one day's campaign, questioned me as to the deeds and behaviour of all my companions in misfortune. I satisfied their curiosity amply, being the only one of the set who could speak Spanish.

To enlist their good will, I also questioned them at length upon the subject of their village, on the work that they did there, on smuggling, their principal sources of employment, &c. &c. They answered my questions with the loquacity common to country rustics. The next day our guards were replaced by some others who were inhabitants of the same village. " In my business of a roving merchant," I said to these last, " I have been at Cadaquès ; " and then I began to talk to them of what I had learnt the night before, of such an individual, who gave himself up to smuggling with more success than others, of his beautiful residence, of the property which he possessed near the village,—in short, of a number of particulars which it seemed impossible for any but an inhabitant of Cadaquès to know. My jest produced an unexpected effect. Such circumstantial details, our guards said to themselves, cannot be known by a roving merchant ; this personage, whom we have found here in such singular society, is certainly a native of Cadaquès ;

and the son of the apothecary must be about his age.
He had gone to try his fortune in America; it is evidently he who fears to make himself known, having been
found with all his riches in a vessel on its way to France.
The report spread, became more consistent, and reached
the ears of a sister of the apothecary established at Rosas.
She runs to me, believes she recognizes me, and falls on
my neck. I protest against the identity. "Well played!"
said she to me; "the case is serious, as you have been
found in a vessel coming to France; persist in your denial; circumstances may perhaps take a more favourable
turn, and I shall profit by them to insure your deliverance. In the mean time, my dear nephew, I will let you
want for nothing." And truly every morning M. Berthémie and I received a comfortable repast.

The church having become necessary to the garrison
to serve as a magazine, we were moved on the 25th of
September, 1808, to a Trinity fort, called the *Bouton de
Rosas*, a citadel situated on a little mountain at the entrance of the roads, and we were deposited deep under
ground, where the light of day did not penetrate on any
side. We did not long remain in this infected place,
not because they had pity upon us, but because it offered
shelter for a part of the garrison attacked by the French.
They made us descend by night to the edge of the sea,
and then transported us on the 17th of October to the
port of Palamos. We were shut up in a hulk; we enjoyed, however, a certain degree of liberty;—they allowed
us to go on land, and to parade our miseries and our rags
in the town. It was there that I made the acquaintance
of the dowager Duchess of Orleans, mother of Louis Philippe. She had left the town of Figueras, where she resided, because, she told me, thirty-two bombs sent from

the fortress had fallen in her house. She was then intending to take refuge in Algiers, and she asked me to bring the captain of the vessel to her, of whom, perhaps, she would have to implore protection. I related to my " *raïs* " the misfortunes of the Princess ; he was moved by them, and I conducted him to her. On entering, he took off his slippers from respect, as if he had entered within a mosque, and holding them in his hand, he went to kiss the front of the dress of Madame d'Orleans. The Princess was alarmed at the sight of this manly figure, wearing the longest beard I ever saw ; she quickly recovered herself, and the interview proceeded with a mixture of French politeness and Oriental courtesy.

The sixty francs from Rosas were expended. Madame D'Orleans would have liked much to assist us, but she was herself without money. All that she could gratify us with was a piece of sugarbread. The evening of our visit I was richer than the Princess. To avoid the fury of the people the Spanish Government sent those French who had escaped the first massacres back to France in slight boats. One of the *cartels* came and cast anchor by the side of our hulk. One of the unhappy emigrants offered me a pinch of snuff. On opening the snuff-box I found there " *una onza de oro*," (an ounce of gold,) the sole remains of his fortune. I returned the snuff-box to him, with warm thanks, after having shut up in it a paper containing these words : — " My fellow-countryman who carries this note has rendered me a great service ;—treat him as one of your children." My petition was naturally favourably received ; it was by this bit of paper, the size of the *onza de oro*, that my family learnt that I was still in existence, and it enabled my mother—a model of piety —to cease saying masses for the repose of my soul.

Five days afterwards, one of my hardy compatriots arrived at Palamos, after having traversed the line of posts both French and Spanish, carrying to a merchant who had friends at Perpignan the proposal to furnish me with all I was in need of. The Spaniard showed a great inclination to agree to the proposal; but I did not profit by his good will, because of the occurrence of events which I shall relate presently.

The Observatory at Paris is very near the barrier. In my youth, curious to study the manners of the people, I used to walk in sight of the public-houses which the desire of escaping payment of the duty has multiplied outside the walls of the capital; on these excursions I was often humiliated to see men disputing for a piece of bread, just as animals might have done. My feelings on this subject have very much altered since I have been personally exposed to the tortures of hunger. I have discovered, in fact, that a man, whatever may have been his origin, his education, and his habits, is governed, under certain circumstances, much more by his stomach than by his intelligence and his heart. Here is the fact which suggested these reflections to me.

To celebrate the unhoped-for arrival of *una onza de oro*, M. Berthémie and I had procured an immense dish of potatoes. The ordnance officer of the Emperor was already devouring it with his eyes, when a Moroccan, who was making his ablutions near us with one of his companions, accidentally filled it with dirt. M. Berthémie could not control his anger; he darted upon the clumsy Mussulman, and inflicted upon him a rough punishment.

I remained a passive spectator of the combat, until the second Moroccan came to the aid of his compatriot.

The party no longer being equal, I also took part in the conflict by seizing the new assailant by the beard. The combat ceased at once, because the Moroccan would not raise his hand against a man who could write a petition so rapidly. This conflict, like the struggles of which I had often been a witness outside the barriers of Paris, had originated in a dish of potatoes.

The Spaniards always cherished the idea that the ship and her cargo might be confiscated; a commission came from Girone to question us. It was composed of two civil judges and one inquisitor. I acted as interpreter. When M. Berthémie's turn came, I went to fetch him, and said to him, " Pretend that you can only talk Styrian, and be at ease; I will not compromise you in translating your answers."

It was done as we had agreed; unfortunately the language spoken by M. Berthémie had but little variety, and the *sacrement der Teufel,* which he had learnt in Germany, when he was aide-de-camp to Hautpoul, predominated too much in his discourse. Be that as it may, the judges observed that there was too great a conformity between his answers and those which I had made myself, to render it necessary to continue an interrogatory, which I may say, by the way, disturbed me much. The wish to terminate it was still more decided on the part of the judges, when it came to the turn of a sailor named Mehemet. Instead of making him swear on the Koran to tell the truth, the judge was determined to make him place his thumb on the forefinger so as represent the cross. I warned him that great offence would thus be given; and, accordingly, when Mehemet became aware of the meaning of this sign, he began to spit upon it with inconceivable violence. The meeting ended at once.

The next day things had wholly changed their appearance; one of the judges from Girone came to declare to us that we were free to depart, and to go with our ship wherever we chose. What was the cause of this sudden change? It was this.

During our quarantine in the windmill at Rosas, I had written, in the name of Captain Braham, a letter to the Dey of Algiers. I gave him an account of the illegal arrest of his vessel, and of the death of one of the lions which the Dey had sent to the Emperor. This last circumstance transported the African monarch with rage. He sent immediately for the Spanish Consul, M. Onis, claimed pecuniary damages for his dear lion, and threatened war if his ship was not released directly. Spain had then to do with too many difficulties to undertake wantonly any new ones, and the order to release the vessel so anxiously coveted arrived at Girone, and from thence at Palamos.

This solution, to which our Consul at Algiers, M. Dubois Thainville, had not remained inattentive, reached us at the moment when we least expected it. We at once made preparations for our departure, and on the 28th of November, 1808, we set sail, steering for Marseilles; but, as the Mussulmen on board the vessel declared, it was written above that we should not enter that town. We could already perceive the white buildings which crown the neighbouring hills of Marseilles, when a gust of the " mistral," of great violence, sent us from the north towards the south.

I do not know what route we followed, for I was lying in my cabin, overcome with sea-sickness; I may therefore, though an astronomer, avow without shame, that at the moment when our unqualified pilots supposed them-

3 *

selves to be off the Baléares, we landed, on the 5th of December, at Bougie.

There, they pretended that during the three months of winter, all communication with Algiers, by means of the little boats named *sandalis*, would be impossible, and I resigned myself to the painful prospect of so long a stay in a place at that time almost a desert. One evening I was making these sad reflections while pacing the deck of the vessel, when a shot from a gun on the coast came and struck the side planks close to which I was passing. This suggested to me the thought of going to Algiers by land.

I went next day, accompanied by M. Berthémie and Captain Spiro Calligero, to the Caïd of the town: "I wish," said I to him, "to go to Algiers by land." The man, quite frightened, exclaimed, "I cannot allow you to do so; you would certainly be killed on the road; your Consul would make a complaint to the Dey, and I should have my head cut off."

"Fear not on that ground. I will give you an acquittance."

It was immediately drawn up in these terms: "We, the undersigned, certify that the Caïd of Bougie wished to dissuade us from going to Algiers by land; that he has assured us that we shall be massacred on the road; that notwithstanding his representations, reiterated twenty times, we have persisted in our project. We beg the Algerine authorities, particularly our Consul, not to make him responsible for this event if it should occur. We once more repeat, that the voyage has been undertaken against his will.

*Signed:* ARAGO and BERTHÉMIE.

Having given this declaration to the Caïd, we considered ourselves quit of this functionary; but he came up to me, undid, without saying a word, the knot of my cravat, took it off, and put it into his pocket. All this was done so quickly that I had not time, I will add that I had not even the wish, to reclaim it.

At the conclusion of this audience, which had terminated in so singular a manner, we made a bargain with a Mahomedan priest, who promised to conduct us to Algiers for the sum of twenty "piastres fortes," and a red mantle. The day was occupied in disguising ourselves well or ill, and we set out the next morning, accompanied by several Moorish sailors belonging to the crew of the ship, after having shown the Mahomedan priest that we had nothing with us worth a sou, so that if we were killed on the road he would inevitably lose all reward.

I went, at the last moment, to make my bow to the only lion that was still alive, and with whom I had lived in very good harmony; I wished also to say good-bye to the monkeys, who during nearly five months had been equally my companions in misfortune.* These monkeys during our frightful misery had rendered us a service which I scarcely dare mention, and which will scarcely be guessed by the inhabitants of our cities, who look upon these animals as objects of diversion; they freed us from the vermin which infested us, and showed particularly a remarkable cleverness in seeking out the hideous insects which lodged themselves in our hair.

---

* On my return to Paris I hastened to the Jardin des Plantes to pay a visit to the lion, but he received me with a very unamiable gnashing of the teeth. Think then of the marvellous history of the Florentine lion, the subject of so many engravings, which is offered on the stall of every printseller to the eyes of the moved and astonished passers-by.

Poor animals! they seemed to me very unfortunate in being shut up in the narrow enclosure of the vessel, when, on the neighbouring coast, other monkeys, as if to bully them, came on to the branches of the trees, giving innumerable proofs of their agility.

At the commencement of the day, we saw on the road two Kabyls, similar to the soldiers of Jugurtha, whose harsh appearance powerfully allayed our fancy for wandering. In the evening we witnessed a fearful tumult, which appeared to be directed against us. We learnt afterwards that the Mahomedan priest had been the object of it; that it originated with some Kabyls whom he had disarmed on one of their journeys to Bougie. This incident, which appeared likely to be repeated, inspired us for a moment with the thought of returning; but the sailors were resolute, and we continued our hazardous enterprise.

In proportion as we advanced, our troops became increased by a certain number of Kabyls, who wished to go to Algiers to work there in the quality of seamen, and who dared not undertake alone this dangerous journey.

The third day we encamped in the open air, at the entrance of a forest. The Arabs lighted a very large fire in the form of a circle, and placed themselves in the middle. Towards eleven o'clock, I was awakened by the noise which the mules made, all trying to break their fastenings. I asked what was the cause of this disturbance. They answered me that a "*sebâá*" had come roaming in the neighbourhood. I was not aware then that a "*sebâá*" was a lion, and I went to sleep again. The next day, in traversing the forest, the arrangement of the caravan was changed. It was grouped in the smallest space possible; one Kabyl was at the head, his gun ready for service; another was in the rear, in the same position. I inquired of the owner of the mule the cause of these unusual precautions. He answered me, that they were dreading an attack from a "*sebââ*," and that if this should occur, one of us would be carried off without having time to put himself on the defensive. "I would rather be a spectator," I said to him, "than an actor in the scene you describe; consequently, I will give you two piastres more if you will keep your mule always in the centre of the moving group." My proposal was accepted. It was then for the first time that I saw that my Arab carried a yatagan under his tunic, which he used for pricking on the mule the whole time that we were in the thicket. Superfluous cautions! The "*sebââ*" did not show himself.

Each village being a little republic, whose territory we could not cross without obtaining permission and a passport from the Mahomedan priest *président*, the priest who conducted our caravan used to leave us in the fields, and went sometimes a good way off to a village to solicit the permission without which it would have been dangerous to continue our route. He remained entire hours without returning to us, and we then had occasion to reflect sadly on the imprudence of our enterprise. We generally slept amongst habitations. Once, we found the streets of a village barricaded, because they were fearing an attack from a neighbouring village. The foremost man of our caravan removed the obstacles; but a woman came out of her house like a fury, and belaboured us with blows from a pole. We remarked that she was fair, of brilliant whiteness, and very pretty.

Another time we lay down in a lurking-place dignified by the beautiful name of caravansary. In the morning, when the sun rose, cries of "*Roumi! Roumi!*" warned us that we had been discovered. The sailor, Mehemet, he who figured in the scene of the oath at Palamos, entered in a melancholy mood the enclosure where we were together, and made us understand that the cries of "Roumi!" vociferated under these circumstances, were equivalent to a sentence of death. "Wait," said he; "a means of saving you has occurred to me." Mehemet entered some moments afterwards, told us that his means had succeeded, and invited me to join the Kabyls, who were going to say prayers.

I accordingly went out, and prostrated myself towards the East. I imitated minutely the gestures which I saw made around me, pronouncing the sacred words,— *La elah il Allah! oua Mahommed raçoul Allah!* It was the scene of Mamamouchi of the "Bourgeois Gentil-homme," which I had so often seen acted by Dugazon,— with this one difference, that this time it did not make me laugh. I was, however, ignorant of the consequences it might have brought upon me on my arrival at Algiers. After having made the profession of faith before Mahom-edans—*There is but one God, and Mahomet is his prophet*, if I had been informed against to the mufti, I must inevitably have become Mussulman, and they would not have allowed me to go out of the Regency.

I must not forget to relate by what means Mehemet had saved us from inevitable death. "You have guessed rightly," said he to the Kabyls; "there are two Christians in the caravansary, but they are Mahomedans at heart, and are going to Algiers to be adopted by the mufti into our holy religion. You will not doubt this when I tell you that I was myself a slave to some Christians, and that they redeemed me with their money."

" In cha Allah ! " they exclaimed with one voice. And
it was then that the scene took place which I have just
described.

We arrived in sight of Algiers the 25th December,
1808. We took leave of the Arab owners of our mules,
who walked on foot by the side of us, and we spurred
them on, in order to reach the town before the closing of
the gates. On our arrival, we learnt that the Dey, to
whom we owed our first deliverance, had been beheaded.
The guard of the palace before which we passed, stopped
us and questioned us as to whence we came. We replied that we came from Bougie by land. " It is not
possible ! " exclaimed all the janissaries at once ; " the
Dey himself would not venture to undertake such a journey ! " " We acknowledge that we have committed a
great imprudence ; that we would not undertake to recommence the journey for millions ; but the fact that we
have just declared is the strict truth."

Arrived at the consular house, we were, as on the first
occasion, very cordially welcomed. We received a visit
from a dragoman sent by the Dey, who asked whether
we persisted in maintaining that Bougie had been our
point of departure, and not Cape Matifou, or some neighbouring port. We again affirmed the truth of our recital ;
it was confirmed, the next day, on the arrival of the proprietors of our mules.

At Palamos, during the various interviews which I had
with the dowager Duchess of Orleans, one circumstance
had particularly affected me. The Princess spoke to me
unceasingly of the wish she had to go and rejoin one of
her sons, whom she believed to be alive, but of whose
death I had been informed by a person belonging to her
household. Hence I was anxious to do all that lay in

my power to mitigate a sorrow which she must experience before long.

At the moment when I quitted Spain for Marseilles, the Duchess confided to me two letters which I was to forward in safety to their addresses. One was destined for the Empress-mother of Russia, the other for the Empress of Austria.

Scarcely had I arrived at Algiers, when I mentioned these two letters to M. Dubois Thainville, and begged him to send them to France by the first opportunity. " I shall do nothing of the sort," he at once answered me. " Do you know that you have behaved in this affair like a young inexperienced man, or, to speak out, like a blunderer? I am surprised that you did not comprehend that the Emperor, with his pettish spirit, might take this much amiss, and consider you, according to the contents of the two letters, as the promoter of an intrigue in favour of the exiled family of the Bourbons." Thus the paternal advice of the French Consul taught me that in all that regards politics, however nearly or remotely, one cannot give himself up without danger to the dictates of the heart and the reason.

I enclosed my two letters in an envelope bearing the address of a trustworthy person, and gave them into the hands of a corsair, who, after touching at Algiers, would proceed to France. I have never known whether they reached their destination.

The reigning Dey, successor to the beheaded Dey, had formerly filled the humble office of " *épileur* " * of dead bodies in the mosques. He governed the Regency

---

* An "*épileur*" is a person who removes superfluous hairs. We have been unable to ascertain what office of this kind is performed in Mohammedan funerals.

with much gentleness, occupying himself with little but his harem. This disgusted those who had raised him to this eminent post, and they resolved upon getting rid of him. We became aware of the danger which menaced him, by seeing the courts and vestibules of the consular house full, according to the custom under such circumstances, of Jews, carrying with them whatever they had of most value. It was a rule at Algiers, that all that happened in the interval comprised between the death of a Dey and the installation of his successor, could not be followed up by justice, and must remain unpunished. One can imagine, then, why the children of Moses should seek safety in the consular houses, the European inhabitants of which had the courage to arm themselves for self-defence as soon as the danger was apparent, and who, moreover, had a janissary to guard them.

Whilst the unfortunate Dey "épileur" was being conducted towards the place where he was to be strangled, he heard the cannon which announced his death and the installation of his successor. "They are in great haste," said he; "what will you gain by carrying matters to extremities? Send me to the Levant; I promise you never to return. What have you to reproach me with?" "With nothing," answered his escort, "but your insignificance. However, a man cannot live as a mere private man, after having been Dey of Algiers." And the unfortunate man perished by the rope.

The communication by sea between Bougie and Algiers was not so difficult, even with the "sandalas," as the Caïd of the former town wished to assure me. Captain Spiro had the cases landed, which belonged to me. The Caïd sought to discover what they contained; and, having perceived through a chink something yellowish,

he hastened to send the news to the Dey, that the
Frenchmen who had come to Algiers by land had among
their baggage cases filled with zechins, destined to revo-
lutionize the Kabylie.    They immediately had these
cases forwarded to Algiers, and at their opening, before
the Minister of Naval Affairs, all the phantasmagoria of
zechins, of treasure, of revolution, disappeared at the
sight of the stands and the limbs of several repeating
circles in copper.

We are now going to sojourn several months in Algiers.    I will take advantage of this to put together some
details of manners which may be interesting as the picture of a state of things anterior to that of the occupation
of the Regency by the French.    This occupation, it must
be remarked, has already fundamentally altered the manners and the habits of the Algerine population.

I am about to report a curious fact, and one which
shows that politics, which insinuate themselves and bring
discord into the bosom of the most united families, had
succeeded, strange to say, in penetrating as far as the
galley-slaves' prison at Algiers.    The slaves belonged to
three nations: there were in 1809 in this prison, Portuguese, Neapolitans, and Sicilians; among these two latter
classes were counted partisans of Murat and those of
Ferdinand of Naples.    One day, at the beginning of the
year, a dragoman came in the name of the Dey to beg
M. Dubois Thainville to go without delay to the prison,
where the friends of the French and their adversaries
had involved themselves in a furious combat; and already several had fallen.    The weapon with which they
struck each other was the heavy long chain attached to
their legs.

Each Consul, as I said above, had a janissary placed

with him as his guard; the one belonging to the French
Consul was a Candiote; he had been surnamed *the Terror.* Whenever some news unfavourable to France was
announced in the cafés, he came to the Consulate to inform himself as to the reality of the fact; and when we
told him that the other janissaries had propagated false
news, he returned to them, and there, yatagan in hand,
he declared himself ready to enter the lists in combat
against those who should still maintain the truth of the
news. As these continual threats might endanger him,
(for they had no support beyond his mere animal courage,) we had wished to render him expert in the handling of arms by giving him some lessons in fencing; but
he could not endure the idea that Christians should touch
him at every turn with foils; he therefore proposed to
substitute for the simulated duel a real combat with the
yatagan.

One may gain an exact idea of this savage nature when
I mention that, having one day heard a pistol-shot, the
sound of which proceeded from his room, people ran, and
found him bathed in his blood; he had just shot off a ball
into his arm to cure himself of a rheumatic pain.

Seeing with what facility the Deys disappeared, I said
one day to our janissary, " With this prospect before your
eyes, would you consent to become Dey ? " " Yes,
doubtless," answered he. " You seem to count as nothing the pleasure of doing all that one likes, if only even
for a single day ! "

When we wished to take a turn in the town of Algiers,
we generally took care to be escorted by the janissary
attached to the consular house; it was the only means of
escaping insults, affronts, and even acts of violence. I
have just said it was the only means. I made a mis-

take; there was one other; that was, to go in the company of a French "lazarist" of seventy years of age, and whose name, if my memory serves me, was Father Joshua; he had lived in this country for half a century. This man, of exemplary virtue, had devoted himself with admirable self-denial to the service of the slaves of the Regency, and had divested himself of all considerations of nationality;—the Portuguese, Neapolitans, Sicilians, all were equally his brethren.

In the times of plague he was seen day and night carrying eager help to the Mussulmans; thus, his virtue had conquered even religious hatreds; and wherever he passed, he and the persons who might accompany him received from multitudes of the people, from the janissaries, and even from the officials of the mosques, the most respectful salutations.

During our long hours of sailing on board the Algerine vessel, and our compulsory stay in the prisons at Rosas, and on the hulk at Palamos, I gathered some ideas as to the interior life of the Moors or the Coulouglous, which, even now when Algiers has fallen under the dominion of France, would perhaps be yet worth preserving. I shall, however, confine myself to recounting, nearly word for word, a conversation which I had with Raïs Braham, whose father was a " *Turc fin*," that is to say, a Turk born in the Levant.

" How is it that you consent," said I to him, " to marry a young girl whom you have never seen, and find in her, perhaps, an excessively ugly woman, instead of the beauty whom you had fancied to yourself? "

" We never marry without having obtained information from the women who serve in the capacity of servants at the public baths. The Jewesses are moreover, in these cases, very useful go-betweens."

"How many legitimate wives have you?"

"I have four, that is to say, the number authorized by the Koran."

"Do they live together on a good understanding?"

"Ah, sir, my house is a hell.  I never enter it without finding them at the step of the door, or at the bottom of the stairs; then, each wants to be the first to make me listen to the complaints which she has to bring against her companions.  I am about to utter blasphemy, but I think that our holy religion ought to prohibit a plurality of wives to those who are not rich enough to give to each a separate habitation."

"But since the Koran allows you to repudiate even legitimate wives, why do you not send back three of them to their parents?"

"Why? because that would ruin me.  On the day of the marriage the father of the young woman to be married stipulates for a dowry, and the half of it is paid. The other half may be exacted the day that the woman is repudiated.  It would then be three half dowries that I should have to pay if I sent back three of my wives. I ought, however, to rectify one inaccuracy in what I said just now, that my four wives had never agreed together. Once, they were agreed among themselves in the feeling of a common hatred.  In going through the market I had bought a young negress.  In the evening, when I retired to rest, I perceived that my wives had prepared no bed for her, and that the unfortunate girl was extended on the ground.  I rolled up my trowsers and laid them under her head as a kind of pillow.  In the morning the distracting cries of the poor slave made me run to her, and I found her nearly sinking under the blows of my four wives; for once they understood each other marvellously well."

In February, 1809, the new Dey, the successor of the
" épileur," a short time after having entered on his functions, claimed from two to three hundred thousand francs,
—I do not remember exactly the sum,—which he pretended was due to him from the French Government.
M. Dubois Thainville answered that he had received the
Emperor's orders not to pay one centime.

The Dey was furious, and decided upon declaring war
against us.  A declaration of war at Algiers used to be
immediately followed by putting all the persons of other
nations into prison.   This time matters were not pushed
to this extreme limit.   Our names might be figuring on
the list of the slaves of the Regency; but in fact, so far
as I was concerned, I remained free in the consular
house.   By means of a pecuniary guarantee, contracted
with the Swedish Consul, M. Norderling, I was even permitted to live at his country house, situated near the
Emperor's fort.

The most insignificant event was sufficient to modify
the ideas of these barbarians.   I had come into the town
one day, and was seated at table at M. Dubois Thainville's, when the English Consul, Mr. Blankley, arrived
in great haste, announcing to our Consul the entrance
into the port of a French prize.   " I never will uselessly
add," said he, generously, " to the severities of war; I
came to announce to you, my colleague, that I will give
up your prisoners on a receipt which will insure me the
deliverance of an equal number of Englishmen detained
in France."   " I thank you," answered M. Dubois Thainville; " but I do not the less deplore this event that it
will retard, indefinitely, perhaps, the settlement of the account in which I am engaged with the Dey."

During this conversation, armed with a telescope, I

was looking through the window of the dining-room, trying to persuàde myself at least that the captured vessel
was not one of much importance.   But one must ỷield to
evidence.   It was pierced for a great number of guns.
All at once, the wind having displayed the flags, I perceived with surprise the French flag over the English
flag.   I communicatèd what I observed to Mr. Blankley.
He answered immediately, " You do not surely pretend
to observe better with your bad telescope than I did with
my *Dollond?* "

"And you cannot pretend," said I to him in *my* turn,
" to see better than an astronomer by profession?   I am
sure of my fact.   I beg M. Thainville's permission, and
will go this instant to visit this mysterious prize."

In short, I went there; and this is what I learnt :—

General Duhesme, Governor of Barcelona, wishing to
rid himself of the most ill-disciplined portion of his garrison, formed the principal part into the crew of a vessel,
the command of which he gave to a lieutenant of Babas-
tro, a celebrated corsair of the Mediterranean.

There were amongst these improvised seamen a hussar, a dragoon, two veterans, a miner with his long beard,
&c. &c.   The vessel, leaving Barcelona by night, escaped
the English cruiser, and got to the entrance of Port
Mahon.   An English " lettre de marque " was coming
out of the port.   The crew of the French vessel boarded
her; and a furious combat on the deck ensued, in which
the French got the upper hand.   It was this " lettre de
marque " which had now arrived at Algiers.

Invested with full power by M. Dubois Thainville, I
announced to the prisoners that they were about to be
immediately given up to their Consul.   I respected even
the trick of the captain, who, wounded by several sabre-

cuts, had contrived to cover up his head with his principal flag.  I re-assured his wife; but my chief care was
especially devoted to a passenger whom I saw with one
arm amputated.

"Where is the surgeon," I said to him, "who operated
on you?"

"It was not our surgeon," he answered.  "He basely
fled with a part of the crew, and saved himself on land."

"Who, then, cut off your arm?"

"It was the hussar whom you see here."

"Unhappy man!" I exclaimed; "what could lead
you, when it was not your profession, to perform this
operation?"

"The pressing request of the wounded man.  His arm
had already swollen to an enormous size.  He wanted
some one to cut it off for him with a blow of a hatchet.
I told him that in Egypt, when I was in hospital, I had
seen several amputations made; that I would imitate
what I had seen, and might perhaps succeed.  That at
any rate it would be better than the blow of a hatchet.
All was agreed; I armed myself with the carpenter's
saw; and the operation was done."

I went off immediately to the American consul, to claim
the assistance of the only surgeon worthy of confidence
who was then in Algiers.  M. Triplet—I think I recollect that that was the name of the man of the distinguished art whose aid I invoked—came at once on board
the vessel, examined the dressing of the wound, and declared, to my very lively satisfaction, that all was going
on well, and that the Englishman would survive his horrible injury.

The same day we had the wounded men carried on
litters to Mr. Blankley's house; this operation, executed

with somewhat of ceremony, modified, though slightly, the feelings of the Dey in our favour, and his sentiments became yet more favourable towards us in consequence of another maritime occurrence, although a very insignificant one.

One day a corvette was seen in the horizon armed with a very great number of guns, and shaping her way towards the port of Algiers; there appeared immediately after an English brig of war, in full sail; a combat was therefore expected, and all the terraces of the town were covered with spectators; the brig appeared to be the best sailer, and seemed to us likely to reach the corvette, but the latter tacked about, and seemed desirous to engage in battle; the English vessel fled before her; the corvette tacked about a second time, and again directed her course towards Algiers, where, one would have supposed, she had some special mission to execute. The brig, in her turn now changed her course, but held herself constantly beyond the reach of shot from the corvette; at last the two vessels arrived in succession in the port, and cast anchor, to the lively disappointment of the Algerine population, who had hoped to be present without danger at a maritime combat between the "Christian dogs," belonging to two nations equally detested in a religious point of view; but shouts of laughter could not be repressed when it was seen that the corvette was a merchant vessel, and that she was only armed with wooden imitations of cannon. It was said in the town that the English sailors were furious, and had been on the point of mutiny against their too prudent captain.

I have very little to tell in favour of the Algerines; hence I must do an act of justice by mentioning, that the corvette departed the next day for the Antilles, her destination, and that the brig was not permitted to set sail until the next day but one.

Bakri often came to the French Consulate to talk of our affairs with M. Dubois Thainville :. " What can you want ? " said the latter, "you are an Algerine ; you will be the first victim of the Dey's obstinacy. I have already written to Livorno that your families and your goods are to be seized. When the vessels laden with cotton, which you have in this port, arrive at Marseilles, they will be immediately confiscated ; it is for you to judge whether it would not better suit you to pay the sum which the Dey claims, than to expose yourself to tenfold and certain loss."

Such reasoning was unanswerable ; and whatever it might cost him, Bakri decided on paying the sum that was demanded of France.

Permission to depart was immediately granted to us ; I embarked the 21st of June, 1809, on board a vessel in which M. Dubois Thainville and his family were passengers.

The evening before our departure from Algiers, a corsair deposited at the consul's the Majorcan mail, which he had taken from a vessel which he had captured. It was a complete collection of the letters which the inhabitants of the Baléares had been writing to their friends on the Continent.

" Look here," said M. Dubois Thainville to me, " here is something to amuse you during the voyage,—you who generally keep your room from sea-sickness,—break the seals and read all these letters, and see whether they contain any accounts by which we might profit how to aid the unhappy soldiers who are dying of misery and despair in the little island of Cabrera."

Scarcely had we arrived on board the vessel, when I set myself to the work, and acted without scruple or remorse the part of an official of the black chamber, with this sole difference, that the letters were unsealed without taking any precautions. I found amongst them several dispatches, in which Admiral Collingwood signified to the Spanish Government the ease with which the prisoners might be delivered. Immediately on our arrival at Marseilles these letters were sent to the minister of naval affairs, who, I believe, did not pay much attention to them.

I knew almost every one at Palma, the capital of Majorca. I leave it to be imagined with what curiosity I read the missives in which the beautiful ladies of the town expressed their hatred against *los malditos cavachios*, (French,) whose presence in Spain had rendered necessary the departure for the Continent of a magnificent regiment of hussars; how many persons might I not have embroiled, if under a mask I had found myself with them at the opera ball!

Many of the letters made mention of me, and were particularly interesting to me; I was sure in this instance there was nothing to constrain the frankness of those who had written them. It is an advantage which few people can boast having enjoyed to the same degree.

The vessel in which I was, although laden with bales of cotton, had some corsair papers of the Regency, and was the reputed escort of three richly laden merchant vessels which were going to France.

We were off Marseilles on the 1st of July, when an English frigate came to stop our passage: "I will not take you," said the English captain; "but you will go towards the Hyères Islands, and Admiral Collingwood will decide on your fate."

"I have received," answered the Barbary captain, "an express commission to conduct these vessels to Marseilles, and I will execute it."

"You, individually, can do what may seem to you best," answered the Englishman; "as to the merchant vessels under your escort, they will be, I repeat to you, taken to Admiral Collingwood." And he immediately gave orders to those vessels to set sail to the East.

The frigate had already gone a little distance when she perceived that we were steering towards Marseilles. Having then learnt from the crews of the merchant vessels that we were ourselves laden with cotton, she tacked about to seize us.

She was very near reaching us, when we were enabled to enter the port of the little island of Pomègue. In the night she put her boats to sea to try to carry us off; but the enterprise was too perilous, and she did not dare attempt it.

The next morning, 2d of July, 1809, I disembarked at the lazaretto.

At the present day they go from Algiers to Marseilles in four days; it had taken me eleven months to make the same voyage. It is true that here and there I had made involuntary sojourns.

My letters sent from the lazaretto at Marseilles were considered by my relatives and friends as certificates of resurrection, they having for a long time past supposed me dead. A great geometer had even proposed to the Bureau of Longitude no longer to pay my allowance to my authorized representative; which appears the more cruel inasmuch as this representative was my father.

The first letter which I received from Paris was full of sympathy and congratulations on the termination of

my laborious and perilous adventures; it was from a
man already in possession of an European reputation, but
whom I had never seen: M. de Humboldt, after what
he had heard of my misfortunes, offered me his friendship. Such was the first origin of a connection which
dates from nearly forty-two years back, without a single
cloud ever having troubled it.

M. Dubois Thainville had numerous acquaintances in
Marseilles; his wife was a native of that town, and her
family resided there. They received, therefore, both of
them, numerous visits in the parlour of the lazaretto.
The bell which summoned them, for me alone was dumb;
and I remained as solitary and forsaken, at the gates of a
town peopled with a hundred thousand of my countrymen, as if I had been in the heart of Africa. One day,
however, the parlour-bell rang three times (the number
of times corresponding to the number of my room); I
thought it must be a mistake. I did not, however, allow
this to appear. I traversed proudly under the escort of
my guard of health the long space which separates the
lazaretto, properly so called, from the parlour; and there
I found, with very lively satisfaction, M. Pons, the director of the Observatory at Marseilles, and the most
celebrated discoverer of comets of whom the annals of
Astronomy have ever had to register the success.

At any time a visit from the excellent M. Pons, whom
I have since seen director of the Observatory at Florence,
would have been very agreeable to me; but, during my
quarantine, I felt it unappreciably valuable. It proved
to me that I had returned to my native soil.

Two or three days before our admission to freedom,
we experienced a loss which was deeply felt by each of
us. To pass away the heavy time of a severe quarantine,

the little Algerine colony was in the habit of going to an
enclosure near the lazaretto, where a very beautiful
gazelle, belonging to M. Dubois Thainville, was confined;
she bounded about there in full liberty with a grace which
excited our admiration. One of us endeavoured to stop
this elegant animal in her course; he seized her unluckily
by the leg, and broke it. We all ran, but only, alas! to
witness a scene which excited the deepest emotion in us.

The gazelle, lying on her side, raised her head sadly;
her beautiful eyes (the eyes of a gazelle!) shed torrents
of tears; no cry of complaint escaped her mouth; she
produced that effect upon us which is always felt when a
person who is suddenly struck by an irreparable misfortune, resigns himself to it, and shows his profound an-
guish only by silent tears.

Having ended my quarantine, I went at once to Perpignan, to the bosom of my family, where my mother,
the most excellent and pious of women, caused numerous
masses to be said to celebrate my return, as she had done
before to pray for the repose of my soul, when she
thought that I had fallen under the daggers of the
Spaniards. But I soon quitted my native town to return to Paris; and I deposited at the Bureau of Longitude and the Academy of Sciences my observations,
which I had succeeded in preserving amidst the perils
and tribulations of my long campaign.

A few days after my arrival, on the 18th of September, 1809, I was nominated an academician in the place
of Lalande. There were fifty-two voters; I obtained
forty-seven voices, M. Poisson four, and M. Nouet one.
I was then twenty-three years of age.

A nomination made with such a majority would appear,
at first sight, as if it could give rise to no serious difficul-

ties; but it proved otherwise. The intervention of M. de Laplace, before the day of ballot, was active and incessant to have my admission postponed until the time when a vacancy, occurring in the geometry section, might enable the learned assembly to nominate M. Poisson at the same time as me. The author of the *Mécanique Céleste* had vowed to the young geometer an unbounded attachment, completely justified, certainly, by the beautiful researches which science already owed to him.* M. de Laplace could not support the idea that a young astronomer, younger by five years than M. Poisson, a pupil, in the presence of his professor at the Polytechnic School, should become an academician before him. He proposed to me, therefore, to write to the Academy that I would not stand for election until there should be a second place to give to Poisson. I answered by a formal refusal, and giving my reasons in these terms: "I care little to be nominated at this moment. I have decided upon leaving shortly with M. de Humboldt for Thibet. In those savage regions the title of member of the Institute will not smooth the difficulties which we shall have to encounter. But I would not be guilty of any rudeness towards the Academy. If they were to receive the declaration for which I am asked, would not the savans who compose this illustrious body have a right to say to me: 'How are you certain that we have thought of you? You refuse what has not yet been offered to you.' "

On seeing my firm resolution not to lend myself to the inconsiderate course which he had advised me to follow, M. de Laplace went to work in another way; he maintained that I had not sufficient distinction for admission into the Academy. I do not pretend that, at the age of three-and-twenty, my scientific attainments were very

considerable, if estimated in an *absolute* manner; but
when I judged by *comparison*, I regained courage, especially on considering that the three last years of my life
had been consecrated to the measurement of an arc of
the meridian in a foreign country; that they were passed
amid the storms of the war with Spain; often enough in
dungeons, or, what was yet worse, in the mountains of
Kabylia, and at Algiers, at that time a very dangerous
residence.

Here is, therefore, my statement of accounts for that
epoch. I make it over to the impartial appreciation of
the reader.

On leaving the Polytechnic School, I had made, in
conjunction with M. Biot, an extensive and very minute
research on the determination of the coefficient of the
tables of atmospheric refraction.

We had also measured the refraction of different gases,
which, up to that time, had not been attempted.

A determination, more exact than had been previously
obtained, of the relation of the weight of air to the
weight of mercury, had furnished a direct value of the
coefficient of the barometrical formula which served for
the calculation of the heights.

I had contributed, in a regular and very assiduous
manner, during nearly two years, to the observations
which were made day and night with the transit telescope
and with the mural quadrant at the Paris Observatory.

I had undertaken, in conjunction with M. Bouvard, the
observations relating to the verification of the laws of the
moon's libration. All the calculations were prepared; it
only remained for me to put the numbers into the formulæ, when I was, by order of the Bureau of Longitude,
obliged to leave Paris for Spain. I had observed vari-

ous comets, and calculated their orbits.   I had, in concert
with M. Bouvard, calculated, according to Laplace's formula, the table of refraction which has been published in
the *Recueil des Tables* of the Bureau of Longitude, and
in the *Connaissance des Temps.*   A research on the
velocity of light, made with a prism placed before the
object end of the telescope of the mural circle, had
proved that the same tables of refraction might serve for
the sun and all the stars.

Finally, I had just terminated, under very difficult circumstances, the grandest triangulation which had ever
been achieved, to prolong the meridian line from France
as far as the island of Formentera.

M. de Laplace, without denying the importance and
utility of these labours and these researches, saw in them
nothing more than indications of promise ; M. Lagrange
then said to him explicitly :—

"Even you, M. de Laplace, when you entered the
Academy, had done nothing brilliant; you only gave
promise.   Your grand discoveries did not come till afterwards."

Lagrange was the only man in Europe who could with
authority address such an observation to him.

M. de Laplace did not reply upon the ground of the
personal question, but he added,—"I maintain that it is
useful to young savans to hold out the position of member of the Institute as a future recompense, to excite
their zeal."

"You resemble," replied M. Hallé, "the driver of the
hackney coach, who, to excite his horses to a gallop, tied
a bundle of hay at the end of his carriage pole; the poor
horses redoubled their efforts, and the bundle of hay

4 *

always flew on before them.  After all, his plan made
them fall off, and soon after brought on their death."

Delambre, Legendre, Biot, insisted on the devotion,
and what they termed the courage, with which I had
combated arduous difficulties, whether in carrying on the
observations, or in saving the instruments and the results
already obtained.  They drew an animated picture of the
dangers I had undergone.  M. de Laplace ended by
yielding when he saw that all the most eminent men of
the Academy had taken me under their patronage, and
on the day of the election he gave me his vote.  It would
be, I must own, a subject of regret with me even to this
day, after a lapse of forty-two years, if I had become
member of the Institute without having obtained the vote
of the author of the *Mécanique Céleste*.

The Members of the Institute were always presented
to the Emperor after he had confirmed their nominations.
On the appointed day, in company with the presidents,
with the secretaries of the four classes, and with the
academicians who had special publications to offer to the
Chief of the State, they assembled in one of the saloons
of the Tuileries.  When the Emperor returned from
mass, he held a kind of review of these savans, these
artists, these literary men, in green uniform.

I must own that the spectacle which I witnessed on
the day of my presentation did not edify me.  I even experienced real displeasure in seeing the anxiety evinced
by members of the Institute to be noticed.

"You are very young," said Napoleon to me on coming
near me; and without waiting for a flattering reply,
which it would not have been difficult to find, he added,
—"What is your name?"  And my neighbour on the

right, not leaving me time to answer the simple enough question just addressed to me, hastened to say,—

" *His* name is Arago? "

" What science do you cultivate? "

My neighbour on the left immediately replied,—

" *He* cultivates astronomy."

" What have you done? "

My neighbour on the right, jealous of my left hand neighbour for having encroached on his rights at the second question, now hastened to reply, and said,—

" *He* has just been measuring the line of the meridian in Spain."

The Emperor imagining doubtless that he had before him either a dumb man or an imbecile, passed on to another member of the Institute. This one was not a novice, but a naturalist well known through his beautiful and important discoveries; it was M. Lamarck. The old man presented a book to Napoleon.

" What is that? " said the latter, " it is your absurd *meteorology*, in which you rival Matthieu Laensberg. It is this ' annuaire' which dishonours your old age. Do something in Natural History, and I should receive your productions with pleasure. As to this volume, I only take it in consideration of your white hair. Here! " And he passed the book to an aide-de-camp.

Poor M. Lamarck, who, at the end of each sharp and insulting sentence of the Emperor, tried in vain to say, " It is a work on Natural History which I present to you," was weak enough to fall into tears.

The Emperor immediately afterwards met with a more energetic antagonist in the person of M. Lanjuinais. The latter had advanced, book in hand. Napoleon said to him, sneeringly :—

" The entire Senate, then, is to merge in the Institute ? "   " Sire," replied Lanjuinais, " it is the body of the state to which most time is left for occupying itself with literature."

The Emperor, displeased at this answer, at once quitted the civil uniforms, and busied himself among the great epaulettes which filled the room.

Immediately after my nomination, I was exposed to strange annoyances on the part of the military authorities. I had left for Spain, still holding the title of pupil of the Polytechnic School.   My name could not remain on the books more than four years; consequently I had been enjoined to return to France to go through the examinations necessary on quitting the school.   But in the meantime Lalande died, and thus a place in the Bureau of Longitude became vacant.   I was named assistant astronomer.   These places were submitted to the nomination of the Emperor.   M. Lacuée, Director of the Conscription, thought that, through this latter circumstance, the law would be satisfied, and I was authorized to continue my operations.

M. Matthieu Dumas, who succeeded him, looked at the question from an entirely different point of view ; he enjoined me either to furnish a substitute, or else to set off myself with the contingent of the twelfth arrondissement of Paris.

All my remonstrances and those of my friends having been fruitless, I announced to the honourable General that I should present myself in the Place de l'Estrapade, whence the conscripts had to depart, in the costume of a member of the Institute ; and that thus I should march on foot through the city of Paris.   General Matthieu Dumas was alarmed at the effect which this scene would produce on the Emperor, himself a member of the Institute, and hastened, under fear of my threat, to confirm the decision of General Lacuée.

In the year 1809, I was chosen by the "conseil du perfectionnement" of the Polytechnic School, to succeed M. Monge, in his chair of Analysis applied to Geometry. The circumstances attending that nomination have remained a secret; I seize the first opportunity which offers itself to me to make them known.

M. Monge took the trouble to come to me one day, at the Observatory, to ask me to succeed him. I declined this honour, because of a proposed journey which I was going to make into Central Asia with M. de Humboldt. "You will certainly not set off for some months to come," said the illustrious geometer; "you could, therefore, take my place temporarily." "Your proposal," I replied, "flatters me infinitely; but I do not know whether I ought to accept it. I have never read your great work on partial differential equations; I do not, therefore, feel certain that I should be competent to give lessons to the pupils of the Polytechnic School on such a difficult theory." "Try," said he, "and you will find that that theory is clearer than it is generally supposed to be." Accordingly, I did try; and M. Monge's opinion appeared to me to be well founded.

The public could not comprehend, at that time, how it was that the benevolent M. Monge obstinately refused to confide the delivery of his course to M. Binet, (a private teacher under him,) whose zeal was well known. It is this motive which I am going to reveal.

There was then in the "Bois de Boulogne" a residence named the *Grey House*, where there assembled round M. Coessin, the high-priest of a new religion, a

number of adepts, such as Lesueur, the musician, Colin,
private teacher of chemistry at the school, M. Binet, &c.
A report from the prefect of police had signified to the
Emperor that the frequenters of the Grey House were
connected with the Society of Jesuits. The Emperor
was uneasy and irritated at this. " Well," said he to M.
Monge, "there are your dear pupils become disciples of
Loyola ! " And on Monge's denial, " You deny it," answered the Emperor; " well, then, know that the private
teacher of your course is in that clique." Every one
can understand that after such a remark, Monge could
not consent to being succeeded by M. Binet.

Having entered the academy, young, ardent, and impassioned, I took much greater part in the nominations
than may have been suitable for my position and my time
of life. Arrived at an epoch of life whence I examine
retrospectively all my actions with calmness and impartiality, I can render this amount of justice to myself, that,
excepting in three or four instances, my vote and interest
were always in favour of the most deserving candidate,
and more than once I succeeded in preventing the Academy from making a deplorable choice. Who could blame
me for having maintained with energy the election of
Malus, considering that his competitor, M. Girard, unknown as a physicist, obtained twenty-two votes out of
fifty-three, and that an addition of five votes would have
given him the victory over the savant who had just discovered the phenomenon of polarization by reflection,
over the savant whom Europe would have named by ac-
clamation? The same remarks are applicable to the
nomination of Poisson, who would have failed against
this same M. Girard if four votes had been otherwise
given. Does not this suffice to justify the unusual ardour

of my conduct? Although in a third trial the majority of the Academy was decided in favour of the same engineer, I cannot regret that I supported up to the last moment with conviction and warmth the election of his competitor, M. Dulong.

I do not suppose that, in the scientific world, any one will be disposed to blame me for having preferred M. Liouville to M. de Pontécoulant.

Sometimes it happened that the Government wished to influence the choice of the Academy; with a strong sense of my rights I invariably resisted all dictation. Once this resistance acted unfortunately on one of my friends—the venerable Legendre; as to myself, I had prepared myself beforehand for all the persecutions of which I could be made the object. Having received from the Minister of the Interior an invitation to vote for M. Binet against M. Navier on the occurrence of a vacant place in the section of mechanics, Legendre nobly answered that he would vote according to his soul and his conscience. He was immediately deprived of a pension which his great age and his long services rendered due to him. The *protégé* of the authorities failed; and, at the time, this result was attributed to the activity with which I enlightened the members of the Academy as to the impropriety of the Minister's proceedings.

On another occasion the King wished the Academy to name Dupuytren, the eminent surgeon, but whose character at the time lay under grave imputations. Dupuytren was nominated, but several blanks protested against the interference of the authorities in academic elections.

I said above that I had saved the Academy from some deplorable choices; I will only cite a single instance, on which occasion I had the sorrow of finding myself in opposition to M. de Laplace. The illustrious geometer wished a vacant place in the astronomical section to be granted to M. Nicollet,—a man without talent, and, moreover, suspected of misdeeds which reflected on his honour in the most serious degree. At the close of a contest, which I maintained undisguisedly, notwithstanding the danger which might follow from thus braving the powerful protectors of M. Nicollet, the Academy proceeded to the ballot; the respected M. Damoiseau, whose election I had supported, obtained forty-five votes out of forty-eight. Thus M. Nicollet had collected but three.

"I see," said M. de Laplace to me, "that it is useless to struggle against young people; I acknowledge that the man who is called the *great elector* of the Academy is more powerful than I am."

"No," replied I; "M. Arago can only succeed in counterbalancing the opinion justly preponderating for M. de Laplace, when the right is found to be without possible contradiction on his side."

A short time afterwards M. Nicollet had run away to America, and the Bureau of Longitude had a warrant passed to expel him ignominiously from its bosom.

I would warn those savans, who, having early entered the Academy, might be tempted to imitate my example, to expect nothing beyond the satisfaction of their conscience. I warn them, with a knowledge of the case, that gratitude will almost always be found wanting.

The elected academician, whose merits you have sometimes exalted beyond measure, pretends that you have done no more than justice to him; that you have only fulfilled a duty, and that he therefore owes you no thanks.

Delambre died the 19th August, 1822. After the necessary delay, they proceeded to fill his place. The situation of Perpetual Secretary is not one which can long be left vacant. The Academy named a commission to present it with candidates; it was composed of Messrs. de Laplace, Arago, Legendre, Rossel, Prony, and Lacroix. The list presented was composed of the names of Messrs. Biot, Fourier, and Arago. It is not necessary for me to say with what obstinacy I opposed the inscription of my name on this list; I was compelled to give way to the will of my colleagues, but I seized the first opportunity of declaring publicly that I had neither the expectation nor the wish to obtain a single vote; that, moreover, I had on my hands already as much work as I could get through; that in this respect M. Biot was in the same position; and that, in short, I should vote for the nomination of M. Fourier.

It was supposed, but I dare not flatter myself that it was the fact, that my declaration exercised a certain influence on the result of the ballot. The result was as follows: M. Fourier received thirty-eight votes, and M. Biot ten. In a case of this nature each man carefully conceals his vote, in order not to run the risk of future disagreement with him who may be invested with the authority which the Academy gives to the perpetual secretary. I do not know whether I shall be pardoned if I recount an incident which amused the Academy at the time.

M. de Laplace, at the moment of voting, took two plain pieces of paper; his neighbour was guilty of the indiscretion of looking, and saw distinctly that the illustrious geometer wrote the name of Fourier on both of them. After quietly folding them up, M. de Laplace put the papers into his hat, shook it, and said to this same curious neighbour: "You see, I have written two papers; I am going to tear up one, I shall put the other into the urn; I shall thus be myself ignorant for which of the two candidates I have voted."

All went on as the celebrated academician had said; only that every one knew with certainty that his vote had been for Fourier; and "the calculation of probabilities" was in no way necessary for arriving at this result.

After having fulfilled the duties of secretary with much distinction, but not without some feebleness and negligence in consequence of his bad health, Fourier died the 16th of May, 1830. I declined several times the honour which the Academy appeared willing to do me, in naming me to succeed him. I believed, without false modesty, that I had not the qualities necessary to fill this important place suitably. When thirty-nine out of forty-four voters had appointed me, it was quite time that I should give in to an opinion so flattering and so plainly expressed. On the 7th of June, 1830, I, therefore, became perpetual secretary of the Academy for the Mathematical Sciences; but, conformably to the plea of an accumulation of offices, which I had used as an argument to support, in November, 1822, the election of M. Fournier, I declared that I should give in my resignation of the Professorship in the Polytechnic School. Neither the solicitations of Marshal Soult, the Minister of War, nor those of the most eminent members of the Academy, could avail in persuading me to renounce this resolution.

# BAILLY.

BIOGRAPHY READ AT THE PUBLIC SITTING OF THE ACADEMY OF SCIENCES, THE 26TH OF FEBRUARY, 1844.

## INTRODUCTION.

GENTLEMEN, — The learned man, illustrious in so many ways, whose life I am going to relate, was taken from France half a century ago. I hasten to make this remark, so as thoroughly to show that I have selected this subject without being deterred by complaints which I look upon as unjust and inapplicable. The glory of the members of the early Academy of Sciences is an inheritance for the present Academy. We must cherish it as we would the glory of later days ; we must hallow it with the same respect, we must devote to it the same worship : the word *prescription* would here be synonymous with ingratitude.

If it had happened, Gentlemen, that amongst the academicians who preceded us, a man, already illustrious by his labours, and, without personal ambition, yet thrown, despite himself, into the midst of a terrible revolution, exposed to a thousand unrestrained passions, had cruelly disappeared in the political effervescence—oh ! then, any negligence, any delay in studying the facts would be in-excusable ; the honourable contemporaries of the victim would soon be no longer there to shed the light of their honest and impartial memory on obscure events ; an ex-istence devoted to the cultivation of reason and of truth would come to be appreciated only from documents, on which, for my part, I would not blindly draw, until it shall be proved that, in revolutionary times, we can trust to the uprightness of parties.

I felt in duty bound, Gentlemen, to give you a sketch of the ideas that have led me to present to you a detailed account of the life and labours of a member of the early Academy of Sciences. The biographies which will soon follow this, will show that the studies I have undertaken respecting Carnot, Condorcet, and Bailly, have not pre-vented me from attending seriously to our illustrious contemporaries.

To render them a loyal and truthful homage, is the first duty of the secretaries of the Academy, and I will religiously fulfil it ; without binding myself, however, to observe a strict chronological order, or to follow the civil registers step by step.

Eulogies, said an ancient authority, should be deferred until we have lost the true measure of the dead. Then we could make giants of them without any one opposing us. On the contrary, I am of opinion that biographers, especially those of academicians, ought to make all pos-sible haste, so that every one may be represented accord-ing to his true measure, and that well-informed people may have the opportunity of rectifying the mistakes which, notwithstanding every care, almost inevitably slip into this sort of composition. I regret that our former secretaries did not adopt this rule. By deferring from year to year to analyze the scientific and political life of Bailly with their scruples, and with their usual talents, they allowed time for inconsiderateness, prejudice, and passions of every kind, to impregnate our minds with a multitude of serious errors, which have added considerably to the difficulty of my task. When I was led to form very different opinions from those that are found spread through some of the most celebrated works, on the events of the great revolution of 1789, in which our fellow-academician took an active part, I could not be so conceited as to expect to be believed on my own word. To propound my opinions then was insufficient; I had also to combat those of the historians with whom I differed. This necessity has given to the biography that I am going to read an unusual length. I solicit the kind sympathy of the assembly on this point. I hope to obtain it, I acknowledge, when I consider that my task is to analyze before you the scientific and literary claims of an illustrious colleague, to depict the uniformly noble and patriotic conduct of the first President of the National Assembly; to follow the first Mayor of Paris in all the acts of an administration, the difficulties of which appeared to be above human strength; to accompany the virtuous magistrate to the very scaffold, to unroll the mournful phases of the cruel martyrdom that he was made to undergo; to retrace, in a word, some of the greatest, some of the most terrible events of the French Revolution.

INFANCY OF BAILLY.—HIS YOUTH.—HIS LITERARY ESSAYS.—HIS MATHEMATICAL STUDIES.

John Sylvain Bailly was born at Paris in 1736. His parents were James Bailly and Cecilia Guichon.

The father of the future astronomer had charge of the king's pictures. This post had continued in the obscure but honest family of Bailly for upwards of a century.

Sylvain, while young, never quitted his paternal home. His mother would not be separated from him; it was not that she could give him the instruction required from masters in childhood, but a tenderness, allowed to run to the utmost extreme, entirely blinded her. Bailly then formed his own mind, under the eye of his parents. Nothing could be better, it seemed, than the boyhood of our brother academician, to verify the oft-repeated theory, touching the influence of imitation on the development of our faculties. Here, the result, attentively examined, would not by a great deal agree with the old hypothesis. I know not but, every thing considered, whether it would rather furnish 'powerful weapons to whoever would wish to maintain that, in its early habits, childhood rather seeks for contrasts.

James Bailly had an idle and light character; whilst young Sylvain from the beginning showed strong reasoning powers, and a passion for study.

The grown man felt in his own element while in noisy gayety.

But the boy loved retirement.

To the father, solitude would have been fatal; for to him life consisted in motion, sallies, witty conversations, free and easy parties, the little gay suppers of those days.

The son, on the contrary, would remain alone and quite silent for whole days. His mind sufficed to itself; he never sought the fellowship of companions of his own age. Extreme steadiness was at once his habit and his taste.

The warder of the king's pictures drew remarkably

well, but did not appear to have troubled himself much with the principles of art.

His son Sylvain studied those principles deeply, and to some purpose; he became a theoretic artist of the first class, but he never could either draw or paint even moderately well.

There are few young people who would not, at some time or other, have wished to escape from the scrutinizing eyes of their parents. The contrary was the case in Bailly's family, for James used sometimes to say to his friends or to his servants, " Do not mention this peccadillo to my son. Sylvain is worth more than I am; his morals are very strict. Under the most respectful exterior, I should perceive in his manner a censure which would grieve me. I wish to avoid his tacit reproaches, even when he does not say a word."

The two characters resembled each other only in one point—in their taste for poetry, or perhaps we ought to say versification, but even here we shall perceive differences.

The father composed songs, little interludes, and farces that were acted at the *Italian Comedy;* but the son commenced at the age of sixteen by a serious work of time,—a tragedy.

This tragedy was entitled *Clothaire.* The subject, drawn from the early centuries of the French History, had led Bailly by a curious and touching coincidence to relate the tortures inflicted on a Mayor of Paris by a deluded and barbarous multitude. The work was modestly submitted to the actor Lanoue, who, although he bestowed flattering encouragement on Bailly, dissuaded him frankly from exposing *Clothaire* to the risk of a public representation. On the advice of the comedian-author, the young poet took *Iphygenia in Tauris* for the subject of his second composition. Such was his ardour, that by the end of three months, he had already written the last line of the fifth act of his new tragedy, and hastened to Passy, to solicit the opinion of the author of *Mahomet II.* This time Lanoue thought he perceived that his confiding young friend was not intended by nature for the drama, and he declared it to him without disguise. Bailly heard the fatal sentence with more resignation than could have been expected from a youth whose budding self-esteem received so violent a shock. He even threw his two tragedies immediately into the fire. Under similar circumstances, Fontenelle showed less docility in his youth. If the tragedy of *Aspar* also disappeared in the flames, it was not only in consequence of the criticism of a friend; for the author went so far as to call forth the noisy judgment of the pit.

Certainly no astronomer will regret that any opinions either off-hand or well digested, on the first literary productions of Bailly, contributed to throw him into the pursuit of science. Still, for the sake of principle, it seems just to protest against the praises given to the foresight of Lanoue, to the sureness of his judgment, to the excellence of his advice. What was it in fact? A lad of sixteen or seventeen years of age, composes two tolerable tragedies, and these essays are made irrevocably to decide on his future fate. We have then forgotten that Racine had already reached the age of twenty-two, when he first appeared, producing *Theagenes and Charicles,* and the *Inimical Brothers;* that Crébillon was nearly forty years of age when he composed a tragedy on *The Death of the Sons of Brutus,* of which not a single verse has been preserved; finally, that the two first comedies of Molière, *The three rival Doctors* and *The Schoolmaster*, are no longer known but by their titles.  Let us recall to mind that reflection of Voltaire's : " It is very difficult to succeed before the age of thirty in a branch of literature that requires a knowledge of the world and of the human heart."

A happy chance showed that the sciences might open an honourable and glorious path to the discouraged poet. M. de Moncaville offered to teach him mathematics, in exchange for drawing-lessons that his son received from the warder of the king's pictures.  The proposal being accepted, the progress of Sylvain Bailly in these studies was rapid and brilliant.

BAILLY BECOMES THE PUPIL OF LACAILLE.—HE IS ASSOCIATED WITH HIM IN HIS ASTRONOMICAL LABOURS.

The mathematical student soon after had one of those providential meetings which decide a young man's future fate.  Mademoiselle Lejeuneux cultivated painting.  It was at the house of this female artist, known afterwards as Madame La Chenaye, that Lacaille saw Bailly.  The attentive, serious, and modest demeanour of the student charmed the great astronomer.  He showed it in a most unequivocal manner, by offering, though so avaricious of his time, to become the guide of the future observer, and also to put him in communication with Clairaut.

It is said that from his first intercourse with Lacaille, Bailly showed a decided vocation for astronomy.  This fact appears to me incontestable.  At his first appearance in this line, I find him associated in the most laborious, difficult, and tiresome investigations of that great observer.

5

These epithets may perhaps appear extraordinary; but they will be so only to those who have learnt the science of the stars in ancient poems, either in verse or in prose.

The Chaldæans, luxuriously reclining on the perfumed terraced roofs of their houses in Babylon, under a constantly azure sky, followed with their eyes the general and majestic movements of the starry sphere; they ascertained the respective displacements of the planets, the moon, the sun; they noted the date and hour of eclipses; they sought out whether simple periods would not enable them to foretell these magnificent phenomena a long time beforehand. Thus the Chaldæans created, if I may be allowed the expression, *Contemplative Astronomy*. Their observations were neither numerous nor exact; they both made and discussed them without labour and without trouble.

Such is not, by a great deal, the position of modern astronomers. Science has felt the necessity of the celestial motions being studied in their minutest details. Theories must explain these details; it is their touchstone; it is by details that theories become confirmed or fall to the ground. Besides, in Astronomy, the most important truths, the most astonishing results, are based on the measurement of quantities of extreme minuteness. Such measures, the present bases of the science, require very fatiguing attention, infinite care, to which no learned man would bind himself, were he not sustained, and encouraged by the hope of attaining some capital determination, through an ardent and decided devotion to the subject.

The modern astronomer, really worthy of the name, must renounce the distractions of society, and even the refreshment of uninterrupted sleep. In our climates during the inclement season, the sky is almost constantly overspread by a thick curtain of clouds. Under pain of postponing by some centuries the verification of this or that theoretic point, we must watch the least clearing off, and avail ourselves of it without delay.

A favourable wind arises and dissipates the vapours in the very direction where some important phenomenon will manifest itself, and is to last only a few seconds. The astronomer, exposed to all the transitions of weather, (it is one of the conditions of accuracy,) the body painfully bent, directs the telescope of a great graduated circle in haste upon the star that he impatiently awaits. His lines for measuring are a spider's threads. If in looking he makes a mistake of half the thickness of one of these threads, the observation is good for nothing; judge what his uneasiness must be; at the critical moment, a puff of wind occasioning a vibration in the artificial light adapted to his telescope, the threads become almost invisible; the star itself, whose rays reach the eye through atmospheric strata of various density, temperature, and refrangibility, will appear to oscillate so much as to render the true position of it almost unassignable; at the very moment when extremely good definition of the object becomes indispensable to insure correctness of measures, all becomes confused, either because the eye-piece gets steamed with vapour, or that the vicinity of the very cold metal occasions an abundant secretion of tears in the eye applied to the telescope; the poor observer is then exposed to the alternative of abandoning to some other more fortunate person than himself, the ascertaining a phenomenon that will not recur during his lifetime, or introducing into the science results of problematical correctness. Finally, to complete the observation, he must read off the microscopical divisions of the graduated circle, and for what opticians call *indolent vision* (the only sort that the ancients ever required) must substitute *strained vision*, which in a few years brings on blindness.*

When he has scarcely escaped from this physical and moral torture, and the astronomer wishes to know what degree of utility is deducible from his labours, he is obliged to plunge into numerical calculations of a repelling length and intricacy. Some observations that have been made in less than a minute, require a whole day's work in order to be compared with the tables.

Such was the view that Lacaille, without any softening, exhibited to his young friend; such was the profession into which the adolescent poet plunged with great ardour, and without having been at all prepared for the transition.

A useful calculation constituted the first claim of our tyro to the attention of the learned world.

The year 1759 had been marked by one of those great events, the memory of which is religiously preserved in scientific history. A comet, that of 1682, had returned at the epoch foretold by Clairaut, and very nearly in the region that mathematical analysis had indicated to him. This reappearance raised comets out of the category of sublunary meteors; it gave them definitely closed curves

* This long list of supposed difficulties in making an exact observation is hardly worthy of a zealous astronomer. Our author shows no enthusiasm for his subject here, and ends by ascribing the whole feremiad to Lacaille, a man of very great practical perseverance. It is to be regretted that Arago never refers to observations of his own, but constantly quotes from others, nor does he always select the best. — *Translator's Note.*

as orbits, instead of parabolas, or even mere straight lines ; attraction confined them within its immense domain ; in short, these bodies ceased for ever to be liable to superstition regarding them as prognostics.

The stringency, the importance of these results, would naturally increase in proportion as the resemblance between the announced orbit and the real orbit became more evident.

This was the motive that determined so many astronomers to calculate the orbit of the comet minutely, from the observations made in 1759, throughout Europe. Bailly was one of those zealous calculators. In the present day, such a labour would scarcely deserve special mention ; but we must remark that the methods at the close of the eighteenth century were far from being so perfect as those that are now in use, and that they greatly depended on the personal ability of the individual who undertook them.

Bailly resided in the Louvre. Being determined to make the theory and practice of astronomy advance together, he had an observatory established from the year 1760, at one of the windows in the upper story of the south gallery. Perhaps I may occasion surprise by giving the pompous name of *Observatory* to the space occupied by a window, and the small number of instruments that it could contain. I admit this feeling, provided it be extended to the Royal Observatory of the epoch, to the old imposing and severe mass of stone that attracts the attention of the promenaders in the great walk of the Luxembourg. There also, the astronomers were obliged to stand in the hollow of the windows ; there also they said, like Bailly : I cannot verify my quadrants either by the horizon or by the zenith, for I can neither see the

horizon nor the zenith. This ought to be known, even
if it should disturb the wild reveries of two or three
writers, who have no scientific authority: France did
not possess an observatory worthy of her, nor worthy of
the science, and capable of rivalling the other observatories of Europe, until within these ten or twelve years.

The earliest observations made by Bailly, from one of
the windows in the upper story of the Louvre gallery
that looks out on the Pont des Arts, are dated in the beginning of 1760. The pupil of Lacaille was not yet
twenty-four years old. Those observations relate to an
opposition of the planet Mars. In the same year he determined the oppositions of Jupiter and of Saturn, and
compared the results of his own determinations with the
tables.

The subsequent year I see him associated with Lacaille
in observing the transit of Venus over the sun's disk. It
was an extraordinary piece of good fortune, Gentlemen,
at the very commencement of his scientific life, to witness in succession two of the most interesting astronomical events: the first predicted and well established return
of a comet; and one of those partial eclipses of the sun
by Venus, that do not recur till after the lapse of a hundred and ten years, and from which science has deduced
the indirect but exact method, without which we should
still be ignorant of the fact that the sun's mean distance
from our earth is thirty-eight millions of leagues.

I shall have completed the enumeration of Bailly's
astronomical labours performed before he became an
academician, when I have added, from observations of
the comet of 1762, the calculation of its parabolic orbit;
the discussion of forty-two observations of the moon by
La Hire, a detailed labour destined to serve as a start-

ing point for any person occupying himself with the lunar theory; finally, also the reduction of 515 zodiacal stars, observed by Lacaille in 1760 and 1761.

## BAILLY A MEMBER OF THE ACADEMY OF SCIENCES.— HIS RESEARCHES ON JUPITER'S SATELLITES.

Bailly was named member of the Academy of Sciences the 29th January, 1763. From that moment his astronomical zeal no longer knew any bounds. The laborious life of our fellow-academician might, on occasion, be set up against a line, more fanciful than true, by which an ill-natured poet stigmatized academical honours. Certainly no one would say of Bailly, that after his election,

> "Il s'endormit et ne fit qu'un somme."
> "He fell asleep and made but one nap (or sum)."

On the contrary, we cannot but be surprised at the multitude of literary and scientific labours that he accomplished in a few years.

Bailly's earliest researches on Jupiter's satellites began in 1763.

The subject was happily chosen. Studying it in all its generalities, he showed himself both an indefatigable computer, a clear-sighted geometer, and an industrious and able observer. Bailly's researches on the satellites of Jupiter, will always be his first and chief claim to scientific glory. Before him, the Maraldis, the Bradleys, the Wargentins had discovered empirically some of the principal perturbations that those bodies undergo, in their revolving motions around the powerful planet that rules them; but they had not been traced up to the principles of universal attraction. The initiative honour in this respect belongs to Bailly. Nor is this honour decreased by the ulterior and considerable improvements that the science has since received; even the discoveries of Lagrange and of Laplace have left this honour intact.

The knowledge of the satellitic motions rests almost entirely on the observation of the precise moment when each of those bodies disappears, by entering into the conical shadow, which the immense opaque globe of Jupiter projects on the opposite side from the sun. In the course of discussing a multitude of these eclipses, Bailly was not long in perceiving that the computers of the Satellitic Tables worked on numerical data that were not at all comparable with each other. This seemed of little consequence previous to the birth of the theory; but, after the analytical discovery of the perturbations, it became desirable to estimate the possible errors of observation, and to suggest means for remedying them. This was the object of the very considerable work that Bailly presented to the Academy in 1771.

In this beautiful memoir, the illustrious astronomer developes the series of experiments, by the aid of which each observation may give the instant of the real disappearance of a satellite, distinguished from the instant of the apparent disappearance, whatever be the power of the telescope used, whatever be the altitude of the eclipsed body above the horizon, and consequently, whatever be the transparency of the atmospheric strata through which the phenomenon is observed, also whatever be the distance from that body to the sun, or to the planet; finally, whatever be the sensibility of the observer's sight, all which circumstances considerably influence the time of apparent disappearance. The same series of ingenious and delicate observations led the author, very curiously, to the determination of the true diameters of the satellites, that is to say, of small luminous points, which, with the telescopes then in use, showed no perceptible diameter.

I will rest contented with these general considerations; only remarking, in addition, that the diaphragms used by Bailly. were not intended only to diminish the quantity of light contributing to the formation of the images, but that they considerably increase the diameter, and in a variable way, at least in the instance of stars.

Under this new aspect, it will be requisite to submit the question to a new examination.

Any geometers and astronomers who wish to know all the extent of Bailly's labours, must not content themselves with consulting the collections in the Academy of Sciences; for he published, at the beginning of 1766, a separate work under the modest title of *Essay on the Theory of Jupiter's Satellites.*

The author commences with the *Astronomical History of the Satellites.* This history contains an almost complete analysis of the discoveries by Maraldi, by Bradley, by Wargentin. The labours of Galileo and his contemporaries are given with less detail and exactness. I have thought that I ought to fill up the lacunæ, by availing myself of some very precious documents published a few years since, and which were unknown to Bailly.

But this I will do in a separate notice, free from all preconceived ideas, and free from all party spirit; I will not forget that an honest man ought not to calumniate any one, not even the agents of the Inquisition.

5 *

When Bailly entered the Academy of Sciences, the
perpetual secretary was Grandjean de Fouchy. The
bad health of this estimable scholar occasioned an early
vacancy to be foreseen.  D'Alembert cast his views on
Bailly, hinted to him the survivorship to Fouchy, and
proposed to him, by way of preparing the way, to write
some biographies.  Bailly followed the advice of the
illustrious geometer, and chose as the subject of his
studies, the éloges proposed by several academies, though
principally by the French Academy.

From the year 1671 to the year 1758, the prize subjects proposed by the French Academy related to questions of religion and morality.  The eloquence of the
candidates had therefore had to exercise itself successively on the knowledge of salvation; on the merit and
dignity of martyrdom; on the purity of the soul and of
the body ; on the danger there is in certain paths that
appear safe, &c. &c.  It had even to paraphrase the
*Ave Maria.*  According to the literal intentions of the
founder, (Balzac,) each discourse was ended by a short
prayer.  Duclos thought in 1758, that five or six volumes
of similar sermons must have exhausted the matter, and
on his proposal the Academy decided that, in future, it
would give as the subject of the eloquence prize, the
eulogiums of the great men of the nation.  Marshal
Saxe, Duguay Trouin, Sully, D'Aguesseau, Descartes,
figured first on this list.  Later, the Academy felt itself
authorized to propose the éloge of kings themselves; it

entered on this new branch at the beginning of 1767, by asking for the éloge of Charles V.

Bailly entered the lists, but his essay obtained only an honourable mention.

Nothing is more instructive than to search out at what epoch originated the principles and opinions of persons who have acted an important part on the political scene, and how those opinions developed themselves. By a fatality much to be regretted, the elements of these investigations are rarely numerous or faithful. We shall not have to express these regrets relative to Bailly. Each composition shows us the serene, candid, and virtuous mind of the illustrious writer, in a new and true point of view. The éloge of Charles V. was the starting point, followed by a long series of works, and it ought to arrest our attention for a while.

The writings, crowned with the approbation of the French Academy, did not reach the public eye till they had been submitted to the severe censure of four Doctors in Theology. A special and digested approbation by the high dignitaries of the Church, whom the illustrious assembly always possessed among her members, was not a sufficient substitute for the humbling formality. If we are sure that we possess the éloge of Charles V. such as it flowed from the author's pen; if we have not reason to fear that the thoughts have undergone some mutilation, we owe it to the little favour that the discourse of Bailly enjoyed in the sitting of the Academy in 1767. Those thoughts, however, would have defied the most squeamish mind, the most shadowy susceptibility. The panegyrist unrolls with emotion the frightful misfortunes that assailed France during the reign of King John. The temerity, the improvidence of that monarch; the dis-

graceful passions of the King of Navarre; his treach-
eries; the barbarous avidity of the nobility; the seditious
disposition of the people; the sanguinary depredations of
the great companies; the ever recurring insolence of
England; all this is expressed without disguise, yet with
extreme moderation. No trait reveals, no fact even fore-
shadows in the author, the future President of a reform-
ing National Assembly, still less the Mayor of Paris,
during a revolutionary effervescence. The author may
make Charles V. say that he will discard favour, and
will call in renown to select his representatives; it will
appear to him that taxes ought to be laid on riches and
spared on poverty; he may even exclaim that oppression
awakens ideas of equality. His temerity will not over-
leap this boundary. Bossuet, Massillon, Bourdaloue,
made the Chair resound with bold words of another
description.

I am far from blaming this scrupulous reserve; when
moderation is united to firmness, it becomes power. In
a word, however, Bailly's patriotism might, I was about
to say ought to, have shown itself more susceptible, more
ardent, prouder. When in the elegant prosopopœia
which closes the éloge, the King of England has recalled with arrogance the fatal day of Poitiers, ought
he not instantly to have restrained that pride within just
limits? ought he not to have cast a hasty glance on the
components of the Black Prince's army? to examine
whether a body of troops, starting from Bordeaux, recruiting in Guienne, did not contain more Gascons than
English? whether France, now bounded by its natural
limits, in its magnificent unity, would not have a right,
every thing being examined, to consider that battle almost
as an event of civil war? ought he not, in short, to have

pointed out, in order to corroborate his remarks, that the knight to whom King John surrendered himself, Denys de Morbecque, was a French officer banished from Artois ?

Self-reliance on the field of battle is the first requisite for obtaining success; now, would not our self-reliance be shaken, if the men most likely to know the facts, and to appreciate them wisely, appeared to think that the Frank race were nationally inferior to other races who had peopled this or that region, either neighbouring or distant ? This, let it be well remarked, is not a puerile susceptibility. Great events may, on a given day, depend on the opinion that the nation has formed of itself. Our neighbours on the other side of the Channel, afford examples on this subject that it would be well to imitate.

In 1767, the Academy of Berlin proposed a prize for an éloge of Leibnitz. The public was somewhat surprised at it. It was generally supposed that Leibnitz had been admirably praised by Fontenelle, and that the subject was exhausted. But from the moment that Bailly's essay, crowned in Prussia, was published, former impressions were quite changed. Every one was anxiously asserting that Bailly's appreciation of his subject might be read with pleasure and benefit, even after Fontenelle's. The éloge composed by the historian of Astronomy will not, certainly, make us forget that written by the first Secretary of the Academy of Sciences. The style is, perhaps, too stiff; perhaps it is also rather declamatory; but the biography, and the analysis of his works, are more complete, especially if we consider the notes; the *universal* Leibnitz is exhibited under more varied points of view.

In 1768, Bailly obtained the award of the prize of

eloquence proposed by the Academy of Rouen. The subject was the éloge of Peter Corneille. In reading this work of our fellow-academician, we may be somewhat surprised at the immense distance that the modest, the timid, the sensitive Bailly puts between the great Corneille, his special favourite, and Racine.

When the French Academy, in 1768, proposed an éloge of Molière for competition, our candidate was vanquished only by Chamfort. And yet, if people had not since that time treated of the author of " Tartufe " to satiety, perhaps I would venture to maintain, notwithstanding some inferiority of style, that Bailly's discourse offered a neater, truer, and more philosophic appreciation of the principal pieces of that immortal poet.

## DEBATES RELATIVE TO THE POST OF PERPETUAL SECRETARY OF THE ACADEMY OF SCIENCES.

We have seen D'Alembert, ever since the year 1763, encouraging Bailly to exercise himself in a style of literary composition then much liked, the style of éloge, and holding out to him in prospect the situation of Perpetual Secretary of the Academy of Sciences. Six years after, the illustrious geometer gave the same advice, and perhaps held out the same hopes, to the young Marquis de Condorcet. This candidate, docile to the voice of his protector, rapidly composed and published the éloges of the early founders of the Academy, of Huyghens, of Mariotte, of Roëmer, &c.

At the beginning of 1773, the Perpetual Secretary, Grandjean de Fouchy, requested that Condorcet should be nominated his successor, provided he survived him. D'Alembert strongly supported this candidateship. Buffon supported Bailly with equal energy; the Academy presented for some weeks the aspect of two hostile camps. There was at last a strongly disputed electoral battle ; the result was the nomination of Condorcet.

I should regret if we had to judge of the sentiments of Bailly, after this defeat, by those of his adherents. Their anger found vent in terms of unpardonable asperity. They said that D'Alembert had "basely betrayed friendship, honour, and the first principles of probity."

They here alluded to a promise of protection, support, coöperation, dating ten years back. But was his promise absolute ? Engaging himself personally to Bailly for a situation that might not become vacant for ten or fifteen years, had D'Alembert, contrary to his duty as an academician, declared beforehand, that any other candidate, whatever might be his talents, would be to him as not existing?

This is what ought to have been ascertained, before giving themselves up to such violent and odious imputations.

Was it not quite natural that the geometer D'Alembert, having to pronounce his opinion between two honourable learned men, gave the preference to the candidate who seemed to him most imbued with the higher mathematics ? The éloges of Condorcet were, besides, by their style, much more in harmony with those that the Academy had approved during three quarters of a century. Before the declaration of the vacancy on the 27th of February, 1773, D'Alembert said to Voltaire, relative to the recueil by Condorcet, "Some one asked me the other day what I thought of that work. I answered by writing on the frontispiece, 'Justice, propriety, learning, clearness, precision, taste, elegance, and nobleness.'" And Voltaire wrote, on the 1st of March, "I have read, while dying, the little book by M. de Condorcet; it is as good in its departments as the éloges by Fontenelle. There is a more noble and more modest philosophy in it, though bold."

And excitement in words and action could not be legitimately reproached in a man who had felt himself supported by a conviction of such distinct and powerful influence.

Among the éloges by Bailly, there is one, that of the Abbé de Lacaille, which not having been written for a literary academy, shows no longer any trace of inflation or declamation, and might, it seems to me, compete with some of the best éloges by Condorcet. Yet, it is curious, that this excellent biography contributed, perhaps as much as D'Alembert's opposition, to make Bailly's claims fail. Vainly did the celebrated astronomer flatter himself in his exordium, "that M. de Fouchy, who, as Secretary of the Academy, had already paid his tribute to Lacaille, would not be displeased at his having followed him in the same career . . . . . that he would not be blamed for repeating the praises due to an illustrious man."

Bailly, in fact, was not blamed aloud; but when the hour for retreat had sounded in M. de Fouchy's ear, without any fuss, without showing himself offended in his self-love, remaining apparently modest, this learned man, in asking for an assistant, selected one who had not undertaken to repeat his éloges; who had not found his biographies insufficient. This preference ought not to be, and was not, uninfluential in the result of the competition.

Bailly, if Perpetual Secretary of the Academy, would

have been obliged to reside constantly at Paris. But Bailly, as member of the Astronomical Section, might retire to the country, and thus escape those thieves of time, as Byron called them, who especially abound in the metropolis. Bailly settled at Chaillot. It was at Chaillot that our fellow-academician composed his best works, those that will sail down the stream of time.

Nature had endowed Bailly with the most happy memory. He did not write his discourses till he had completed them in his head. His first copy was always a clean copy. Every morning Bailly started early from his humble residence at Chaillot; he went to the Bois de Boulogne, and there, walking for many hours at a time, his powerful mind elaborated, coördinated, and robed in all the pomps of language, those high conceptions destined to charm successive generations. Biographers inform us that Crébillon composed in a similar way. And this was, according to several critics, the cause of the incorrectness, of the asperity of style, which disfigure several pieces by that tragic poet. The works of Bailly, and especially the discourses that complete the *History of Astronomy*, invalidate this explanation. I could also appeal to the elegant and pure productions of that poet whom France has just lost and weeps for. No one indeed can be ignorant of his works; Casimir Delavigne, like Bailly, never committed his verses to paper until he had worked them up in his mind to that harmonious perfection which procured for them the unanimous suffrages of all people of taste. Gentlemen, pardon this reminiscence. The heart loves to connect such names as those of Bailly and of Delavigne; those rare and glorious symbols, in whom we find united talent, virtue, and an invariable patriotism.

HISTORY OF ASTRONOMY.—LETTERS ON THE ATLANTIS
    OF PLATO AND ON THE ANCIENT HISTORY OF
    ASIA.

In 1775, Bailly published a quarto volume, entitled
*History of Ancient Astronomy, from its Origin up to the
Establishment of the Alexandrian School.* An analogous
work for the lapse of time, comprised between the Alexandrian School and 1730, appeared in 1779, in two volumes. An additional volume appeared three years later,
entitled the *History of Modern Astronomy up to the Epoch
of* 1782. The fifth part of this immense composition, the
*History of Indian Astronomy,* was published in 1787.

When Bailly undertook this general history of Astronomy, the science possessed nothing of the sort. Erudition
had seized upon some special questions, some detailed
points, but no commanding view had presided over these
investigations.

Weidler's book, published in 1741, was a mere simple
nomenclature of the astronomers of every age, and of
every country; the dates of their birth and death; the
titles of their works. The utility of this precise enumeration of dates and titles did not alter the character of the
book.

Bailly sketches the plan of his work with a masterly
hand in a few lines; he says, "It is interesting to transport one's self back to the times when Astronomy began;
to observe how discoveries were connected together, how
errors have got mixed up with truth, have delayed the
knowledge of it, and retarded its progress; and, after
having followed the various epochs and traversed every
climate, finally to contemplate the edifice founded on the
labours of successive centuries and of various nations."

This vast plan essentially led to the minute discussion and comparison of a multitude of passages both ancient and modern. If the author had mixed up these discussions with the body of the work, he would have laboured for astronomers only. If he had suppressed all discussions, the book would have interested amateurs only. To avoid this double rock, Bailly decided on writing a connected narrative with the quintessence of the facts, and to place the proofs and the discussions of the merely conjectural parts, under the appellation of explanations in separate chapters. Bailly's History, without forfeiting the character of a serious and erudite work, became accessible to the public in general, and contributed to disseminate accurate notions of Astronomy both among literary men and among general society.

When Bailly declared, in the beginning of his book, that he would go back to the very commencement of Astronomy, the reader might expect some pages of pure imagination. I know not, however, whether any body would have expected a chapter of the first volume to be entitled, *Of Antediluvian Astronomy.*

The principal conclusion to which Bailly comes, after an attentive examination of all the positive ideas that antiquity has bequeathed to us is, that we find rather the ruins than the elements of a science in the most ancient Astronomy of Chaldæa, of India, and of China.

After treating of certain ideas of Pluche, Bailly says, "The country of possibilities is immense, and although truth is contained therein, it is not often easy to distinguish it."

Words so reasonable would authorize me to inquire whether the calculations of our fellow-labourer, intended to establish the immense antiquity of the Indian Tables,

are beyond all criticism. But the question has been sufficiently discussed in a passage of *The Exposition of the
System of the World,* on which it would be useless to
insist here. Whatever came from the pen of M. de Laplace was always marked by the stamp of reason and of
evidence. In the first lines of his magnificent work,
after having remarked that "the history of Astronomy
forms an essential part of the history of the human
mind," Bailly observes, "that it is perhaps the true
measure of man's intelligence, and a proof of what he
can do with time and genius." I shall allow myself to
add, that no study offers to reflecting minds more striking
or more curious relations.

When by measurements, in which the evidence of the
method advances equally with the precision of the results,
the volume of the earth is reduced to the millionth part
of the volume of the sun; when the sun himself, transported to the region of the stars, takes up a very modest
place among the thousands of millions of those bodies
that the telescope has revealed to us; when the 38,000,000
of leagues which separate the earth from the sun, have
become, by reason of their comparative smallness, a base
totally insufficient for ascertaining the dimensions of the
visible universe; when even the swiftness of the luminous rays (77,000 leagues per second) barely suffices for
the common valuations of science; when, in short, by a
chain of irresistible proofs, certain stars have retired to
distances that light could not traverse in less than a million of years; we feel as if annihilated by such immensities.
In assigning to man, and to the planet that he inhabits,
so small a position in the material world, Astronomy seems
really to have made progress only to humble us.

But if, on the other hand, we regard the subject from

the opposite point of view, and reflect on the extreme
feebleness of the natural means by the help of which so
many great problems have been attacked and solved; if
we consider that to obtain and measure the greater part
of the quantities now forming the basis of astronomical
computation, man has had greatly to improve the most
delicate of his organs, to add immensely to the power of
his eye; if we remark that it was not less requisite for
him to discover methods adapted to measuring very long
intervals of time, up to the precision of tenths of seconds;
to combat against the most microscopic effects that constant variations of temperature produce in metals, and
therefore in all instruments; to guard against the innumerable illusions that a cold or hot atmosphere, dry or
humid, tranquil or agitated, impresses on the medium
through which the observations have inevitably to be
made; the feeble being resumes all his advantage; by
the side of such wonderful labours of the mind, what
signifies the weakness, the fragility of our body; what
signify the dimensions of the planet, our residence, the
grain of sand on which it has happened to us to appear
for a few moments!

The thousands of questions on which Astronomy has
thrown its dazzling light belong to two entirely distinct
categories; some offered themselves naturally to the
mind, and man had only to seek the means for solving
them; others, according to the beautiful expression of
Pliny, were enveloped in the majesty of nature! When
Bailly lays down in his book these two kinds of problems,
it is with the firmness, the depth, of a consummate
astronomer; and when he shows their importance, their
immensity, it is always with the talent of a writer of the
highest order; it is sometimes with a bewitching elo-

quence. If in the beautiful work we are alluding to,
Astronomy unavoidably assigns to man an imperceptible
place in the material world, she assigns him, on the other
hand, a vast share in the intellectual world. The writings which, supported by the invincible deductions of
science, thus elevate man in his own eyes, will find grateful readers in all climes and times.

In 1775, Bailly sent the first volume of his history to
Voltaire. In thanking him for his present, the illustrious
old man addressed to the author one of those letters that
he alone could write, in which flattering and enlivening
sentences were combined without effort with high reasoning powers. " I have many thanks to return you, (said
the Patriarch of Ferney,) for having on the same day
received a large book on medicine and yours, while I was
still ill; I have not opened the first, I have already read
the second almost entirely, and feel better."

Voltaire, indeed, had read Bailly's work pen in hand,
and he proposed to the illustrious astronomer some queries, which proved both his infinite perspicacity, and
wonderful variety of knowledge. Bailly then felt the
necessity of developing some ideas which in his *History
of Ancient Astronomy* were only accessories to his principal subject. This was the object of the volume that
he published in 1776, under the title of *Letters on the
Origin of the Sciences and of the People of Asia, addressed to M. de Voltaire.* The author modestly announced that " to lead the reader by the interest of the
style to the interest of the question discussed," he would
place at the head of his work three letters from the
author of *Merope*, and he protested against the idea that
he had been induced to play with paradoxes.

According to Bailly, the present nations of Asia are

heirs of an anterior people, who understood Astronomy perfectly. Those Chinese, those Hindoos, so renowned for their learning, would thus have been mere depositaries; we should have to deprive them of the title of inventors. Certain astronomical facts, found in the annals of those southern nations, appear to have belonged to a higher latitude. By these means we discover the true site on the globe of the primitive people, proving against the received opinion that learning came southward from the north.

Bailly also found that the ancient fables, considered physically, appeared to belong to the northern regions of the earth.

In 1779, Bailly published a second collection, forming a sequel to the former, and entitled *Letters on the Atlantis of Plato, and on the Ancient History of Asia.*

Voltaire died before these new letters could be communicated to him. Bailly did not think that this circumstance ought to make him change the form of the discussion already employed in the former series; it is still Voltaire whom he addresses.

The philosopher of Ferney thought it strange that there should be no knowledge of this ancient people, who, according to Bailly, had instructed the Indians. To answer this difficulty, the celebrated astronomer undertakes to prove that some nations have disappeared, without their existence being known to us by any thing beyond tradition. He cites five of these, and in the first rank the Atlantidæ.

Aristotle said that he thought Atlantis was a fiction of Plato's: "He who created it also destroyed it, like the walls that Homer built on the shores of Troy, and then made them disappear." Bailly does not join in this

skepticism. According to him, Plato spoke seriously to
the Athenians of a learned, polished people, but destroyed
and forgotten. Only, he totally repudiates the idea of
the Canaries being the remains of the ancient country of
the Atlantidæ, and now engulfed. Bailly rather places
that nation at Spitzbergen, Greenland, or Nova Zembla,
whose climate may have changed. We should also have
to seek for the Garden of the Hesperides near the Pole ;
in short, the fable of the Phœnix may have arisen in the
Gulf of the Obi, in a region where we must suppose the
sun to have been annually absent during sixty-five days.

It is evident, in many passages, that Bailly is himself
surprised at the singularity of his own conclusions, and
fears that his readers may rather regard them as jokes.
He therefore exclaims, "My pen would not find expressions for thoughts which I did not believe to be true."
Let us add, that no effort is painful to him. Bailly calls
successively to his aid astronomy, history, supported by
vast erudition, philology, the systems of Mairan, of Buffon, relatively to the heat appertaining to the earth. He
does not forget, using his own words, " that in the human
species, still more sensitive than curious, more anxious
for pleasure than for instruction, nothing pleases generally, or for a long time, unless the style is agreeable ;
that dry truth is killed by ennui ! " Yet Bailly makes
few proselytes ; and a species of instinct determines men
of science to despise the fruits of so persevering a labour;
and D'Alembert goes so far as to tax them with poverty,
even with hollow ideas, with vain and ridiculous efforts ;
he goes so far as to call Bailly, relatively to his letters,
the *illuminated brother.* Voltaire is, on the contrary,
very polite and very academical in his communications
with our author. The renown of the Brahmins is dear

to him ; yet this does not prevent his discussing closely the proofs, the arguments of the ingenious astronomer. We could also now enter into a serious discussion. The mysterious veil that in Bailly's time covered the East, is in great part raised. We now know the Astronomy of the Chinese and the Hindoos in all its detail. We know up to what point the latter had carried their mathematical knowledge. The theory of central heat has in a few years made an unhoped-for progress ; in short, comparative philology, prodigiously extended by the invaluable labours of Sacy, Rémusat, Quatremère, Burnouf, and Stanislaus Julien, have thrown strong lights on some historical and geographical questions, where there reigned before a profound darkness. Armed with all these new means of investigation, it might easily be established that the systems relative to an ancient unknown people, first creator of all the sciences, and relative to the Atlantidæ, rest on foundations devoid of solidity. Yet, if Bailly still lived, we should be only just in saying to him, as Voltaire did, merely changing the tense of a verb, " Your two books *were*, Sir, treasures of the most profound erudition and the most ingenious conjectures, adorned with an eloquence of style, which is always suitable to the subject."

FIRST INTERVIEW OF BAILLY WITH FRANKLIN.—HIS ENTRANCE INTO THE FRENCH ACADEMY IN 1783. —HIS RECEPTION. — DISCOURSE. — HIS RUPTURE WITH BUFFON.

Bailly became the particular and intimate friend of Franklin at the end of 1777. The personal acquaintance of these two distinguished men began in the strangest manner.

One of the most illustrious members of the Institute,

Volney, on returning from the New World, said : " The Anglo-Americans tax the French with lightness, with indiscretion, with chattering." (Volney, preface to *The Table of the Climate of the United States*.) Such is the impression, in my opinion very erroneous, at least by comparison, under which the Ambassador Franklin arrived in France. All the world knows that he halted at Chaillot. As an inhabitant of the Commune, Bailly thought it his duty to visit without delay the illustrious guest thus received. He was announced, and Franklin, knowing him by reputation, welcomed him very cordially, and exchanged with his visitor the eight or ten words usual on such occasions. Bailly seated himself by the American philosopher, and discreetly awaited some question to be put to him. Half an hour passed, and Franklin had not opened his mouth. Bailly drew out his snuff-box, and presented it to his neighbour without a word ; the traveller signed with his hand that he did not take snuff. The dumb interview was then prolonged during a whole hour. Bailly finally rose. Then Franklin, as if delighted to have found a Frenchman who could remain silent, extended his hand to him, pressed his visitor's affectionately, exclaiming : " Very well, Monsr. Bailly, very well ! "

After having recounted the anecdote as our academician used amusingly to relate it, I really fear being asked how I look upon it. Well, Gentlemen, whenever this question may be put to me, I shall answer that Bailly and Franklin discussing together some scientific question from the moment of their meeting, would have appeared to me much more worthy of each other, than the two actors of the scene at Chaillot. I will, moreover, grant that we may draw the following inference,—that even men of genius are liable to cross humours; but I must at the same time add that the example is not dangerous, dumbness not being an efficacious method of making one's self valued, or of distinguishing ourselves to advantage.

Bailly was nominated member of the French Academy in the place of M. de Tressan, in November, 1783. The same day, M. de Choiseul Gouffier succeeded to D'Alembert. Thanks to the coincidence of the two nominations, Bailly escaped the sarcasms which the expectant academicians never fail to pour out, with or without reason, against those who have obtained a double crown. This time they vented their spleen exclusively on the great man, thus enabling the astronomer to take possession of his new dignity without raising the usual storm. Let us carefully collect, Gentlemen, from the early years of our academician's life, all that may appear an anticipated compensation for the cruel trials that we shall have to relate in the sequel.

The admission of the eloquent author of the *History of Astronomy* into the Academy, was more difficult than could be supposed by those who have remarked to what slight works certain early and recent writers have owed the same favour. Bailly failed three times. Fontenelle had before him unsuccessfully presented himself once oftener; but Fontenelle underwent these successive checks without ill-humour, and without being discouraged. Bailly, on the contrary, with or without reason, seeing in these unfavourable results of the elections the immediate effect of D'Alembert's enmity, showed himself much more hurt at it, perhaps, than was suitable for a philosopher. In these somewhat envenomed contests, Buffon always gave Bailly a cordial and able support.

Bailly pronounced his reception-discourse in February,

1784. The merits of M. de Tressan were therein celebrated with grace and delicacy. The panegyrist identified himself with his subject. A select public loaded
with praises various passages wherein just and profound
ideas were clothed in all the richness of a forcible and
harmonious style.

Did any one ever speak with more eloquence of the
scientific power revealed by a contemporary discovery!
Listen, Gentlemen, and judge.

" That which the sciences can add to the privileges of
the human race has never been more marked than at the
present moment. They have acquired new domains for
man. The air seems to become as accessible to him as
the waters, and the boldness of his enterprises equals
almost the boldness of his thoughts. The name of
Montgolfier, the names of those hardy navigators of the
new element, will live through time ; but who among us,
on seeing these superb experiments, has not felt his soul
elevated, his ideas expanded, his mind enlarged ? "

I know not whether, all things considered, the satisfaction of self-love which may be attached to academical
titles, to his success in public and important meetings,
ever completely rewarded Bailly for the heartaches he
experienced in his literary career.

A kind and tender intimacy had grown up between the
great naturalist Buffon and the celebrated astronomer.
An academical nomination broke it up. You know it,
Gentlemen ; amongst us a nomination is the apple of
discord ; notwithstanding the most opposite views, every
one then thinks that he is acting for the true interest of
science or of letters ; every one thinks that he is proceeding in the line of strict justice ; every one endeavours
earnestly to make proselytes. So far all is legitimate.

But what is much less so, is forgetting that a vote is a decision, and that in this sense the academician, like the magistrate, may say to the suitor, whether an academician or not, "I give decrees, and not services."

Unfortunately, considerations of this sort, notwithstanding their justice, would make but little impression on the haughty and positive mind of Buffon. That great naturalist wished to have the Abbé Maury nominated; his associate Bailly thought he ought to vote for Sedaine. Let us place ourselves in the ordinary course of things, and it will appear difficult to see in this discordancy a sufficient cause for a rupture between two superior men. *The Unforeseen Wager* and *The Unconscious Philosopher*, considerably balanced the, then very light, weight of Maury. The comic poet had already reached his sixty-sixth year; the Abbé was young. The high character, the irreproachable conduct of Sedaine, might, without disparagement, be put in comparison with what the public knew of the character of the official and the private life of the future cardinal. Whence then had the illustrious naturalist derived such a great affection for Maury, such violent antipathies against Sedaine? It may be surmised that they arose from aristocratic prejudices of rank. Nor is it impossible but that M. le Comte de Buffon instinctively foresaw, with some repugnance, his approaching confraternity with a man formerly a lapidary; but was not Maury the son of a shoemaker? This very small incident of our literary history seemed doomed to remain in obscurity; chance has, I believe, given me the key to it.

You remember, Gentlemen, that aphorism continually quoted by Buffon, and of which he seemed very proud,—

" Style makes the man."

I have discovered that Sedaine made a counterpart of it. The author of *Richard Cœur de Lion* and of *The Deserter* said,—

"Style is nothing, or next to it!"

Place this heresy, in imagination, under the eyes of the immortal writer, whose days and nights were passed in polishing his style, and if you then ask me why he detested Sedaine, I shall have a right to answer: You do not know the human heart.

Bailly firmly resisted the imperious solicitations of his former patron, and refused even to absent himself from the Academy on the day of the nomination. He did not hesitate to sacrifice the attractions and advantages of an illustrious friendship to the performance of a duty; he answered to him who wanted to be master, "I will be free." Honour be to him!

The example of Bailly warns timid men never to listen to mere entreaties, whatever may be their source; not to yield but to good arguments. Those who have thought so little of their own tranquillity as to do any more in academical elections than to give a silent and secret vote, will see on their part, in the noble and painful resistance of an honest man, how culpable they become in trying to substitute authority for persuasion, in wishing to subject conscience to gratitude.

On the occurrence of a similar discord, the astronomer Lemonnier, of the Academy of Sciences, said one day to Lalande, his fellow-academician and former pupil, " I enjoin you not to put your foot again within my door during the semi-revolution of the lunar orbital nodes." Calculation shows this to be nine years. Lalande submitted to the punishment with a truly astronomical punctuality;

but the public, despite the scientific form of the sentence, thought it excessively severe.   What then will be said of that which was pronounced by Buffon?—"We will never see each other more, Sir!"   These words will appear at once both harsh and solemn, for they were occasioned by a difference of opinion on the comparative merits of Sedaine and the Abbé Maury.   Our friend resigned himself to this separation, nor ever allowed his just resentment to be perceived.   I may even remark, that after this brutal disruption he showed himself more attentive than ever to seize opportunities of paying a legitimate homage to the talents and eloquence of the French Pliny.

### REPORT ON ANIMAL MAGNETISM.

We are now going to see the astronomer, the savant, the man of letters, struggling against passions of every kind, excited by the famous question of animal magnetism.

At the beginning of the year 1778, a German doctor established himself at Paris.   This physician could not fail of succeeding in what was then styled high society. He was a stranger.   His government had expelled him; acts of the greatest effrontery and unexampled charlatanism were imputed to him.

His success, however, exceeded all expectations.   The Gluckists and the Piccinists themselves forgot their differences, to occupy themselves exclusively with the new comer.

Mesmer, since we must call him by his name, pretended to have discovered an agent till then totally unknown both in the arts and in physics; an universally distributed fluid, and serving thus as a means of communication and of influence among the celestial globes;—a fluid capable of flux and reflux, which introduced itself more or less abundantly into the substance of the nerves, and acted on them in a useful manner,— thence the name of animal magnetism given to this fluid.

Mesmer said: "Animal magnetism may be accumulated, concentrated, transported, without the aid of any intermediate body. It is reflected like light; musical sounds propagate and augment it."

Properties so distinct, so precise, seemed as if they must be capable of experimental verification. It was requisite, then, to be prepared for some instance of want of success, and Mesmer took good care not to neglect it. The following was his declaration: "Although the fluid be universal, all animated bodies do not equally assimilate it into themselves; there are some even, though very few in number, that by their very presence destroy the effects of this fluid in the surrounding bodies."

So soon as this was admitted, as soon it was allowed to explain instances of non-success by the presence of neutralizing bodies, Mesmer no longer ran any risk of being embarrassed. Nothing prevented his announcing, in full security, "that animal magnetism could immediately cure diseases of the nerves, and mediately other diseases; that it afforded to doctors the means of judging with certainty of the origin, the nature, and the progress of the most complicated maladies; that nature, in short, offered in magnetism a universal means of curing and preserving mankind."

Before quitting Vienna, Mesmer had communicated his systematic notions to the principal learned societies of Europe. The Academy of Sciences at Paris, and the

Royal Society of London, did not think proper to answer. The Academy of Berlin examined the work, and wrote to Mesmer that he was in error.

Some time after his arrival in Paris, Mesmer tried again to get into communication with the Academy of Sciences. This society even acceded to a rendezvous. But, instead of the empty words that were offered them, the academicians required experiments. Mesmer stated —I quote his words—that *it was child's play ;* and the conference had no other result.

The Royal Society of Medicine, being called upon to judge of the pretended cures performed by the Austrian doctor, thought that their agents could not give a well-founded opinion " without having first duly examined the patients to ascertain their state." Mesmer rejected this natural and reasonable proposal. He wished that the agents should be content with the word of honour and attestations of the patients. In this respect, also, the severe letters of the worthy Vicq-d'Azyr put an end to communications which must have ended unsatisfactorily.

The faculty of medicine showed, we think, less wisdom. It refused to examine any thing ; it even proceeded in legal form against one of its regent doctors who had associated himself, they said, with the charlatanism of Mesmer.

These barren debates evidently proved that Mesmer himself was not thoroughly sure of his theory, nor of the efficacy of the means of cure that he employed. Still the public showed itself blind. The infatuation became extreme. French society appeared at one moment divided into magnetizers and magnetized. From one end of the kingdom to the other agents of Mesmer were seen, who, with receipt in hand, put the weak in intellect under contribution.

The magnetizers had had the address to intimate that the mesmeric crises manifested themselves only in persons endowed with a certain sensitiveness. From that moment, in order not to be ranged among the insensible, both men and women, when near the *rod*, assumed the appearance of epileptics.

Was not Father Hervier really in one of those paroxysms of the disease when he wrote, "If Mesmer had lived contemporary with Descartes and Newton, he would have saved them much labour : those great men suspected the existence of the universal fluid; Mesmer has discovered the laws of its action "?

Count de Gébelin showed himself stranger still. The new doctrine would naturally seduce him by its connection with some of the mysterious practices of ancient times; but the author of *The Primitive World* did not content himself with writing in favour of Mesmerism with the enthusiasm of an apostle. Frightful pain, violent griefs, rendered life insupportable to him; Gébelin saw death approaching with satisfaction, so from that moment he begged earnestly that he might not be carried to Mesmer's, where assuredly "he could not die." We must just mention, however, that his request was not attended to; he was carried to Mesmer's, and died while he was being magnetized.

Painting, sculpture, and engraving were constantly repeating the features of this Thaumaturgus. Poets wrote verses to be inscribed on the pedestals of the busts, or below the portraits. Those by Palisot deserve to be quoted, as one of the most curious examples of poetic licences :—

" Behold that man—the glory of his age!
Whose art can all Pandora's ills assuage.
In skill and tact no rival pow'r is known—
E'en Greece, in him, would Æsculapius own." *

Enthusiasm having thus gone to the last limits in verse,
enthusiasm had but one way left to become remarkable
in prose: that is, violence.  Is it not thus that we must
characterize the words of Bergasse?—"The adversaries
of animal magnetism are men who must one day be
doomed to the execration of all time, and to the punishment of the avenging contempt of posterity."

It is rare for violent words not to be followed by violent acts.  Here every thing proceeded according to the
natural course of human events.  We know, indeed, that
some furious admirers of Mesmer attempted to suffocate
Berthollet in the corner of one of the rooms of the Palais
Royal, for having honestly said that the scenes he had
witnessed did not appear to him demonstrative.  We
have this anecdote from Berthollet himself.

The pretensions of the German doctor increased with
the number of his adherents.  To induce him to permit
only three learned men to attend his meetings, M. de
Maurepas offered him, in the name of the king, 20,000
francs a year for life, and 10,000 annually for house-rent.
Yet Mesmer did not accept this offer, but demanded, as
a national recompense, one of the most beautiful châteaux
in the environs of Paris, together with all its territorial
dependencies.

Irritated at finding his claims repulsed, Mesmer quitted

* " Le voilà, ce mortel, dont le siècle s'honore,
Par qui sont replongés au séjour infernal
Tous les fléaux vengeurs que déchaîna Pandore;
Dans son art bienfaisant il n'a pas de rival,
Et la Grèce l'eut pris pour le dieu d'Epidaure."

France, angrily vowing her to the deluge of maladies from which it would have been in his power to save her. In a letter written to Marie Antoinette, the Thaumaturgus declared that he had refused the government offers through austerity.

Through austerity!!! Are we then to believe that, as it was then pretended, Mesmer was entirely ignorant of the French language ; that in this respect his meditations had been exclusively centered on the celebrated verse—

" Fools are here below for our amusement?" *

However this may be, the austerity of Mesmer did not prevent his being most violently angry when he learnt at Spa that Deslon continued the magnetical treatments at Paris. He returned in all haste. His partisans received him with enthusiasm, and set on foot a subscription of 100 louis per head, which produced immediately near 400,000 francs, (16,000*l.*) We now feel some surprise to see, among the names of the subscribers, those of Messrs. de Lafayette, de Ségur, d'Eprémesnil.

Mesmer quitted France a second time about the end of 1781, in quest of a more enlightened government, who could appreciate superior minds. He left behind him a great number of tenacious and ardent adepts, whose importunate conduct at last determined the government to submit the pretended magnetic discoveries to be examined by four Doctors of the Faculty of Paris. These distinguished physicians solicited to have added to them some members of the Academy of Sciences. M. de Breteuil then recommended Messrs. Le Roy, Bory, Lavoisier, Franklin, and Bailly, to form part of the mixed commission. Bailly was finally named reporter.

* " Les sots sont ici-bas pour nos menus plaisirs."

The work of our brother-academician appeared in
August, 1784. Never was a complex question reduced
to its characteristic traits with more penetration and tact;
never did more moderation preside at an examination,
though personal passions seemed to render it impossible;
never was a scientific subject treated in a more dignified
and lucid style.

Nothing equals the credulity of men in whatever
touches their health. This aphorism is an eternal truth.
It explains how a portion of the public has returned to
mesmeric practices; how I shall still perform an interesting task by giving a detailed analysis of the magnificent labours published by our fellow-academician sixty
years ago. This analysis will show, besides, how daring
those men were, who recently, in the bosom of another
academy, constituted themselves passionate defenders of
some old women's tales, which one would have supposed
had been permanently buried in oblivion.

The commissioners go in the first place to the treatment by M. Deslon, examine the famous rod, describe it
carefully, relate the means adopted to excite and direct
magnetism. Bailly then draws out a varied and truly
extraordinary table of the state of the sick people. His
attention is principally attracted by the convulsions that
they designated by the name of *crisis*. He remarked that
in the number of persons in the crisis state, there were
always a great many women, and very few men; he does
not imagine any deceit, however; holds the phenomena
as established, and passes on to search out their causes.

According to Mesmer and his partisans, the cause of
the crisis and of the less characteristic effects, resided in
a particular fluid. It was to search out proofs of the existence of this fluid, that the commissioners had first to

devote their efforts. Indeed, Bailly said, "Animal magnetism may exist without being useful, but it cannot be
useful if it does not exist."

The animal magnetic fluid is not luminous and visible,
like electricity; it does not produce marked and manifest
effects on inert matter, as the fluid of the ordinary mag-
net does; finally, it has no taste. Some magnetizers
asserted that it had a smell; but repeated experiments
proved that they were in error. The existence, then, of
the pretended fluid, could be established only by its effects
on animated beings.

Curative effects would have thrown the commission
into an inextricable dædalus, because nature alone, without any treatment, cures many maladies. In this system
of observations, they could not have hoped to learn the
exact part performed by magnetism, until after a great
number of cures, and after trials oftentimes repeated.

The commissioners, therefore, had to limit themselves
to instantaneous effects of the fluid on the animal organ-
ism.

They then submitted themselves to the experiments,
but using an important precaution. "There is no individual," says Bailly, "in the best state of health, who, if
he closely attended to himself, would not feel within him
an infinity of movements and variations, either of exceedingly slight pain, or of heat, in the various parts of his
body. . . . These variations, which are continually taking
place, are independent of magnetism. . . . The first care
required of the commissioners was, not to be too attentive to what was passing within them. If magnetism is
a real and powerful cause, we have no need to think
about it to make it act and manifest itself; it must, so to
say, force the attention, and make itself perceived by
even a purposely distracted mind."

The commissioners, magnetized by Deslon, felt no effect. After the healthy people, some ailing ones followed, taken of all ages, and from various classes of society. Among these sick people, who amounted to fourteen, five felt some effects. On the remaining nine, magnetism had no effect whatever.

Notwithstanding the pompous announcements, magnetism already could no longer be considered as a certain indicator of diseases.

Here the reporter made a capital remark: magnetism appeared to have no effect on incredulous persons who had submitted to the trials, nor on children. Was it not allowable to think, that the effects obtained in the others proceeded from a previous persuasion as to the efficacy of the means, and that they might be attributed to the influence of imagination? Thence arose another system of experiments. It was desirable to confirm or to destroy this suspicion; "it became therefore requisite to ascertain to what degree imagination influences our sensations, and to establish whether it could have been in part or entirely the cause of the effects attributed to magnetism."

There could be nothing neater or more demonstrative than this portion of the work of the commissioners. They go first to Dr. Jumelin, who, let it be observed, obtains the same effects, the same crises as Deslon and Mesmer, by magnetizing according to an entirely different method, and not restricting himself to any distinction of poles; they select persons who seem to feel the magnetic action most forcibly, and put their imagination at fault by now and then bandaging their eyes.

What happens then?

When the patients see, the seat of the sensations is

exactly the part that is magnetized; when their eyes are bandaged, they locate these same sensations by chance, sometimes in parts very far away from those to which the magnetizer is directing his attention. The patient, whose eyes are covered, often feels marked effects at a time when they are not magnetizing him, and remains, on the contrary, quite passive while they are magnetizing him, without his being aware of it.

Persons of all classes offer similar anomalies. An instructed physician, subjected to these experiments, "feels effects whilst nothing is being done, and often does not feel effects while he is being acted upon. On one occasion, thinking that they had been magnetizing him for ten minutes, this same doctor fancied that he felt a heat in his lumbi, which he compared to that of a stove."

Sensations thus felt, when no magnetizing was exerted, must evidently have been the effect of imagination.

The commissioners were too strict logicians to confine themselves with these experiments. They had established that imagination, in some individuals, can occasion pain, and heat—even a considerable degree of heat—in all parts of the body; but practical female Mesmerizers did more; they agitated certain people to that pitch, that they fell into convulsions. Could the effect of imagination go so far?

Some new experiments entirely did away with these doubts.

A young man was taken to Franklin's garden at Passy, and when it was announced to him that Deslon, who had taken him there, had magnetized a tree, this young man ran about the garden, and fell down in convulsions, but it was not under the magnetized tree: the crisis seized him while he was embracing another tree, very far from the former.

Deslon selected, in the treatment of poor people, two women who had rendered themselves remarkable by their sensitiveness around the famous rod, and took them to Passy. These women fell into convulsions whenever they thought themselves mesmerized, although they were not. At Lavoisier's, the celebrated experiment of the cup gave analogous results. Some plain water engendered convulsions occasionally, when magnetized water did not.

We must really renounce the use of our reason, not to perceive a proof in this collection of experiments, so well arranged that imagination alone can produce all the phenomena observed around the mesmeric rod, and that mesmeric proceedings, cleared from the delusions of imagination, are absolutely without effect. The commissioners, however, recommence the examination on these last grounds, multiply the trials, adopt all possible precautions, and give to their conclusions the evidence of mathematical demonstrations. They establish, finally and experimentally, that the action of the imagination can both occasion the crises to cease, and can engender their occurrence.

Foreseeing that people with an inert or idle mind would be astonished at the important part assigned to the imagination by the commissioners' experiments in the production of mesmeric phenomena, Bailly instanced: sudden affection disturbing the digestive organs; grief giving the jaundice; the fear of fire restoring the use of their legs to paralytic patients; earnest attention stopping the hiccough; fright blanching people's hair in an instant, &c.

The touching or stroking practised in mesmeric treatments, as auxiliaries of magnetism, properly so called,
required no direct experiments, since the principal agent,
—since magnetism itself, had disappeared.  Bailly,
therefore, confined himself, in this respect, to anatomical
and physiological considerations, remarkable for their
clearness and precision.  We read, also, with a lively interest, in his report, some ingenious reflections on the
effects of imitation in those assemblages of magnetized
people.  Bailly compares them to those of theatrical
representations.  He says: "Observe how much stronger the impressions are when there are a great many
spectators, and especially in places where there is the
liberty of applauding.  This sign of particular emotions
produces a general emotion, participated in by everybody according to their respective susceptibility.  This
is also observed in armies on the day of battle, when the
enthusiasm of courage, as well as panic-terrors, propagate themselves with so much rapidity.  The sound of
the drum and of military music, the noise of the cannon,
of the musquetry, the cries, the disorder, stagger the
organs, impart the same movement to men's minds, and
raise their imaginations to a similar degree.  In this
unity of intoxication, an impression once manifested becomes universal; it encourages men to charge, or determines men to fly."  Some very curious examples of
imitation close this portion of Bailly's report.

The commissioners finally examined whether these
convulsions, occasioned by the imagination or by magnetism, could be useful in curing or easing the suffering persons.  The reporter said: "Undoubtedly, the imagination
of sick people often influences the cure of their maladies
very much. . . . There are cases in which every thing

must first be disordered, to enable us to restore order
. . . . but the shock must be unique . . . . whereas in
the public treatment by magnetism . . . . the habit of
the crises cannot but be injurious.

This thought related to the most delicate considerations. It was developed in a report addressed to the
king personally. This report was to have remained
secret, but it was published some years since. It should
not be regretted; the magnetic treatment, regarded in a
certain point of view, pleased sick people much; they
are now aware of all its dangers.

In conclusion, Bailly's report completely upsets an
accredited error. This was an important service, nor
was it the only one. In searching for the imaginary
cause of animal magnetism, they ascertained the real
power that man can exert over man, without the immediate and demonstrable intervention of any physical
agent; they established that "the most simple actions
and signs sometimes produce most powerful effects; that
man's action on the imagination may be reduced to an
art . . . . at least in regard to persons who have faith."
This work finally showed how our faculties should be
experimentally studied; in what way psychology may
one day come to be placed among the exact sciences.

I have always regretted that the commissioners did not
judge it expedient to add a historical chapter to their
excellent work. The immense erudition of Bailly would
have given it an inestimable value. I figure to myself,
also, that in seeing the Mesmeric practices that have now
been in use during upwards of two thousand years, the
public would have asked itself whether so long an interval of time had ever been required to push a good and
useful thing forward into estimation. By circumscribing

himself to this point of view, a few traits would have sufficed.

Plutarch, for example, would have come to the aid of the reporter. He would have showed him Pyrrhus curing complaints of the spleen, by means of frictions made with the great toe of his right foot. Without giving one's self up to a wild spirit of interpretation, we might be permitted to see in that fact the germ of animal magnetism. I admit that one circumstance would have rather unsettled the savant: this was the white cock that the King of Macedon sacrificed to the gods before beginning these frictions.

Vespasian, in his turn, might have figured among the predecessors of Mesmer, in consequence of the extraordinary cures that he effected in Egypt by the action of his foot. It is true that the pretended cure of an old blindness, only by the aid of a little of that emperor's saliva, would have thrown some doubt on the veracity of Suetonius.

Homer and Achilles are not too far back but we might have invoked their names. Joachim Camerarius, indeed, asserted having seen, on a very ancient copy of the Iliad, some verses that the copyists sacrificed because they did not understand them, and in which the poet alluded, not to the heel of Achilles (its celebrity has been well established these three thousand years,) but to the medical properties possessed by the great toe of that same hero's right foot.

What I regret most is, the chapter in which Bailly might have related how certain adepts of Mesmer's had the hardihood to magnetize the moon, so as, on a given day, to make all the astronomers devoted to observing that body fall into a syncope; a perturbation, by the way, that no geometer, from Newton to Laplace, had thought of.

The work of Bailly gave rise to trouble, spite, and anger, among the Mesmerists. It was for many months the target for their combined attacks. All the provinces of France saw refutations of the celebrated report arise : sometimes under the form of calm discussions, decent and moderate ; .but generally with all the characteristics of violence, and the acrimony of a pamphlet.

It would be labour thrown away now to go to the dusty shelves of some special library, to hunt up hundreds of pamphlets, even the titles of which are now completely forgotten. The impartial analysis of that ardent controversy does not call for such labour; I believe at least that I shall attain my aim, by concentrating my attention on two or three writings which, by the strength of the arguments, the merit of the style, or the reputation of their authors, have left some trace in men's minds.

In the first rank of this category of works we must place the elegant pamphlet published by Servan, under the title of *Doubts of a Provincial, proposed to the Gentlemen Medical Commissioners commanded by the King to examine into Animal Magnetism.*

The appearance of this little work of Servan's was saluted in the camp of the Mesmerists with cries of triumph and joy. Undecided minds fell back into doubt and perplexity. Grimm wrote in Nov. 1784: "No cause is desperate. That of magnetism seemed as if it must fall under the reiterated attacks of medicine, of philosophy, of experience and of good sense. ; . . Well, M. Servan, formerly the Attorney-General at Grenoble, has been proving that with talent we may recover from any thing, even from ridicule."

Servan's pamphlet seemed at the time the anchor of salvation for the Mesmerists. The adepts still borrow from it their principal arguments. Let us see, then, whether it has really shaken Bailly's report.

From the very commencing lines, the celebrated Attorney-General puts the question in terms deficient in exactness. If we believe him, the commissioners were called to establish a parallel between magnetism and medicine; " they were to weigh on both sides the errors and the dangers; to indicate with wise discernment what it would be desirable to preserve, and what to retrench, in the two sciences." Thus, according to Servan, the sanative art altogether would have been questioned, and the impartiality of the physicians might appear suspicious. The clever magistrate took care not to forget, on such an occasion, the eternal maxim, no one can be both judge and client. Physicians, then, ought to have been excepted.

There then follows a legitimate homage to the nongraduated academicians, members of the commission: " Before Franklin and Bailly," says the author, " every knee must bend. The one has invented much, the other has discovered much; Franklin belongs to the two worlds, and all ages seem to belong to Bailly." But arming himself afterwards with more cleverness than uprightness, with these words of the reporter, " The commissioners, especially the doctors, made an infinity of experiments," he insinuates under every form that the commissioners accepted of a very passive line of conduct. Thus, putting aside the most positive declarations, pretending even to forget the name, the titles of the reporter, Servan no longer sees before him but one class of adversaries, regent doctors of the Faculty of Paris, and then

he gives full scope to his satirical vein. He holds it even
as an honour that they do not regard him as impartial.
" The doctors have killed me ; what it has pleased them
to leave me of life is not worth, in truth, my seeking a
milder term. . . . . . For these twenty years I have
always been worse through the remedies administered to
me than through my maladies. . . . . . Even were
animal magnetism a chimera, it should be tolerated ; it
would still be useful to mankind, by saving many individuals among them from the incontestable dangers of
vulgar medicine. . . . . I wish that medicine, so long
accustomed to deceive itself, should still deceive itself
now, and that the famous report be nothing but a great
error. . . . . ." Amidst these singular declarations,
there are hundreds of epigrams still more remarkable by
their ingenious and lively turn than by their novelty. If
it were true, Gentlemen, that the medical corps had ever
tried, knowingly, to impose on the vulgar, to hide the
uncertainty of their knowledge, the weakness of their
theories, the vagueness of their conceptions, under an
obscure and pedantic jargon, the immortal and laughable
sarcasms of Molière would not have been more than an
act of strict justice. In all cases every thing has its day ;
now, towards the end of the eighteenth century, the most
delicate, the most thorny points of doctrine were discussed
with an entire good faith, with perfect lucidity, and in a
style that placed many members of the faculty in the
rank of our best speakers. Servan, however, goes beyond the limits of a scientific discussion, when, without
any sort of excuse, he accuses his adversaries of being
anti-mesmerists through esprit de corps, and, what is
worse, through cupidity.

Servan is more in his element when he points out that

the present best established medical theories occasioned
at their birth prolonged debates; when he reminds us
that several medicines have been alternately proscribed
and recommended with vehemence: the author might
even have more deeply undermined this side of his subject. Instead of some unmeaning jokes, why did he not
show us, for example, in a neighbouring country, two
celebrated physicians, Mead and Woodward, deciding,
sword in hand, the quarrel that had arisen between them
as to the purgative treatment of a patient? We should
then have heard Woodward, pierced through and through,
rolling on the ground, and drenched in blood, say to his
adversary with an exhausted voice: "The blow was
harsh, but yet I prefer it to your medicine!"

It is not truth alone that has the privilege of rendering
men passionate. Such was the legitimate result of these
retrospective views. I now ask myself whether, by
labouring to put the truth of this aphorism in full light,
the passionate advocate of Mesmerism showed proof of
ability!

Gentlemen, let us put all these personal attacks aside,
all these recriminations against science and its agents,
who unfortunately had not succeeded in restoring the
health of the morose magistrate. What remains then of
his pamphlet? Two chapters, only two chapters, in
which Bailly's report is treated seriously. The medical
commissioners and the members of the Academy had not
seen, in the real effects of Mesmerism anything more than
was occasioned by imagination. The celebrated magistrate exclaims on this subject, "Any one hearing this
proposition spoken of would suppose, before reading the
report, that the commissioners had treated and cured, or
considerably relieved by the force of imagination, large

tumours, inveterate obstructions, gutta serenas, and strong paralyses." Servan admitted, in short, that magnetism had effected most wonderful cures. But there lay all the question. The cures being admitted, the rest followed as a matter of course.

However incredible these cures might be, they must be admitted, they said, when numerous witnesses certified their truth. Was it owing to chance that attestations were wanting for the miracles at the Cemetery of St. Médard? Did not the counsellor to the parliament, Montgeron, state, in three large quarto volumes, the names of a great multitude of individuals who protested on their honour as illuminati, that the tomb of the Deacon, Páris, had restored sight to the blind, hearing to the deaf, strength to the paralytic; that in a twinkling it cured ailing people of gouty rheumatism, of dropsy, of epilepsy, of phthisis, of abscesses, of ulcers, &c.? Did these attestations, although many emanated from persons of distinction, from the Chevalier Folard, for example, prevent the convulsionists from becoming the laughing-stock of Europe? Did they not see the Duchess of Maine herself laugh at their prowess in the following witty couplet?—

> " A scavenger at the palace-gate
> Who, his left heel being lame,
> Obtained as a most special grace,
> That his right should ail the same." *

Was not government, urged to the utmost, at last obliged to interfere, when the multitude, carrying folly to the extremest bounds, was going to try to resuscitate the

---

\* " Un décrotteur à la royale,
Du talon gauche estropié,
Obtint pour grace spéciale
D'être boiteux de l'autre pié."

7

dead? In short, do we not remember the amusing distich, affixed at the time to the gate of the Cemetery of St. Médard?—

"By royal decree, we prohibit the gods
To work any miracles near to these sods." *

Servan must have known better than any one that in regard to testimony, and in questions of complex facts, quality always carries the day over mere numbers; let us add, that quality does not result either from titles of nobility, or from riches, nor from the social position, nor even from a certain sort of celebrity. What we must seek for in a witness is a calmness of mind and of feeling, a store of knowledge, and a very rare thing, notwithstanding the name it bears, common sense; on the other hand, what we must most avoid is the innate taste of some persons for the extraordinary, the wonderful, the paradoxical. Servan did not at all recollect these precepts in the criticism he wrote on Bailly's work.

We have already remarked that the Commissioners of the Academy and of the Faculty did not assert that the Mesmeric meetings were always ineffectual. They only saw in the crises the mere results of imagination; nor did any sort of magnetic fluid reveal itself to their eyes. I will also prove, that imagination alone generated the refutation that Servan gave to Bailly's theory. "You deny," exclaims the attorney-general, "you deny, gentlemen commissioners, the existence of the fluid which Mesmer has made to act such an important part! I maintain, on the contrary, not only that this fluid exists, but also that it is the medium by the aid of which all the vital func-

* "De par le Roi, défense à Dieu
D'opérer miracle en ce lieu!"

tions are excited; I assert that imagination is one of the
phenomena engendered by this agent; that its greater or
less abundance in this or that among our organs, may
totally change the normal intellectual state of individuals."

Everybody agrees that too great a flow of blood towards the brain produces a stupefaction of the mind.
Analogous or inverse effects might evidently be produced by a subtle, invisible, imponderable fluid, by a
sort of nervous fluid, or magnetic fluid (if this term be
preferred), circulating through our organs. And the
commissioners took good care not to speak on this subject of impossibility. Their thesis was more modest;
they contented themselves with saying that nothing demonstrated the existence of such a fluid. Imagination,
therefore, had no share in their report; but in Servan's
refutation, on the contrary, imagination was the chief
actor.

One thing that was still less proved, if possible, than
any of those that we have been speaking of, is the influence that the magnetic fluid of the magnetizer might
exert on the magnetized person.

In magnetism, properly so called, in that which phys-
icists have studied with so much care and success, the
phenomena are constant. They are reproduced exactly
under the same conditions of form, of duration, and of
quantity, when certain bodies, being present to each
other, find themselves exactly in the same relative positions. That is the essential and necessary character of
all purely material and mechanical action. Was it thus
in the pretended phenomena of animal magnetism? In
no way. To-day the crises would occur in the space of
some seconds; to-morrow they may require several en-

tire hours; and finally, on another day, other circumstances remaining the same, the effect would be positively null. A certain magnetizer exercised a brisk action on a certain patient, and was absolutely powerless on another, who, on the contrary, entered into a crisis under the earliest efforts of a second magnetizer. Instead of one or two universal fluids, there must, then, to explain the phenomena, be as many distinct fluids, and constantly acting, as there exist animated or inanimate beings in the world.

The necessity of such a hypothesis evidently upset Mesmerism from its very foundations; yet the illuminati did not judge thus. All bodies became a focus of special emanations, more or less subtle, more or less abundant, and more or less dissimilar. So far the hypothesis found very few contradictors, even among rigorous minds; but soon these individual corporeal emanations were endowed, relatively towards those, (without the least appearance of proof,) either with a great power of assimilation, or with a decided antagonism, or with a complete neutrality; but they pretended to see in these occult qualities the material causes of the most mysterious affections of the soul. Oh! then doubt had a legitimate right to take possession of·all those minds that had been taught by the strict proceedings of science not to rest satisfied with vain words. In the singular system that I have been explaining, when Corneille says,—

> " There are some secret knots, some sympathies,
>   By whose relations sweet assorted souls
>   Attach themselves the one to the other . . . " *

and when the celebrated Spanish Jesuit Balthazar Gra-

* " Il est des nœuds secrets, il est des sympathies,
    Dont par les doux rapports les âmes assorties
    S'attachent l'une à l'autre."

cian spoke of the natural relationship of minds and hearts, both the one and the other alluded, assuredly without suspecting it, to the mixture, penetration, and easy crossing of two atmospheres.

"I love thee not, Sabidus," wrote Martial, "and I know not why; all that I can tell thee is, that I love thee not." Mesmerists would soon have relieved the poet from his doubts. If Martial loved not Sabidus, it was because their atmospheres could not intermingle without occasioning a kind of storm.

Plutarch informs us that the conqueror of Arminius fainted at the sight of a cock. Antiquity was astonished at this phenomenon. What could be more simple, however? the corporeal emanations of Germanicus and of the cock exercised a repulsive action the one on the other.

The illustrious biographer of Cheronea declares, it is true, that the presence of the cock was not requisite, that its crowing produced exactly the same effect on the adopted son of Tiberius. Now, the crowing may be heard a long way off; the crowing, then, would seem to possess the power of transporting the corporeal emanations of the king of the lower court with great rapidity through space. The thing may appear difficult to believe. As for myself, I think it would be puerile to stop at such a difficulty; have we not leaped high over other difficulties far more embarrassing?

The Maréchal d'Albret was still worse off than Germanicus : the atmosphere that made him fall into a syncope exhaled from the head of a wild boar. A live, complete, whole wild boar produced no effect; but on perceiving the head of the animal detached from the body, the Maréchal was struck as if with lightning. You see, gentlemen, to what sad trials military men would be exposed, if the Mesmerian theory of atmospheric conflicts were to regain favour. We ought to be carefully on our guard against a ruse de guerre, of which no one till then had ever thought,—that is, against cocks, wild boars, &c.,—for through them an army might suddenly be deprived of its commander-in-chief. "It would also be requisite not to entrust command," Montaigne says, "to men who would fly from apples more than from arquebusades."

It is not only amongst the corpuscular emanations of living animals that the Mesmerists asserted conflicts to occur. They unhesitatingly extended their speculations to dead bodies. Some ancients dreamt that a catgut cord made of a wolf's intestines would never strike in unison with one made from a lamb's intestine; a discord of atmospheres renders the phenomenon possible. It is still a conflict of corporeal emanations that explains the other aphorism of an ancient philosopher: "The sound of a drum made with a wolf's skin takes away all sonorousness from a drum made with a lamb's skin."

Here I pause, Gentlemen. Montesquieu said: "When God created the brains of human beings, he did not intend to guarantee them."

To conclude: Servan's witty, piquant, agreeably written pamphlet was worthy under this triple claim of the reception with which the public honoured it; but it did not shake, in any one part, the lucid, majestic, elegant report by Bailly. The magistrate of Grénoble has said, that in his long experience he had met men accustomed to reflect without laughing, and other men who only wished to laugh without reflecting. Bailly thought of the first class when he wrote his memorable report.

*Thę Doubts of the Provincial man* were destined only for
the other class.

It was also to these light and laughing souls that Servan exclusively addressed himself some time after, if it
be true that the *Queries of the young Doctor Rhubarbini
de Purgandis* were written by him.

Rhubarbini de Purgandis sets to work manfully.  In
his opinion the report by Franklin, by Lavoisier, by
Bailly, is, in the scientific life of those learned men, what
the *Monades* were for Leibnitz, the *Whirlwinds* for Descartes, the *Commentary on the Apocalypse* for Newton.
These examples may enable us to judge of the rest, and
render all farther refutation unnecessary.

Bailly's report destroyed root and branch the ideas, thè
systems, the practices of Mesmer and of his adepts.  Let
us add sincerely that we have no right to appeal to him
in regard to modern somnambulism.  The greater portion of the phenomena now grouped around that name
were neither known nor announced in 1783.  A magnetizer certainly says the most improbable thing in the
world, when he affirms that a given individual in the
state of somnambulism can see every thing in the most
profound darkness, that he can read through a wall, and
even without the help of his eyes.  But the improbability
of these announcements does not result from the celebrated report, for Bailly does not mention such marvels,
neither in praise nor dispraise ; he does not say one word
about them.  The physicist, the doctor, the merely curious man who gives himself up to experiments in somnambulism, who thinks he must examine whether, in
certain states of nervous excitement, some individuals
are really endowed with extraordinary faculties; with
the faculty, for example, of reading with their stomach,

or with their heel; people who wish to know exactly up
to what point the phenomena so boldly asserted by the
magnetizers of our epoch may be within the domain of
rogues and sharks ; all such people, we say, do not at all
deny the authority of the subject in question, nor do they
put themselves really in opposition to the Lavoisiers, the
Franklins, or the Baillys ; they dive into an entirely new
world, of which those illustrious learned men did not even
suspect the existence.

I cannot approve of the mystery adopted by some
grave learned men, who, in the present day, attend experiments on somnambulism. Doubt is a proof of diffidence, and has rarely been inimical to the progress of
science. We could not say the same of incredulity. He
who, except in pure mathematics, pronounces the word
*impossible,* is deficient in prudence. Reserve is especially requisite when we treat of animal organization.

Our senses, notwithstanding twenty-four centuries of
study, observations, and researches, are far from being
an exhausted subject. Take, for example, the ear. A
celebrated natural philosopher, Wollaston, occupied himself with it; and immediately we learn, that with an
equal sensibility as regards the low notes a certain individual can hear the highest tones, whilst another cannot
hear them at all; and it becomes proved that certain
men, with perfectly sound organs, never heard the cricket
in the chimney-corner, yet did not doubt but that bats
occasionally utter a piercing cry; and attention being
once awakened to these singular results, observers have
found the most extraordinary differences of sensibility
between their right ear and their left ear, &c.

Our vision offers phenomena not less curious, and an
infinitely vaster field of research. Experience has proved,

for example, that some people are absolutely blind to certain colours, as red, and enjoy perfect vision relatively to yellow, to green, and to blue.    If the Newtonian theory of emission be true, we must irrevocably admit that a ray ceases to be light as soon as we diminish its velocity by one ten thousandth part.    Thence flow those natural conjectures, which -are well worthy of experimental examination : all men do not see by the same rays ; decided differences may exist in this respect in the same individual during various nervous states ; it is possible that the calorific rays, the dark rays of one person, may be the luminous rays of another person, and reciprocally ; the calorific rays traverse some substances freely, which are therefore called diathermal, these substances, thus far, had been called opaque, because they transmit no ray commonly called luminous ;  now the words opaque and diathermal have no absolute meaning.    The diathermals allow those rays to pass through which constitute the light of one man ;  and they stop those which constitute the light of another man.    Perhaps in this way the key of many phenomena might be found, that till now have remained without any plausible explanation.

Nothing, in the marvels of somnambulism, raised more doubts than an oft-repeated assertion, relative to the power which certain persons are said to possess in a state of crisis, of deciphering a letter at a distance with the foot, the nape of the neck, or the stomach.    The word *impossible* in this instance seemed quite legitimate.    Still, I do not doubt but some rigid minds would withhold it after having reflected on the ingenious experiments by which Moser produces, also at a distance, very distinct images of all sorts of objects, on all sorts of bodies, and in the most complete darkness.

7 *

When we call to mind in what immense proportion electric or magnetic actions increase by motion, we shall be less inclined to deride the rapid actions of magnetizers.

In here recording these developed reflections, I wished to show that somnambulism must not be rejected *à priori*, especially by those who have kept well up with the recent progress of the physical sciences. I have indicated some facts, some resemblances, by which magnetizers might defend themselves against those who would think it superfluous to attempt new experiments, or even to see them performed. For my part, I hesitate not to acknowledge it, although, notwithstanding the possibilities that I have pointed out, I do not admit the reality of the readings, neither through a wall, nor through any other opaque body, nor by the mere intromission of the elbow, or the occiput,—still, I should not fulfil the duties of an academician if I refused to attend the meetings where such phenomena were promised me, provided they granted me sufficient influence as regards the proofs, for me to feel assured that I was not become the victim of mere jugglery.

Nor did Franklin, Lavoisier, or Bailly believe in Mesmeric magnetism before they became members of the Government Commission, and yet we may have remarked with what minute and scrupulous care they varied the experiments. True philosophers ought to have constantly before their eyes those two beautiful lines :—

" To suppose that every thing has been discovered is a profound error: It is mistaking the horizon for the limits of the world." *

* " Croire tout découvert est un erreur profonde:
    C'est prendre l'horizon pour les bornes du monde."

ELECTION OF BAILLY INTO THE ACADEMY OF IN-
SCRIPTIONS.

In speaking of the pretended identity of the Atlantis, or of the kingdom of Ophir under Solomon with America, Bailly says, in his fourteenth letter to Voltaire: "Those ideas belonged to the age of learned men, but not to the philosophic age." And elsewhere (in the twenty-first letter) we read these words: "Do not fear that I shall fatigue you by heavy erudition." To have supposed that erudition could be heavy and be deficient in philosophy, was for certain people of a secondary order an unpardonable crime. And thus we saw men, excited by a sentiment of hate, arm themselves with a critical microscope, and painfully seek out imperfections in the innumerable quotations with which Bailly had strengthened himself. The harvest was not abundant; yet, these eager ferrets succeeded in discovering some weak points, some interpretations that might be contested. Their joy then knew no bounds. Bailly was treated with haughty disdain: "His literary erudition was very superficial; he had not the key of the sanctuary of antiquity; he was everywhere deficient in languages."

That it might not be supposed that these reproaches had any reference to Oriental literature, Bailly's adversaries added: "that he had not the least tincture of the ancient languages; that he did not know Latin."

He did not know Latin? And do you not see, you stupid enemies of the great Astronomer, that if it had been possible to compose such learned works as *The History of Astronomy*, and *The Letters on the Atlantis*, without referring to the original texts, by using translations only, you would no longer have preserved any importance in the literary world.    How is it that you did not remark, that by despoiling Bailly (and very arbitrarily) of the knowledge of Latin, you showed the inutility of studying that language to become both one of your best writers, and one of the most illustrious philosophers of the age ?

The Academy of Inscriptions and Belles Lettres, far from participating in these puerile rancours, in the blind prejudices of some lost children of erudition, called Bailly to its bosom in 1785.    Till then, Fontenelle alone had had the honour of belonging to the three great Academies of France.    Bailly always showed himself very proud of a distinction which associated his name in an unusual manner with that of the illustrious writer, whose eulogies contributed so powerfully to make science and scientific men known and respected.

Independently of this special consideration, Bailly, as member of the French Academy, could all the better appreciate the suffrages of the Academy of Inscriptions, since there existed at that time between those two illustrious Societies a strong and inexplicable feeling of rivalry.    This had even proceeded so far, that by a most solemn deliberation of the Academy of Inscriptions, any of its members would have ceased to belong to it, would have been irrevocably expelled, if they had even only endeavoured to be received into the French Academy; and the king having annulled this deliberation, fifteen academicians bound themselves by oath to observe all its stipulations notwithstanding; furthermore, in 1783, Choiseul Gouffier, who was accused of having adhered to the principles of the fifteen confederates, and then of having allowed himself to be nominated by the rival Academy, was summoned by Anquetil to appear before the Tribunal of the Marshals of France for having broken his word of honour.

But, I may be allowed here to remark, superior men have always had the privilege of upsetting, by the mere influence of their name, the obstacles that routine, prejudices, and jealousy wished to oppose to the progress and the union of souls.

## REPORT ON THE HOSPITALS.

Scientific tribunals, which should pronounce in the first instance while awaiting the definitive judgment of the public, were one of the requisites of our epoch; and thus, without any formal prescription of its successive regulations, the Academy of Sciences has been gradually led on to appoint committees to examine all the papers that have been presented to it, and to pronounce on their novelty, merit, and importance. This labour is generally an ungrateful one, and without glory, but talent has immense privileges; entrust Bailly with those simple Academical Reports, and their publication becomes an event.

M. Poyet, architect and comptroller of buildings in Paris, presented to Government in the course of the year 1785, a paper wherein he strove to establish the necessity of removing the Hôtel Dieu, and building a new hospital in another locality. This document, submitted by order of the king to the judgment of the Academy, gave rise, directly or indirectly, to three deliberations. The Academic Commissioners were, Lassone, Tenou, Tillet, Darcet, Daubenton, Bailly, Coulomb, Laplace, and Lavoisier. It was Bailly, however, who constantly held the pen. His reports have been honoured with a great and just celebrity. The progress of science would

now perhaps allow of some modification being made in
the ideas of the illustrious commissioners. Their views
on warming-rooms, on their size, on ventilation, on general health, might, for example, receive some real ameliorations; but nothing could add to the sentiments of
respect inspired by Bailly's work. What clearness of
exposition! What neatness, what simplicity of style!
Never did a writer put himself more completely out of
view; never did a man more sincerely seek to make the
sacred cause of humanity triumph. The interest that
Bailly takes in the poor is deep, but always exempt
from parade; his words are moderate, full of gentleness,
even where hasty feelings of anger and indignation would
have been legitimate. Of anger and of indignation! Yes,
Gentlemen; listen, and decide!

I have cited the names of the commissioners. At no
time, and in no country, could more virtue and learning
have been united. These select men, regulating themselves in this respect according to the most common logic,
felt that the task of pronouncing on a reform of the Hôtel
Dieu imposed on them the necessity of examining that
establishment. "We have asked," said their interpreter,
"we have asked the Board of Administration to permit
us to see the hospital in detail, and accompanied by some
one who could guide and instruct us . . . . . we required
to know several particulars; we asked for them, but we
obtained nothing."

We have obtained nothing! These are the sad, the
incredible words, that men so worthy of respect are obliged to insert in the first line of their report!

What then was the authority that allowed itself to be
so deficient in the most usual respect towards commissioners invested with the confidence of the King, the

Academy, and the Public? This authority consisted of several administrators (the type of them, it is said, is not quite lost), who looked upon the poor as their patrimony, who devoted to them a disinterested but unproductive activity; who were impatient at any amelioration, the germ of which had not developed itself either in their own heads, or in those of certain men, philanthropic by nature, or by the privilege of their station. Ah! if by enlightened and constant care that vast asylum, opened to poverty and sickness, near Notre-Dame, had been then conducted, now sixty years ago, only in a tolerable way, we should have understood how, in taking human nature into consideration, the promoters of this great benefit would have repelled an examination that seemed to throw a doubt on their zeal and on their good sense. But alas! let us take from Bailly's work a few traits of the moderate and faithful picture that he drew of the Hôtel Dieu, and you shall decide, Gentlemen, whether the susceptibility of the administrators was authorized; whether, on the contrary, they ought not themselves to have anticipated the unhoped-for help from the king's power, united to science, which was now offered to them; whether by retarding certain ameliorations by a single day, they did not commit the crime of lèse-humanity.

In 1786, infirmities of all sorts were treated at the Hôtel Dieu: surgical maladies, chronic maladies, contagious maladies, female diseases, infantine diseases, &c. Every thing was admitted, but all presented an inevitable confusion.

A patient on arriving was often laid in the bed and in the sheets of a man who had had the itch, and had just died.

The department reserved for madmen being very con-

fined, two were put to sleep together. Two madmen in
the same sheets! Nature revolts at the very thought of
it.

In the ward of St. Francis, reserved exclusively for
men having the smallpox, there were sometimes, for
want of other space, as many as six adults or eight children in a bed not a mètre and a half wide.

The women attacked with this frightful disease were
mixed in the ward of St. Monique with others who had
only a simple fever, and the latter fell an inevitable prey
to the hideous contagion, in the very place where, full of
confidence, they had hoped to recover their health.

'Women with child, women in their confinement, were
equally crowded, pell-mell, on narrow and infected
truckle-beds.

Nor let it be supposed that I have borrowed from
Bailly's Report some purely exceptional cases, belonging
to those cruel times, when whole populations, suffering
under some epidemic, were tried beyond all human an-
ticipation. In their usual state, the beds of the Hôtel
Dieu, which were not a mètre and a half wide, contained
four, and often six patients; they were placed alternately
head and feet, the feet of one touching the shoulders of
the next; each had only for his share of space 25 centimetres (9 inches); now, a man of medium size, lying
with his arms close to his body, is 48 centimetres (16
inches) broad at the shoulders. The poor patients then
could not keep within the bed but by lying on their side
perfectly immovable; no one could turn without pushing,
without waking his neighbour; they therefore used to
agree, as far as their illness would allow, for some of
them to remain up part of the night in the space between
the beds, whilst the others slept; and when the ap-

proaches of death nailed these unfortunate people to
their place, did they not energetically curse that help,
which in such a situation could only prolong their painful agony.

But it was not only that beds thus placed were a
source of discomfort, of disgust; that they prevented
rest and sleep; that an insupportable heat occasioned
and propagated diseases of the skin and frightful vermin;
that the fever patient bedewed his neighbours with his
profuse perspirations; and that in the critical moment
he might be chilled by contact with those whose hot fit
would occur later, &c. Still more serious effects resulted from the presence of many sick in the same bed;
the food, the medicines, intended for one person, often
found their way to another. In short, Gentlemen, in
those beds of multiple population, the dead often lay for
hours, and sometimes whole nights, intermingled with the
living. The principal charitable establishment in Paris
thus offered those dreadful coincidences, that the poets
of Rome, that ancient historians have represented under
King Mezentius, as the utmost extreme of barbarism.

Such was, Gentlemen, the normal state of the old
Hôtel Dieu. One word, one word only, will suffice to
tell what was the exceptional state: they placed some
patients on the tops or testers of those same beds, where
we have found so much suffering, so many authorized
maledictions.

Now, Gentlemen, let us, together with our fellow academician, cast a glance on the ward of surgical operations.

This ward was full of patients. The operations were
performed in their presence. Bailly says, " We see
there the preparations for the torment; there are heard

the cries of the tormented. He who has to suffer the next day has before him a picture of his own future sufferings ; he who has passed through this terrible trial, must be deeply moved at those cries so similar to his own, and must feel his agonies repeated ; and these terrors, these emotions, he experiences in the midst of the progress of inflammation or suppuration, retarding his recovery, and at the hazard of his life." . . . . " To what purpose," Bailly justly exclaims, " would you make an unfortunate man suffer, if there is not a probability of saving him, and unless we increase that probability by all possible precautions ? "

The heart aches, the mind becomes confused, at the sight of so much misery ; and yet this hospital, so little in harmony with its intended purpose, still existed sixty years ago. It is in a capital, the centre of the arts, of knowledge, of polished manners ; it is in an age renowned for the development of public wealth, for the progress of luxury, for the ruinous creation of a crowd of establishments devoted to amusements, to worldly and futile pleasures ; it is by the side of the palace of an opulent archbishop ; it is at the gate of a sumptuous cathedral, that the unfortunate, under the deceitful mask of charity, underwent such dreadful tortures. To whom should we impute the long duration of this vicious and inhuman organization ?

To the professors of the art ? No, no, Gentlemen ! By an inconceivable anomaly the physicians, the surgeons, never obtained more than a secondary, a subordinate influence over the administration of the hospitals. No, no, the sentiments of the medical body for the poor could not be doubted, at an epoch and in a country where Dr. Anthony Petit thus answered the irritated

queen, Marie Antoinette : "Madam, if I came not yesterday to Versailles, it was because I was attending the
lying-in of a peasant, who was in the greatest danger.
Your Majesty errs, however, in supposing that I neglect
the Dauphin for the poor; I have hitherto treated the
young child with as much attention and care as if he
had been the son of one of your grooms."

Preference was granted to the most suffering, to those
in most danger, disregarding rank and fortune; such
was, you see, Gentlemen, the sublime rule of the French
Medical Corps; and such is still its gospel.   I want no
other proof of it than those admirable words addressed
by our fellow labourer Larrey, to his friend Tanchou,
when wounded at the Battle of Montmirail : " Your
wound is slight, sir; we have only room and straw in
this ambulance for serious wounds.   They will take you
into that stable."

The medical corps could not, therefore, with any reason be accused or suspected in regard to the old Hôtel
Dieu of Paris.

If economy be invoked, I find an answer quite à-pro-
pos in Bailly : the daily allowance for the patients at the
Hôtel Dieu was notably higher than in other establishments in the capital more charitably organized.

Would any one go so far as to assert that the sick condemned to seek refuge in the hospitals, having their sen-
sibilities blunted by labour, by misery, by their daily
sufferings, would but faintly feel the effects of the horrible arrangements that the old Hôtel Dieu revealed to all
clear-sighted people ?   I will quote from the report of
our colleague ; " The maladies continue nearly double
the time at the Hôtel Dieu, compared with those at the
Charité : the mortality there is also nearly double ! . . . .

All the trepanned die in that hospital; whilst this operation is tolerably successful in Paris, and still more so at
Versailles."

The maladies continue double the time! The mortality there is double! All those who are trepanned die!
The lying-in women die in a frightful proportion, &c.
These are the sinister words that strike the eye periodically in the statements of the Hôtel Dieu; and yet, let
us repeat it, years passed away, and nothing was altered
in the organization of the great hospital! Why persist
in remaining in a condition that so openly wounds humanity? Must we, together with Cabanis, who also
abused the old Hôtel Dieu severely, " must we exclaim,
that abuses known by all the world, against which every
voice is raised, have secret supporters who know how to
defend them, in a manner to tire out well-meaning people? Must we speak of false characters, perverse hearts,
that seemed to regard errors and abuses as their patrimony?" Let us dare to acknowledge it, Gentlemen,
evil is generally perpetrated in a less wicked manner:
it is done without the intervention of any strong passion;
by vulgar, yet all-powerful routine, and ignorance. I
observe the same thought, though couched in the calm
and cleverly circumspect language of Bailly: "The
Hôtel Dieu has existed perhaps since the seventh century, and if this hospital is the most imperfect of all, it
is because it is the oldest. From the earliest date of
this establishment, good has been sought, the desire has
been to adhere to it, and constancy has appeared a duty.
From this cause, all useful novelties have with difficulty
found admission; any reform is difficult; there is a numerous administration to convince; there is an immense
mass to move."

The immensity of the mass, however, did not discourage the old Commissioners of the Academy. Let this conduct serve as an example to learned men, to administrators, who might be called upon to cast an investigating eye on the whole of our beneficent and humane establishments. Undoubtedly, the abuses, if any yet exist, have not individually any thing to be compared to those to which Bailly's report did justice; but would it be impossible for them to have sprung up afresh in the course of half a century, and that in proportion to their multiplicity, they should still make enormous and deplorable breaches in the patrimony of the poor?

I shall modify very slightly, Gentlemen, the concluding words of our illustrious colleague's report, and I shall not in the least alter their innate meaning, if I say, in finishing this long analysis: " Each poor man is now laid alone in a bed, and he owes it principally to the gifted, persevering, and courageous efforts of the Academy of Sciences. The poor man ought to know it, and the poor man will not forget it." Happy, Gentlemen, happy the academy that can adorn itself with such reminiscences!

## REPORT ON THE SLAUGHTER-HOUSES.

An attentive glance at the past has been, in all ages and in all countries, the infallible means of rightly appreciating the present. When we direct this glance to the sanitary state of Paris, the name of Bailly will again present itself in the first line amongst the promoters of a capital amelioration, which I shall point out in a few words.

Notwithstanding the numerous acts of parliament,—notwithstanding the positive police regulations, which dated back to Charles IX., to Henry III., to Henry IV.,

slaughter-houses still existed in the interior of the capital
in 1788; for instance, at l'Apport-Paris, La Croix-Rouge,
in the streets of the Butcheries, Mont-Martre, Saint-Mar-
tin, Traversine, &c. &c.   The oxen were, consequently,
driven in droves through frequented parts of the town;
enraged by the noise of the carriages, by the excitements
of the children, by the attacks or barking of the wandering dogs, they often sought to escape,—entered houses or
alleys, spread alarm everywhere, gored people, and committed great damage.   Fetid gases exhaled from buildings too small and badly ventilated; the offal that had to
be carried away gave out an insupportable smell; the
blood flowed through the gutters of the neighbourhood,
with other remains of the animals, and putrefied there.
The melting of tallow, an inevitable annexation of all
slaughter-houses, spread around disgusting emanations,
and occasioned a constant danger of fire.

So inconvenient, so repulsive a state of things, awakened the solicitude of individuals and of the public administration; the problem was submitted to our predecessors,
and Bailly, as usual, became the reporter of the Academical Committee.   The other members were Messrs. Tillet,
Darcet, Daubenton, Coulomb, Lavoisier, and Laplace.

When Napoleon, wishing to liberate Paris from the
dangerous and insalubrious results of internal slaughter-
houses, decreed the construction of the fine slaughter-
houses known by everybody, he found the subject already
well examined, exhibited in all its points of view, in
Bailly's excellent work.   "We ask," said the reporter of
the Academical Commission in 1788, "we ask that the
shambles be removed to a distance from the interior of
Paris;" and these interior shambles have disappeared
accordingly.   Does it create surprise that it required more

than fifteen years to obtain the grant of this most reasonable demand? I will further remark that, unfortunately, there was nothing exceptional in this; he who sows a thought in a field rank with prejudices, with private interests, and with routine, must never expect an early harvest.

## BIOGRAPHIES OF COOK AND OF GRESSET.

The publication of the five quarto volumes of which *the History of Astronomy* consists, together with the two powerful *reports* that I have just described, had worn out Bailly. To relax and amuse his mind, he resumed the style of composition that had enchanted him in his youth; he wrote some biographies, amongst others, that of Captain Cook, proposed as a prize-subject by the Academy of Marseilles, and the Life of Gresset.

The biography of Gresset first appeared anonymously. This circumstance gave rise to a singular scene, which the author used to relate with a smile. I will here myself repeat the principal traits of it, if it be only to deter writers, whoever they may be, from launching their works into the world without affixing their names to them.

The Marchioness of Créqui was a lady in the high circles of society, to whom a copy of the eulogium of the author of *Vert-Vert* was presented as an offering. Some days after Bailly went to pay her a visit; did he hope to hear her speak favourably of the new work? I know not. At all events, our predecessor would have been ill rewarded for his curiosity.

" Do you know," said the great lady as soon as she saw him, " a Eulogy of Gresset recently published? The author has sent me a copy of it, without naming himself.

He will probably come to see me; he may, perhaps, have come already. What could I say to him? I do not think any one ever wrote worse. He mistakes obscurity for profundity; it is the darkness before the creation."

Notwithstanding all Bailly's efforts to change the subject of the conversation, perhaps on account of those very efforts, the Marchioness rose, goes in search of the pam-phlet, puts it into the author's hands, and begs of him to read aloud, if it be but the first page—quite enough, she said, to enable one to judge of the rest.

Bailly used to read remarkably well. I leave it to be guessed whether, on this occasion, he was able to exercise this talent. Superfluous trouble! Madame de Créqui interrupted him at each sentence by the most disagreeable commentaries, by exclamations such as the following: " Detestable style!" " Confusion worse confounded!" and other similar amenities. Bailly did not succeed in extorting any indulgences from Madame de Créqui, when, fortunately, the arrival of another visitor put an end to this insupportable torture.

Two years after this, Bailly having become the first personage in the city, some booksellers collected all his opuscula and published them. This time, the Marchioness, who had lost all recollection of the scene that I have been describing, overpowered the Mayor of Paris with compliments and felicitations on account of this same eulogy, which she had before treated with such inhuman rigour.

Such a contrast excited the mirth of the author. Still, might I dare to say so, Madame de Créqui was, perhaps, sincere on both occasions; had the exaggerations of praise and of criticism been put aside, it would not have been

impossible to defend both opinions.  The early pages of
the pamphlet might appear embarrassed and obscure,
whilst in the rest there might be found great refinement,
elegance, and appreciations full of taste.

### ASSEMBLY OF THE NOTABLES.—BAILLY IS NAMED FIRST DEPUTY OF PARIS ; AND SOON AFTER DEAN OR SENIOR OF THE DEPUTIES OF THE COMMUNES.

The Assembly of the Notables had no other effect than
to show in a stronger light the disorder of the finances,
and the other wounds that were galling France.  It was
then that the Parliament of Paris asked for the convocation of the States General.  This demand was unfavour-
ably received by Cardinal de Brienne.  Soon afterwards
the convocation became a necessity, and Necker, now in
the ministry, announced, in the month of November,
1788, that it was decreed in Council, and that the king
had even granted to the third estate a double representation, which had been so imprudently disputed by the
courtiers.

The districts were formed, on the king's convocation,
the 21st of April, 1789.  That day was the first day of
Bailly's political life.  It was on the 21st of April that
the Citizen of Chaillot, entering the Hall of the *Feuil-
lants*, imagined, he said, that " he breathed a new atmosphere," and regarded " as a phenomenon that he should
have become something in the body-politic, merely from
his being a citizen."

The elections were to be made in two gradations.
Bailly was named first elector of his district.  A few
days after, at the general meeting, the Assembly called
him to the Board in quality of secretary.  Thus it was
our fellow-academician who, in the beginning, drew up

8

the celebrated *procès-verbal* of the meetings of the electors of Paris, so often quoted by the historians of the
revolution.

Bailly also took an active part in drawing up the records of his district, and the records of the body of electors.  The part he acted in these two capacities could
not be doubtful, if we judge of it by the three following
short quotations extracted from his memoirs: "The nation must remember that she is sovereign and mistress to
order every thing. . . . . It is not when reason awakes,
that we should allege ancient privileges and absurd prejudices. . . . . I shall praise the electors of Paris who
were the first to conceive the idea of prefacing the
French Constitution with a declaration of the Rights of
Man."

Bailly had always been so extremely reserved in his
conduct and in his writings, that it was difficult to sur-
mise under what point of view he would consider the
national agitation of '89.   Hence, at the very beginning, the Abbé Maury, of the French Academy, proposed to unite himself to Bailly, and that they should
reside at Versailles, and have an apartment in common
between them.   It is difficult to avoid a smile when one
compares the conduct of the eloquent and impetuous
Abbé with the categorical declarations, so distinct and so
progressive, of the learned astronomer.

On Tuesday, the 12th of May, the general assembly
of the electors proceeded to ballot for the nomination of
the first deputy of Paris.   Bailly was chosen.

This nomination is often quoted as a proof of the high
intelligence, and of the wisdom of our fathers, two qualities which, since that epoch, must have been constantly
on the decline, if we are to believe the blind Pessimists.

Such an accusation imposed on me the duty of carrying the appreciation of this wisdom, of this intelligence that is held up against us, even to numerical correctness. The following is the result: the majority of the votes was 159; Bailly obtained 173; this was fourteen more than he required. If fourteen votes had changed sides the result would have been different. Was this an incident, I ask, to exclaim so much against?

Bailly showed himself deeply affected by this mark of the confidence with which he was regarded. His sensibility, his gratitude, did not prevent him, however, from recording in his memoirs the following *naive* observation: " I observed in the Assembly of the Electors a great dislike for literary men, and for the academicians."

I recommend this remark to all studious men who, by circumstances or by a sense of duty, may be thrown into the whirlpool of politics. Perhaps I may yield to the temptation of developing it, when I shall have to characterize Bailly's connection with his co-laborers in the first municipality of Paris.

The great question on the verification of the powers was already strongly agitated, the day that Bailly and the other Deputies of Paris for the first time were able to go to Versailles; our academician had only spoken once in that majestic assembly, viz: to induce the adoption of the method of voting by members being *seated* or *standing*,—when, on the 3d of June, he was named Senior of the Deputies of the Communes (or Commons). Formerly, the right of presiding in the third house of the kingdom belonged to the provost of the merchants. Bailly in his diffidence thought that the assembly, in assigning the chair to him, had wished to compensate the capital for the loss of an old privilege. This considera-

tion induced him to accept of a duty that he thought
above his powers,—he who always depicted himself as
timid to an extreme, and not possessing a facility of
speaking.

Men's minds were more animated, more ardent in 1789
than those would admit who always see in the present a
faithful image of the past. But calumny, that murderous arm of political party, already respected no position.
Knowledge, loyalty, virtue, did not suffice to shelter any
one from its poisoned darts. Bailly experienced it on
the very day after his nomination to such an eminent post
as President of the Communes.

On the 29th of May, the Communes had voted an
address to the king on the constantly recurring difficulties that the nobility opposed to the union of the States
General in one assembly. In order to carry out this
most solemn deliberation, Bailly solicited an audience, in
which the moderate and respectful expression of the anxiety of six hundred loyal deputies was to be presented to
the monarch. In the midst of these strifes the Dauphin
died. Without taking the trouble to consult dates, the
court party immediately represented Bailly as a stranger
to the commonest proprieties, and totally deficient in feeling ; he ought, they said, to have respected the most allowable of griefs ; his importunities had been barbarous.

I had imagined that such ridiculous accusations were
no longer thought of; the categorical explanations that
Bailly himself gave on this topic, seemed to me as if they
would have suffced to convince the most prejudiced. I
was deceived, Gentlemen ; the reproach of violence, of
brutal insensibility, has just been repeated by the pen of
a clever and a conscientious man. I will give his recital :
" Scarcely two hours had elapsed since the royal child

had breathed his last sigh, when Bailly, President of the
Third Estate, insisted on admission to the king, who had
prohibited any one being allowed to intrude upon him.
But so positive was the demand, that they were obliged
to yield, and Louis XVI. exclaimed, ' There are then no
fathers in that chamber of the Third Estate.' The
chamber very much applauded this trait of brutal insensibility in Bailly, which they termed a trait of Spartan
stoicism."

As many errors as words. The following is the truth.
The illness of the Dauphin had not prevented the two
privileged orders from being received by the king. This
preference offended the Communes. They ordered the
President to solicit an audience. He discharged his duty
with great caution. All his proceedings were concerted
with two ministers, Necker and M. de Barentin. The
king answered, " It is impossible for me to see M. Bailly
in the situation in which I am to-night, nor to-morrow
morning, nor to fix a day for receiving the deputation of
the Third Estate." The note ends with these words :
" Show my note to M. Bailly for his vindication."

Thus, on the day of these events the Dauphin was not
dead ; thus the king was not obliged to yield, he did not
receive Bailly; thus the chamber had no act of insensibility to applaud ; thus Louis XVI. perceived so clearly
that the President of the Communes was fulfilling the
duties of his office, that he felt it requisite to give him
an exoneration.

The death of the Dauphin happened on the 4th of
June. As soon as the assembly of the Third Estate
were informed of it, they charged the President, I quote
the very words, " to report to their majesties the deep
grief with which this news had penetrated the Communes."

A deputation of twenty members, having Bailly at their head, was received on the 6th. The President thus expressed himself: " Your faithful Communes are deeply moved by the circumstance in which your majesty has the goodness to receive their deputation, and they take the liberty to address to you the expression of all their regrets, and of their respectful sensibility."

Such language can, I think, be delivered without uneasiness to the appreciation of all good men.

Let us be correct; the Communes did not obtain at once the audience that they demanded on account of the difficulties of the ceremonial. They would have wished to make the Third Estate speak kneeling. " This custom," said M. de Barentin, " has existed from time immemorial, ánd if the king wished . . . ." " And if twenty-five millions of men do not wish it," exclaimed Bailly, interrupting the minister, " where are the means to force them ? " " The two privileged orders," replied the Guard of the Seals, somewhat stunned by the apostrophe, " no longer require the Third Estate to bend the knee ; but, after having formerly possessed immense privileges in the ceremonial, they limit themselves now to asking some difference. This difference I cannot find." " Do not take the trouble to seek for it," replied the President hastily : " however slight the difference might be, the Communes will not suffer it."

This digression was required through a grave and recent error. The memory of Bailly will not suffer by it, since it has afforded me the opportunity of establishing, beyond any reply, that in our fellow academician a noble firmness was on occasions allied to urbanity, mildness, and politeness. But what will be said of the puerilities which I have been obliged to recall, of the mean pretensions of the courtiers on the eve of an immense revolution ?   When the Greeks of the Lower Empire, instead of going on the ramparts valiantly to repel the attacks of the Turks, remained night and day collected around some sophists in their lyceums and academies, their sterile debates at least related to some intellectual questions ; but at Versailles, there was nothing in action, on the part of two out of three orders, but the most miserable vanity.

By an express arrangement, decreed from the beginning, among the Members of the Communes, the Dean or President had to be renewed every week.   Notwithstanding the incessant representations of Bailly, this legislative article was long neglected, so fortunate did the Assembly feel in having at their head this eminent man, who to undeniable knowledge, united sincerity, moderation, and a degree of patriotism not less appreciated.

He thus presided over the Third Estate on the memorable days that determined the march of our great revolution.

On the 17th of June, for instance, when the Deputies of the Communes, worn out with the tergiversations of the other two orders, showed that in case of need they would act without their concurrence, and resolutely adopted the title of National Assembly,—they provided against presumed projects of dissolution, by stamping as illegal all levies of contribution which were not granted by the Assembly.

Again, on the 20th of June, when the Members of the National Assembly, affronted at the Hall having been closed and their meetings suspended without an official notification, with only the simple form of placards and public criers, as if a mere theatre was in question, they assembled at a tennis-court, and " took an oath never to separate, but to assemble wherever circumstances might render it requisite, until the Constitution of the Kingdom should be established and confirmed on solid foundations."

Once more, Bailly was still at the head of his colleagues on the 23d of June, when, by an inexcusable inconsistency, and which perhaps was not without some influence on the events of that day, the Deputies of the Third Estate were detained a long time at the servants' door of the Hall of Meeting, and in the rain ; while the deputies of the other two orders, to whom a more convenient and more suitable entrance had been assigned, were already in their places.

The account that Bailly gave of the celebrated royal meeting on the 23d of June, does not exactly agree with that of most historians.

The king finished his speech with the following imprudent words : " I order you, Gentlemen, to separate immediately."

The whole of the nobility and a portion of the clergy retired ; while the Deputies of the Communes remained quietly in their places. The Grand Master of the Ceremonies having remarked it, approaching Bailly said to him, " You heard the king's order, Sir ? " The illustrious President answered, " I cannot adjourn the Assembly until it has deliberated on it." " Is that indeed your answer, and am I to communicate it to the king ? " " Yes, Sir," replied Bailly, and immediately addressing the Deputies who surrounded him, he said, " It appears to me that the assembled nation cannot receive an order."

It was after this debate, at once both firm and moderate, that Mirabeau addressed from his place the well-known apostrophe to M. de Brézé. The President disapproved both of the basis and the form of it; he felt that there was no sufficient motive; for, said he, the Grand Master of the Ceremonies made use of no menace; he had not in any way insinuated that there was an intention to resort to force; he had not, above all, spoken of bayonets. At all events, there is an essential difference between the words of Mirabeau as related in almost all the Histories of the Revolution, and those reported by Bailly. According to our illustrious colleague the impetuous tribune exclaimed, " Go tell those who sent you, that the force of bayonets can do nothing against the will of the nation." This is, to my mind, much more energetic than the common version. The expression, " We will only retire by the force of bayonets ! " had always appeared to me, notwithstanding the admiration conceded to it, to imply only a resistance which would cease on the arrival of a corporal and half-a-dozen soldiers.

Bailly quitted the chair of President of the National Assembly on the 2d of July. His scientific celebrity, his virtue, his conciliating spirit, had not been superfluous in habituating certain men to see a member of the Communes preside over an assembly in which there was a prince of the blood, a prince of the church, the greatest lords of the kingdom, and all the high dignitaries of the clergy. The first person named to succeed to Bailly was the Duke d'Orléans. After his refusal, the Assembly chose the Archbishop of Vienne (Pompignan).

Bailly recalls to mind with sensibility, in his memoirs, the testimonies of esteem that he obtained through his difficult and laborious presidency. The 3d of July, on

8 *

the proposition of the Duke de la Rochefoucauld and of the Archbishop of Bordeaux, the National Assembly sent a deputation to their illustrious ex-president, to thank him (these are the precise words) " for his noble, wise, and firm conduct." The electoral body of Bordeaux had been beforehand with these homages. The Chamber of Commerce of that town, at the same time, decided that the portrait of the great citizen should decorate their hall of meeting. The Academy of Sciences, the Academy of Inscriptions and Belles Lettres, did not remain insensible to the glory that one of their members had acquired in the career of politics, and testified it by numerous deputations. Finally, Marmontel, in the name of the French Academy, expressed to Bailly " how proud that assembly was to count among its members an Aristides that no one was tired of calling the Just."

I shall not excite surprise, I hope, by adding, after such brilliant testimonies of sympathy, that the inhabitants of Chaillot celebrated the return of Bailly amongst them by fêtes, and fireworks, and that even the curate of the parish and the churchwardens, unwilling to be surpassed by their fellow-citizens, nominated the historian of antediluvian astronomy honorary churchwarden. I will, at all events, repress the smile that might arise from such private reminiscences, by reminding the reader that a man's moral character is better appreciated by his neighbours, to whom he shows himself daily without disguise, than that of more considerable persons, who are only seen on state occasions, and in official costume.

BAILLY BECOMES MAYOR OF PARIS. — SCARCITY. —
MARAT DECLARES HIMSELF INIMICAL TO THE
MAYOR. — EVENTS OF THE 6TH OF OCTOBER.

The Bastille had been taken on the 14th of July.
That event, on which, during upwards of half a century,
there have been endless discussions, on opposite sides,
was characterized in the following way, in the address to
the National Assembly, drawn up by M. Moreau de
Saint Méry, in the name of the City Committee :—

" Yesterday will be for ever memorable by the taking
of a citadel, consequent on the Governor's perfidy. The
bravery of the people was irritated by the breaking of
the word of honour. This act (the strongest proof that
the nation who knows best how to obey, is jealous of its
just liberties,) has been followed by incidents that from
the public misfortunes might have been foreseen."

Lally Tollendal said to the Parisians, on the 15th of
July : " In the disastrous circumstances that have just
occurred, we did not cease to participate in your griefs ;
and we have also participated in your anger ; it was just."

The National Assembly solicited and obtained permission from the king on the 15th of July, to send a deputation to Paris, which they flattered themselves would
restore order and peace in that great city, then in a con-
vulsed state. Madame Bailly, always influenced by
fear, endeavoured, though vainly, to dissuade her husband from joining the appointed deputies. The learned
academician naïvely replied, " After a presidency that
has been applauded, I am not sorry to show myself to my
fellow-citizens." You see, Gentlemen, that Bailly always
admits the future reader of his Posthumous Memoirs
confidentially into his most secret feelings.

The deputation completed its mandate at the Town Hall, to the entire satisfaction of the Parisian populace ; the Archbishop of Paris, its President, had already proposed to go in procession to the Cathedral to sing *Te Deum ;* they were preparing to depart, when the Assembly, giving way to a spontaneous enthusiasm, with an unanimous voice, proclaimed Bailly Mayor of Paris, and Lafayette Commander-in-Chief of the National Guard, the creation of which had just been authorized.

The official minutes of the Municipality state, that on being thus unexpectedly named, Bailly bent forward to the Assembly, his eyes bathed in tears, and that amidst his sobs he could only utter a few unconnected words to express his gratitude. The Mayor's own recital differs very little from this official relation. Still I shall quote it as a model of sincerity and of modesty.

" I know not whether I wept, I know not what I said ; but I remember well that I was never so surprised, so confused, and so beneath myself. Surprise adding to my usual timidity before a large assembly, I rose, I stammered out a few words that were not heard, and that I did not hear myself, but which my agitation, much more than my mouth, rendered expressive. Another effect of my sudden stupidity was, that I accepted without knowing what a burden I was taking on myself."

Bailly having become Mayor, and being tacitly accepted by the National Assembly, even from the 16th of July, availed himself of his intimacy with Vicq-d'Azyr, the Queen's physician, to persuade Louis XVI. to show himself to the Parisians. This advice was listened to. On the 17th the new magistrate addressed the king near the barrière de la Conférence, in a discourse that began thus :—

" I bring to your Majesty the keys of your good city
of Paris. They are the same that were presented to
Henry IV. He had reconquered his people, here the
people have reconquered their king."

The antithesis : " he had reconquered his people, here
the people have reconquered their king," was universally
applauded. But since then, it has been criticized with
bitterness and violence. The enemies of the Revolution
have striven to discover in it an intention of committing
an outrage, to which the character of Bailly, and still
more so the first glance at an examination of the rest of
his discourse, give a flat contradiction. I will acknowledge, Gentlemen, I think that I have even a right to decline the epithet of " unfortunate," which one of our most
respectable colleagues in the French Academy has pronounced relative to this celebrated phrase, while doing
justice at the same time to the sentiments of the author.
The poison contained in the few words that I have quoted,
was very inoffensive, since more than a year passed without any courtier, though furnished like a microscope with
all the monarchical susceptibilities, beginning to suspect
its existence.

The Mayor of Paris was at the Hôtel de Ville in the
midst of those same Parisian citizens who inspired him,
a few months before, with the mortifying reflection already
quoted : " I remarked in the Assembly of Electors a dislike to literary people and Academicians." The feeling
did not appear to be changed.

The political movement in 1789, had been preceded
by two very serious physical perturbations which had
great influence on the march of events. Every one is
aware, that the excessively rigorous winter of 1788–89
was the cause of severe sufferings to the people. But it

may not be so generally known, that on the 13th of July, 1788, a fall of hail of unprecedented size and quantity, in a few hours completely ravaged the two parallel zones lying between the department of the Charente and the frontiers of the Pays-Bas, and that in consequence of this frightful hail, the wheat partly failed, both in the north and in the west of France, until after the harvest of 1789.

The scarcity was already severely felt, when Bailly on the 15th of July accepted the appointment of Mayor of Paris. That day, it had been ascertained, from an examination of the quantity of corn at the Market Hall and of the private stocks of the bakers, that the supply of grain and flour would be entirely exhausted in three days. The next day, the 16th of July, all the overseers in the victualling administration had disappeared. This flight, the natural consequence of the terrible intimidation that hovered over those who were in any way connected with the furnishing of provisions, interrupted the operations which had been commenced, and exposed the city of Paris to famine.

Bailly, a magistrate of only one day's standing, considered that the multitude understands nothing, hears nothing when bread fails ; that a scarcity, either real or supposed, is the great promoter of riots; that all classes of the population grant their sympathy to whoever cries, *I am hungry ;* that this lamentable cry soon unites individuals of all ages, of both sexes, of every condition, in one common sentiment of blind fury ; that no human power could maintain order and tranquillity in the bosom of a population that dreads the want of food ; he therefore resolved to devote his days and his nights to provisioning the capital; to deserve, as he himself said, the title of the *Father nourisher of the Parisians,*—that title of which he showed himself always so proud, after having painfully gained it.

Bailly day by day recorded in his Memoirs a statement of his actions, of his anxieties, and of his fears. It may be good for the instruction of the more fortunate administrators of the present epoch, to insert here a few lines from the journal of our colleague.

"18th August. Our provisions are very much reduced. Those of the morrow depend strictly on the arrangements made on the previous evening; and now amidst this distress, we learn that our flour-wagons have been stopped at Bourg-la-Reine; that some banditti are pillaging the markets in the direction of Rouen, that they have seized twenty wagons of flour that were destined for us; . . . that the unfortunate Sauvage was massacred at Saint Germain-en-Laye; . . . . that Thomassin escaped with difficulty from the fury of the populace at Choisy."

By repeating either these literal words, or something equivalent to them, for every day of distress throughout the year 1789, an exact idea may be formed of the anxieties that Bailly experienced from the morning after his installation as mayor. I deceive myself; to complete the picture we ought also to record the unreflecting and inconsiderate actions of a multitude of people whose destiny appeared to be, to meddle with every thing and to spoil every thing. I will not resist the wish to show one of these self-important men, starving (or very nearly so) the city of Paris.

"21st August. The store of victuals, Bailly says, was so scanty, that the lives of the inhabitants of Paris depended on the somewhat mathematical precision of our arrangements. Having learnt that a barge with eighteen

hundred sacks of flour had arrived at Poissy, I immediately despatched a hundred wagons from Paris to
fetch them.   And behold, in the evening, an officer without powers and without orders, related before me, that
having met some wagons on the Poissy road, he made
them go back, because he did not think that there was a
wharf for any loaded barge on the Seine.   It would be
difficult for me to describe the despair and the anger
into which this recital threw me.   We were obliged to
put sentinels at the bakers' doors ! "

The despair and the anger of Bailly were very natural.
Even now, after more than half a century, no one thinks
without a shudder of that obscure individual who, from
not believing that a loaded barge could get up to Poissy,
was going, on the 21st August, 1789, to plunge the capital into bloody disorders.

By means of perseverance, devotedness, and courage,
Bailly succeeded in overcoming all the difficulties that
the real scarcity, and the fictitious one, which was still
more redoubtable, caused daily to arise.   He succeeded,
but his health from that epoch was deeply injured; his
mind had undergone several of those severe shocks that
we can never entirely recover from.   Our colleague
said, " when I used to pass the bakers' shops during the
scarcity, and saw them besieged by a crowd, my heart
sunk within me ; and even now that abundance has been
restored to us, the sight of one of those shops strikes me
with a deep emotion."

The administrative conflicts, the source of which lay
in the very bosom of the Council of the Commune, daily
drew from Bailly the following exclamation, a faithful
image of his mind : *I have ceased to be happy.*   The
embarrassments that proceeded from external sources

touched him much less, and yet they were far from contemptible.   Let us surmount our repugnance, although a
reasonable one; let us cast a firm look on the sink where
the unworthy calumnies were manufactured, of which
Bailly was for some time the object.

Several years before our first revolution, a native of
Neufchatel quitted his mountains, traversed the Jura,
and lighted upon Paris.   Without means, without any
recognized talent, without eminence of any sort, repulsive
in appearance, of a more than negligent deportment, it
seemed unlikely that he should hope, or even dream, of
success; but the young traveller had been told to have
full confidence, although a celebrated academician had
not yet given that singular definition of our country,
" France is the home of foreigners."   At all events, the
definition was not erroneous in this instance, for soon
after his arrival, the Neufchatelois was appointed physician to the household of one of the princes of the royal
family, and formed strict intimacies with the greater part
of the powerful people about the court.

This stranger thirsted for literary glory.   Amongst his
early productions, a medico-philosophical work figured in
three volumes, relative to the reciprocal influences of the
mind and the body.   The author thought he had produced a *chef d'œuvre;* even Voltaire was not thought to
be above analyzing it suitably; let us hasten to say that
the illustrious old man, yielding to the pressing solicitations of the Duke de Praslin, one of the most active
patrons of the Swiss doctor, promised to study the work
and give his opinion of it.

The author was at the acmé of his wishes.   After having pompously announced that the seat of the soul is in
the *meninges* (cerebral membrane), could there be any

thing to fear from the liberal thinker of Ferney? He had only forgotten that the patriarch was above all a man of good taste, and that the book on the body and soul offended all the proprieties of life. Voltaire's article appeared. He began with this severe and just lesson— " We should not be prodigal of contempt towards others, and of esteem for ourselves, to such a degree as will be revolting to our readers." The end was still more overwhelming. " We see harlequin everywhere cutting capers to amuse the pit."

Harlequin had received a sufficient dose. Not having succeeded in literature, he threw himself upon the sciences.

On betaking himself to this new career, the doctor of Neufchatel attacked Newton. But unluckily his criticisms were directed precisely to those points wherein optics may vie in evidence with geometry itself. This time the patron was M. de Maillebois, and the tribunal the Academy of Sciences.

The Academy pronounced its judgment gravely, without inflicting a word of ridicule ; for example, it did not speak of harlequin ; but it did not therefore remain the less established that the pretended experiments, intended, it was said, to upset Newton's, on the unequal refrangibility of variously coloured rays, and the explanation of the rainbow, &c., had absolutely no scientific value.

Still the author would not allow himself to have been beaten. He even conceived the possibility of retaliation ; and, availing himself of his intimacy with the Duke de Villeroy, governor of the second city in the kingdom, he got the Academy of Lyons to propose for competition all the questions in optics, which for several years past had been the subjects of its disquisitions ; he even furnished the amount of the prize out of his own pocket, under an assumed name.

The prize so longed for, and so singularly proposed, was not obtained, however, by the Duke de Villeroy's candidate, but by the astronomer Flaugergues. From that instant, the pseudo-physicist became the bitter enemy of the scientific bodies of the whole universe, of whoever bore the title of an academician. Putting aside all shame, he no longer made himself known in the field of natural philosophy, merely by imaginary experiments, or by juggleries; he had recourse to contemptible practices, with the object of throwing doubt upon the clearest and best proved principles of science; for example, the metallic needles discovered by the academician Charles, and which the foreign doctor had adroitly concealed in a cake of resin, in order to contradict the common opinion of the electric non-conductibility of that substance.

These details were necessary. I could not avoid characterizing the journalist who by his daily calumnies contributed most to undermine the popularity of Bailly. It was requisite besides, once for all, to strip him in this circle of the epithet of philosopher, with which men of the world, and even some historians, inconsiderately gratified him. When a man reveals himself by some brilliant and intelligent works, the public is pleased to find them united with good qualities of the heart. Nor should its joy be less hearty on discovering the absence of all intellectual merit in a man who had before shown himself despicable by his passions, or his vices, or even only by serious blemishes of character.

If I have not yet named the enemy of our colleague, if I have contented myself with recounting his actions, it is in order to avoid as much as I can the painful feeling

that his name must raise here.    Judge, Gentlemen,
weigh, my scruples : the furious persecutor of Bailly, of
whom I have been talking to you for some minutes, was
Marat.

The revolution of '89 just occurred in time to relieve
the abortive author, physiologist, and physicist from the
intolerable position into which he had been thrown by his
inability and his quackery.

As soon as the revolution had assumed a decided
movement, great surprise was occasioned by the sudden
transformations excited in the inferior walks of the political world.   Marat was one of the most striking examples
of these hasty changes of principles.   The Neufchatel
physician had shown himself a violent adversary to those
opinions that occasioned the convocation of the assembly
of Notables, and the national commotion in '89.   At that
time democratical institutions had not a more bitter or
more violent censor.   Marat liked it to be believed that
in quitting France for England, he fled especially from
the spectacle of social renovation which was odious to
him.   Yet a month after the taking of the Bastille, he
returned to Paris, established a journal, and from its very
beginning left far behind him, even those who, in the
hope of making themselves remarkable, thought they
must push exaggeration to its very farthest limits.   The
former connection of Marat with M. de Calonne was
perfectly well known; they remembered these words of
Pitt's : "The French must go through liberty, and then
be brought back to their old government by licence;"
the avowed adversaries of revolution testified by their
conduct, by their votes, and even by their imprudent
words, that according to them, *the worst* was the only
means of returning to what they call *the good ;* and yet

these instructive comparisons struck only eight or ten members of our great assemblies, so small a share has suspicion in the national character, so painful is distrust to French sincerity. The historians of our troubles themselves have but skimmed the question that I have just raised—assuredly a very important and very curious one. In such matters, the part of a prophet is tolerably hazardous; yet I do not hesitate to predict, that a minute study of the conduct and of the discourses of Marat, would lead the mind more and more to those chapters in a treatise on the chase, wherein we see depicted bad species of falcons and hawks, at first only pursuing the game by a sign from the master, and for his advantage; but by degrees taking pleasure in these bloody struggles, and entering on the sport at last with passion and for their own profit.

Marat took good care not to forget that during a revolution, men, naturally suspicious, act in their more immediate affairs so as to render those persons suspected whose duty it is to watch over them. The Mayor of Paris, the General Commandant of the National Guard, were the first objects, therefore, at which the pamphleteer aimed. As an academician, Bailly had an extra claim to his hate.

Among men of Marat's disposition, the wounds of self-love never heal. Without the hateful passions derived from this source, who would believe that an individual, whose time was divided between the superintendence of a daily journal, the drawing up of innumerable placards with which he covered the walls of Paris, together with the struggles of the Convention, the disputes not less fierce of the clubs; that an individual who, besides, had given himself the task of imposing an Agrarian law on

the country, could find time to write the very long letters
against the old official adversaries of his bad experiments,
his absurd theories, his lucubrations devoid both of erudition and of talent; letters in which the Monges, the La-
places, the Lavoisiers are treated with such an entire
neglect of justice and of truth, and with such a cynical
spirit, that my respect for this assembly prevents my
quoting a single expression.

It was not then only the Mayor of Paris whom the
pretended friend of the people persecuted; it was also
the Academician Bailly. But the illustrious philosopher,
the virtuous magistrate, gave no hold for positive and
decided criminations. The hideous pamphleteer understood this well; and therefore he adopted vague insinua-
tions, that allowed of no possible refutation, a method
which, we may remark by the way, has not been without
imitators. Marat exclaimed every day: " Let Bailly
send in his accounts!" and the most powerful figure of
rhetoric, as Napoleon said, repetition, finally inspires
doubts in a stupid portion of the public, in some feeble,
ignorant, and credulous minds in the Council of the
Commune; and the scrupulous magistrate wished, in
fact, to send in his accounts. Here they are in two
lines: Bailly never had the handling of any public funds.
He left the Hôtel de Ville, after having spent there two
thirds of his patrimony. If his functions had been long
protracted, he would have retired completely ruined.
Before the Commune assigned him any salary, the expenses of our colleague in charities already exceeded
30,000 livres.

That was, Gentlemen, the final result. The details
would be more striking, and the name of Bailly would
ennoble them. I could show our colleague entering only

once with his wife, to regulate the furnishing of the apartments that the Commune assigned him; rejecting all that
had the appearance of luxury or even of elegance; to
replace sets of china by sets of earthenware, new carpets
by the half-used ones of M. de Crosnes, writing tables
of mahogany by writing tables of walnut, &c. But all
this would appear an indirect criticism, which is far from
my thoughts. From the same motives, I will not say,
that inimical to all sinecures, of all plurality of appoint-
ments, when the functions are not fulfilled, the Mayor of
Paris, since he no longer regularly attended the meetings
of the National Assembly, no longer fingered the pay of
a deputy, and that this was proved, to the great confusion
of the idiots, whose minds had been disturbed by Marat's
clamours. Yet I will record that Bailly refused all that
in the incomes of his predecessors had proceeded from
an impure source; as, for example, the allowances from
the lotteries, the amount of which was by his orders
constantly paid into the coffers of the Commune.

You see, Gentlemen, that no trouble was required to
show that the disinterestedness of Bailly was great,
enlightened, dictated by virtue, and that it was at least
equal to his other eminent qualities. In the series of
accusations that I have extracted from the pamphlets
of that epoch, there is one, however, as to which, all
things considered, I will not attempt to defend Bailly.
He accepted a livery from the city; on this point no
blame was attached to him; but the colours of the livery
were very gaudy. Perhaps the inventors of these bright
shades had imagined, that the insignia of the first magistrate of the metropolis, in a ceremony, in a crowd, should,
like the light from a Pharos, strike even inattentive
eyes. But these explanations regard those who would

make of Bailly a perfectly rational being, a man absolutely faultless; I, although his admirer, I resign myself
to admit that in a laborious life, strewed with so many
rocks, he committed the horrible crime, unpardonable let
it be called, of having accepted from the Commune a
livery of gaudy colours.

Bailly figured in the events of the month of October
1789, only by the unsuccessful efforts he made at Paris,
to arrange with Lafayette how to prevent a great crowd
of women from going to Versailles. When this crowd,
considerably increased, returned on the 6th October very
tumultuously escorting the carriages of the royal family,
Bailly harangued the king at the Barrière de la Conférence. Three days after, he also complimented the Queen
at the Tuileries in the name of the Municipal Council.

On retiring from the National Assembly, which he
then called a Cavern of Anthropophagi, Lally Tollendal
published a letter in which he found bitter fault with
Bailly on account of these discourses. Lally was angry,
recollecting that the day when the king reëntered his
capital as a prisoner, surrounded by a very disrespectful
crowd, and preceded by the heads of his body-guards,
had appeared to Bailly a fine day!

If the two heads had been in the procession, Bailly
becomes inexcusable; but the two epochs, or rather hours
(to speak more correctly), have been confounded; the
wretched men, who after a conflict with the body-guard,
brought their barbarous trophies to Paris, left Versailles
in the morning; they were arrested and imprisoned, by
order of the municipality, as soon as they had entered
the barriers of the capital. Thus the hideous circumstance reported by Lally was the dream of a wild imagination.

## A GLANCE AT THE POSTHUMOUS MEMOIR OF BAILLY.

Bailly's Memoirs have thus far served me as a guide and check; now that this resource fails me, let us refer to his posthumous work.

I could only consult those Memoirs as far as they related to the public or private life of our colleague. Historians may consult them in a more general point of view. They will find some valuable facts in them, related without prejudice; ample matter for new and fruitful reflections on the way in which revolutions are generated, increase, and lead to catastrophes. Bailly is less positive, less absolute, less slashing, than the generality of his contemporaries, even respecting those events in which circumstances assigned to him the principal part to be acted; hence when he points out some low intrigue, in distinct and categorical terms, he inspires full confidence.

When the occasion will allow of it, Bailly praises with enthusiasm; a noble action fills him with joy; he puts it together and relates it with relish. This disposition of mind is sufficiently rare to deserve mention.

The day, still far off, when we shall finally recognize that our great revolution presented, even in the interior, even during the most cruel epochs, something besides anarchical and sanguinary scenes: the day when, like the intrepid fishermen in the Gulf of Persia and on the coasts of Ceylon, a zealous and impartial writer will consent to plunge head-foremost into the ocean of facts of all sorts, of which our fathers were witnesses, and exclusively seize the pearls, disdainfully rejecting the mud,—Bailly's Memoirs will furnish a glorious contingent to this national work. Two or three quotations will explain my ideas,

9

and will show, besides, how scrupulously Bailly registered all that could shed honour on our country.

I will take the first fact from the military annals; a grenadier of the French Guard saves his commanding officer's life, although the people thought that they had great reason of complaint against him. " Grenadier, what is your name?" exclaimed the Duke de Châtelet, full of gratitude. The soldier replied, " Colonel, my name is that of all my comrades."

I will borrow the second fact from the civil annals: Stephen de Larivière, one of the electors of Paris, had gone on the 20th of July, to fetch Berthier de Sauvigny, who had been fatally arrested at Compiègne, on the false report that the Assembly of the Town Hall wished to prosecute him as intendant of the army, by which a few days before the capital had been surrounded. The journey was performed in an open cabriolet, amidst the insults of a misled population, who imputed to the prisoner the scarcity and bad quality of the bread. Twenty times, guns, pistols, sabres, would have put an end to Berthier's life, if, twenty times, the member of the Commune of Paris had not voluntarily covered him with his body. When they reached the streets of the capital, the cabriolet had to penetrate through an immense and compact crowd, whose exasperation bordered on delirium, and who evidently wished to perpetrate the utmost extremities; not knowing which of the two travellers was the Intendant of Paris, they betook themselves to crying out, " let the prisoner take off his hat!" Berthier obeyed, but Larivière uncovered his head also at the same instant.

All parties would gain by the production of a work, that I desire to see most earnestly. For my part, I acknowledge, I should be sorry not to see in it the answer made to Francis II. by one of the numerous officers who committed the fault, so honestly acknowledged afterwards,—a fault that no one would commit now,—that of joining foreigners in arms. The Austrian prince, after his coronation, attempted, at a review, to induce our countrymen to admire the good bearing of his troops, and finally exclaimed, "There are materials wherewith to crush the Sans-culottes." "That remains to be seen!" instantly answered the émigré officer.

May these quotations lead some able writer to erect a monument still wanting to the glory of our country! There is in this subject, it seems to me, enough to inspire legitimate ambition. Did not Plutarch immortalize himself by preserving noble actions and fine sentiments from oblivion?

### EXAMINATION OF BAILLY'S ADMINISTRATION AS MAYOR.

The illustrious Mayor of Paris had not the leisure to continue writing his reminiscences beyond the date of the 2d of October, 1789. The analysis and appreciation of the events subsequent to that epoch will remain deprived of that influential sanction, pure as virtue, concise and precise as truth, which I found in the handwriting of our colleague. Xenocrates, historians say, who was celebrated among the Greeks for his honesty, being called to bear witness before a tribunal, the judges with common consent stopped him as he was advancing towards the altar according to the usual custom, and said, "These formalities are not required from you; an oath would add nothing to the authority of your words." Such, Bailly presents himself to the reader of his Posthumous Memoirs. None of his assertions leave any room for indecision or doubt. He needs not high-flown expressions or protestations in order to convince ; nor would an oath add authority to his words. He may be deceived, but he is never the deceiver.

I will spare no effort to give to the description of the latter part of Bailly's life, all the correctness which can result from a sincere and conscientious comparison of the writings published as well by the partisans as by the enemies of our great revolution. Such, however, is my desire to prevent two phases, though very distinct, being confounded together, that I shall here pause, in order to cast a scrupulous glance on the actions and on the various publications of our colleague. I shall moreover thus have an easy opportunity of filling up some important lacunæ.

I read in a biographical article, otherwise very friendly, that Bailly was nominated the very day of, and immediately after, the assassination of M. de Flesselles; and in this identity the wish was to insinuate that the first Mayor of Paris received this high dignity from the bloody hands of a set of wretches. The learned biographer, notwithstanding his good will, has ill repelled the calumny. With a little more attention he would have succeeded better. A simple comparison of dates would have sufficed. The death of M. de Flesselles occurred on the 14th of July ; Bailly was nominated two days after.

I will address the same remark to the authors of a Biographical Dictionary still more recent, in which they speak of the ineffectual efforts that Bailly made to prevent the multitude from murdering the governor of the Bastille (de Launay). But Bailly had no opportunity of making an effort, for he was then at Versailles ; no duty called him to Paris, nor did he become Mayor till two

days after the taking of the fortress.  It is really inexcusable not to have compared the two dates, by which
these errors would have been avoided.

Many persons very little acquainted with contempo-
raneous history, fancy that during the whole duration of
Bailly's administration, Paris was quite a cut-throat place.
That is a romance; the following is the truth:—

Bailly was Mayor during two years and four months.
In that time there occurred four political assassinations;
those of Foulon and of Berthier de Sauvigny, his son-in-
law, at the Hôtel de Ville; that of M. Durocher, a respectable officer of the gendarmerie, killed at Chaillot, by
a musket-shot, in August, 1789 ; and that of a baker
massacred in a riot in the month of October of the same
year.  I do not speak of the assassination of two unfortunate men on the Champ de Mars in July, 1791, as that
deplorable fact must be considered separately.

The individuals guilty of the assassination of the baker
were seized, condemned to death, and executed.  The
family of the unfortunate victim became the object of
the anxious care of all the authorities, and obtained a
pension.

The death of M. Durocher was attributed to some
Swiss soldiers who had revolted.

The horrible and ever to be deplored assassinations
of Foulon and of Berthier, are among those·misfortunes
which, under certain given circumstances, no human
power could prevent.

In times of scarcity, a slight word, either true or unfounded, suffices to create a terrible commotion.

Réveillon is made to say, that a workman can live
upon fifteen sous per diem, and behold his manufactory
destroyed from top to bottom.

They ascribe to Foulon the barbarous vaunt; "I will force the people to eat hay;" and without any order from the constituted authorities, some peasants, neighbours of the old minister, arrest him, take him to Paris, his son-in-law experiences the same fate, and the famished populace immolates both of them.

In proportion as the multitude appear to me unjust and culpable, in attacking certain men respecting a scarcity of provisions, when it is the manifest consequence of the severity of the seasons, I should be disposed to excuse their rage against the authors of factitious scarcities. Well, Gentlemen, at the time that Foulon was assassinated, the people, deceived by some impassioned orators of the Assembly, might, or let us rather say, ought to believe, that they were wilfully famished. Foulon perished the 22d of July, 1789; on the 15th, that is to say, seven days before, Mirabeau had addressed the following incendiary words to the inhabitants of the capital, from the National Tribune :—

"Henry IV. allowed provisions to be taken into besieged and rebellious Paris; but now, some perverse ministers intercept convoys of provisions destined for famished and obedient Paris."

Yet people have been so inconsiderate as to be astonished at the assassinations of Foulon and of Berthier. Going back in thought to the month of July, 1789, I perceive in the imprudent apostrophe of the eloquent tribune, more sanguinary disorders than the contemporary history has had to record.

One of the most honourable, one of the most respectable and the most respected members of the institute, having been led, in a recent work, to relate the assassination of Foulon, has thrown on the conduct of Bailly, under those cruel circumstances, an aspersion that I read with surprise and grief. Foulon was detained in the Hôtel de Ville. Bailly went down into the square, and succeeded for a moment in calming the multitude. "I did not imagine," said the Mayor in his memoirs, " that they could have forced the Hôtel de Ville, a well-guarded post, and an object of respect to all the citizens. I therefore thought the prisoner in perfect safety; I did not doubt but the waves of this storm would finally subside, and I departed."

The honourable author of the *History of the Reign of Louis XVI.* opposes to this passage the following words taken from the official minutes of the Hôtel de Ville: " The electors (those who had accompanied Bailly out to the square) reported in the Hall the certainty that the calm would not last long." The new historian adds: " How could the Mayor alone labour under this delusion? It is too evident, that on such a day, the public tranquillity was much too uncertain, to allow of the chief magistrate of the town absenting himself without deserving the reproach of weakness." The remainder of the passage shows too evidently, that in the author's estimation, weakness here was synonymous with cowardice.

It is against this, Gentlemen, that I protest with heartfelt earnestness. Bailly absented himself because he did not think that the Hôtel de Ville could be forced. The electors in the passage quoted do not enunciate a different opinion: where then is the contradiction?

Bailly deceived himself in this expectation, for the multitude burst into the Hôtel de Ville. We will grant that there was an error of judgment in this; but nothing in the world authorizes us to call in question the courage of the Mayor.

To decide after the blow, with so little hesitation or consideration, that Bailly ought not to have absented himself from the House of the Commune, we must forget that, under such circumstances, the obligations of the first magistrate of the city were quite imperious and very numerous; it is requisite, above all, not to remember that each day, the provision of flour required for the nourishment of seven or eight hundred thousand inhabitants, depended on the measures adopted on the previous evening. M. de Crosne, who on quitting the post of Lieutenant of Police, had not ceased to be a citizen, was during some days a very enlightened and zealous councillor for Bailly; but on the day that Foulon was arrested, this dismissed magistrate thought himself lost. He and his family made an appeal to the gratitude and humanity of our colleague. It was to procure a refuge for them, that Bailly employed the few hours of absence with which he was so much reproached: those hours during which that catastrophe happened which the Mayor could not have prevented, since even the superhuman efforts of General Lafayette, commanding an armed force, proved futile. I will add, that to spare M. de Crosne an arbitrary arrest, the imminent danger of which alas! was too evident in the death of Berthier, Bailly absented himself again from the Hôtel de Ville on the night of the 22d to the 23d of July, to accompany the former Lieutenant of Police to a great distance from Paris.

There is not a more distressing spectacle than that of one honest man wrongfully attacking another honest man. Gentlemen, let us never willingly leave the satisfaction and the advantage of it to the wicked.

To appreciate the actions of our predecessors with impartiality and justice, it would be indispensable to keep

constantly before our eyes the list of unheard-of difficulties that the revolution had to surmount, and to remember
the very restricted means of repression placed at the
disposal of the authorities in the beginning.

The scarcity of food gave rise to many embarrassments, to many a crisis; but causes of quite another
nature had not less influence on the march of events.

In his memoirs, Bailly speaks of the manœuvres of a
redoubtable faction labouring for . . . . . . under the
name of the . . . . . The names are blank. A certain
editor of the work filled up the lacunæ. I have not the
same hardihood. I only wished to remark that Bailly
had to combat at once both the spontaneous effervescence of the multitude, and the intrigues of a crowd of
secret agents, who distributed money with a liberal hand.

Some day, said our colleague, the infernal genius who
directed those intrigues and *le bailleur de fonds* will be
known. Although the proper names are wanting, it is
certain that some persons inimical to the revolution urged
it to deplorable excesses.

These enemies had collected in the capital thirty or
forty thousand vagabonds. What could be opposed to
them? The Tribunals? They had no moral power, and
were declared enemies to the revolution. The National
Guard? It was only just formed; the officers scarcely
knew each other, and moreover scarcely knew the men
who were to obey them. Was it at least permitted to
depend on the regular armed force? It consisted of six
battalions of French Guards without officers; of six
thousand soldiers who, from every part of France, had
flocked singly to Paris, on reading in the newspapers the
following expressions from General Lafayette: "They
talk of deserters! The real deserters are those men who

9 *

have not abandoned their standards." There were finally six hundred Swiss Guards in Paris, deserters from their regiments ; for, let us speak freely, the celebrated monument of Lucerne will not prevent the Swiss themselves from being recognized by impartial and intelligent historians, as having experienced the revolutionary fever.

Those who, with such poor means of repression, flattered themselves that they could entirely prevent any disorder, in a town of seven or eight hundred thousand inhabitants in exasperation, must have been very blind. Those, on the other hand, who attempt to throw the responsibility of the disorders on Bailly, would prove by this alone, that good people should always keep aloof from public affairs during a revolution.

The administrator, a being of modern creation, now declares, with the most ludicrous self-sufficiency, that Bailly was not equal to the functions of a Mayor of Paris. It is, he says, by undeserved favour that his statue has been placed on the façade of the Hôtel de Ville. During his magistracy, Bailly did not create any large square in the capital, he did not open out any large streets, he elevated no splendid monument ; Bailly would therefore have done better had he remained an astronomer or erudite scholar.

The enumeration of all the public erections that Bailly did not execute is correct. It might also have been added, that far from devoting the municipal funds to building, he had the vast and threatening castle of the Bastille demolished down to its very foundations ; but this would not deprive Bailly of the honour of having been one of the most enlightened magistrates that the city of Paris could boast.

Bailly did not enlarge any street, did not erect any

palace during the twenty-eight months of his administration! No, undoubtedly! for, first it was necessary to
give bread to the inhabitants of Paris ; now the revenues
of the town, added to the daily sums furnished by Necker,
scarcely sufficed for those principal wants. Some years
before, the Parisians had been very much displeased at
the establishment of import dues on all alimentary substances. The writers of that epoch preserved the burlesque Alexandrine, which was placarded all over the
town, on the erection of the Octroi circumvallation :

" Le mur murant Paris, rend Paris murmurant." *

The multitude was not content with murmuring; the
moment that a favourable opportunity occurred, it went
to the barriers and broke them down. These were re-
established by the administration with great trouble, and
the smugglers often took them down by main force.
The *Octroi* revenue from the imports, which used to
amount to 70,000 francs, now fell to less than 30,000.
Those persons who have considered the figures of the
present revenue, will assuredly not compare such very
dissimilar epochs.

But it is said that ameliorations in the moral world
may often be effected without expense. What were
those for which the public was indebted to the direct
exertions of Bailly? The question is simple, but re-
pentance will follow the having asked it. My answer
is this: One of the most honourable victories gained by
mathematics over the avaricious prejudices of the ad-
ministrations of certain towns has been, in our own times,
the radical suppression of gambling-houses. I will hasten
to prove that such a suppression had already engaged

* " The wall walling Paris, renders Paris wailing."

Bailly's attention, that he had partly effected it, and that no one ever spoke of those odious dens with more eloquence and firmness.

"I declare," wrote the Mayor of Paris on the 5th of May, 1790, "that the gambling-houses are in my opinion a public scourge. I think that these meetings not only should not be tolerated, but that they ought to be sought out and prosecuted, as much as the liberty of the citizens, and the respect due to their homes, will admit.

"I regard the tax that has been levied from such houses as a disgraceful tribute. I do not think that it is allowable to employ a revenue derived from vice and disorder, even to do good. In consequence of these principles, I have never granted any permit to gambling-houses; I have constantly refused them. I have constantly announced that not only they would not be tolerated, but that they would be sought out and prosecuted."

If I add that Bailly suppressed all spectacles of animal-fighting, at which the multitude cannot fail to acquire ferocious and sanguinary habits, I shall have a right to ask of every superficial writer, how he would justify the epithet of sterile, applied with such assurance to the administration of our virtuous colleague.

Anxious to carry out in practice that which had been largely recognized theoretically in the declaration of rights—the complete separation of religion from civil law,—Bailly presented himself before the National Assembly on the 14th of May, 1791, and demanded, in the name of the city of Paris, the abolition of an order of things which, in the then state of men's minds, gave rise to great abuses. If declarations of births, of marriages, and of deaths are now received by civil officers in a form agreeing with all religious opinions, the country is chiefly indebted for it to the intelligent firmness of Bailly.

The unfortunate beings for whom all public men should feel most solicitous, are those prisoners who are awaiting in prison the decrees of the courts of justice. Bailly took care not to neglect such a duty. At the end of 1790, the old tribunals had no moral power; they could no longer act; the new ones were not yet created. This state of affairs distracted the mind of our colleague. On the 18th of November, he expressed his grief to the National Assembly, in terms full of sensibility and kindness. I should be culpable if I left them in oblivion.

" Gentlemen, the prisons are full. The innocent are awaiting their justification, and the criminals an end to their remorse. All breathe an unwholesome air, and disease will pronounce terrible decrees. Despair dwells there : Despair says, either give me death, or judge me. When we visit those prisons, that is what the fathers of the poor and the unfortunate hear; this is what it is their duty to repeat to the fathers of their country. We must tell them that in those asylums of crime, of misery, and of every grief, time is infinite in its duration; a month is a century, a month is an abyss the sight of which is frightful. . . . . . We ask of the tribunals to empty the prisons by the justification of the innocent, or by examples of justice."

Does it not appear to you, Gentlemen, that calm times may occasionally derive excellent lessons, and, moreover, lessons expressed in very good language, from our revolutionary epoch ?

## THE KING'S FLIGHT.—EVENTS ON THE CHAMP DE MARS.

In the month of April, 1791, Bailly perceived that his influence over the Parisian population was decreasing. The king had announced that he should depart on the 18th, and would remain some days at St. Cloud. The state of his health was the ostensible cause of his departure. Some religious scruples were probably the real cause; the holy week was approaching, and the king would have no communications with the ecclesiastics sworn in for his parish. Bailly was not discomposed at this projected journey; he regarded it even with satisfaction. Foreign courts, said our colleague, looked upon him as a prisoner. The sanction he gives to various decrees, appears to them extorted by violence; the visit of Louis XVI. to Saint Cloud will dissipate all these false reports. Bailly therefore concerted measures with La Fayette for the departure of the royal family; but the inhabitants of Paris, less confiding than their mayor, already saw the king escaping from St. Cloud, and seeking refuge amidst foreign armies. They therefore rushed to the Tuileries, and notwithstanding all the efforts of Bailly and his colleague, the court carriages could not advance a step. The king and queen therefore, after waiting for an hour and a half in their carriage, reascended into the palace.

To remain in power after such a check, was giving to the country the most admirable proof of devotion.

In the night of the 20th to the 21st of June, 1791, the king quitted the Tuileries. This flight, so fatal to the monarchy, irretrievably destroyed the ascendency that Bailly had exercised over the capital. The populace usually judges from the event. The king, they said, with the queen and their two children, were freely allowed to go out of the palace. The Mayor of Paris was their accomplice, for he has the means of knowing every thing; otherwise he might be accused of carelessness, or of the most culpable negligence.

These attacks were not only echoed in the shops, in the streets, but also in the strongly organized clubs. The Mayor answered in a peremptory manner, but without entirely effacing the first impression. During several days after the king's flight, both Bailly and La Fayette were in personal danger. The National Assembly had often to look to their safety.

I have now reached a painful portion of my task, a frightful event, that led finally to Bailly's cruel death; a bloody catastrophe, the relation of which will perhaps oblige me to allow a little blame to hover over some actions of this virtuous citizen, whom thus far it has been my delight to praise without any restriction.

The flight of the king had an immense influence on the progress of our first revolution. It threw into the republican party some considerable political characters who, till then, had hoped to realize the union of a monarchy with democratical principles.

Mirabeau, a short time before his death, having heard this projected flight spoken of, said to Cabanis: "I have defended monarchy to the last; I defend it still, although I think it lost. . . . . . But, if the king departs, I will mount the tribune, have the throne declared vacant, and proclaim a Republic."

After the return from Varennes, the project of substituting a republican government for a monarchical government was very seriously discussed by the most moderate members of the National Assembly, and we now know that the Duke de La Rochefoucauld and Dupont (de Némours) for example, were decidedly in favour of a republic. But it was chiefly in the clubs that the idea of such a radical change had struck root. When the Commission of the National Assembly had expressed itself, through M. Muguet, at the sitting of the 13th of July, 1791, against the forfeiture of Louis XVI., there was a great fermentation in Paris. Some agents of the Cordeliers (Shoemakers') Club were the first to ask for signatures to a petition on the 14th of July, against the proposed decision. The Assembly refused to read and even to receive it. On the motion of Laclos, the club of the Jacobins got up another. This, after undergoing some important modifications, was to be signed on the 17th on the Champ de Mars, on the altar of their country. These projects were discussed openly, in full daylight. The National Assembly deemed them anarchical. On the 16th of July it called to its bar the municipality of Paris, enjoining it to have recourse to force, if requisite, to repress any culpable movements.

The Council of the Commune on the morning of the 17th placarded a proclamation that it had prepared according to the orders of the National Assembly. Some municipal officers went about preceded by a trumpeter, to read it in various public squares. Around the Hotel de Ville, the military arrangements, commanded by La Fayette, led to the expectation of a sanguinary conflict. All at once, on the opening of the sitting of the National Assembly, a report was circulated that two good citizens having dared to tell the people collected around their country's altar, that they must obey the law, had been put to death, and that their heads, stuck upon pikes, were carried through the streets. The news of this attack excited the indignation of all the deputies, and under this impression, Alexander Lameth, then President of the Assembly, of his own accord transmitted to Bailly very severe new orders, a circumstance which, though only said *en passant*, has been but recently known.

The municipal body, as soon as it was informed, about eleven o'clock, of the two assassinations, deputed three of its members, furnished with full powers, to reëstablish order. Strong detachments accompanied the municipal officers. About two o'clock it was reported that stones had been thrown at the National Guard. The Municipal Council instantly had martial law proclaimed on the Place de Grève, and the red flag suspended from the principal window of the Hotel de Ville. At half-past five o'clock, just when the municipal body was about to start for the Champ de Mars, the three councillors, who had been sent in the morning to the scene of disorder, returned, accompanied by a deputation of twelve persons, taken from among the petitioners. The explanations given on various sides occasioned a new deliberation of the Council. The first decision was maintained, and at six o'clock the municipality began its march with the red flag, three pieces of cannon, and numerous detachments of the National Guard.

Bailly, as chief of the municipality, found himself at this time in one of those solemn and perilous situations, in which a man becomes responsible in the eyes of a whole nation, in the eyes of posterity, for the inconsiderate or even culpable actions of the passionate multitude that surrounds him, but which he scarcely knows, and over which he has little or no influence.

The National Guard, in that early epoch of the revo-

lution, was very troublesome to lead and to rule. Insubordination appeared to be the rule in its ranks; and
hierarchical obedience a very rare exception. My remark may perhaps appear severe: well, Gentlemen, read
the contemporary writings, Grimm's Correspondence, for
example, and you will see, under date of November 1790,
a dismissed captain replying to the regrets of his company in the following style: "Console yourselves, my
companions, I shall not quit you; only, henceforward I
shall be a simple fusilier; if you see me resolved to be
no longer your chief, it is because I am content to command in my turn."

It is allowable besides to suppose that the National
Guard of 1791 was deficient, in the presence of such
crowds, of that patience, that clemency, of which the
French troops of the line have often given such perfect
examples. It was not aware that, in a large city, crowds
are chiefly composed of the unemployed and the idly
curious.

It was half-past seven o'clock when the municipal
body arrived at the Champ de Mars. Immediately some
individuals placed on the glacis exclaimed: "Down with
the red flag! down with the bayonettes!" and threw
some stones. There was even a gun fired. A volley
was fired in the air to frighten them; but the cries soon
recommenced; again some stones were thrown; then
only the fatal fusillade of the National Guard began!

These, Gentlemen, are the deplorable events of the
Champ de Mars, faithfully analyzed from the relation that
Bailly himself gave of the 18th July to the Constituent
Assembly. This recital, the truth of which no one as-
suredly will question any more than myself, labours under
some involuntary but very serious omissions. I will

indicate them, when the march of events leads us, in following our unfortunate colleague, to the revolutionary tribunal.

BAILLY QUITS THE MAYORALTY THE 12TH OF NOVEM-
BER, 1791.—THE ESCHEVINS.—EXAMINATION OF
THE REPROACHES THAT MIGHT BE ADDRESSED
TO THE MAYOR.

I resume the biography of Bailly at the time when he quitted the Hôtel de Ville after a magistracy of about two years.

On the 12th November, 1791, Bailly convoked the Council of the Commune, rendered an account of his administration, solemnly entreated those who thought themselves entitled to complain of him, to say so without reserve; so resolved was he to bow to any legitimate complaints; installed his successor Pétion, and retired. This separation did not lead to any of those heartfelt demonstrations from the co-labourers of the late Mayor, which are the true and the sweetest recompense to a good man.

I have sought for the hidden cause of such a constant and undisguised hostility towards the first Mayor of Paris. I asked myself first, whether the magistrate's manners had possibly excited the susceptibilities of the Eschevins.* The answer is decidedly in the negative. Bailly showed in all the relations of life a degree of patience, a suavity, a deference to the opinions of others, that would have soothed the most irascible selflove.

Must we suspect jealousy to have been at work? No, no; the persons who constituted the town-council were

* *Eschevin* was a sort of town-councilman, peculiar to Paris and to Rotterdam, acting under a mayor.

too obscure, unless they were mad, to attempt to vie in public consideration and glory with the illustrious author of *the History of Astronomy*, with the philosopher, the writer, the erudite scholar who belonged to our three principal academies, an honour that Fontenelle alone had enjoyed before him.

Let us say it aloud, for such is our conviction, nothing personal excited the evil proceedings, the acts of insubordination with which Bailly had daily to reproach his numerous assistants. It is even presumable, that in his position, any one else would have had to register more numerous and more serious complaints. Let us be truthful: when the *aristocracy of the ground-floor*, according to the expression of one of the most illustrious members of the French Academy, was called by the revolutionary movements to replace the *aristocracy of the first-floor*, it became giddy. Have I not, it said, conducted the business of the warehouse, the workshop, the counting-house, &c., with probity and success; why then should I not equally succeed in the management of public affairs? And this swarm of new statesmen were in a hurry to commence work; hence all control was irksome to them, and each wished to be able to say on returning home, "I have framed such or such an act that will tie the hands of faction for ever; I have repressed this or that riot; I have, in short, saved the country by proposing such or such a measure for the public good, and by having it adopted." The pronoun *I* so agreeably tickles the ear of a man lately risen from obscurity.

What the thorough-bred Eschevin, whether new or old, dreads above every thing else, is specialties. He has an insurmountable antipathy towards men, who have in the face of the world gained the honourable titles of historian, geometer, mechanician, astronomer, physician, chemist, or geologist, &c. . . . . . . His desire, his will, is to speak on every thing.  He requires, therefore, colleagues who cannot contradict him.

If the town constructs an edifice, the Eschevin, losing sight of the question, talks away on the aspect of the façades.  He declares with the imperturbable assurance inspired by a fact that he had heard speak of whilst on the knees of his nurse, that on a particular side of the future building, the moon, an active agent of destruction, will incessantly corrode the stones of the frontage, the shafts of the columns, and that it will efface in a few years all the projecting ornaments; and hence the fear of the moon's voracity will lead to the upsetting of all the views, the studies, and the well-digested plans of several architects.  Place a meteorologist on the council, and, despite the authority of the nurses, a whole scaffolding of gratuitous suppositions will be crumbled to dust by these few categorical and strict words of science; the moon does not exert the action that is attributed to it.

At another time, the Eschevin hurls his anathema at the system of warming by steam.  According to him, this diabolical invention is an incessant cause of damp to the wood-work, the furniture, the papers, and the books. The Eschevin fancies, in short, that in this way of warm- ing, torrents of watery vapour enter into the atmosphere of the apartments.  Can he love a colleague, I ask, who after having had the cunning patience to let him come to the conclusion of his discourse, informs him that, although vapour, the vehicle of an enormous quantity of latent heat, rapidly conveys this caloric to every floor of the largest edifice, it has never occasion therefore to escape from those impermeable tubes through which the circu- lation is effected !

Amidst the various labours that are required by every large town, the Eschevin thinks, some one day, that he has discovered an infallible way of revenging himself of specialties. Guided by the light of modern geology, it has been proposed to go with an immense sounding line in hand, to seek in the bowels of the earth the incalculable quantities of water, that from all eternity circulate there without benefiting human nature, to make them spout up to the surface, to distribute them in various directions, in large cities, until then parched, to take advantage of their high temperature, to warm economically the magnificent conservatories of the public gardens, the halls of refuge, the wards of the sick in hospitals, the cells of madmen. But according to the old geology of the Eschevin, promulgated perhaps by his nurse, there is no circulation in subterranean water; at all events, subterranean water cannot be submitted to an ascending force and rise to the surface; its temperature would not differ from that of common well-water. The Eschevin, however, agrees to the expensive works proposed. Those works, he says, will afford no material result; but once for all, such fantastic projects will receive a solemn and rough contradiction, and we shall then be liberated for ever from the odious yoke under which science wants to enslave us.

However, the subterranean water appears. It is true that a clever engineer had to bore down 548 mètres (or 600 yards) to find it; but thence it comes transparent as crystal, pure as if the product of distillation, warmed as physical laws had shown that it would be, more abundant indeed than they had dared to foresee, it shot up thirty-three mètres above the ground.

Do not suppose, Gentlemen, that putting aside wretched views of self-love, the Eschevin would applaud such a result. He shows himself, on the contrary, deeply humiliated. And he will not fail in future to oppose every undertaking that might turn out to the honour of science. Crowds of such incidents occur to the mind. Are we to infer thence, that we ought to be afraid of seeing the administration of a town given up to the stationary and exclusive spirit of the old Eschevinage—to people who have learnt nothing and studied nothing? Such is not the result of these long reflections. I wished to enable people to foresee the struggle, not the defeat. I even hasten to add, that by the side of the surly, harsh, rude, positive Eschevin, the type of whom, to say the truth, is fortunately becoming rare, an honourable class of citizens exists, who, content with a moderate fortune laboriously acquired, live retired, charm their leisure with study, and magnanimously place themselves, without any interested views, at the service of the community. Everywhere similar auxiliaries fight courageously for truth as soon as they perceive it. Bailly constantly obtained their concurrence; as is proved by some touching testimonies of gratitude and sympathy. As to the counsellors who so often occasioned trouble, confusion, and anarchy in the Hôtel de Ville in the years '89 and '90, I am inclined to blame the virtuous magistrate for having so patiently, so diffidently endured their ridiculous pretensions, their unbearable assumption of power.

From the earliest steps in the important study of nature, it becomes evident that facts unveiled to us in the lapse of centuries, are but a very small fraction, if we compare them with those that still remain to be discovered. Placing ourselves in that point of view, deficiency in diffidence would just be the same as deficiency in judgment. But, by the side of positive diffidence, if I

may be allowed the expression, relative diffidence comes
in.   This is often a delusion; it deceives no one, yet
occasions a thousand difficulties.   Bailly often confounded
them.   We may regret, I think, that in many instances,
the learned academician disdained to throw in the face
of his vain fellow-labourers these words of an ancient
philosopher : " When I examine myself, I find I am but
a pigmy; when I compare myself, I think I am a giant."

If I were to cover with a veil that which appeared to
me susceptible of criticism in the character of Bailly, I
should voluntarily weaken the praises that I have bestowed on several acts of his administration.   I will not
commit this fault, no more than I have done already in
alluding to the communications of the mayor with the
presuming Eschevins.

I will therefore acknowledge that on several occasions,
Bailly, in my opinion, showed himself influenced by a
petty susceptibility, if not about his personal preroga-
tives, yet about those of his station.

I think also that Bailly might be accused of an occasional want of foresight.

Imaginative and sensitive, the philosopher allowed his
thoughts to centre too exclusively on the difficulties of
the moment.   He persuaded himself, from an excess of
good-will, that no new storm would follow the one that
he had just overcome.   After every success, whether
great or small, against the intrigues of the court, or
prejudices, or anarchy, whether President of the National
Assembly or Mayor of Paris, our colleague thought the
country saved.   Then his joy overflowed; he would
have wished to spread it over all the world.   It was thus
that on the day of the definite reunion of the nobility
with the other two orders, the 27th of June, 1789, Bailly

going from Versailles to Chaillot, after the close of the session, leaned half his body out of his carriage door, and announced the happy tidings with loud exclamations to all whom he met on the road. At Sèvres, it is from himself that I borrow the anecdote, he did not see without painful surprise that his communication was received with the most complete indifference by a group of soldiers assembled before the barrack door; Bailly laughed much on afterwards learning that this was a party of Swiss soldiers, who did not understand a word he said.

Happy the actors in a great revolution, in whose conduct we find nothing to reprehend until after having entered into so minute an analysis of their public and private conduct.

BAILLY'S JOURNEY FROM PARIS TO NANTES, AND THEN FROM NANTES TO MÉLUN.—HIS ARREST IN THE LAST TOWN.—HE IS TRANSFERRED TO PARIS.

After having quitted the Mayorality of Paris, Bailly retired to Chaillot, where he hoped again to find happiness in study; but upwards of two years passed amidst the storms of public life had deeply injured his health; it was therefore requisite to obey the advice of physicians, and undertake a journey. About the middle of June, 1792, Bailly quitted the capital, made some excursions in the neighbouring departments, went to Niort to visit his old colleague and friend, M. de Lapparent, and soon after went on far as Nantes, where the due influence of another friend, M. Gelée de Prémion, seemed to promise him protection and tranquillity. Determined to establish himself in this last town, Bailly and his wife took a small lodging in the house of some distinguished people, who could understand and appreciate them.

10

They hoped to live there in peace; but news from Paris soon dissipated this illusion. The Council of the Commune decreed, that the house previously occupied, in consequence of a formal decision, by the Mayor of Paris, and by the public offices of the town, ought to have paid a tax of 6,000 livres, and strange enough, that Bailly was responsible for it. The pretended debt was claimed with harshness. They demanded the payment of it without delay. To free himself Bailly was obliged to sell his library, to abandon to the chances of an auction that multitude of valuable books, from which he had sought out, in the silence of his study, and with such remarkable perseverance, the most recondite secrets of the firmament.

This painful separation was followed by two acts that did not afflict him less.

The central government (then directed, it must be allowed, by the Gironde party) placed Bailly under surveillance. Every eight days the venerable academician was obliged to present himself at the house of the Syndic Procurator of the Departmental Administration of the Lower-Loire, like a vile malefactor, whose every footstep it would be to the interest of society to watch. What was the true motive for such a strange measure? This secret has been buried in a tomb where I shall not allow myself to dig for it.

Though painful to me to say so, the odious assimilation of Bailly to a dangerous criminal had not exhausted the rancour of his enemies. A letter from Roland, the Minister of the Interior, announced very dryly to the unfortunate proscribed man, that the apartments in the Louvre, which his family had occupied for upwards of half a century, had been withdrawn from him. They had even proceeded so far as to furnish a tipstaff with the order to clear the rooms.

A short time before this epoch, Bailly had found himself obliged to sell his house at Chaillot. The old Mayor of Paris then had no longer a hearth or a home in the great city which had been the late scene of his devotion, his solicitude, and his sacrifices. When this reflection occurred to his mind, his eyes filled with tears.

But the grief that Bailly experienced on seeing himself the daily object of odious persecutions, left his patriotic convictions intact. Vainly did they endeavour several times to transform a legitimate hatred towards individuals into an antipathy towards principles. They still remember in Brittany the debate raised, by one of these attempts, between our colleague and a Vendéan physician, Dr. Blin. Never, in the season of his greatest popularity, did the president of the National Assembly express himself with more vivacity; never had he defended our first revolution with more eloquence. Not long since, in the same place, I pointed out to public attention another of our colleagues (Condorcet), who already under the blow of a capital condemnation, devoted his last moments to restore to the light of day the principles of eternal justice, which the fashions and the follies of men had but too much obscured. At a time of weak or interested convictions, and disgraceful capitulations of conscience, those two examples of unchangeable convictions deserved to be remarked. I am happy in having found them in the bosom of the Academy of Sciences.

Tranquillity of mind is not less requisite than vigour of intellect, to those who undertake great works. Thus during his residence at Nantes, Bailly did not even try to add to his numerous scientific or literary productions.

This celebrated astronomer passed his time in reading novels. He sometimes said with a bitter smile: "My day has been well occupied; since I got up, I have put myself in a position to give an analysis of the two, or of the three first volumes of the new novel that the reading-room has just received." From time to time these abstractions were of a more elevated tone ; he owed them to two young persons, who having reached an advanced age may now be listening to my words. Bailly discoursed with them of Homer, of Plato, of Aristotle, of the principal works in our literature, of the rapid progress of the sciences, and chiefly of those of astronomy. What our colleague chiefly appreciated in these two young friends, was a true sensibility, and great warmth of feeling. I know that years have not effaced or weakened these rare qualities in the bosoms of those two Brétons. M. Pariset, our colleague, and M. Villenave, will therefore think it natural in me to thank them here, in the name of science and literature, in the name of humanity, for the few moments of sweet peace and happiness that they afforded to our learned colleague, at a time when the inconstancy and ingratitude of men were lacerating his heart.

Louis XVI. had perished ; dark clouds hung over the horizon; some acts of odious brutality showed our proscribed philosopher how little he must thenceforward depend on public sympathy; how much times had changed since the memorable meeting (of the 7th of October, 1791), at which the National Assembly decided that the bust of Bailly should be placed in the hall of their meetings ! The storm appeared near and very menacing; even persons usually of little foresight were meditating where to find shelter.

During these transactions, Charles Marquis de Casaux,

known by various productions on literature and on economical politics, went and requested our colleague, together with his wife, to take a passage on board a ship that he had freighted for himself and his family. "We will first go to England," said M. Casaux; "we will then, if you prefer it, pass our exile in America. Have no anxiety, I have property; I can, without inconvenience to myself, undertake all the expenses. Pythagoras said: 'In solitude the wise man worships echo;' but this no longer suffices in France; the wise man must fly from a land that threatens to devour its children."

These warm solicitations, and the prayers of his weeping companion, could not shake the firm resolution of Bailly. "From the day that I became a public character," he said, "my fate has become irrevocably united with that of France; never will I quit my post in the moment of danger. Under any circumstances my country may depend on my devotion. Whatever may happen, I shall remain."

By regulating his conduct on such fine generous maxims, a citizen does himself honour, but he exposes himself to fall under the blows of faction.

Bailly was still at Nantes on the 30th of June, 1793, when eighty thousand Vendéans, commanded by Cathelineau and Charette, went to besiege that city.

Let us imagine to ourselves the position of the President of the sitting of the "Jeu de Paume," of the first Mayor of Paris, in a city besieged by the Vendéans! We cannot presume that the unfavourable opinion of the Convention under which he was labouring, and the rigorous surveillance to which he was subjected, would have saved him from harsh treatment if the town had been taken. No one can therefore be surprised that after the

victory of Nanteans, our colleague hastened to follow
out his project, formed a short time before, of withdraw-
ing from the insurgent provinces.

Up to the beginning of July 1793, Mélun had enjoyed
perfect tranquillity.  Bailly knew it through M. de Laplace, who, living retired in that chief town of the department, was there composing the immortal work in which
the wonders of the heavens are studied with so much
depth and genius.  He also knew that the great geometer, hoping to be still more retired in a cottage on the
banks of the Seine, and out of the town, was going to
dispose of his house in Mélun.  It is easy to guess that
Bailly would be charmed with the prospect of residing
far away from political agitation, and near to his illustrious friend !

The arrangements were promptly made, and on the
6th of July, M. and Madame Bailly quitted Nantes in
company with M. and Madame Villenave, who were
going to Rennes.

At this same time, a division of the revolutionary army
was marching to Mélun.  As soon as the terrible news
was known, Madame Laplace wrote to Bailly, persuading him, under covert expressions, to give up the intended
project.  The house, she said, is at the water's edge :
there is extreme dampness in the rooms : Madame Bailly
would die there.  A letter so different from those that
had preceded it, could not fail of its effect ; such at least
was the hope with which M. and Madame Laplace flattered themselves, when about the end of July they perceived, with inexpressible alarm, Bailly crossing the
garden path.  " Great God, you did not then understand
our last letter ! " exclaimed at the same instant our colleague's two friends.  "I understood perfectly," Bailly

replied with the greatest calm; "but on the one hand, the two servants who followed me to Nantes, having heard that I was going to be imprisoned, quitted me; on the other hand, If I am to be arrested, I wish it to be in a house that I have occupied some time. I will not be described in any act as an individual without a domicile!" Can it be said, after this, that great men are not subject to strange weaknesses?

These minute details will be my only answer to some culpable expressions that I have met with in a work very widely spread: "M. Laplace," says the anonymous writer "knew all the secrets of geometry; but he had not the least notion of the state France was in, he therefore imprudently advised Bailly to go and join him."

What is to be here deplored as regards imprudence, is, that a writer, without exactly knowing the facts, should authoritatively pronounce such severe sentences against one of the most illustrious ornaments of our country.

Bailly did not even enjoy the puerile satisfaction of taking rank among the domiciled citizens of Mélun. For two days after his arrival in that town, a soldier of the revolutionary army having recognized him, brutally ordered him to accompany him to the municipality: "I am going there," coolly replied Bailly; "you may follow me there."

The municipal body of Mélun had at that time an honest and very courageous man at its head, M. Tarbé des Sablons. This virtuous magistrate endeavoured to prove to the multitude, (with which the Hôtel de Ville was immediately filled by the news, rapidly propagated, of the arrest of the old Mayor of Paris,) that the passports granted at Nantes, countersigned at Rennes, showed nothing irregular; that according to the terms of the law, he could not but set Bailly at liberty, under pain of for-feiture. Vain efforts ! To avoid a bloody catastrophe, it was necessary to promise that reference would be made to Paris, and that in the mean time he should be guarded — à vue—in his own house.

The surveillance, perhaps purposely, was not at all strict ; to escape would have been very easy. Bailly utterly discarded the notion. He would not at any price have compromised M. Tarbé, nor even his guard.

An order from the Committee of Public Safety en-joined the authorities of Mélun to transfer Bailly to one of the prisons of the capital. On the day of departure, Madame Laplace paid a visit to our unfortunate colleague. She represented to him again the possibility of escape. The first scruples no longer existed ; the escort was already waiting in the street. But Bailly was inflexible. He felt perfectly safe. Madame Laplace held her son in her arms ; Bailly took the opportunity of turning the conversation to the education of children. He treated the subject, to which he might well have been thought a stranger, with a remarkable superiority, and ended even with several amusing anecdotes that would deserve a place in the witty and comic gallery of "les Enfants terribles."

On arriving at Paris, Bailly was imprisoned at the Madelonnettes, and some days after at La Force. They there granted him a room, where his wife and his nephews were permitted to visit him.

Bailly had undergone only one examination of little importance, when he was summoned as a witness in the trial of the queen.

BAILLY IS CALLED AS A WITNESS IN THE TRIAL OF
THE QUEEN. — HIS OWN TRIAL BEFORE THE REV-
OLUTIONARY TRIBUNAL. — HIS CONDEMNATION TO
DEATH. — HIS EXECUTION. — IMAGINARY DETAILS
ADDED BY ILL-INFORMED HISTORIANS TO WHAT
THAT ODIOUS AND FRIGHTFUL EVENT ALREADY
PRESENTED.

Bailly, under the weight of a capital accusation, and
precisely on account of a portion of the acts imputed to
Marie Antoinette, was heard as a witness in the trial of
that princess.   The annals of tribunals, either ancient
or modern, never offered any thing like this.   What did
they hope for?   To lead our colleague to make inexact
declarations, or to concealments from a feeling of imminent personal danger?   To suggest the thought to him
to save his own head at the expense of that of an unhappy woman?   To make virtue finally stagger?   At
all events, this infernal combination failed; with a man
like Bailly it could not succeed.

" Do you know the accused?" said the President to
Bailly.   "Oh! yes, I do know her!" answered the
witness, in a tone of emotion, and bowing respectfully to
Marie Antoinette.   Bailly then protested with horror
against the odious imputations that the act of accusation
had put into the mouth of the young dauphin.   From
that moment Bailly was treated with great harshness.
He seemed to have lost in the eyes of the tribunal the
character of a witness, and to have become the accused.
The turn that the debates took would really authorize us
to call the sitting in which the queen was condemned, (in
which she figured ostensibly as the only one accused,) the
trial of Marie Antoinette and of Bailly.   What signified,

10 *

after all, this or that qualification of this monstrous trial?
in the judgment of any man of feeling, never did Bailly
prove himself more noble, more courageous, more worthy,
than in this difficult situation.

Bailly appeared again before the Revolutionary Tribunal, and this time as the accused, the 10th of November 1793. The accusation bore chiefly on the pretended
participation of the Mayor of Paris in the escape of Louis
XVI. and his family, and in the catastrophe that occurred
in the Champ de Mars.

If any thing in the world appeared evident, even in
1793, even before the detailed revelations of the persons
who took a more or less direct part in the event, it is,
that Bailly did not facilitate the departure of the royal
family; it is that, in proportion to the suspicions that
reached him, he did all that was in his power to prevent
their departure; it is, that the President of the sitting of
the Jeu de Paume had not, and could never have had in
any case, an intention of going to join the fugitive family
in a strange country; it is that, finally, any act emanating
from a public authority in which such expressions as the
following could be found: "The deep wickedness of
Bailly . . . . . Bailly thirsted for the people's blood!"
must have excited the disgust and indignation of good
men, whatever might be their political opinions.

The accusation, as far as it regarded the murderous
fusillade on the Champ de Mars, had more weight; this
event had as counterpoises, the 10th of August and the
31st of May; La Fayette says in his memoirs, that those
two days were a retaliation. It is at least certain that
the terrible scenes of the 17th of July cost Bailly his life;
they left deep impressions in people's minds, which were
still perceptible after the revolution of 1830, and which,

on more than one occasion, rendered the position of La
Fayette one of great delicacy. I have therefore studied
them most attentively, with a very sincere and lively
desire to dissipate, once for all, the clouds that seemed to
have obscured this point, this sole point, in the life of
Bailly. I have succeeded, Gentlemen, without ever having had a wish or occasion to veil the truth. I do no
Frenchman the injustice to suppose that I need define to
him an event of the national history that has been so influential on the progress of our revolution, but perhaps,
there may be some foreigners present at this sitting. It
will be therefore for them only that I shall here relate
some details. We must bring to mind some deplorable
circumstances of the evening of the 17th July, when the
multitude had assembled on the Champ de Mars or
Champ de la Fédération, around the altar of their
country, the remains of the wooden edifice that had been
raised to celebrate the anniversary of the 14th of July.
Part of this crowd signed a petition tending to ask the
forfeiture of the throne by Louis XVI., then lately re-
conducted from Varennes, and on whose fate the Constituent Assembly had been enacting regulations. On
that occasion martial law was proclaimed. The National
Guard, with Bailly and La Fayette at their head, went
to the Champ de Mars; they were assailed by clamours,
by stones, and by the firing of a pistol; the Guard fired;
many victims fell, without its being possible to say exactly
how many, for the estimates, according to the effect that
the reporters wished to produce, varied from eighty to
two thousand!

The Revolutionary Tribunal heard several witnesses
relative to the events on the Champ de Mars: amongst
them I find Chaumette, Procurator of the Commune of

Paris; Lullier, the Syndic Procurator General of the
Department; Coffinhal, Judge of the Revolutionary Tribunal; Dufourny, manufacturer of gunpowder; Momoro,
a printer.

All these witnesses strongly blamed the old Mayor of
Paris ; but who is there that does not know how much
arbitrariness and cruelty these individuals, whom I have
mentioned above, showed during our misfortunes ? Their
declarations, therefore, must be received with great suspicion.

The sincere admirers of Bailly would be relieved of a
great weight, if the event of the Champ de la Fédération
had been darkened only by the testimonies of Chaumettes
and Coffinhals. Unfortunately, the public accuser produced some very grave documents during the debates,
which the impartial historian cannot overlook. Let us
say, however, just to correct one error out of a thousand,
that on the day of Bailly's trial, the public accuser was
Naulin, and not Fouquier Tinville, notwithstanding all
that has been written on this subject by persons calling
themselves well-informed, and even some of the accused's
intimate friends.

The catastrophe of the Champ de Mars, when impar-
tially examined in its essential phases, presents some very
simple problems :

Was a petition to the Constituent Assembly illegal that
was got up on the 17th of July, 1791, against a decree
issued on the 15th ?

Had the petitioners, by assembling on the Champ de
Mars, violated any law ?

Could the two murders committed in the morning be
imputed to these men ?

Had projects of disorder and rebellion been manifested

with sufficient evidence to justify the proclamation of martial law, and especially the putting it into practice?

I say it, Gentlemen, with deep grief, these problems will be answered in the negative by whoever takes the trouble to analyze without passion, and without preconceived opinions, some authentic documents, which people in general seem to have made it a point to leave in oblivion. But I hasten to add, that considering the question as to intention, Bailly will continue to appear, after this examination, quite as humane, quite as honourable, quite as pure as we have found him to be in the other phases of a public and private life, which might serve as a model.

In the best epochs of the National Assembly, no one who belonged to it would have dared to maintain, that to draw up and sign a petition, whatever might be the object of it, were rebellious acts. Never, at that time, would the President of that great Assembly have called down hate, public vengeance, or a sanguinary repression upon those who attempted, said Charles Lameth, in the sitting of the 16th of July, " to oppose their individual will to the law, which is an expression of the national will." The right of petition seemed as if it ought to be absolute, even if contrary to sanctioned and promulgated laws in full action, and even more so against legislative arrangements still under discussion, or scarcely voted.

The petitioners of the Champ de Mars asked the Constituent Assembly to revise a decree that they had issued two days before. We have no occasion to examine whether the act was reasonable, opportune, dictated by an enlightened view of the public good. The question is simple ; in soliciting the Assembly to revise a decree, they violated no law. Perhaps it will be thought that the petitioners at least committed an unusual act, contrary to all custom. Even this would be unfounded. In ten various instances, the National Assembly modified or annulled its own decrees; in twenty others, it had been entreated to revise them, without any cry of anarchy being raised.

It is well ascertained, that the crowd on the Champ de Mars availed itself of a right that the constitution recognized, that of getting up and signing a petition against a decree which, right or wrong, it thought was opposed to the true interests of the country. Still, the exercise of the right of petitioning was always wisely subjected to certain forms. Had these forms been violated? Was the meeting illegal?

In 1791, according to the decrees, every meeting that wished to exercise the right of petition must consist of unarmed citizens, and be announced to the competent authorities twenty-four hours beforehand.

Well, on the 16th of July, twelve persons had gone as a deputation to the municipality, in order to declare, according to law, that the next day, the 17th, numerous citizens would meet, without arms, on the Champ de Mars, where they wished to sign a petition. The deputation obtained an acknowledgment of its declaration from the hand of the syndic procurator Desmousseaux, who addressed them besides with these solemn words: " The law shields you with its inviolability."

The acknowledgment was presented to Bailly on the day of his condemnation.

Had they committed some assassinations? Yes, undoubtedly; they had committed two; but in the morning, very early; but at the Gros Caillou, and not on the Champ de Mars. Those horrid murders could not legitimately be imputed to the petitioners who, eight or

ten hours after, surrounded the altar of their country ;
to the crowd who fell by the fusillade of the National
Guard.  By changing the date of these crimes, and dis-
placing also the localities where these crimes were committed, some historians of our revolution, and amongst
others the best known of all, have given, without intending it, to the meeting in the afternoon, a character that
cannot be honestly concurred in.

It is requisite we should know at what hour, in what
place, and how, these misfortunes happened, before we
hazard an opinion on the sanguinary acts of that day, the
17th of July.

A young man had gone that day very early to the altar
of his country.  This young man wished to copy several
inscriptions.  All at once he heard a singular noise, and
very soon after the worm of a wimble shot up from the
planked floor on which he was standing.  The youth
went and sought the guard, who raised the plank, and
found beneath the altar two ill-looking individuals, lying
down and furnished with provisions.  One of these men
was an invalid with a wooden leg.  The guard seized
them, and took them to the Gros Caillou, to the section,
to the Commissary of Police.  On the way, the barrel of
water with which these unfortunate men had provided
themselves under the altar of their country, was transformed, according to the ordinary course of things, into a
barrel of gunpowder.  The inhabitants of that quarter of
the town collected together ; it was on a Sunday.  The
women especially showed themselves very much irritated
when the purpose of the auger-holes was told them, as
declared by the invalid.  When the two prisoners came
out of the hall to be conducted to the Hôtel de Ville, the
crowd tore them from the guard, massacred them, and
paraded their heads on pikes !

It cannot be too often repeated, that these hideous assassinations, this execution of two old vagabonds by the barbarous and blinded population of the Gros Caillou, evidently had no relation to, no connection with, the events which, in the evening, carried mourning into the Champ de la Fédération.

On the evening of the 17th of July, from five to seven o'clock, had the crowd which was collected around the altar of their country an aspect of turbulence, giving reason to fear a riot, sedition, violence, or any anarchical enterprise?

Relative to this point, we have the written declaration of three councillors, whom the municipality had sent in the morning to the Gros Caillou, on the first intimation of the two assassinations of which I have just spoken. This declaration was presented to Bailly on the day of his condemnation. We read therein, " that the assembled citizens on the Champ de Mars had in no way acted contrary to law; that they only asked for time to sign their petition before they retired; that the crowd had shown all possible respect to the commissaries, and given proofs of submission to the law and its agents." The Municipal Councillors, on their return to the Hôtel de Ville, accompanied by a deputation of twelve of the petitioners, protested strongly against the proclamation of martial law; they declared that if the red flag was unfurled, they would be regarded, and with some appearance of reason, as traitors and faithless men.

Vain efforts; the anger of the councillors, confined since the morning at the Hôtel de Ville, carried the day over the enlightened opinion of those who had been sent scrupulously to study the state of affairs, who had mixed in the crowd, who returned after having reassured it by promises.

I might invoke the testimony of one of my honourable colleagues. Led by the fine weather, and somewhat also by curiosity, towards the Champ de Mars, he was enabled to observe all; and he has assured me that there never was a meeting which showed less turbulence or seditious spirit; that especially the women and children were very numerous. Is it not, besides, perfectly proved now, that on the morning of the 17th July, the Jacobin club, by means of printed placards, disavowed any intention of petitioning; and that the influential men of the Jacobins and of the Cordeliers,—those men whose presence might have given to this concourse the dangerous character of a riot,—not only did not appear there, but had started in the night for the country?

By thus connecting together all the circumstances whence it is proved that martial law was proclaimed and put in practice on the 17th of July without legitimate motives, a most terrible responsibility seems at first sight to be cast on the memory of Bailly. But reassure yourselves, Gentlemen; the events which are now grouped together, and are exhibited to our eyes with complete evidence, were not known on that inauspicious day at the Hôtel de Ville, until they had been distorted by the spirit of party.

In the month of July, 1791, after the king had returned from Varennes, the monarchy and the republic began for the first time to be dangerously opposed to each other; in an instant passion took the place of cool reason in the minds of the respective partisans of the two different forms of government. The terrible formula: *We must make an end of it!* was in everybody's mouth.

Bailly was surrounded by those passionate politicians who, without the least scruple as to the honesty or legal-ity of the means, are determined to make an end of the adversaries who annoy them, as soon as circumstances seem to promise them victory.

Bailly had still near him some Eschevins long accustomed to regard him as a magistrate for show.

The former gave the Mayor false, or highly coloured intelligence. The others, by long habit, did not conceive themselves obliged to communicate any thing to him.

On the bloody day of July, 1791, of all the inhabitants of Paris, perhaps Bailly was the man who knew with least detail or correctness the events of the morning and of the evening.

Bailly, with his deep horror for falsehood, would have thought that he was most cruelly insulting the magistrates, if he had not attributed to them similar sentiments to his own. His uprightness prevented his being sufficiently on the watch against the machinations of parties. It was evidently by false reports that he was induced to unfurl the red flag on the 17th of July: "It was from the reports that followed each other," he said to the Revolutionary Tribunal, on being questioned by the President, "and became more and more alarming every hour, that the council adopted the measure of marching with the armed force to the Champ de Mars."

In all his answers Bailly insisted on the repeated orders he had received from the President of the National Assembly; on the reproaches addressed to him for not sufficiently watching the agents of foreign powers; it was against these pretended agents and their creatures, that the Mayor of Paris thought he was marching when he put himself at the head of a column of National Guards.

Bailly did not even know the cause of the meeting; he had not been informed that the crowd wished to sign a petition ; and that the previous evening, according to the decree of the law, there had been a declaration made to this effect before the competent authority. His answers to the Revolutionary Tribunal leave not the least doubt on this point !

Oh Eschevins, Eschevins ! when your vain pretensions only were treated of, the public could forgive you ; but the 17th of July, you took advantage of Bailly's confidence ; you induced him to take sanguinary measures of repression, after having fascinated him with false reports ; you committed a real crime. If it was the duty of the Revolutionary Tribunal, of deplorable memory, to demand in 1793 from any one an explanation of the massacres of the Champ de Mars, it was not Bailly assuredly who ought to have been accused in the first place.

The political party whose blood flowed on the 17th of July, pretended to have been the victim of a plot concocted by its adversaries. When interrogated by the President of the Revolutionary Tribunal, Bailly answered : " I had no knowledge of it, but experience has since given me reason to think that such a plot did exist at that time."

Nothing more serious has ever been written against the promoters of the sanguinary violences on the 17th of July.

The blame that has been thrown on the events of the Champ de Mars has not been confined solely to the fact of proclaiming martial law ; the repressive measures that followed that proclamation have been criticized with equal bitterness.

The municipal administration was especially reproached for having hoisted a red flag much too small ; a flag that was called in the Tribunal *a pocket flag ;* for not

having placed this flag at the head of the column, as the
law commands, but in such a position, that the public on
whom the column was advancing could not see it; for
having made the armed force enter the Champ de Mars,
by all the gates on the side towards the town, a manœuvre
that seemed rather intended to surround the multitude,
than to disperse it; for having ordered the National
Guard to load their arms, even on the Place de Grève;
for having made the guard fire before the three required
summonses were made, and fire upon the people around
the altar, whilst the stones and the pistol shot, which were
assigned as the motive for the sanguinary order, came
from the steps and benches; for allowing some people
who were endeavouring to escape on the side towards
l'Ecole Militaire, and others who had actually jumped
into the Seine, to be pursued, shot, and bayonetted.

It results clearly from one of Bailly's publications,
from his answers to the questions put to him by the President of the Revolutionary Tribunal, from the writings of
the day:

That the Mayor of Paris gave no order for the troops
to be collected on the 17th of July; that he had had no
conference on that day with the military authority; that
if any arrangements, culpable and contrary to law were
adopted, as to the situation of the cavalry, of the red flag,
and of the Municipal Body, in the column marching on
the Champ de Mars, they could not without injustice be
imputed to him; that Bailly was not aware of the National Guard having loaded their muskets with ball before quitting the square of the Hôtel de Ville; that he
was not aware even of the existence of the red flag,
with whose small dimensions he had been so severely
reproached; that the National Guard fired without his

order; that he made every effort to stop the firing, to
stop the pursuit, and make the soldiers resume their
ranks; that he congratulated the troops of the line, who
under the command of Hulin, entered by the gate of
l'Ecole Militaire, and not only did not fire, but tore many
of the unfortunate people from the hands of the National
Guard, whose exasperation amounted to delirium. In
short, it might be asked, relative to any want of exactness attributable to Bailly in that unfortunate affair,
whether it was just to impute it to him who, in his letters to Voltaire on the origin of the sciences, wrote as
follows in 1776:

"I am unfortunately short-sighted. I am often humiliated in the open country. Whilst I with difficulty can
distinguish a house at the distance of a hundred paces, my
friends relate to me what they see at the distance of five
or six hundred. I open my eyes, I fatigue myself without seeing any thing, and I am sometimes inclined to think
that they amuse themselves at my expense."

You begin to see, Gentlemen, the advantage that a
firm and able lawyer might have drawn from the authentic facts that I have just been relating. But Bailly knew
the pretended jury before whom he had to appear. This
jury was not a collection of drunken cobblers, whatever
some passionate writers may have asserted; it was worse
than that, Gentlemen, notwithstanding the deservedly
celebrated names that were occasionally interspersed
among them: it was—let us cut the subject short—an
odious commission.

The very circumscribed list from which chance in 1793
and 1794 drew the juries of the Revolutionary Tribunals,
did not embrace, as the sacred word *jury* seems to imply,
all one class of citizens. The authorities formed it, after

a prefatory and very minute inquiry, of their adherents only. The unfortunate defendants were thus judged not by impartial persons free from any preconceived system, but by political enemies, which is as much as to say, by that which is the most cruel and remorseless in the world.

Bailly would not be defended. After his appearance as a witness in the trial of Marie Antoinette, the ex-Mayor only wrote and had printed for circulation, a paper entitled *Bailly to his fellow-citizens*. It closes with these affecting words :

" I have only gained by the Revolution that which my fellow-citizens have gained: liberty and equality. I have lost by it some useful situations, and my fortune is nearly destroyed. I could be happy with what remains of it to me and a clear conscience; but to be happy in the repose of my retreat, I require, my dear fellow-citizens, your esteem : I know well that, sooner or later, you will do me justice ; but I require it while I live, and while I am yet amongst you."

Our colleague was unanimously condemned. We should despair of the future, unless such a unanimity struck all friends of justice and humanity with stupor, if it did not increase the number of decided adversaries to all political tribunals.

When the President of the Tribunal interrogated the accused, already declared guilty, as to whether he had any reclamations to make relative to the execution of the sentence, Bailly answered :

" I have always carried out the law ; I shall know how to submit myself to it, since you are its organ."

The illustrious convict was led back to his cell.

Bailly had said in his éloge on M. de Tressan : " French gaiety produces the same effect as stoicism."

These words occurred to my memory at the time when I was gathering from various sources the proof that on re-entering the Conciergerie after his condemnation, Bailly showed himself at once both gay and stoical.

He desired his nephew, M. Batbéda, to play a game at piquet with him as usual. He thought of all the circumstances connected with the frightful morrow with such coolness, that he even said with a smile to M. Batbéda during the game: "Let us rest awhile, my friend, and take a pinch of snuff; to-morrow I shall be deprived of this pleasure, for I shall have my hands tied behind my back."

I will quote some words which, while testifying to a similar degree Bailly's serenity of mind, are more in harmony with his grave character, and more worthy of being preserved in history.

One of the companions of the illustrious academician's captivity, on the evening of the 11th of November, with tears in his eyes and moved by a tender veneration, exclaimed: "Why did you let us fancy there was a possibility of acquittal? You deceived us then?"—Bailly answered: "No, I was teaching you never to despair of the laws of your country."

In the paroxysms of wild despair, some of the prisoners reviewing the past, went so far as to regret that they had never infringed the laws of the strictest honesty.

Bailly brought back these minds, erring for the moment from the path of duty, by repeating to them maxims which both in form and substance would not disparage the collections of the most celebrated moralists:

"It is false, very false, that a crime can ever be useful. The trade of an honest man is the safest, even in times of revolution. Enlightened egotism suffices to put any

intelligent individual into the path of justice and truth.
Whenever innocence can be sacrificed with impunity,
crime is not sure of succeeding. There is so great a
difference between the death of a good man and that of
a wicked man, that the multitude is incapable of estimat-
ing it."

Cannibals devouring their vanquished enemies seem to
me less hideous, less contrary to nature, than those
wretches, the refuse of the population of large towns,
who, too often alas! have carried their ferocity so far, as
to disturb by their clamorous and infamous raillery the
last moments of the unhappy victims about to be struck
by the sword of the law. The more humiliating this
picture of the degradation of the human species may be,
the more we should beware of overcharging the colour-
ing. With few exceptions, the historians of Bailly's last
agony appear to me to have forgotten this duty. Was
the truth, the strict truth, not sufficiently distressing?
Was it requisite, without any sort of proof, to impute to
the mass of the people the infernal cynicism of cannibals?
Should they lightly make just sentiments of disgust and
indignation rest upon an immense class of citizens? I
think not, Gentlemen, and I will therefore avoid the
cruelty and poignancy of chaining the thoughts for a long
time on such scenes; I will prove that by rendering the
drama a little less atrocious, I have only sacrificed imaginary details, which are the envenomed fruits of the
spirit of the party.

I will not shut my ears to the questions that already
hum around me. People will say to me, What are your
claims for daring to modify a page of our revolutionary
history, on which every one seemed agreed? What right
have you to weaken contemporary testimonies, you, who

at the time of Bailly's death, were scarcely born; you,
who lived in an obscure valley of the Pyrenees, two
hundred and twenty leagues from the capital?

These questions do not embarrass me at all. In short,
I do not ask that the relation of what seems to me to be
the expression of the truth, should be adopted upon my
word. I enumerate my proofs, I express my doubts.
Within these limits there is no one but has claims to bring
forward; the discussion is open to all the world, the public will pronounce its definitive judgment.

As a general thesis, I will add that by concentrating
our researches on one circumscribed and special object,
we have a better chance of seeing it correctly and knowing it well, all other things being equal, than by scattering our attention in all directions.

As to the merit of contemporaneous narratives, it seems
to me very dubious. Political passions do not allow us
to see objects in their real dimensions, nor in their true
forms, nor in their natural colours. Moreover, have not
unpublished and very valuable documents come to shed
bright colours, just where the spirit of party had spread a
thick veil?

The account that Riouffe gave of the death of Bailly
has almost blindly led all the historians of our revolution.
What does it consist of " at bottom." The prisoner of la
Conciergerie said it himself; of tales related by execu-
tioners' valets, repeated by turnkeys.

I would willingly allow this account to be set against
me, notwithstanding the horrid sewer from which Riouffe
had been obliged to draw, if it were not evident that this
clever writer saw all the revolutionary events through the
just anger that an ardent and active young man must feel
after an iniquitous imprisonment; if this current of senti-

11

ments and ideas had not led him into some manifest errors.

Who has not, for example, read with tears in their eyes, in the *Mémoires sur les Prisons*, what the author relates of the fourteen girls of Verdun ? " Of those girls," he said, " of unparalleled fairness, and who appeared like young virgins dressed for a public fête. They disappeared," added Riouffe, " all at once, and were mowed down in the spring of life. The court occupied by the women the day after their death, had the appearance of a garden that had been despoiled of its flowers by a storm. I have never seen amongst us a despair equal to that excited by this barbarity."

Far be from me the intention to weaken the painful feelings which the catastrophe related by Riouffe must naturally inspire; but every one has remarked that the report of this writer is very circumstantial; the author appears to have seen all with his own eyes. Yet he has been guilty of the gravest inaccuracy.

Out of the fourteen unfortunate women who were sentenced after Verdun was retaken from the Prussians, two girls of seventeen years of age were not condemned to death on account of their youth.

This first circumstance was well worth recording. Let us go farther. A historian having lately consulted the official journals of that epoch, and the bulletin of the Revolutionary Tribunal, discovered with some surprise that among the twelve *young girls* who were condemned, there were seven either married or widows, whose ages varied from forty-one to sixty-nine !

Contemporary accounts then, even those of Riouffe, may be submitted without irreverence to earnest discussion. When a tenth part of the funds annually devoted to researches in and examination of old chronicles, is applied to making extracts from the registers relative to the French Revolution, we shall certainly see many other hideous circumstances that revolt the soul, disappear from our contemporary history.    Look at the massacres of September! The historians most in vogue report the number of victims that fell in that butchery to have been from six to twelve thousand; whilst a writer who has lately taken the trouble to analyze the prison registers in the gaoler's books, cannot make the whole amount to one thousand.    Even this number is very large; but, for my part, I thank the author of this recent publication for having reduced the number of assassinations in September to less than a tenth part of what had been generally admitted.

When the discussion which I have here undertaken becomes known to the public, it will be seen how many and how important are the retrenchments to be made from that lugubrious page of our history.    Another important circumstance may be appreciated, which appears to me to arise from all these facts.    After having weighed my proofs, every one I hope will join me in seeing that the wretches around the scaffold of Bailly were but the refuse of the population, fulfilling for pay the part that had been assigned them by three or four wealthy cannibals.

The sentence pronounced against Bailly by the Revolutionary Tribunal was to be executed on the 12th of November, 1793.    The reminiscences recently published by a fellow-prisoner of our colleague, the reminiscences of M. Beugnot, will enable us to penetrate into the Conciergerie, on the morning of that inauspicious day.

Bailly had risen early, after having slept as usual, the sleep of the just.    He took some chocolate, and conversed a long time with his nephew. The young man was a prey to despair, but the illustrious prisoner preserved all his serenity. The previous evening in returning from the Tribunal, he remarked, with admirable coolness, though springing from a certain disquietude, " that the spectators of his trial had been strongly excited against him. I fear," he added, "that the mere execution of the sentence will no longer satisfy them, which might be dangerous in its consequences. Perhaps the police will provide against it." These reflections having recurred to Bailly's mind on the 12th, he asked for, and drank hastily, two cups of coffee without milk. These precautions were a sinister omen. To his friends who surrounded him at this awful moment, and were sobbing aloud, he said, " Be calm; I have rather a difficult journey to perform, and I distrust my constitution. Coffee excites and reanimates; I hope, however, to reach the end properly."

Noon had just struck. Bailly addressed a last and tender adieu to his companions in captivity, wished them a better fate, followed the executioner without weakness as well as without bravado, mounted the fatal cart, his hands tied behind his back. Our colleague was accustomed to say: " We must entertain a bad opinion of those who, in their dying moments, have not a look to cast behind them." Bailly's last look was towards his wife. A gendarme of the escort feelingly listened to his last words, and faithfully repeated them to his widow. The procession reached the entrance to the Champ de Mars, on the side towards the river, at a quarter past one o'clock. This was the place where, according to the words of the sentence, the scaffold had been raised. The blinded crowd collected there, furiously exclaimed that the sacred ground of the Champ de la Fédération should not be

soiled by the presence and by the blood of him whom they
called a great criminal.    Upon their demand (I had
almost said their orders), the scaffold was taken down
again, and carried piecemeal into one of the fosses, where
it was put up afresh.    Bailly remained the stern witness
of these frightful preparations, and of these infernal
clamours.    Not one complaint escaped from his lips.
Rain had been falling all the morning; it was cold; it
drenched the body, and especially the bare head, of the
venerable man.    A wretch saw that he was shivering,
and cried out to him, " *Thou tremblest, Bailly.*"—"*I am
cold, my friend,*" mildly answered the victim.    These
were his last words.

Bailly descended into the moat, where the executioner
burnt before him the red flag of the 17th July; he then
with a firm step mounted the scaffold.    Let us have the
courage to say it, when the head of our venerable colleague fell, the paid witnesses whom this horrid execution
had assembled on the Champ de Mars burst into infamous
acclamations.

I had announced a faithful recital of the martyrdom of
Bailly; I have kept my word.    I said that I should ban-
ish many circumstances without reality, and that the
drama would thus become less atrocious.    If I am to trust
your aspect, I have not accomplished the second part of
my promise.    The imagination perhaps cannot reach beyond the cruel facts on which I have been obliged to
dilate.    You ask what I can have retrenched from former
relations, whilst what remains is so deplorable.

The order for execution addressed by Fouquier Tinville to the executioner has been seen by several persons
now living.    They all declare that if it differs from the
numerous orders of a similar nature that the wretch sent

off daily, it was only by the substitution of the following words: "Esplanade du Champ de Mars," for the usual designation of " Place de la Revolution." Now, the Revolutionary Tribunal has deserved many anathemas, but I never remarked its being reproached with not having known how to enforce obedience.

I felt myself relieved from an immense weight, Gentlemen, when I could dispel from my thoughts the image of a melancholy march on foot of two hours, because with it there disappeared two hours of corporeal ill-usage, which, according to those same accounts, our virtuous colleague must have endured from the Conciergerie to the Champ de Mars.

An illustrious writer asserts that they conducted Bailly to the Place de la Revolution, that the scaffold there was taken to pieces on the multitude demanding it, and that the victim was then led to the Champ de Mars. This relation is not correct. The sentence expressed in positive terms, that, as an exception, the Square of the Revolution was not to be the scene of Bailly's execution. The procession went direct to the place designated.

The historian already quoted affirms that the scaffold on being put up again on the bank of the Seine was erected on a heap of rubbish; that this operation lasted some hours, and that Bailly meanwhile was drawn round the Champ de Mars several times.

These promenades are imaginary. Those men who on the arrival of the lugubrious procession vociferated that the presence of the old Mayor of Paris would soil the Champ de la Fédération, could not the next minute force him to make the circuit of it. In fact, the illustrious victim remained in the road. The cruel idea, so knowingly attributed to the actors of those hideous scenes, to raise the fatal instrument on a heap of rubbish on the river bank, so that Bailly might in his last moments see the house at Chaillot where he had composed his works, was so far from occurring to the mind of the multitude, that the sentence was executed in the moat between two walls.

I have not thought it my duty, Gentlemen, to represent the condemned man forced to carry some parts of the scaffold himself, because he had his hands tied behind his back.  In my recital nobody waves the burning red flag over Bailly's head, because this barbarity is not mentioned in the narratives, otherwise so shocking, drawn up by some friends of our colleague shortly after the event; nor have I consented, with the author of *The History of the French Revolution*, to represent one of the soldiers forming the escort asking the question that led the victim to make, we must say so, the theatrical answer : "Yes, I tremble, but it is with cold ;" but the more touching answer, so characteristic of Bailly; "Yes, my friend, I am cold."

Far be it from me, Gentlemen, to suppose that no soldier in the world would be capable of a despicable and culpable act.  I do not ask, assuredly, the suppression of all courts-martial ; but to be induced to attribute to a man dressed in a military uniform, a personal part in this frightful drama, proofs or contemporary testimonies would be required, of which I have found no trace.

If the fact had occurred, its results would certainly have become known to the public.  I take to witness an event which is found related in Bailly's Memoirs.

On the 22d of July, 1789, on the square of the Hôtel de Ville, a dragoon with his sabre mutilated the corpse of Berthier.  His comrades, feeling outraged by this barbarity, all showed themselves instantly resolved to fight him in succession, and so wash out in his blood the disgrace he had thrown on the whole corps. The dragoon fought that same evening and was killed.

In his *History of Prisons*, Riouffe says that "Bailly exhausted the ferocity of the populace, of whom he had been the idol, and was basely abandoned by the people, though they had never ceased to esteem him."

Nearly the same idea is found expressed in *The History of the Revolution*, and in several other works.

What is called the populace rarely read and did not write. To attack it and calumniate it therefore was a convenient thing, since no refutation need to be feared. I am far from supposing that the historians whose works I have quoted, ever gave way to such considerations; but I affirm, with entire certainty, that they have deceived themselves. In the sanguinary drama that has been unrolled before your eyes, the atrocities had a quite different source from the sentiments common to the barbarians that were swarming in the dregs of society and always ready to soil it with every crime; in plainer words, it is not to the unfortunate people who have neither property, nor capital, living by the work of their hands, to the *prolétaires*, that we are to impute the deplorable incidents which marked Bailly's last moments. To put forward an opinion so remote from received opinions, is imposing on one's self the duty of proving its truth.

After his condemnation, our·colleague exclaimed, says La Fayette: "I die for the sitting of the Jeu de Paume, and not for the fatal day at the Champ de Mars." I do not here intend to expound these mysterious words in the glimpses they give us by a half-light; but, whatever

meaning we may attribute to them, it is evident that the
sentiments and passions of the lower class have no share
in them ; it is a point beyond discussion.

On reëntering the Conciergerie, the evening before his
death, Bailly spoke of the efforts that must have been
made to excite the passions of the auditors, who followed
the various phases of his trial.   Factitious excitement is
always the produce of corruption.   The working classes
are without money; they then cannot have been the cor-
ruptors or direct promoters of the distressing scenes of
which Bailly complained.

The implacable enemies of the former President of the
National Assembly had procured for pay some auxiliaries
among the turnkeys of the Conciergerie.   M. Beugnot
informs us that when the venerable magistrate was con-
signed to the gendarmes who were to conduct him to the
Tribunal, " these wretches pushed him violently, sending
him from one to the other like a drunken man, calling
out: *Hold there, Bailly! Catch, Bailly, there!* and that
they laughed and shouted at the grave demeanour the
philosopher maintained amidst the insults of those cannibals."

To confirm my statement that these violences (in comparison with which, in truth, those of the Champ de Mars
lose their virulence,) were fomented by pay, I have more
than the formal declaration of our colleague's fellow prisoner.   For in fact I find that no other prisoner or convict
underwent such treatment; not even the man called the
Admiral, when he was taken to the Conciergerie for having attempted to assassinate Collot-d'Herbois.

Besides, it is not only on indirect considerations that
my decided opinion is founded relative to the intervention
of rich and influential people in those scenes of indescrib-

able barbarity on the Champ de Mars.  Mérard St. Just,
the intimate friend of Bailly, has alluded by his initials
to a wretch who, the very day of our colleague's death,
publicly boasted of having electrified the few acolytes
who, together with him, insisted on the removal of the
scaffold ; the day after the execution, the meeting of the
Jacobins reëchoed with the name of another individual
of the Gros Caillou, who also claimed his share of influence in the crime.

I have progressively unrolled before you the series of
events in our revolution, in which Bailly took an active
part; I have scrupulously searched out the smallest circumstances of the deplorable affair on the Champ de
Mars; I have followed our colleague in his proscription
to the Revolutionary Tribunal, and to the foot of the
scaffold.  We had seen him before, surrounded by esteem,
by respect, and by glory, in the bosom of our principal
academies.  Yet the work is not complete; several essential traits are still wanting.

I will therefore claim a few more minutes of your kind
attention.  The moral life of Bailly is like those master-
pieces of ancient sculpture, that deserve to be studied in
every point of view, and in which new beauties are continually discovered, in proportion as the contemplation is
prolonged.

### PORTRAIT OF BAILLY.—HIS WIFE.

Nature did not endow Bailly generously with those
exterior advantages that please us at first sight.  He was
tall and thin.  His visage compressed, his eyes small and
sunk, his nose regular, but of unusual length, and a very
brown complexion, constituted an imposing whole, severe
and almost glacial.  Fortunately, it was easy to perceive

through this rough bark, the inexhaustible benevolence of the good man; the kindness that always accompanies a serene mind, and even some rudiments of gayety.

Bailly early endeavoured to model his conduct on that of the Abbé de Lacaille, who directed his first steps in the career of astronomy. And therefore it will be found that in transcribing five or six lines of the very feeling eulogy that the pupil dedicated to the memory of his revered master, I shall have made known at the same time many of the characteristic traits of the panegyrist:

" He was cold and reserved towards those of whom he knew little; but gentle, simple, equable, and familiar in the intercourse of friendship. It is there that, throwing off the grave exterior which he wore in public, he gave himself up to a peaceful and amiable gayety."

The resemblance between Bailly and Lacaille goes no farther. Bailly informs us that the great astronomer proclaimed truth on all occasions, without disquieting himself as to whom it might wound. He would not consent to put vice at its ease, saying:

" If good men thus showed their indignation, bad men being known, and vice unmasked, could no longer do harm, and virtue would be more respected." This Spartan morality could not accord with Bailly's character; he admired but did not adopt it.

Tacitus took as a motto: " To say nothing false, to omit nothing true." Our colleague contented himself in society with the first half of the precept. Never did mockery, bitterness, or severity issue from his lips. His manners were a medium between those of Lacaille and the manners of another academician who had succeeded in not making a single enemy, by adopting the two axioms: " Every thing is possible, and everybody is in the right."

Crébillon obtained permission from the French Academy to make his reception discourse in verse. At the moment when that poet, then almost sixty years of age, said, speaking of himself,

"No gall has ever poisoned my pen,"

the hall reëchoed with approbation.

I was going to apply this line by the author of *Rhadamistus* to our colleague, when accident offered to my sight a passage in which Lalande reproaches Bailly for having swerved from his usual character, in 1773, in a discussion that they had together on a point in the theory of Jupiter's Satellites. I set about the search for this discussion; I found the article by Bailly in a journal of that epoch, and I affirm that this dispute does not contain a word but what is in harmony with all our colleague's published writings. I return therefore to my former idea, and say of Bailly, with perfect confidence,

"No gall had ever poisoned his pen."

Diffidence is usually the trait that the biographers of studious men endeavour most to put in high relief. I dare assert, that in the common acceptation, this is pure flattery. To merit the epithet of diffident, must we think ourselves beneath the competitors of whom we are at least the equals? Must we, in examining ourselves, fail in the tact, in the intelligence, in the judgment, that nature has awarded us, and of which we make so good a use in appreciating the works of others? Oh! then, few learned men can be said to be diffident. Look at Newton: his diffidence is almost as celebrated as his genius. Well, I will extract from two of his letters, scarcely known, two paragraphs which, put side by side, will excite some surprise; the first confirms the general opinion; the second

seems with equal force to contradict it. Here are the
two passages :

" We are diffident in the presence of Nature."

" We may nobly feel our own strength in the face of
man's works."

In my opinion, the opposition in these two passages is
only apparent; it will be explained by means of a distinction which I have already slightly indicated.

Bailly's diffidence required the same distinction. When
people praised him to his face on the diversity of his
knowledge, our colleague did not immediately repel the
compliment; but soon after, he would stop his panegyrist,
and whisper in his ear with an air of mystery : " I will
confide a secret to you, pray do not take advantage of it :
I am only a very little less ignorant than another man."

Never did a man act more in harmony with his principles. Bailly was led to reprimand severely a man belonging to the humblest and poorest class of society.
Anger does not make him forget that he speaks to a citizen, to a man. " I ask pardon," says the first magistrate
of the capital, addressing himself to a rag-gatherer; " I
ask your pardon, if I am angry; but your conduct is so
reprehensible, that I cannot speak to you otherwise."

Bailly's friends were wont to say that he devoted too
much of his patrimony to pleasure. This word was
calumniously interpreted. Mérard Saint Just has given
the true sense of it : " Bailly's pleasure was beneficence."

So eminent a mind could not fail to be tolerant. Such
in fact Bailly constantly showed himself in politics, and
what is almost equally rare, in regard to religion. In
the month of June, 1791, he checked in severe terms the
fury with which the multitude appeared to be excited, at
the report that at the Théatines some persons had taken

the Communion two or three times in one day. " The accusation is undoubtedly false," said the Mayor of Paris; " but if it were true, the public would not have a right to inquire into it. Every one should have the free choice of his religion and his creed." Nothing would have been wanting in the picture, if Bailly had taken the trouble to remark how strange it was, that these violent scruples against repeated Communions emanated from persons who probably never took the Sacrament at all.

The reports on animal magnetism, on the hospitals, on the slaughter-houses, had carried Bailly's name into regions, whence the courtiers knew very cleverly how to discard true merit. *Madame* then wished to attach the illustrious academician to her person as a cabinet secretary. Bailly accepted. It was an entirely honorary title. The secretary saw the princess only once, that was on the day of his presentation.

Were more important functions reserved for him? We must suppose so; for some influential persons offered to procure Bailly a title of nobility and a decoration. This time the philosopher flatly refused, saying, in answer to the earnest negotiators: " I thank you, but he who has the honour of belonging to the three principal academies of France is sufficiently decorated, sufficiently noble in the eyes of rational men; a cordon, or a title, could add nothing to him."

The first secretary of the Academy of Sciences had, some years before, acted as Bailly did. Only he gave his refusal in such strong terms, that I could not easily believe them to have been written by the timid pen of Fontenelle, if I did not find them in a perfectly authentic document, in which he says: " Of all the titles in this world, I have never had any but of one sort, the titles of

Academician, and they have not been profaned by an
admixture of any others, more worldly and more osten-
tatious."

Bailly married, in November, 1787, an intimate friend
of his mother's, already a widow, only two years younger
than himself. Madame Bailly, a distant relation of the
author of the *Marseillaise*, had an attachment for her
husband that bordered on adoration. She lavished on
him the most tender and affectionate attention. The
success that Madame Bailly might have had in the fashionable world by her beauty, her grace, by her ineffable
goodness, did not tempt her. She lived in almost absolute retirement, even when the learned academician was
most in society. The Mayor's wife appeared only at
one public ceremony : the day of the benediction of the
colours of the sixty battalions of the National Guard by
the Archbishop of Paris, she accompanied Madame de
Lafayette to the Cathedral. She said : " My husband's
duty is to show himself in public wherever there is any
good to be done, or sound advice to be given ; mine is to
remain at home." This rare retiring and respectable
conduct did not disarm some hideous pamphleteers.
Their impudent sarcasms were continually attacking the
modest wife on her domestic hearth, and troubling her
peace of mind. In their logic of the tavern they fancied
that an elegant and handsome woman, who avoided society, could not fail to be ignorant and stupid. Thence
arose a thousand imaginary stories, ridiculous both as to
their matter and form, thrown out daily to the public,
more, indeed, to offend and disgust the upright magistrate than to humble his companion.

The axe that ended our colleague's life, with the same
stroke, and almost as completely, crushed in Madame

Bailly, after so many poignant agitations and unexampled misfortunes, all that was left of strength of mind and power of intellect. A strange incident also aggravated the sadness of Madame Bailly's situation. On a day of trouble, during her husband's lifetime, she had placed the assignats resulting from the sale of their house at Chaillot, amounting to about thirty thousand francs, in the wadding of a dress. The enfeebled memory of the unfortunate widow did not recall to her the existence of this treasure, even in the time of her greatest distress. When the age of the material which had secreted them began to reveal them to daylight, they were no longer of any value.

The widow of the author of one of the best works of the age, of the learned member of our three great academies, of the first President of the National Assembly, of the first Mayor of Paris, found herself thus reduced, by an unheard-of turn of fortune, to implore help from public pity. It was the geometer Cousin, member of this academy, who by his incessant solicitations got Madame Bailly's name inserted at the Board of Charity in his arrondissement. The support was distributed in kind. Cousin used to receive the articles at the Hôtel de Ville, where he was a Municipal Councillor, and carried them himself to the street de la Sourdière. It was, in short, in the street de la Sourdière that Madame Bailly had obtained two rooms gratis, in the house of a compassionate person, whose name I very much regret not having learnt. Does it not appear to you, Gentlemen, that the academician Cousin, who crossed the whole of Paris, with the bread under his arm and the meat and the candle, intended for the unfortunate widow of an illustrious colleague, did himself more honour than if he had

come to one of the sittings bringing in his portfolio the
results of some fine scientific research? Such noble
actions are certainly worth good " Papers."

Affairs proceeded thus up to the revolution of the 18th
Brumaire. On the 21st, the public criers were announcing everywhere, even in the street de la Sourdière, that
General Bonaparte was Consul, and M. de Laplace Minister of the Interior. This name, so well known by the
respectable widow, reached even the room that she in-
habited, and caused her some emotion. That same evening, the new minister (this was a noble beginning, Gentlemen) asked for a pension of 2000 francs for Madame
Bailly. The Consul granted the demand, adding to it
this express condition, that the first half year should be
paid in advance, and immediately. Early on the 22d,
a carriage stopped in the street de la Sourdière; Madame
de Laplace descends from it, carrying in her hand a
purse filled with gold. She rushed to the staircase, runs
to the humble abode, that had now for several years witnessed irremediable sorrow and severe misery; Madame
Bailly was at the window : " My dear friend, what are
you doing there so early? " exclaimed the wife of the
minister. " Madam," replied the widow, " I heard the
public crier yesterday, and I was expecting you ! "

If after having, from a sense of duty, expatiated upon
anarchical, odious, and sanguinary scenes, the historian
of our civil discords has the good fortune to meet on his
progress with an incident that gratifies the mind, raises
the soul, and fills the heart with pleasing emotions, he
stops there, Gentlemen, as the African traveller halts in
an oasis !

# HERSCHEL.

WILLIAM HERSCHEL, one of the greatest astronomers that ever lived in any age or country, was born at Hanover, on the 15th of November, 1738. The name of Herschel has become too illustrious for people to neglect searching back, up the stream of time, to learn the social position of the families that have borne it. Yet the just curiosity of the learned world on this subject has not been entirely satisfied. We only know that Abraham Herschel, great-grandfather of the astronomer, resided at Mähren, whence he was expelled on account of his strong attachment to the Protestant faith; that Abraham's son Isaac was a farmer in the vicinity of Leipzig; that Isaac's eldest son, Jacob Herschel, resisted his father's earnest desire to see him devote himself to agriculture, that he determined on being a musician, and settled at Hanover.

Jacob Herschel, father of William, the astronomer, was an eminent musician; nor was he less remarkable for the good qualities of his heart and of his mind. His very limited means did not enable him to bestow a complete education on his family, consisting of six boys and four girls. But at least, by his care, his ten children all became excellent musicians. The eldest, Jacob, even acquired a rare degree of ability, which procured for him the appointment of Master of the Band in a Hanoverian regiment, which he accompanied to England.  The third son, William, remained under his father's roof.  Without neglecting the fine arts, he took lessons in the French language, and devoted himself to the study of metaphysics, for which he retained a taste to his latest day.

In 1759, William Herschel, then about twenty-one years old, went over to England, not with his father, as has been erroneously published, but with his brother Jacob, whose connections in that country seemed likely to favour the young man's opening prospects in life. Still, neither London nor the country towns afforded him any resource in the beginning, and the first two or three years after his expatriation were marked by some cruel privations, which, however, were nobly endured.  A fortunate chance finally raised the poor Hanoverian to a better position; Lord Durham engaged him as Master of the Band in an English regiment which was quartered on the borders of Scotland.  From this moment the musician Herschel acquired a reputation that spread gradually, and in the year 1765 he was appointed organist at Halifax (Yorkshire).  The emoluments of this situation, together with giving private lessons both in the town and the country around, procured a degree of comfort for the young William.  He availed himself of it to remedy, or rather to complete, his early education.  It was then that he learnt Latin and Italian, though without any other help than a grammar and a dictionary.  It was then also that he taught himself something of Greek.  So great was the desire for knowledge with which he was inspired while residing at Halifax, that Herschel found means to continue his hard philological exercises, and at the same time to study deeply the learned but very obscure mathematical work on the theory of music by R.

Smith. This treatise, either explicitly or implicitly, supposed the reader to possess some knowledge of algebra
and of geometry, which Herschel did not possess, but of
which he made himself master in a very short time.

In 1766, Herschel obtained the appointment of organist to the Octagon Chapel at Bath. This was a more
lucrative post than that of Halifax, but new obligations
also devolved on the able pianist. He had to play incessantly either at the Oratorios, or in the rooms at the
baths, at the theatre, and in the public concerts. Then,
being immersed in the most fashionable circle in England,
Herschel could no longer refuse the numerous pupils who
wished to be instructed in his school. It is difficult to
imagine how, among so many duties, so many distractions
of various kinds, Herschel could continue so many studies,
which already at Halifax had required in him so much
resolution, so much perseverance, and a very uncommon
degree of talent. We have already seen that it was by
music that Herschel was led to mathematics; mathematics in their turn led him to optics, the principal and
fertile source of his illustrious career. The hour finally
struck, when his theoretic knowledge was to guide the
young musician into a laborious application of principles
quite foreign to his habits; and the brilliant success of
which, as well as their excessive hardihood, will excite
reasonable astonishment.

A telescope, a simple telescope, only two English feet
in length, falls into the hands of Herschel during his
residence at Bath. This instrument, however imperfect,
shows him a multitude of stars in the sky that the naked
eye cannot discern; shows him also some of the known
objects, but now under their true dimensions; reveals
forms to him that the richest imaginations of antiquity

had never suspected. Herschel is transported with enthusiasm. He will, without delay, have a similar instrument but of larger dimensions. The answer from London is delayed for some days : these few days appear as many centuries to him. When the answer arrives, the price that the optician demands proves to be much beyond the pecuniary resources of a mere organist. To any other man this would have been a clap of thunder. This unexpected difficulty on the contrary, inspired Herschel with fresh energy; he cannot buy a telescope, then he will construct one with his own hands. The musician of the Octagon Chapel rushes immediately into a multitude of experiments, on metallic alloys that reflect light with the greatest intensity, on the means of giving the parabolic figure to the mirrors, on the causes that in the operation of polishing affect the regularity of the figure, &c. So rare a degree of perseverance at last receives its reward. In 1774 Herschel has the happiness of being able to examine the heavens with a Newtonian telescope of five English feet focus, entirely made by himself. This success tempts him to undertake still more difficult enterprises. Other telescopes of seven, of eight, of ten, and even of twenty feet focal distance, crown his efforts. As if to answer in advance those critics who would have accused him of a superfluity of apparatus, of unnecessary luxury, in the large size of the new instruments, and his extreme minutiæ in their execution, Nature granted to the astronomical musician, on the 13th of March 1781, the unheard-of honour of commencing his career of observation with the discovery of a new planet, situated on the confines of our solar system. Dating from that moment, Herschel's reputation, no longer in his character of musician, but as a constructor of telescopes and as an astronomer, spread throughout the world. The King, George III., a great lover of science, and much inclined besides to protect and patronize both men and things of Hanoverian origin, had Herschel presented to him; he was charmed with the simple yet lucid and modest account that he gave of his repeated endeavours; he caught a glimpse of the glory that so penetrating an observer might reflect on his reign, ensured to him a pension of 300 guineas a year, and moreover a residence near Windsor Castle, first at Clay Hall and then at Slough. The visions of George III. were completely realized. We may confidently assert, relative to the little house and garden of Slough, that it is the spot of all the world where the greatest number of discoveries have been made. The name of that village will never perish; science will transmit it religiously to our latest posterity.

I will avail myself of this opportunity to rectify a mistake, of which ignorance and idleness wish to make a triumphant handle, or, at all events, to wield in their cause as an irresistible justification. It has been repeated to satiety, that at the time when Herschel entered on his astronomical career he knew nothing of mathematics. But I have already said, that during his residence at Bath, the organist of the Octagon Chapel had familiarized himself with the principles of geometry and algebra; and a still more positive proof of this is, that a difficult question on the vibration of strings loaded with small weights had been proposed for discussion in 1779: Herschel undertook to solve it, and his dissertation was inserted in several scientific collections of the year 1780.

The anecdotic life of Herschel, however, is now closed. The great astronomer will not quit his observatory any more, except to go and submit the sublime results of his laborious vigils to the Royal Society of London. These results are contained in his memoirs; they constitute one of the principal riches of the celebrated collection known under the title of *Philosophical Transactions.*

Herschel belonged to the principal Academies of Europe, and about 1816 he was named Knight of the Guelphic order of Hanover. According to the English habit, from the time of that nomination the title of Sir William took the place, in all this illustrious astronomer's memoirs, already honoured with so much celebrity, of the former appellation of Doctor William. Herschel had been named a Doctor (of laws) in the University of Oxford in 1786. This dignity, by special favour, was conferred on him without any of the obligatory formalities of examination, disputation, or pecuniary contribution, usual in that learned corporation.

I should wound the elevated sentiments that Herschel professed all his life, if I were not here to mention two indefatigable assistants that this fortunate astronomer found in his own family. The one was Alexander Herschel, endowed with a remarkable talent for mechanism, always at his brother's orders, and who enabled him to realize without delay any ideas that he had conceived ; * the other was Miss Caroline Herschel, who deserves a still more particular and detailed mention.

Miss Caroline Lucretia Herschel went to England as soon as her brother became special astronomer to the king. She received the appellation there of Assistant Astronomer, with a moderate salary. From that moment

---

* When age and infirmities obliged Alexander Herschel to give up his profession as a musician, he quitted Bath, and returned to Hanover, very generously provided by Sir William with a comfortable independence for life.

she unreservedly devoted herself to the service of her brother, happy in contributing night and day to his rapidly increasing scientific reputation. Miss Caroline shared in all the night-watches of her brother, with her eye constantly on the clock, and the pencil in her hand; she made all the calculations without exception; she made three or four copies of all the observations in separate registers; coördinated, classed, and analyzed them. If the scientific world saw with astonishment how Herschel's works succeeded each other with unexampled rapidity during so many years, they were specially indebted for it to the ardour of Miss Caroline. Astronomy, moreover, has been directly enriched by several comets through this excellent and respectable lady. After the death of her illustrious brother, Miss Caroline retired to Hanover, to the house of Jahn Dietrich Herschel, a musician of high reputation, and the only surviving brother of the astronomer.

William Herschel died without pain on the 23d of August 1822, aged eighty-three. Good fortune and glory never altered in him the fund of infantine candour, inexhaustible benevolence, and sweetness of character, with which nature had endowed him. He preserved to the last both his brightness of mind and vigour of intellect. For some years Herschel enjoyed with delight the distinguished success of his only son,* Sir John Herschel. At his last hour he sunk to rest with the pleasing conviction that his beloved son, heir of a great name, would not allow it to fall into oblivion, but adorn it with fresh lustre,

---

* Sir W. Herschel had married Mary, the widow of John Pitt, Esq., possessed of a considerable jointure, and the union proved a remarkable accession of domestic happiness. This lady survived Sir William by several years. They had but this son.—*Translator's Note.*

and that great discoveries would honour his career also. No prediction of the illustrious astronomer has been more completely verified.

The English journals gave an account of the means adopted by the family of William Herschel, for preserving the remains of the great telescope of thirty-nine English feet (twelve metres) constructed by that celebrated astronomer.

The metal tube of the instrument carrying at one end the recently cleaned mirror of four feet ten inches in diameter, has been placed horizontally in the meridian line, on solid piers of masonry, in the midst of the circle, where formerly stood the mechanism requisite for manœuvring the telescope. The first of January 1840, Sir John Herschel, his wife, their children, seven in number, and some old family servants, assembled at Slough. Exactly at noon, the party walked several times in procession round the instrument; they then entered the tube of the telescope, seated themselves on benches that had been prepared for the purpose, and sung a requiem, with English words composed by Sir John Herschel himself. After their exit, the illustrious family ranged themselves around the great tube, the opening of which was then hermetically sealed. The day concluded with a party of intimate friends.

I know not whether those persons who will only appreciate things from the peculiar point of view from which they have been accustomed to look, may think there was something strange in several of the details of the ceremony that I have just described. I affirm at least that the whole world will applaud the pious feeling which actuated Sir John Herschel; and that all the friends of science will thank him for having consecrated the humble garden

12

where his father achieved such immortal labours, by a monument more expressive in its simplicity than pyramids or statues.

## CHRONOLOGICAL TABLE

OF THE MEMOIRS OF WILLIAM HERCHEL.*

1780. *Philosophical Transactions*, vol. lxx.—Astronomical Observations on the Periodical Star in the Neck of the Whale.—Astronomical Observations relative to the Lunar Mountains.

1781. *Phil. Trans.*, vol. lxxi.—Astronomical Observations on the Rotation of the Planets on their Axes, made with a View to decide whether the Daily Rotation of the Earth be always the same.—On the Comet of 1781, afterwards called the *Georgium Sidus*.

1782. *Phil. Trans.*, vol. lxxii.—On the Parallax of the Fixed Stars.—Catalogue of Double Stars.—Description of a Lamp Micrometer, and the Method of using it.—Answers to the Doubts that might be raised to the high magnifying Powers used by Herschel.

1783. *Phil. Trans.*, vol. lxxiii.—Letter to Sir Joseph Banks on the Name to be given to the new Planet.—On the Diameter of the Georgium Sidus, followed by the Description of a Micrometer with luminous or dark Disks.—On the proper Motion of the Solar System, and the various Changes that have occurred among the Fixed Stars since the Time of Flamsteed.

1784. *Phil. Trans.*, vol. lxxiv.—On some remarkable Appearances in the Polar Regions of Mars, the Inclination of its Axis, the Position of its Poles, and its Spheroïdal Form.—Some Details on the real Diameter of Mars, and on its Atmosphere.—Analysis of some Observations on the Constitution of the Heavens.

1785. *Phil. Trans.*, vol. lxxv.—Catalogue of Double Stars.—On the Constitution of the Heavens.

1786. *Phil. Trans.* vol., lxxvi.—Catalogue of a Thousand Nebulæ and Clusters of Stars.—Researches on the Cause of a Defect of Definition in Vision, which has been attributed to the Smallness of the Optic Pencils.

* These titles are copied direct from the Philosophical Transactions, instead of being retranslated.—*Translator's Note.*

1787. *Phil. Trans.*, vol. lxxvii.—Remarks on the new Comet.—Discovery of Two Satellites revolving round George's Planet.—On Three Volcanoes in the Moon.

1788. *Phil. Trans.*, vol. lxxviii.—On George's Planet (Uranus) and its Satellites.

1789. *Phil. Trans.*, vol. lxxix.—Observations on a Comet. Catalogue of a Second Thousand new Nebulæ and Clusters of Stars.—Some Preliminary Remarks on the Constitution of the Heavens.

1790. *Phil. Trans.*, vol. lxxx.—Discovery of Saturn's Sixth and Seventh Satellites; with Remarks on the Constitution of the Ring, on the Planet's Rotation round an Axis, on its Spheroïdal Form, and on its Atmosphere.—On Saturn's Satellites, and the Rotation of the Ring round an Axis.

1791. *Phil. Trans.*, vol. lxxxi.—On the Nebulous Stars and the Suitableness of this Epithet.

1792. *Phil. Trans.*, vol. lxxxii.—On Saturn's Ring, and the Rotation of the Planet's Fifth Satellite round an Axis.—Mixed Observations.

1793. *Phil. Trans.*, vol. lxxxiii.—Observations on the Planet Venus.

1794. *Phil. Trans.*, vol. lxxxiv.—Observations on a Quintuple Band in Saturn.—On some Peculiarities observed during the last Solar Eclipse.—On Saturn's Rotation round an Axis.

1795. *Phil. Trans.*, vol. lxxxv.—On the Nature and Physical Constitution of the Sun and Stars.—Description of a Reflecting Telescope forty feet in length.

1796. *Phil. Trans.*, vol. lxxxvi.—Method of observing the Changes that happen to the Fixed Stars; Remarks on the Stability of our Sun's Light.—Catalogue of Comparative Brightness, to determine the Permanency of the Lustre of Stars.—On the Periodical Star *a* Herculis, with Remarks tending to establish the Rotatory Motion of the Stars on their Axes; to which is added a second Catalogue of the Brightness of the Stars.

1797. *Phil. Trans.*, vol. lxxxvii.—A Third Catalogue of the comparative Brightness of the Stars; with an Introductory Account of an Index to Mr. Flamsteed's Observations of the Fixed Stars, contained in the Second Volume of the Historia Cœlestis to which are added several useful Results derived from that Index.—Observations of the changeable Brightness of the Satellites of Jupiter, and of the Variation in their apparent Magnitudes; with a Determination of the Time of their rotary Motions on their Axes, to which is added a Measure of the Diameter of the Second Satellite, and an Estimate of the comparative Size of the Fourth.

1798. *Phil. Trans.*, vol. lxxxviii.—On the Discovery of Four additional Satellites of the Georgium Sidus. The retrograde Motion of its old Satellites announced; and the Çause of their Disappearance at certain Distances from the Planet explained.

1799. *Phil. Trans.*, vol. lxxxix.—A Fourth Catalogue of the comparative Brightness of the Stars.

1800. *Phil. Trans.* vol. xc.—On the Power of penetrating into Space by Telescopes, with a comparative Determination of the Extent of that Power in Natural Vision, and in Telescopes of various Sizes and Constructions; illustrated by select Observations.—Investigation of the Powers of the Prismatic Colours to heat and illuminate Objects; with Remarks that prove the different Refrangibility of radiant Heat; to which is added an Inquiry into the Method of viewing the Sun advantageously with Telescopes of large Apertures and high magnifying Powers.—Experiments on the Refrangibility of the Invisible Rays of the Sun.—Experiments on the Solar and on the Terrestrial Rays that occasion Heat; with a comparative View of the Laws to which Light and Heat, or rather the Rays which occasion them, are subject, in order to determine whether they are the same or different.

1801. *Phil. Trans.*, vol. xci.—Observations tending to investigate the Nature of the Sun, in order to find the Causes or Symptoms of its variable Emission of Light and Heat; with Remarks on the Use that may possibly be drawn from Solar Observations.—Additional Observations tending to investigate the Symptoms of the variable Emission of the Light and Heat of the Sun; with Trials to set aside darkening Glasses, by transmitting the Solar Rays through Liquids, and a few Remarks to remove Objections that might be made against some of the Arguments contained in the former paper.

1802. *Phil. Trans.*, vol. xcii.—Observations on the two lately discovered celestial Bodies (Ceres and Pallas).—Catalogue of 500 new Nebulæ and Clusters of Stars, with Remarks on the Construction of the Heavens.

1803. *Phil. Trans.*, vol. xciii.—Observations of the Transit of Mercury over the Disk of the Sun; to which is added an Investigation of the Causes which often prevent the proper Action of Mirrors.—Account of the Changes that have happened during the last Twenty-five Years in the relative Situation of Double Stars; with an Investigation of the Cause to which they are owing.

1804. *Phil. Trans.*, vol. xciv.—Continuation of an Account of the Changes that have happened in the relative Situation of Double Stars.

1805. *Phil. Trans.*, vol. xcv.—Experiments for ascertaining how far Telescopes will enable us to determine very small Angles, and to distinguish the real from the spurious Diameters of Celestial and Terrestrial Objects: with an Application of the Result of these Experiments to a Series of Observations on the Nature and Magnitude of Mr. Harding's lately discovered Star.—On the Direction and Velocity of the Motion of the Sun and Solar System.—Observation on the singular Figure of the Planet Saturn.

1806. *Phil. Trans.*, vol. xcvi.—On the Quantity and Velocity of the Solar Motion.—Observations on the Figure, the Climate, and the Atmosphere of Saturn and its Ring.

1807. *Phil. Trans.*, vol. xcvii.—Experiments for investigating the Cause of the Coloured Concentric Rings, discovered by Sir Isaac Newton between two Object-glasses laid one upon another.—Observations on the Nature of the new celestial Body discovered by Dr. Olbers, and of the Comet which was expected to appear last January in its Return from the Sun.

1808. *Phil. Trans.*, vol. xcviii.—Observations of a Comet, made with a view to investigate its Magnitude, and the Nature of its Illumination. To which is added, an Account of a new Irregularity lately perceived in the Apparent Figure of the Planet Saturn.

1809. *Phil. Trans.*, vol. xcix.—Continuation of Experiments for investigating the Cause of Coloured Concentric Rings, and other Appearances of a similar Nature.

1810. *Phil. Trans.*, vol. c.—Supplement to the First and Second Part of the Paper of Experiments for investigating the Cause of Coloured Concentric Rings between Object-glasses, and other Appearances of a similar Nature.

1811. *Phil. Trans.*, vol. ci.—Astronomical Observations relating to the Construction of the Heavens, arranged for the Purpose of a critical Examination, the Result of which appears to throw some new Light upon the Organization of the Celestial Bodies.

1812. *Phil. Trans.*, vol. cii.—Observations of a Comet, with Remarks on the Construction of its different Parts.—Observations of a Second Comet, with Remarks on its Construction.

1814. *Phil. Trans.*, vol. civ.—Astronomical Observations relating to the Sidereal Part of the Heavens, and its Connection with the Nebulous Part; arranged for the Purpose of a critical Examination.

1815. *Phil. Trans.*, vol. cv.—A Series of Observations of the Satellites of the Georgian Planet, including a Passage through the Node of their Orbits; with an Introductory Account of the Telescopic Apparatus that has been used on this Occasion, and a final Exposition of some calculated Particulars deduced from the Observations.

1817. *Phil. Trans.*, vol. cvii.—Astronomical Observations and Experiments tending to investigate the Local Arrangement of the Celestial Bodies in Space, and to determine the Extent and Condition of the Milky Way.

1818. *Phil. Trans.*, vol. cviii.—Astronomical Observations and Experiments selected for the Purpose of ascertaining the relative Distances of Clusters of Stars, and of investigating how far the Power of Telescopes may be expected to reach into Space, when directed to ambiguous Celestial Objects.

1822. *Memoirs of the Astronomical Society of London.*—On the Positions of 145 new Double Stars.

The chronological and detailed analysis of so many labours would throw us into numerous repetitions. A systematic order will be preferable; it will more distinctly fix the eminent place that Herschel will never cease to occupy in the small group of our contemporary men of genius, whilst his name will reëcho to the most distant posterity. The variety and splendour of Herschel's labours vie with their extent. The more we study them, the more we must admire them. It is with great men, as it is with great movements in the arts, we cannot understand them without studying them under various points of view.

Let us here again make a general reflection. The memoirs of Herschel are, for the greater part, pure and simple extracts from his inexhaustible journals of observations at Slough, accompanied by a few remarks. Such a table would not suit historical details. In these respects the author has left almost every thing to his biographers to do for him. And they must impose on themselves the task of assigning to the great astronomer's predecessors the portion that legitimately belongs to them, out of the mass of discoveries, which the public (we must say) has got into an erroneous habit of referring too exclusively to Herschel.

At one time I thought of adding a note to the analysis

of each of the illustrious observer's memoirs, containing a detailed indication of the improvements or corrections that the progressive march of science has brought on. But in order to avoid an exorbitant length in this biography, I have been obliged to give up my project. In general I shall content myself with pointing out what belongs to Herschel, referring to my *Treatise on Popular Astronomy* for the historical details. The life of Herschel had the rare advantage of forming an epoch in an extensive branch of astronomy; it would require us almost to write a special treatise on astronomy, to show thoroughly the importance of all the researches that are due to him.

### IMPROVEMENTS IN THE MEANS OF OBSERVATION.

The improvements that Herschel made in the construction and management of telescopes have contributed so directly to the discoveries with which that observer enriched astronomy, that we cannot hesitate to bring them forward at once.

I read the following passage in a Memoir by Lalande, printed in 1783, and forming part of the preface to vol. viii. of the *Ephemerides of the Celestial Motions.*

" Each time that Herschel undertakes to polish a mirror (of a telescope), he condemns himself to ten, or twelve, or even fourteen hours' constant work. He does not quit his workshop for a minute, not even to eat, but receives from the hands of his sister that nourishment without which one could not undergo such prolonged fatigue. Nothing in the world would induce Herschel to abandon his work; for, according to him, it would be to spoil it."

The advantages that Herschel found in 1783, 1784,

and 1785, in employing telescopes of twenty feet and with large apertures, made him wish to construct much larger still. The expense would be considerable; King George III. provided for it. The work, begun about the close of 1785, was finished in August, 1789. This instrument had an iron cylindrical tube, thirty-nine feet four inches English in length, and four feet ten inches in diameter. Such dimensions are enormous compared with those of telescopes made till then. They will appear but small, however, to persons who have heard the report of a pretended ball given in the Slough telescope. The propagators of this popular rumour had confounded the astronomer Herschel with the brewer Meux, and a cylinder in which a man of the smallest stature could scarcely stand upright, with certain wooden vats, as large as a house, in which beer is made and kept in London.

Herschel's telescope, forty English feet * in length, allowed of the realization of an idea, the advantages of which would not be sufficiently appreciated if I did not here recall to mind some facts.

In any telescope, whether refracting or reflecting, there are two principal parts: the part that forms the aërial images of the distant objects, and the small lens by the aid of which these images are enlarged just as if they consisted of radiating matter. When the image is produced by means of a lenticular glass, the place it occupies will be found in the prolongation of the line that extends from the object to the centre of the lens. The astronomer, furnished with an eye-piece, and wishing to

---

* Conforming to general usage, and to Sir W. Herschel himself, we shall allude to this instrument as the *forty-foot* telescope, though M. Arago adheres to thirty-nine feet and drops the inches, probably because the Parisian foot is rather longer than the English.— *Translator's Note.*

examine that image, must necessarily place himself *beyond* the point where the rays that form it have crossed each other; *beyond*, let us carefully remark, means *farther off* from the object-glass. The observer's head, his body, cannot then injure the formation or the brightness of the image, however small may be the distance from which we have to study it. But it is no longer thus with the image formed by means of reflection. For the image is now placed between the object and the reflecting mirror; and when the astronomer approaches in order to examine it, he inevitably intercepts, if not the totality, at least a very considerable portion of the luminous rays, which would otherwise have contributed to give it great splendour. It will now be understood, why in optical instruments where the images of distant objects are formed by the reflection of light, it has been necessary to carry the images, by the aid of a second reflection, out of the tube that contains and sustains the principal mirror. When the small mirror, on the surface of which the second reflection is effected, is plane, and inclined at an angle of 45° to the axis of the telescope; when the image is reflected laterally, through an opening made near the edge of the tube and furnished with an eyepiece; when, in a word, the astronomer looks definitively in a direction perpendicular to the line described by the luminous rays coming from the object and falling on the centre of the great mirror, then the telescope is called *Newtonian*. But in the *Gregorian* telescope, the image formed by the principal mirror falls on a second mirror, which is very small, slightly curved, and parallel to the first. The small mirror reflects the first image and throws it beyond the large mirror, through an opening made in the middle of that principal mirror.

Both in the one and in the other of these two telescopes, the small mirror interposed between the object
and the great mirror forms relative to the latter a sort of
screen which prevents its entire surface from contributing
towards forming the image. The small mirror, also, in
regard to intensity, gives some trouble.

Let us suppose, in order to clear up our ideas, that the
material of which the two mirrors are made, reflects only
half of the incident light. In the course of the first
reflection, the immense quantity of rays that the aperture
of the telescope had received, may be considered as reduced to half. Nor is the diminution less on the small
mirror. Now, half of half is a quarter. Therefore the
instrument will send to the eye of the observer only a
quarter of the incident light that its aperture had received. These two causes of diminished light not existing in a refracting telescope, it would give, under parity
of dimensions, four times more * light than a Newtonian
or Gregorian telescope gives.

Herschel did away with the small mirror in his large
telescope. The large mirror is not mathematically centred
in the large tube that contains it, but is placed rather
obliquely in it. This slight obliquity causes the images
to be formed not in the axis of the tube, but very near
its circumference, or outer mouth, we may call it. The
observer may therefore look at them there direct, merely
by means of an eye-piece. A small portion of the astronomer's head, it is true, then encroaches on the tube; it
forms a screen, and interrupts some incident rays. Still,
in a large telescope, the loss does not amount to half by
a great deal; which it would inevitably do if the small
mirror were there.

* It would be more correct to say four times *as much* light.—
$lator

Those telescopes, in which the observer, placed at the anterior extremity of the tube, looks direct into the tube and turns his back to the objects, were called by Herschel *front view telescopes.* In vol. lxxvi. of the *Philosophical Transactions* he says, that the idea of this construction occurred to him in 1776, and that he then applied it unsuccessfully to a ten-foot telescope; that during the year 1784, he again made a fruitless trial of it in a twenty-foot telescope. Yet I find that on the 7th of September 1784, he recurred to *a front view* in observing some nebulæ and groups of stars. However discordant these dates may be, we cannot without injustice neglect to remark, that a front view telescope was already described in 1732, in volume vi. of the collection entitled *Machines and Inventions approved by the Academy of Sciences.* The author of this innovation is Jaques Lemaire, who has been unduly confounded with the English Jesuit, Christopher Maire, assistant to Boscovitch, in measuring the meridian comprised between Rome and Rimini. Jaques Lemaire having only telescopes of moderate dimensions in view, was obliged, in order not to sacrifice any of the light, to place the great mirror so obliquely, that the image formed by its surface should fall entirely outside the tube of the instrument. So great a degree of inclination would certainly deform the objects. The *front view* construction is admissible only in very large telescopes.

I find in the *Transactions* for 1803, that in solar observations, Herschel sometimes employed telescopes, the great mirror of which was made of glass. It was a telescope of this sort that he used for observing the transit of Mercury on the 9th of November, 1802. It was seven English feet long, and six inches and three tenths in diameter.

Practical astronomers know how much the mounting of a telescope contributes to produce correct observations. The difficulty of a solid yet very movable mounting, increases rapidly with the dimensions and weight of an instrument. We may then conceive that Herschel had to surmount many obstacles, to mount a telescope suitably, of which the mirror alone weighed upwards of 1000 kilogrammes (*a ton*). But he solved this problem to his entire satisfaction by the aid of a combination of spars, of pulleys, and of ropes, of all which a correct idea may be formed by referring to the woodcut we have given in our *Treatise on Popular Astronomy* (vol. i.). This great apparatus, and the entirely different stands that Herschel imagined for telescopes of smaller dimensions, assign to that illustrious observer a distinguished place amongst the most ingenious mechanics of our age.

Persons in general, I may even say the greater part of astronomers, know not what was the effect that the great forty-foot telescope had in the labours and discoveries of Herschel. Still, we are not less mistaken when we fancy that the observer of Slough always used this telescope, than in maintaining with Baron von Zach (see *Monatliche Correspondenz*, January, 1802), that the colossal instrument was of no use at all, that it did not contribute to any one discovery, that it must be considered as a mere object of curiosity. These assertions are distinctly contradicted by Herschel's own words. In the volume of *Philosophical Transactions* for the year 1795 (p. 350), I read for example: "On the 28th of August 1789, having directed my telescope (of forty feet) to the heavens, I discovered the sixth satellite of Saturn, and I perceived the spots on that planet, better than I had been able to do before." (See also, relative to this sixth satellite, the *Philosophical Transactions* for 1790, p. 10.) In that same volume of 1790, p. 11, I find: "The great light of my forty-foot telescope was then so useful, that on the 17th of September 1789, I remarked the seventh satellite, then situated at its greatest western elongation."

The 10th of October, 1791, Herschel saw the ring of Saturn and the fourth satellite, looking in at the mirror of his forty-foot telescope, with his naked eye, without any sort of eye-piece.

Let us acknowledge the true motives that prevented Herschel from oftener using his telescope of forty feet. Notwithstanding the excellence of the mechanism, the manœuvring of that instrument required the constant aid of two labourers, and that of another person charged with noting the time at the clock. During some nights when the variation of temperature was considerable, this telescope, on account of its great mass, was always behind-hand with the atmosphere in thermometric changes, which was very injurious to the distinctness of the images.

Herschel found that in England, there are not above a hundred hours in a year during which the heavens can be advantageously observed with a telescope of forty feet, furnished with a magnifying power of a thousand. This remark led the celebrated astronomer to the conclusion, that, to take a complete survey of the heavens with his large instrument, though each successive field should remain only for an instant under inspection, would not require less than eight hundred years.

Herschel explains in a very natural way the rare occurrence of the circumstances in which it is possible to make good use of a telescope of forty feet, and of very large aperture.

A telescope does not magnify real objects only, but magnifies also the apparent irregularities arising from atmospheric refractions; now, all other things being equal, these irregularities of refraction must be so much the stronger, so much the more frequent, as the stratum of air is thicker through which the rays have passed to go and form the image.

Astronomers experienced extreme surprise, when in 1782, they learned that Herschel had applied linear magnifying powers of a thousand, of twelve hundred, of two thousand two hundred, of two thousand six hundred, and even of six thousand times, to a reflecting telescope of seven feet in length. The Royal Society of London experienced this surprise, and officially requested Herschel to give publicity to the means he had adopted for ascertaining such amounts of magnifying power in his telescopes. Such was the object of a memoir that he inserted in vol. lxxii. of the *Philosophical Transactions;* and it dissipated all doubts. No one will be surprised that magnifying powers, which it would seem ought to have shown the Lunar mountains, as the chain of Mont Blanc is seen from Maçon, from Lyons, and even from Geneva, were not easily believed in. They did not know that Herschel had never used magnifying powers of three thousand, and six thousand times, except in observing brilliant stars; they had not remembered that light reflected by planetary bodies, is too feeble to continue distinct under the same degree of magnifying power as the actual light of the fixed stars does.

Opticians had given up, more from theory than from careful experiments, attempting high magnifying powers, even for reflecting telescopes. They thought that the image of a small circle cannot be distinct, cannot be sharp at the edges, unless the pencil of rays coming from the object in nearly parallel lines, and which enters the eye after having passed through the eye-piece, be sufficiently broad.  This being once granted, the inference followed, that an image ceases to be well defined, when it does not strike at least two of the nervous filaments of the retina with which that organ is supposed to be overspread. These gratuitous circumstances, grafted on each other, vanished in presence of Herschel's observations.  After having put himself on his guard against the effects of diffraction, that is to say, against the scattering that light undergoes when it passes the terminal angles of bodies, the illustrious astronomer proved, in 1786, that objects can be seen well defined by means of pencils of light whose diameter does not equal five tenths of a millimetre.

Herschel looked on the almost unanimous opinion of the double lens eye-piece being preferable to the single lens eye-piece, as a very injurious prejudice in science. For experience proved to him, notwithstanding all theoretic deductions, that with equal magnifying powers, in reflecting telescopes at least (and this restriction is of some consequence), the images were brighter and better defined with single than with double eye-pieces.  On one occasion, this latter eye-piece would not show him the bands of Saturn, whilst by the aid of a single lens they were perfectly visible.  Herschel said : " The double eye-piece must be left to amateurs and to those who, for some particular object, require a large field of vision." (*Philosophical Transactions*, 1782, *pages* 94 *and* 95.)

It is not only relative to the comparative merit of single or double eye-pieces that Herschel differs from the general opinions of opticians ; he thinks, moreover,

that he has proved by decisive experiments, that concave
eye-pieces (like that used by Galileo) surpass the convex
eye-piece by a great deal, both as regards clearness and
definition.

Herschel assigns the date of 1776 to the experiments
which he made to decide this question. (*Philosophical
Transactions*, year 1815, p. 297.) Plano-concave and
double concave lenses produced similar effects. In what
did these lenses differ from the double convex lenses?
In one particular only : the latter received the rays reflected by the large mirror of the telescope, after their
union at the focus, whereas the concave lenses received
the same rays before that union. When the observer
made use of a convex lens, the rays that went to the
back of the eye to form an image on the retina, had
crossed each other before in the air ; but no crossing of
this kind took place when the observer used a concave
lens. Holding the double advantage of this latter sort
of lens over the other, as quite proved, one would be inclined, like Herschel, to admit, " that a certain mechanical
effect, injurious to clearness and definition, would accompany the focal crossing of the rays of light." *

This idea of the crossing of the rays suggested an experiment to the ingenious astronomer, the result of which
deserves to be recorded.

A telescope of ten English feet was directed towards
an advertisement covered with very small printing, and
placed at a sufficient distance. The convex lens of the

* On comparing the Cassegrain telescopes with a small convex
mirror, to the Gregorian telescopes with a small concave mirror, Captain Kater found that the former, in which the luminous rays do not
cross each other before falling on the small mirror, possess, as to intensity, a marked advantage over the latter, in which this crossing
takes place.

eye-piece was carried not by a tube properly so called, but by four rigid fine wires placed at right angles. This arrangement left the focus open in almost every direction. A concave mirror was then placed so that it threw a very condensed image of the sun laterally on the very spot where the image of the advertisement was formed. The solar rays, after having crossed each other, finding nothing on their route, went on and lost themselves in space. A screen, however, allowed the rays to be intercepted at will before they united.

This done, having applied the eye to the eye-piece and directed all his attention to the telescopic image of the advertisement, Herschel did not perceive that the taking away and then replacing the screen made the least change in the brightness or definition of the letters. It was therefore of no consequence, in the one instance as well as in the other, whether the immense quantity of solar rays crossed each other at the very place where, *in another direction*, the rays united that formed the image of the letters. I have marked in Italics the words that especially show in what this curious experiment differs from the previous experiments, and yet does not entirely contradict them. In this instance the rays of various origin, those coming from the advertisement and from the sun, crossed each other respectively in almost rectangular directions; during the comparative examination of the stars with convex and with concave eye-pieces, the rays that seemed to have a mutual influence, had a common origin and crossed each other at very acute angles. There seems to be nothing, then, in the difference of the results at which we need to be much surprised.

Herschel increased the catalogue, already so extensive, of the mysteries of vision, when he explained in what manner we must endeavour to distinguish separately the two members of certain double stars very close to each other. He said if you wish to assure yourself that η Coronæ is a double star, first direct your telescope to α Geminorum, to ζ Aquarii, to μ Draconis, to ρ Herculis, to α Piscium, to ε Lyræ. Look at those stars for a long time, so as to acquire the habit of observing such objects. Then pass on to ξ Ursæ majoris, where the closeness of the two members is still greater. In a third essay select ι Bootis (marked 44 by Flamsteed and i in Harris's maps) *, the star that precedes α Orionis, n of the same constellation, and you will then be prepared for the more difficult observation of η Coronæ. Indeed η Coronæ is a sort of miniature of i Bootis, which may itself be considered as a miniature of α Gem. (*Philosophical Transactions*, 1782, p. 100.)

As soon as Piazzi, Olbers, and Harding had discovered three of the numerous telescopic planets now known, Herschel proposed to himself to determine their real magnitudes ; but telescopes not having then been applied to the measurement of excessively small angles, it became requisite, in order to avoid any illusion, to try some experiments adapted to giving a scale of the powers of those instruments. Such was the labour of that indefatigable astronomer, of which I am going to give a compressed abridgment.

* In the selection of i Bootis as a test, Arago has taken the precaution of giving its corresponding denomination in other catalogues, and Bailey appends the following note, No. 2062, to 44 Bootis. " In the British Catalogue this star is not denoted by any letter: but Bayer calls it i, and on referring to the earliest MS. Catalogue in MSS. vol. xxv., I find it is there so designated; I have therefore restored the letter." (See Bailey's Edition of Flamsteed's British Catalogue of Stars, 1835.) The distance between the two members of this double star is 3″ ·7 and position 23° ·5. See " Bedford Cycle."—*Translator*.

The author relates first, that in 1774, he endeavoured to ascertain experimentally, with the naked eye and at the distance of distinct vision, what angle a circle must subtend to be distinguished by its form from a square of similar dimensions. The angle was never smaller than 2′ 17″; therefore at its maximum it was about one fourteenth of the angle subtended by the diameter of the moon.

Herschel did not say, either of what nature the circles and squares of paper were that he used, nor on what background they were projected. It is a lacuna to be regretted, for in those phenomena the intensity of light must be an important feature. However it may have been, the scrupulous observer not daring to extend to telescopic vision what he had discovered relative to vision with the naked eye, he undertook to do away with all doubt, by direct observations.

On examining some pins' heads placed at a distance in the open air, with a three-foot telescope, Herschel could easily discern that those bodies were round, when the subtended angles became, after their enlargement, 2′ 19″. This is almost exactly the result obtained with the naked eye.

When the globules were darker; when, instead of pins' heads, small globules of sealing-wax were used, their spherical form did not begin to be distinctly visible till the moment when the subtended magnified angles, that is, the moment when the natural angle multiplied by the magnifying power, amounted to five minutes.

In a subsequent series of experiments, some globules of silver placed very far from the observer, allowed their globular form to be perceived, even when the magnified angle remained below two minutes.

Under equality of subtended angle, then, the telescopic vision with strong magnifying powers showed itself superior to the naked eye vision. This result is not unimportant.

If we take notice of the magnifying powers used by Herschel in these laborious researches, powers that often exceeded five hundred times, it will appear to be established that the telescopes possessed by modern astronomers, may serve to verify the round form of distant objects, the form of celestial bodies even when the diameters of those bodies do not subtend naturally (to the naked eye), angles of above three tenths of a second: and 500, multiplied by three tenths of a second, give 2′ 30.″

Refracting telescopes were still ill understood instruments, the result of chance, devoid of certain theory, when they already served to reveal brilliant astronomical phenomena. Their theory, in as far as it depended on geometry and optics, made rapid progress. These two early phases of the problem leave but little more to be wished for; it is not so with a third phase, hitherto a good deal neglected, connected with physiology, and with the action ·of light on the nervous system. Therefore, we should search in vain in old treatises on optics and on astronomy, for a strict and complete discussion on the comparative effect that the size and intensity of the images, that the magnifying power and the aperture of a telescope may have, by night and by day, on the visibility of the faintest stars. This lucana Herschel tried to fill up in 1799; such was the aim of the memoir entitled, *On the space-penetrating Power of Telescopes.*

This memoir contains excellent things; still, it is far from exhausting the subject. The author, for instance, entirely overlooks the observations made by day. I also find, that the hypothetical part of the discussion is not perhaps so distinctly separated from the rigorous part as it might be; that disputable numbers, though given with a degree of precision down to the smallest decimals, do not look well as terms of comparison with some results which, on the contrary, rest on observations bearing mathematical evidence.

Whatever may be thought of these remarks, the astronomer or the physicist who would like again to undertake the question of visibility with telescopes, will find some important facts in Herschel's memoir, and some ingenious observations, well adapted to serve them as guides.

## LABOURS IN SIDEREAL ASTRONOMY.

The curious phenomenon of a periodical change of intensity in certain stars, very early excited a keen attention in Herschel. The first memoir by that illustrious observer presented to the Royal Society of London and inserted in the *Philosophical Transactions* treats precisely of the changes of intensity of the star *o* in the neck of the Whale.

This memoir was still dated from Bath, May, 1780. Eleven years after, in the month of December, 1791, Herschel communicated a second time to that celebrated English Society the remarks that he had made by sometimes directing his telescopes to the mysterious star. At both those epochs the observer's attention was chiefly applied to the absolute values of the *maxima* and *minima* of intensity.

The changeable star in the Whale was not the only periodical star with which Herschel occupied himself. His observations of 1795 and of 1796 proved that *a* Herculis also belongs to the category of variable stars, and that the time requisite for the accomplishment of all the changes of intensity, and for the star's return to any given state, was sixty days and a quarter. When Herschel obtained this result, about ten changeable stars were already known; but they were all either of very long or very short periods. The illustrious astronomer considered that, by introducing between two groups that exhibited very short and very long periods, a star of somewhat intermediate conditions,—for instance, one requiring sixty days to accomplish all its variations of intensity,—he had advanced the theory of these phenomena by an essential step; the theory at least that attributes every thing to a movement of rotation round their centres which the stars may undergo.

Sir William Herschel's catalogues of double stars offer a considerable number to which he ascribes a decided green or blue tint. In binary combinations, when the small star appears very blue or very green, the large one is usually yellow or red. It does not appear that the great astronomer took sufficient interest in this circumstance. I do not find, indeed, that the almost constant association of two complementary colours (of yellow and blue, or of red and green), ever led him to suspect that one of those colours might not have any thing real in it, that it often might be a mere illusion, a mere result of contrast. It was only in 1825, that I showed that there are stars whose contrast really explains their apparent colour; but I have proved besides, that blue is incontestably the colour of certain insulated stars, or stars that have only white ones, or other blue ones in their vicinity. Red is the only colour that the ancients ever distinguished from white in their catalogues.

Herschel also endeavoured to introduce numbers in

the classification of stars as to magnitude ; he has en-
deavoured, by means of numbers, to show the comparative intensity of a star of first magnitude, with one of
second, or one of third magnitude, &c.

In one of the earliest of Herschel's memoirs, we find,
that the apparent sidereal diameters are proved to be for
the greater part factitious, even when the best made telescopes are used. Diameters estimated by seconds, that
is to say, reduced according to the magnifying power,
diminish as the magnifying power is increased. These
results are of the greatest importance.

In the course of his investigation of sidereal parallax,
though without finding it, Herschel made an important
discovery; that of the proper motion of our system. To
show distinctly the direction of the motion of the solar
system, not only was a displacement of the sidereal
perspective required, but profound mathematical knowledge, and a peculiar tact. This peculiar tact Herschel
possessed in an eminent degree. Moreover, the result
deduced from the very small number of proper motions
known at the beginning of 1783, has been found almost
to agree with that found recently by clever astronomers,
by the application of subtile analytical formulæ, to a considerable number of exact observations.

The proper motions of the stars have been known and
proved for more than a century, and already Fontenelle
used to say in 1738, that the sun probably also moved
in a similar way. The idea of partly attributing the
displacement of the stars to a motion of the sun, had suggested itself to Bradley and to Mayer. And Lambert
especially had been very explicit on the subject. Until
then, however, there were only conjectures and mere

probabilities. Herschel passed those limits. He himself proved that the sun positively moves ; and that, in this respect also, that immense and dazzling body must be ranged among the stars ; that the apparently inextricable irregularities of numerous sidereal proper motions arise in great measure from the displacement of the solar system ; that, in short, the point of space towards which we are annually advancing, is situated in the constellation of Hercules.

These are magnificent results. The discovery of the proper motion of our system will always be accounted among Herschel's highest claims to glory, even after the mention that my duty as historian has obliged me to make of the anterior conjectures by Fontenelle, by Bradley, by Mayer, and by Lambert.

By the side of this great discovery we should place another, that seems likely to expand in future. The results which it allows us to hope for will be of extreme importance. The discovery here alluded to was announced to the learned world in 1803 ; it is that of the reciprocal dependence of several stars, connected the one with the other, as the several planets and their satellites of our system are with the sun.

Let us to these immortal labours add the ingenious ideas that we owe to Herschel on the nebulæ, on the constitution of the Milky-way, on the universe as a whole ; ideas which almost by themselves constitute the actual history of the formation of the worlds, and we cannot but have a deep reverence for that powerful genius that has scarcely ever erred, notwithstanding an ardent imagination.

## LABOURS RELATIVE TO THE SOLAR SYSTEM.

Herschel occupied himself very much with the sun, but only relative to its physical constitution. The observations that the illustrious astronomer made on this subject, the consequences that he deduced from them, equal the most ingenious discoveries for which the sciences are indebted to him.

In his important memoir in 1795, the great astronomer declares himself convinced that the substance by the intermediation of which the sun shines, cannot be either a liquid, or an elastic fluid. It must be analogous to our clouds, and float in the transparent atmosphere of that body. The sun has, according to him, two atmospheres, endowed with motions quite independent of each other. An elastic fluid of an unknown nature is being constantly formed on the dark surface of the sun, and rising up on account of its specific lightness, it forms the *pores* in the stratum of reflecting clouds ; then, combining with other gases, it produces the wrinkles in the region of luminous clouds. When the ascending currents are powerful, they give rise to the *nuclei*, to the *penumbræ*, to the *faculæ*. If this explanation of the formation of solar spots is well founded, we must expect to find that the sun does not constantly emit similar quantities of light and heat. Recent observations have verified this conclusion. But large nuclei, large penumbræ, wrinkles, faculæ, do they indicate an abundant luminous and calorific emission, as Herschel thought; that would be the result of his hypothesis on the existence of very active ascending currents, but direct experience seems to contradict it.

The following is the way in which a learned man,

13

Sir David Brewster, appreciates this view of Herschel's:
"It is not conceivable that luminous clouds, ceding to
the lightest impulses and in a state of constant change,
can be the source of the sun's devouring flame and of
the dazzling light which it emits; nor can we admit
besides, that the feeble barrier formed by planetary
clouds would shelter the objects that it might cover,
from the destructive effects of the superior elements."

Sir D. Brewster imagines that the non-luminous rays
of caloric, which form a constituent part of the solar
light, are emitted by the dark nucleus of the sun; whilst
the visible coloured rays proceed from the luminous
matter by which the nucleus is surrounded. "From
thence," he says, "proceeds the reason of light and heat
always appearing in a state of combination: the one
emanation cannot be obtained without the other. With
this hypothesis we should explain naturally why it is
hottest when there are most spots, because the heat of
the nucleus would then reach us without having been
weakened by the atmosphere that it usually has to traverse." But it is far from being an ascertained fact,
that we experience increased heat during the apparition
of solar spots; the inverse phenomenon is more probably true.

Herschel occupied himself also with the physical constitution of the moon. In 1780, he sought to measure
the height of our satellite's mountains. The conclusion
that he drew from his observations was, that few of the
lunar mountains exceed 800 metres (or 2600 feet).
More recent selenographic studies differ from this conclusion. There is reason to observe on this occasion
how much the result surmised by Herschel differs from
any tendency to the extraordinary or the gigantic, that

has been so unjustly assigned as the characteristic of the illustrious astronomer.

At the close of 1787, Herschel presented a memoir to the Royal Society, the title of which must have made a strong impression on people's imaginations. The author therein relates that on the 19th of April, 1787, he had observed in the non-illuminated part of the moon, that is, in the then dark portion, three volcanoes in a state of ignition. Two of these volcanoes appeared to be on the decline, the other appeared to be active. Such was then Herschel's conviction of the reality of the phenomenon, that the next morning he wrote thus of his first observation: " The volcano burns with more violence than last night." The real diameter of the volcanic light was 5000 metres (16,400 English feet). Its intensity appeared very superior to that of the nucleus of a comet then in apparition. The observer added : " The objects ...uated near the crater are feebly illuminated by the light that emanates from it." Herschel concludes thus: "In short, this eruption very much resembles the one I witnessed on the 4th of May, 1783."

How happens it, after such exact observations, that few astronomers now admit the existence of active volcanoes in the moon? I will explain this singularity in a few words.

The various parts of our satellite are not all equally reflecting. Here, it may depend on the form, elsewhere, on the nature of the materials. Those persons who have examined the moon with telescopes, know how very considerable the difference arising from these two causes may be, how much brighter one point of the moon sometimes is than those around it. Now, it is quite evident that the relations of intensity between the faint parts

and the brilliant parts must continue to exist, whatever
be the origin of the illuminating light. In the portion
of the lunar globe that is illuminated by the sun, there
are, everybody knows, some points, the brightness of
which is extraordinary compared to those around them ;
those same points, when they are seen in that portion of
the moon that is only lighted by the earth, or in the ash-
coloured part, will still predominate over the neighbouring regions by their comparative intensity. Thus we
may explain the observations of the Slough astronomer,
without recurring to volcanoes. Whilst the great observer was studying in the non-illuminated portion of
the moon, the supposed volcano of the 20th of April,
1787, his nine-foot telescope showed him in truth, by
the aid of the secondary rays proceeding from the earth,
even the darkest spots.

Herschel did not recur to the discussion of the supposed actually burning lunar volcanoes, until 1791. In
the volume of the *Philosophical Transactions* for 1792,
he relates that, in directing a twenty-foot telescope,
magnifying 360 times, to the entirely eclipsed moon on
the 22d of October, 1790, there were visible, over the
whole face of the satellite, about a hundred and fifty
very luminous red points. The author declares that he
will observe the greatest reserve relative to the simi-
larity of all these points, their great brightness, and
their remarkable colour.

Yet is not red the usual colour of the moon when
eclipsed, and when it has not entirely disappeared?
Could the solar rays reaching our satellite by the effect
of refraction, and after an absorption experienced in the
lowest strata of the terrestrial atmosphere, receive another tint? Are there not in the moon, when freely

illuminated, and opposite to the sun, from one to two hundred little points, remarkable by the brightness of their light? Would it be possible for those little points not to be also distinguishable in the moon, when it receives only the portion of solar light which is refracted and coloured by our atmosphere?

Herschel was more successful in his remarks on the absence of a lunar atmosphere. During the solar eclipse of the 5th September, 1793, the illustrious astronomer particularly directed his attention to the shape of the acute horn resulting from the intersection of the limbs of the moon and of the sun. He deduced from his observation that if towards the point of the horn there had been a deviation of only one second, occasioned by the refraction of the solar light in the lunar atmosphere, it would not have escaped him.

Herschel made the planets the object of numerous researches. Mercury was the one with which he least occupied himself; he found its disk perfectly round on observing it during its projection, that is to say, in astronomical language, during its transit over the sun on the 9th of November, 1802. He sought to determine the time of the rotation of Venus since the year 1777. He published two memoirs relative to Mars, the one in 1781, the other in 1784, and the discovery of its being flattened at the poles we owe to him. After the discovery of the small planets, Ceres, Pallas, Juno, and Vesta, by Piazzi, Olbers, and Harding, Herschel applied himself to measuring their angular diameter. He concluded from his researches that those four new bodies did not deserve the name of planets, and he proposed to call them asteroïds. This epithet was subsequently adopted; though bitterly criticized by a historian of the

Royal Society of London, Dr. Thomson, who went so far as to suppose that the learned astronomer "had wished to deprive the first observers of those bodies, of all idea of rating themselves as high as him (Herschel) in the scale of astronomical discoverers." I should require nothing farther to annihilate such an imputation, than to put it by the side of the following passage, extracted from a memoir by this celebrated astronomer, published in the *Philosophical Transactions*, for the year 1805: "The specific difference existing between planets and asteroïds appears now, by the addition of a third individual of the latter species, to be more completely established, and that circumstance, in my opinion, has added more to the *ornament* of our system than the discovery of a new planet could have done."

Although much has not resulted from Herschel's having occupied himself with the physical constitution of Jupiter, astronomy is indebted to him for several important results relative to the duration of that planet's rotation. He also made numerous observations on the intensities and comparative magnitudes of its satellites.

The compression of Saturn, the duration of its rotation, the physical constitution of this planet and that of its ring, were, on the part of Herschel, the object of numerous researches which have much contributed to the progress of planetary astronomy. But on this subject two important discoveries especially added new glory to the great astronomer.

Of the five known satellites of Saturn at the close of the 17th century, Huygens had discovered the fourth; Cassini the others.

The subject seemed to be exhausted, when news from Slough showed what a mistake this was.

On the 28th of August, 1789, the great forty-foot telescope revealed to Herschel a satellite still nearer to the ring than the other five already observed. According to the principles of the nomenclature previously adopted, the small body of the 28th August ought to have been called the first satellite of Saturn, the numbers indicating the places of the other five would then have been each increased by a unity. But the fear of introducing confusion into science by these continual changes of denomination, induced a preference for calling the new satellite the sixth.

Thanks to the prodigious powers of the forty-foot telescope, a last satellite, the seventh, showed itself on the 17th of September, 1789, between the sixth and the ring.

This seventh satellite is extremely faint. Herschel, however, succeeding in seeing it whenever circumstances were very favourable, even by the aid of the twenty-foot telescope.

The discovery of the planet Uranus, the detection of its satellites, will always occupy one of the highest places among those by which modern astronomy is honoured.

On the 13th of March, 1781, between ten and eleven o'clock at night, Herschel was examining the small stars near H Geminorum with a seven-foot telescope, bearing a magnifying power of 227 times. One of these stars seemed to him to have an unusual diameter. The celebrated astronomer, therefore, thought it was a comet. It was under this denomination that it was then discussed at the Royal Society of London. But the researches of Herschel and of Laplace showed later that the orbit of the new body was nearly circular, and Uranus was elevated to the rank of a planet.

The immense distance of Uranus, its small angular diameter, the feebleness of its light, did not allow the hope, that if that body had satellites, the magnitudes of which were, relatively to its own size, what the satellites of Jupiter, of Saturn are, compared to those two large planets, any observer could perceive them, from the earth. Herschel was not a man to be deterred by such discouraging conjectures. Therefore, since powerful telescopes of the ordinary construction, that is to say, with two mirrors conjugated, had not enabled him to discover any thing, he substituted, in the beginning of January, 1787, *front view* telescopes, that is, telescopes throwing much more light on the objects, the small mirror being then suppressed, and with it one of the causes of loss of light is got rid of.

By patient labour, by observations requiring a rare perseverance, Herschel attained (from the 11th of January, 1787, to the 28th of February, 1794,) to the discovery of the six satellites of his planet, and thus to complete the *world* of a system that belongs entirely to himself.

There are several of Herschel's memoirs on comets. In analyzing them, we shall see that this great observer could not touch any thing without making further discoveries in the subject.

Herschel applied some of his fine instruments to the study of the physical constitution of a comet discovered by Mr. Pigott, on the 28th September, 1807.

The nucleus was round and well determined. Some measures taken on the day when the nucleus subtended only an angle of a single second, gave as its real angle $\frac{6}{100}$ of the diameter of the earth.

Herschel saw no phase at an epoch when only $\frac{7}{10}$ of the nucleus could be illuminated by the sun. The nucleus then must shine by its own light.

This is a legitimate inference in the opinion of every one who will allow, on one hand, that the nucleus is a solid body, and on the other, that it would have been possible to observe a phase of $\frac{8}{10}$ on a disk whose apparent total diameter did not exceed one or two seconds of a degree.

Very small stars seemed to grow much paler when they were seen through the coma or through the tail of the comet.

This faintness may have only been apparent, and might arise from the circumstance of the stars being then projected on a luminous background. Such is, indeed, the explanation adopted by Herschel. A gaseous medium, capable of reflecting sufficient solar light to efface that of some stars, would appear to him to possess in each stratum a sensible quantity of matter, and to be, for that reason, a cause of real diminution of the light transmitted, though nothing reveals the existence of such a cause.

This argument, offered by Herschel in favour of the system which transforms comets into self-luminous bodies, has not, as we may perceive, much force. I might venture to say as much of many other remarks by this great observer. He tells us that the comet was very visible in the telescope on the 21st of February, 1808; now, on that day, its distance from the sun amounted to 2·7 times the mean radius of the terrestrial orbit; its distance from the observer was 2·9: "What probability would there be that rays going to such distances, from the sun to the comet, could, after their reflection, be seen by an eye nearly three times more distant from the comet than from the sun?"

13 *

It is only numerical determinations that could give
value to such an argument.  By satisfying himself with
vague reasoning, Herschel did not even perceive that he
was committing a great mistake by making the comet's
distance from the observer appear to be an element of
visibility.  If the comet be self-luminous, its intrinsic
splendour (its brightness for unity of surface) will
remain constant at any distance, as long as the subtended
angle remains sensible.  If the body shines by borrowed
light, its brightness will vary only according to its change
of distance from the sun; nor will the distance of the
observer occasion any change in the visibility; always,
let it be understood, with the restriction that the apparent diameter shall not be diminished below certain
limits.

Herschel finished his observations of a comet that was
visible in January, 1807, with the following remark :—

"Of the sixteen telescopic comets that I have examined, fourteen had no solid body visible at their centre ;
the other two exhibited a central light, very ill defined,
that might be termed a nucleus, but a light that certainly
could not deserve the name of a disk."

The beautiful comet of 1811 became the object of that
celebrated astronomer's conscientious labour.  Large telescopes showed him, in the midst of the gazeous head, a
rather reddish body of planetary appearance, which bore
strong magnifying powers, and showed no sign of phase.
Hence Herschel concluded that it was self-luminous.
Yet if we reflect that the planetary body under consideration was not a second in diameter, the absence of a
phase does not appear a demonstrative argument.

The light of the head had a blueish-green tint.  Was
this a real tint, or did the central reddish body, only

through contrast, make the surrounding vapour appear to be coloured ? Herschel did not examine the question in this point of view.

The head of the comet appeared to be enveloped at a certain distance, on the side towards the sun, by a brilliant narrow zone, embracing about a semicircle, and of a yellowish colour. From the two extremities of the semicircle there arose, towards the region away from the sun, two long luminous streaks which limited the tail. Between the brilliant circular semi-ring and the head, the cometary substance seemed dark, very rare, and very diaphanous.

The luminous semi-ring always presented similar appearances in all the positions of the comet; it was not then possible to attribute to it really the annular form, the shape of Saturn's ring, for example. Herschel sought whether a spherical demi-envelop of luminous matter, and yet diaphanous, would not lead to a natural explanation of the phenomenon. In this hypothesis, the visual rays, which on the 6th of October, 1811, made a section of the envelop, or bore almost tangentially, traversed a thickness of matter of about 399,000 kilometres, (248,000 English miles,) whilst the visual rays near the head of the comet did not meet above 80,000 kilometres (50,000 miles) of it. As the brightness must be proportional to the quantity of matter traversed, there could not fail to be an appearance around the comet, of a semi-ring five times more luminous than the central regions. This semi-ring, then, was an effect of projection, and it has revealed a circumstance to us truly remarkable in the physical constitution of comets.

The two luminous streaks that outlined the tail at its two limits, may be explained in a similar manner; the tail was not flat as it appeared to be ; it had the form of a conoid, with its sides of a certain thickness. The visual lines which traversed those sides almost tangenti- ally, evidently met much more matter than the visual lines passing across. This maximum of matter could not fail of being represented by a maximum of light.

The luminous semi-ring floated ; it appeared one day to be suspended in the diaphanous atmosphere by which the head of the comet was surrounded, at a distance of 518,000 kilometres (322,000 English miles) from the nucleus.

This distance was not constant. The matter of the semi-annular envelop seemed even to be precipitated by slow degrees through the diaphanous atmosphere ; finally it reached the nucleus ; the earlier appearances vanished ; the comet was reduced to a globular nebula.

During its period of dissolution, the ring appeared sometimes to have several branches.

The luminous shreds of the tail seemed to undergo rapid, frequent, and considerable variations of length. Herschel discerned symptoms of a movement of rotation both in the comet and in its tail. This rotatory motion carried unequal shreds from the centre towards the bor- der, and reciprocally. On looking from time to time at the same region of the tail, at the border, for example, sensible changes of length must have been perceptible, which however had no reality in them. Herschel thought, as I have already said, that the beautiful comet of 1811, and that of 1807, were self-luminous. The second comet of 1811 appeared to him to shine only by borrowed light. It must be acknowledged that these conjectures did not rest on any thing demonstrative.

In attentively comparing the comet of 1807 with the

beautiful comet of 1811, relative to the changes of distance from the sun, and the modifications resulting thence, Herschel put it beyond doubt that these modifications have something individual in them, something relative to a special state of the nebulous matter. On one celestial body the changes of distance produce an enormous effect, on another the modifications are insignificant.

## OPTICAL LABOURS.

I shall say very little on the discoveries that Herschel made in physics. In short, everybody knows them. They have been inserted into special treatises, into elementary works, into verbal instruction ; they must be considered as the starting-point of a multitude of important labours with which the sciences have been enriched during several years.

The chief of these is that of the dark radiating heat which is found mixed with light.

In studying the phenomena, no longer with the eye, like Newton, but with a thermometer, Herschel discovered that the solar spectrum is prolonged on the red side far beyond the visible limits. The thermometer sometimes rose higher in that dark region, than in the midst of brilliant zones. The light of the sun then, contains, besides the coloured rays so well characterized by Newton, some invisible rays, still less refrangible than the red. and whose warming power is very considerable. A world of discoveries has arisen from this fundamental fact.

The dark heat emanating from terrestrial objects more or less heated, became also subjects of Herschel's investigations. His work contained the germs of a good number of beautiful experiments since erected upon it in our own day.

By successively placing the same objects in all parts of the solar spectrum Herschel determined the illuminating powers of the various prismatic rays. The general result of these experiments may be thus enunciated:

The illuminating power of the red rays is not very great; that of the orange rays surpasses it, and is in its turn surpassed by the power of the yellow rays. The maximum power of illumination is found between the brightest yellow and the palest green. The yellow and the green possess this power equally. A like assimilation may be laid down between the blue and the red. Finally, the power of illumination in the indigo rays, and above all in the violet, is very weak.

Yet the memoirs of Herschel on Newton's coloured rings, though containing a multitude of exact experiments, have not much contributed to advance the theory of those curious phenomena. I have learnt from good authority, that the great astronomer held the same opinion on this topic. He said that it was the only occasion on which he had reason to regret having, according to his constant method, published his labours immediately, as fast as they were performed.

# LAPLACE.

HAVING been appointed to draw up the report of a
committee of the Chamber of Deputies which was nominated in 1842, for the purpose of taking into consideration the expediency of a proposal submitted to the
Chamber by the Minister of Public Instruction, relative
to the publication of a new edition of the works of Laplace at the public expense, I deemed it to be my
duty to embody in the report a concise analysis of the
works of our illustrious countryman. Several persons,
influenced, perhaps, by too indulgent a feeling towards
me, having expressed a wish that this analysis should not
remain buried amid a heap of legislative documents, but
that it should be published in the *Annuaire du Bureau
des Longitudes,* I took advantage of this circumstance to
develop it more fully so as to render it less unworthy of
public attention. The scientific part of the report presented to the Chamber of Deputies will be found here
entire. It has been considered desirable to suppress the
remainder. I shall merely retain a few sentences containing an explanation of the object of the proposed law,
and an announcement of the resolutions which were
adopted by the three powers of the State.

" Laplace has endowed France, Europe, the scientific
world, with three magnificent compositions: the *Traité*

*de Mécanique Céleste*, the *Exposition du Système du Monde*, and the *Théorie Analytique des Probabilités*. In the present day (1842) there is no longer to be found a single copy of this last work at any bookseller's establishment in Paris. The edition of the *Mécanique Céleste* itself will soon be exhausted. It was painful then to reflect that the time was close at hand when persons engaged in the study of the higher mathematics would be compelled, for want of the original work, to inquire at Philadelphia, at New York, or at Boston for the English translation of the *chef d'œuvre* of our countryman by the excellent geometer Bowditch. These fears, let us hasten to state, were not well founded. To republish the *Mécanique Céleste* was, on the part of the family of the illustrious geometer, to perform a pious duty. Accordingly, Madame de Laplace, who is so justly, so profoundly attentive to every circumstance calculated to enhance the renown of the name which she bears, did not hesitate about pecuniary considerations. A small property near Pont l'Evêque was about to change hands, and the proceeds were to have been applied so that Frenchmen should not be deprived of the satisfaction of exploring the treasures of the *Mécanique Céleste* through the medium of the vernacular tongue.

"The republication of the complete works of Laplace rested upon an equally sure guarantee. Yielding at once to filial affection, to a noble feeling of patriotism, and to the enthusiasm for brilliant discoveries which a course of severe study inspired, General Laplace had long since qualified himself for becoming the editor of the seven volumes which are destined to immortalize his father.

"There are glorious achievements of a character too elevated, of a lustre too splendid, that they should continue to exist as objects of private property. Upon the State devolves the duty of preserving them from indifference and oblivion : of continually holding them up to attention, of diffusing a knowledge of them through a thousand channels; in a word, of rendering them subservient to the public interests.

" Doubtless the Minister of Public Instruction was influenced by these considerations, when upon the occasion of a new edition of the works of Laplace having become necessary, he demanded of you to substitute the great French family for the personal family of the illustrious geometer. We give our full and unreserved adhesion to this proposition. It springs from a feeling of patriotism which will not be gainsayed by any one in this assembly."

In fact, the Chamber of Deputies had only to examine and solve this single question : " Are the works of Laplace of such transcendent, such exceptional merit, that their republication ought to form the subject of deliberation of the great powers of the State ? " An opinion prevailed, that it was not enough merely to appeal to public notoriety, but that it was necessary to give an exact analysis of the brilliant discoveries of Laplace in order to exhibit more fully the importance of the resolution about to be adopted. Who could hereafter propose on any similar occasion that the Chamber should declare itself without discussion, when a desire was felt, previous to voting in favour of a resolution so honourable to the memory of a great man, to fathom, to measure, to examine minutely and from every point of view monuments such as the *Mécanique Céleste* and the *Exposition du Système du Monde*? It has appeared to me that the report drawn up in the name of a committee of one of the three great powers of the State might worthily close this series of biographical notices of eminent astronomers.*

The Marquis de Laplace, peer of France, one of the forty of the French Academy, member of the Academy of Sciences and of the *Bureau des Longitudes,* an asso-. ciate of all the great Academies or Scientific Societies of Europe, was born at Beaumont-en-Auge of parents belonging to the class of small farmers, on the 28th of March, 1749 ; he died on the 5th of March, 1827.

The first and second volumes of the *Mécanique Céleste* were published in 1799 ; the third volume appeared in 1802, the fourth volume in 1805 ; as regards the fifth volume, Books XI. and XII. were published in 1823, Books XIII. XIV. and XV. in 1824, and Book XVI. in 1825. The *Théorie des Probabilités* was published in 1812. We shall now present the reader with the history of the principal astronomical discoveries contained in these immortal works.

Astronomy is the science of which the human mind may most justly boast. It owes this indisputable pre-eminence to the elevated nature of its object, to the grandeur of its means of investigation, to the certainty, the utility, and the unparalleled magnificence of its results.

From the earliest period of the social existence of mankind, the study of the movements of the heavenly bodies has attracted the attention of governments and peoples. To several great captains, illustrious statesmen, philosophers, and eminent orators of Greece and Rome it formed a subject of delight. Yet, let us be permitted to state, astronomy truly worthy of the name is

---

* The author here refers to the series of biographies contained in tome III. of the *Notices Biographiques.— Translator.*

quite a modern science. It dates only from the sixteenth century.

Three great, three brilliant phases, have marked its progress.

In 1543 Copernicus overthrew with a firm and bold hand, the greater part of the antique and venerable scaffolding with which the illusions of the senses and the pride of successive generations had filled the universe. The earth ceased to be the centre, the pivot of the celestial movements; it henceforward modestly ranged itself among the planets; its material importance, amid the totality of the bodies of which our solar system is composed, found itself reduced almost to that of a grain of sand.

Twenty-eight years had elapsed from the day when the Canon of Thorn expired while holding in his faltering hands the first copy of the work which was to diffuse so bright and pure a flood of glory upon Poland, when Würtemberg witnessed the birth of a man who was destined to achieve a revolution in science not less fertile in consequences, and still more difficult of execution. This man was Kepler. Endowed with two qualities which seemed incompatible with each other, a volcanic imagination, and a pertinacity of intellect which the most tedious numerical calculations could not daunt, Kepler conjectured that the movements of the celestial bodies must be connected together by simple laws, or, to use his own expressions, by *harmonic* laws. These laws he undertook to discover. A thousand fruitless attempts, errors of calculation inseparable from a colossal undertaking, did not prevent him a single instant from advancing resolutely towards the goal of which he imagined he had obtained a glimpse. Twenty-two years were employed by him in this investigation, and still he was not weary of it! What, in reality, are twenty-two years of labour to him who is about to become the legislator of worlds; who shall inscribe his name in ineffaceable characters upon the frontispiece of an immortal code; who shall be able to exclaim in dithyrambic language, and without incurring the reproach of any one, "The die is cast; I have written my book; it will be read either in the present age or by posterity, it matters not which; it may well await a reader, since God has waited six thousand years for an interpreter of his works?" *

To investigate a physical cause capable of making the planets revolve in closed curves; to place the principle of the stability of the universe in mechanical forces and not in solid supports such as the spheres of crystal which our ancestors had dreamed of; to extend to the revolutions of the heavenly bodies the general principles of the mechanics of terrestrial bodies,—such were the questions which remained to be solved after Kepler had announced his discoveries to the world.

Very distinct traces of these great problems are perceived here and there among the ancients as well as the

---

* These celebrated laws, known in astronomy as the laws of Kepler, are three in number. The first law is, that the planets describe ellipses around the sun in their common focus; the second, that a line joining the planet and the sun sweeps over equal areas in equal times; the third, that the squares. of the periodic times of the planets are proportional to the cubes of their mean distances from the sun. The first two laws were discovered by Kepler in the course of a laborious examination of the theory of the planet Mars; a full account of this inquiry is contained in his famous work *De Stella Martis*, published in 1609. The discovery of the third law was not effected until, several years afterwards, Kepler announced it to the world in his treatise on Harmonics (1628). The passage quoted below is extracted from that work.— *Translator*.

moderns, from Lucretius and Plutarch down to Kepler, Bouillaud, and Borelli. It is to Newton, however, that we must award the merit of their solution. This great man, like several of his predecessors, conceived the celestial bodies to have a tendency to approach towards each other in virtue of an attractive force, deduced the mathematical characteristics of this force from the laws of Kepler, extended it to all the material molecules of the solar system, and developed his brilliant discovery in a work which, even in the present day, is regarded as the most eminent production of the human intellect.

The heart aches when, upon studying the history of the sciences, we perceive so magnificent an intellectual movement effected without the coöperation of France. Practical astronomy increased our inferiority. The means of investigation were at first inconsiderately entrusted to foreigners, to the prejudice of Frenchmen abounding in intelligence and zeal. Subsequently, intellects of a superior order struggled with courage, but in vain, against the unskilfulness of our artists. During this period, Bradley, more fortunate on the other side of the Channel, immortalized himself by the discovery of aberration and nutation.

The contribution of France to these admirable revolutions in astronomical science, consisted, in 1740, of the experimental determination of the spheroidal figure of the earth, and of the discovery of the variation of gravity upon the surface of our planet. These were two great results; our country, however, had a right to demand more: when France is not in the first rank she has lost her place.*

* The spheroidal figure of the earth was established by the comparison of an arc of the meridian that had been measured in France,

This rank, which was lost for a moment, was brilliantly regained, an achievement for which we are indebted to four geometers.

When Newton, giving to his discoveries a generality which the laws of Kepler did not imply, imagined that the different planets were not only attracted by the sun, but that they also attract each other, he introduced into the heavens a cause of universal disturbance. Astronomers could then see at the first glance that in no part of the universe whether near or distant would the Keplerian laws suffice for the exact representation of the phenomena; that the simple, regular movements with which the imaginations of the ancients were pleased to endue the heavenly bodies would experience numerous, considerable, perpetually changing perturbations.

To discover several of these perturbations, to assign their nature, and in a few rare cases their numerical values, such was the object which Newton proposed to himself in writing the *Principia Mathematica Philosophiæ Naturalis.*

with a similar arc measured in Lapland, from which it appeared that the length of a degree of the meridian increases from the equator towards the poles, conformably to what ought to result upon the supposition of the earth having the figure of an oblate spheroid. The length of the Lapland arc was determined by means of an expedition which the French Government had despatched to the North of Europe for that purpose. A similar expedition had been despatched from France about the same time to Peru in South America, for the purpose of measuring an arc of the meridian under the equator, but the results had not been ascertained at the time to which the author alludes in the text. The variation of gravity at the surface of the earth was established by Richer's experiments with the pendulum at Cayenne, in South America (1673-4), from which it appeared that the pendulum oscillates more slowly—and consequently the force of gravity is less intense—under the equator than in the latitude of Paris.— *Translator.*

Notwithstanding the incomparable sagacity of its author the Principia contained merely a rough outline of the planetary perturbations. If this sublime sketch did not become a complete portrait we must not attribute the circumstance to any want of ardour or perseverance; the efforts of the great philosopher were always superhuman, the questions which he did not solve were incapable of solution in his time. When the mathematicians of the continent entered upon the same career, when they wished to establish the Newtonian system upon an incontrovertible basis, and to improve the tables of astronomy, they actually found in their way difficulties which the genius of Newton had failed to surmount.

Five geometers, Clairaut, Euler, D'Alembert, Lagrange, and Laplace, shared between them the world of which Newton had disclosed the existence. They explored it in all directions, penetrated into regions which had been supposed inaccessible, pointed out there a multitude of phenomena which observation had not yet detected; finally, and it is this which constitutes their imperishable glory, they reduced under the domain of a single principle, a single law, every thing that was most refined and mysterious in the celestial movements. Geometry had thus the boldness to dispose of the future; the evolutions of ages are scrupulously ratifying the decisions of science.

We shall not occupy our attention with the magnificent labours of Euler, we shall, on the contrary, present the reader with a rapid analysis of the discoveries of his four rivals, our countrymen.*

---

* It may perhaps be asked why we place Lagrange among the French geometers? This is our reply : It appears to us that the individual who was named Lagrange Tournier, two of the most character-

If a celestial body, the moon, for example, gravitated solely towards the centre of the earth, it would describe a mathematical ellipse; it would strictly obey the laws of Kepler, or, which is the same thing, the principles of mechanics expounded by Newton in the first sections of his immortal work.

Let us now consider the action of a second force. Let us take into account the attraction which the sun exercises upon the moon, in other words, instead of two bodies, let us suppose three to operate on each other, the Keplerian ellipse will now furnish merely a rough indication of the motion of our satellite. In some parts the attraction of the sun will tend to enlarge the orbit, and will in reality do so; in other parts the effect will be the reverse of this. In a word, by the introduction of a third attractive body, the greatest complication will succeed to a simple regular movement upon which the mind reposed with complacency.

If Newton gave a complete solution of the question of the celestial movements in the case wherein two bodies attract each other, he did not even attempt an analytical investigation of the infinitely more difficult problem of three bodies. The problem of three bodies (this is the name by which it has become celebrated), the problem for determining the movement of a body subjected to the attractive influence of two other bodies, was solved for the first time, by our countryman Clairaut.*

istic French names which it is possible to imagine, whose maternal grandfather was M. Gros, whose paternal great-grandfather was a French officer, a native of Paris, who never wrote except in French, and who was invested in our country with high honours during a period of nearly thirty years;—ought to be regarded as a Frenchman although born at Turin.—*Author*.

* The problem of three bodies was solved independently about the

From this solution we may date the important improvements of the lunar tables effected in the last century.

The most beautiful astronomical discovery of antiquity, is that of the precession of the equinoxes. Hipparchus, to whom the honour of it is due, gave a complete and precise statement of all the consequences which flow from this movement. Two of these have more especially attracted attention.

By reason of the precession of the equinoxes, it is not always the same groups of stars, the same constellations, which are perceived in the heavens at the same season of the year. In the lapse of ages the constellations of winter will become those of summer and reciprocally.

By reason of the precession of the equinoxes, the pole does not always occupy the same place in the starry vault. The moderately bright star which is very justly named in the present day, the pole star, was far removed from the pole in the time of Hipparchus; in the course of a few centuries it will again appear removed from it. The designation of pole star has been, and will be, applied to stars very distant from each other.

When the inquirer in attempting to explain natural phenomena has the misfortune to enter upon a wrong path, each precise observation throws him into new complications. Seven spheres of crystal did not suffice for representing the phenomena as soon as the illustrious astronomer of Rhodes discovered precession. An eighth

same time by Euler, D'Alembert, and Clairaut. The two last-mentioned geometers communicated their solutions to the Academy of Sciences on the same day, November 15, 1747. Euler had already in 1746 published tables of the moon, founded on his solution of the same problem, the details of which he subsequently published in 1753.— *Translator.*

14

sphere was then wanted to account for a movement in which all the stars participated at the same time.

Copernicus having deprived the earth of its alleged immobility, gave a very simple explanation of the most minute circumstances of precession. He supposed that the axis of rotation does not remain exactly parallel to itself; that in the course of each complete revolution of the earth around the sun, the axis deviates from its position by a small quantity ; in a word, instead of supposing the circumpolar stars to advance in a certain way towards the pole, he makes the pole advance towards the stars. This hypothesis divested the mechanism of the universe of the greatest complication which the love of theorizing had introduced into it. A new Alphonse would have then wanted a pretext to address to his astronomical synod the profound remark, so erroneously interpreted, which history ascribes to the king of Castile.

If the conception of Copernicus improved by Kepler had, as we have just seen, introduced a striking improvement into the mechanism of the heavens, it still remained to discover the motive force which, by altering the position of the terrestrial axis during each successive year, would cause it to describe an entire circle of nearly 50° in diameter, in a period of about 26,000 years.

Newton conjectured that this force arose from the action of the sun and moon upon the redundant matter accumulated in the equatorial regions of the earth : thus he made the precession of the equinoxes depend upon the spheroidal figure of the earth ; he declared that upon a round planet no precession would exist.

All this was quite true, but Newton did not succeed in establishing it by a mathematical process. Now this great man had introduced into philosophy the severe and

just rule : Consider as certain only what has been demonstrated. The demonstration of the Newtonian conception of the precession of the equinoxes was, then, a
great discovery, and it is to D'Alembert that the glory of
it is due.* The illustrious geometer gave a complete
explanation of the general movement, in virtue of which
the terrestrial axis returns to the same stars in a period
of about 26,000 years. He also connected with the
theory of gravitation the perturbation of precession discovered by Bradley, that remarkable oscillation which the
earth's axis experiences continually during its movement
of progression, and the period of which, amounting to
about eighteen years, is exactly equal to the time which
the intersection of the moon's orbit with the ecliptic
employs in describing the 360° of the entire circumference.

Geometers and astronomers are justly occupied as
much with the figure and physical constitution which the
earth might have had in remote ages as with its present
figure and constitution.

As soon as our countryman Richer discovered that a
body, whatever be its nature, weighs less when it is
transported nearer the equatorial regions, everybody per-

* It must be admitted that M. Arago has here imperfectly represented Newton's labours on the great problem of the precession of
the equinoxes. The immortal author of the Principia did not merely
*conjecture* that the conical motion of the earth's axis is due to the
disturbing action of the sun and moon upon the matter accumulated
around the earth's equator: he *demonstrated* by a very beautiful and
satisfactory process that the movement must necessarily arise from
that cause; and although the means of investigation, in his time,
were inadequate to a rigorous computation of the quantitative effect,
still, his researches on the subject have been always regarded as
affording one of the most striking proofs of sagacity which is to be
found in all his works.—*Translator.*

ceived that the earth, if it was originally fluid, ought to bulge out at the equator. Huyghens and Newton did more; they calculated the difference between the greatest and least axes, the excess of the equatorial diameter over the line of the poles.*

The calculation of Huyghens was founded upon hypo-

* It would appear that Hooke had conjectured that the figure of the earth might be spheroidal before Newton or Huyghens turned their attention to the subject. At a meeting of the Royal Society on the 28th of February, 1678, a discussion arose respecting the figure of Mercury which M. Gallet of Avignon had remarked to be oval on the occasion of the planet's transit across the sun's disk on the 7th of November, 1677. Hooke was inclined to suppose that the phenomenon was real, and that it was due to the whirling of the planet on an axis " which made it somewhat of the shape of a turnip, or of a solid made by an ellipsis turned round upon its shorter diameter." At the meeting of the Society on the 7th of March, the subject was again discussed. In reply to the objection offered to his hypothesis on the ground of the planet being a solid body, Hooke remarked that " although it might now be solid, yet that at the beginning it might have been fluid enough to receive that shape; and that although this supposition should not be granted, it would be probable enough that it would really run into that shape and make the same appearance; *and that it is not improbable but that the water here upon the earth might do it in some measure by the influence of the diurnal motion, which, compounded with that of the moon, he conceived to be the cause of the Tides.*" (Journal Book of the Royal Society, vol. vi. p. 60.) Richer returned from Cayenne in the year 1674, but the account of his observations with the pendulum during his residence there, was not published until 1679, nor is there to be found any allusion to them during the intermediate interval, either in the volumes of the Academy of Sciences or any other publication. We have no means of ascertaining how Newton was first induced to suppose that the figure of the earth is spheroidal, but we know, upon his own authority, that as early as the year 1667, or 1668, he was led to consider the effects of the centrifugal force in diminishing the weight of bodies at the equator. With respect to Huyghens, he appears to have formed a conjecture respecting the spheroidal figure of the earth independently of Newton; but his method for computing the ellipticity is founded upon that given in the Principia.— *Translator.*

thetic properties of the attractive force which were wholly inadmissible; that of Newton upon a theorem which he ought to have demonstrated; the theory of the latter was characterized by a defect of a still more serious nature : it supposed the density of the earth during the original state of fluidity, to be homogeneous.* When in attempting the solution of great problems we have recourse to such simplifications; when, in order to elude difficulties of calculation, we depart so widely from natural and physical conditions, the results relate to an ideal world, they are in reality nothing more than flights of the imagination.

In order to apply mathematical analysis usefully to the determination of the figure of the earth it was necessary to abandon all idea of homogeneity, all constrained resemblance between the forms of the superposed and unequally dense strata ; it was necessary also to examine the case of a central solid nucleus. This generality increased tenfold the difficulties of the problem ; neither Clairaut nor D'Alembert was, however, arrested by them: Thanks to the efforts of these two eminent geometers, thanks to some essential developments due to their immediate successors, and especially to the illustrious Legendre, the theoretical determination of the figure of the earth has attained all desirable perfection. There now reigns the most satisfactory accordance between the results of calculation and those of direct measurement. The earth, then, was originally fluid: analysis

---

* Newton assumed that a homogeneous fluid mass of a spheroidal form would be in equilibrium if it were endued with an adequate rotatory motion and its constituent particles attracted each other in the inverse proportion of the square of the distance. Maclaurin first demonstrated the truth of this theorem by a rigorous application of the ancient geometry.— *Translator*.

has enabled us to ascend to the earliest ages of our planet.*

In the time of Alexander comets were supposed by the majority of the Greek philosophers to be merely meteors generated in our atmosphere. During the middle ages, persons, without giving themselves much concern about the nature of those bodies, supposed them to prognosticate sinister events. Regiomontanus and Tycho Brahé proved by their observations that they are situate beyond the moon; Hevelius, Dörfel, &c., made them revolve around the sun; Newton established that they move under the immediate influence of the attractive force of that body, that they do not describe right lines, that, in fact, they obey the laws of Kepler. It was necessary, then, to prove that the orbits of comets are curves which return into themselves, or that the same comet has been seen on several distinct occasions. This discovery was reserved for Halley. By a minute investigation of the circumstances connected with the apparitions of all the comets to be met with in the records of history, in ancient chronicles, and in astronomical annals, this eminent philosopher was enabled to prove that the comets of 1682, of 1607, and of 1531, were in reality

---

* The results of Clairaut's researches on the figure of the earth are mainly embodied in a remarkable theorem discovered by that geometer, and which may be enunciated thus:—*The sum of the fractions expressing the ellipticity and the increase of gravity at the pole is equal to two and a half times the fraction expressing the centrifugal force at the equator, the unit of force being represented by the force of gravity at the equator.* This theorem is independent of any hypothesis with respect to the law of the densities of the successive strata of the earth. Now the increase of gravity at the pole may be ascertained by means of observations with the pendulum in different latitudes. Hence it is plain that Clairaut's theorem furnishes a practical method for determining the value of the earth's ellipticity.— *Translator.*

so many successive apparitions of one and the same body.

This identity involved a conclusion before which more than one astronomer shrunk. It was necessary to admit that the time of a complete revolution of the comet was subject to a great variation, amounting to as much as two years in seventy-six.

Were such great discordances due to the disturbing action of the planets?

The answer to this question would introduce comets into the category of ordinary planets or would exclude them for ever. The calculation was difficult : Clairaut discovered the means of effecting it. While success was still uncertain, the illustrious geometer gave proof of the greatest boldness, for in the course of the year 1758 he undertook to determine the time of the following year when the comet of 1682 would reappear. He designated the constellations, nay the stars, which it would encounter in its progress.

This was not one of those remote predictions which astrologers and others formerly combined very skilfully with the tables of mortality, so that they might not be falsified during their lifetime : the event was close at hand. The question at issue was nothing less than the creation of a new era in cometary astronomy, or the casting of a reproach upon science, the consequences of which it would long continue to feel.

Clairaut found by a long process of calculation, conducted with great skill, that the action of Jupiter and Saturn ought to have retarded the movement of the comet ; that the time of revolution compared with that immediately preceding, would be increased 518 days by the disturbing action of Jupiter, and 100 days by the action of Saturn, forming a total of 618 days, or more than a year and eight months.

Never did a question of astronomy excite a more intense, a more legitimate curiosity. All classes of society awaited with equal interest the announced apparition. A Saxon peasant, Palitzch, first perceived the comet. Henceforward, from one extremity of Europe to the other, a thousand telescopes traced each night the path of the body through the constellations. The route was always, within the limits of precision of the calculations, that which Clairaut had indicated beforehand. The prediction of the illustrious geometer was verified in regard both to time and space : astronomy had just achieved a great and important triumph, and, as usual, had destroyed at one blow a disgraceful and inveterate prejudice. As soon as it was established that the returns of comets might be calculated beforehand, those bodies lost for ever their ancient prestige. The most timid minds troubled themselves quite as little about them as about eclipses of the sun and moon, which are equally subject to calculation. In fine, the labours of Clairaut had produced a deeper impression on the public mind than the learned, ingenious, and acute reasoning of Bayle.

The heavens offer to reflecting minds nothing more curious or more strange than the equality which subsists between the movements of rotation and revolution of our satellite. By reason of this perfect equality the moon always presents the same side to the earth. The hemisphere which we see in the present day is precisely that which our ancestors saw in the most remote ages ; it is exactly the hemisphere which future generations will perceive.

The doctrine of final causes which certain philosophers

have so abundantly made use of in endeavouring to account for a great number of natural phenomena was in this particular case totally inapplicable. In fact, how could it be pretended that mankind could have any interest in perceiving incessantly the same hemisphere of the moon, in never obtaining a glimpse of the opposite hemisphere? On the other hand, the existence of a perfect, mathematical equality between elements having no necessary connection—such as the movements of translation and rotation of a given celestial body—was not less repugnant to all ideas of probability. There were besides two other numerical coincidences quite as extraordinary; an identity of direction, relative to the stars, of the equator and orbit of the moon; exactly the same precessional movements of these two planes. This group of singular phenomena, discovered by J. D. Cassini, constituted the mathematical code of what is called the *Libration of the Moon*.

The libration of the moon formed a very imperfect part of physical astronomy when Lagrange made it depend on a circumstance connected with the figure of our satellite which was not observable from the earth, and thereby connected it completely with the principles of universal gravitation.

At the time when the moon was converted into a solid body, the action of the earth compelled it to assume a less regular figure than if no attracting body had been situate in its vicinity. The action of our globe rendered elliptical an equator which otherwise would have been circular. This disturbing action did not prevent the lunar equator from bulging out in every direction, but the prominence of the equatorial diameter directed towards

14 *

the earth became four times greater than that of the diameter which we see perpendicularly.

The moon would appear then, to an observer situate in space and examining it transversely, to be elongated towards the earth, to be a sort of pendulum without a point of suspension. When a pendulum deviates from the vertical, the action of gravity brings it back; when the principal axis of the moon recedes from its usual direction, the earth in like manner compels it to return.

We have here, then, a complete explanation of a singular phenomenon, without the necessity of having recourse to the existence of an almost miraculous equality between two movements of translation and rotation, entirely independent of each other. Mankind will never see but one face of the moon. Observation had informed us of this fact; now we know further that this is due to a physical cause which may be calculated, and which is visible only to the mind's eye,—that it is attributable to the elongation which the diameter of the moon experienced when it passed from the liquid to the solid state under the attractive influence of the earth.

If there had existed originally a slight difference between the movements of rotation and revolution of the moon, the attraction of the earth would have reduced these movements to a rigorous equality. This attraction would have even sufficed to cause the disappearance of a slight want of coincidence in the intersections of the equator and orbit of the moon with the plane of the ecliptic.

The memoir in which Lagrange has so successfully connected the laws of libration with the principles of gravitation, is no less remarkable for intrinsic excellence than style of execution. After having perused this production, the reader will have no difficulty in admitting that the word *elegance* may be appropriately applied to mathematical researches.

In this analysis we have merely glanced at the astronomical discoveries of Clairaut, D'Alembert, and Lagrange. We shall be somewhat less concise in noticing the labours of Laplace.

After having enumerated the various forces which must result from the mutual action of the planets and satellites of our system, even the great Newton did not venture to investigate the general nature of the effects produced by them. In the midst of the labyrinth formed by increases and diminutions of velocity, variations in the forms of the orbits, changes of distances and inclinations, which these forces must evidently produce, the most learned geometer would fail to discover a trustworthy guide. This extreme complication gave birth to a discouraging reflection. Forces so numerous, so variable in position, so different in intensity, seemed to be incapable of maintaining a condition of equilibrium except by a sort of miracle. Newton even went so far as to suppose that the planetary system did not contain within itself the elements of indefinite stability; he was of opinion that a powerful hand must intervene from time to time, to repair the derangements occasioned by the mutual action of the various bodies. Euler, although farther advanced than Newton in a knowledge of the planetary pertubations, refused also to admit that the solar system was constituted so as to endure for ever.

Never did a greater philosophical question offer itself to the inquiries of mankind. Laplace attacked it with boldness, perseverance, and success. The profound and long-continued researches of the illustrious geometer

established with complete evidence that the planetary
ellipses are perpetually variable; that the extremities of
their major axes make the tour of the heavens; that, independently of an oscillatory motion, the planes of their
orbits experienced a displacement in virtue of which
their intersections with the plane of the terrestrial orbit
are each year directed towards different stars. In the
midst of this apparent chaos there is one element which
remains constant or is merely subject to small periodic
changes; namely, the major axis of each orbit, and consequently the time of revolution of each planet. This is
the element which ought to have chiefly varied, according to the learned speculations of Newton and Euler.

The principle of universal gravitation suffices for preserving the stability of the solar system. It maintains
the forms and inclinations of the orbits in a mean condition which is subject to slight oscillations; variety does
not entail disorder; the universe offers the example of
harmonious relations, of a state of perfection which Newton himself doubted. This depends on circumstances
which calculation disclosed to Laplace, and which, upon
a superficial view of the subject, would not seem to be
capable of exercising so great an influence. Instead of
planets revolving all in the same direction in slightly
eccentric orbits, and in planes inclined at small angles
towards each other, substitute different conditions and
the stability of the universe will again be put in jeopardy,
and according to all probability there will result a frightful chaos.*

* The researches on the secular variations of the eccentricities and
inclinations of the planetary orbits depend upon the solution of an
algebraic equation equal in degree to the number of planets whose
mutual action is considered, and the coefficients of which involve the
values of the masses of those bodies. It may be shown that if the

Although the invariability of the mean distances of the planetary orbits has been more completely demonstrated since the appearance of the memoir above referred to, that is to say by pushing the analytical approximations to a greater extent, it will, notwithstanding, always constitute one of the admirable discoveries of the author of the *Mécanique Céleste*. Dates, in the case of such sub-

roots of this equation be equal or imaginary, the corresponding element, whether the eccentricity or the inclination, will increase indefinitely with the time in the case of each planet; but that if the roots, on the other hand, be real and unequal, the value of the element will oscillate in every instance within fixed limits. Laplace proved by a general analysis, that the roots of the equation are real and unequal, whence it followed that neither the eccentricity nor the inclination will vary in any case to an indefinite extent. But it still remained uncertain, whether the limits of oscillation were not in any instance so far apart that the variation of the element (whether the eccentricity or the inclination) might lead to a complete destruction of the existing physical condition of the planet. Laplace, indeed, attempted to prove, by means of two well-known theorems relative to the eccentricities and inclinations of the planetary orbits, that if those elements were once small, they would always remain so, provided the planets all revolved around the sun in one common direction and their masses were inconsiderable. It is to these theorems that M. Arago manifestly alludes in the text. Le Verrier and others have, however, remarked that they are inadequate to assure the permanence of the existing physical condition of several of the planets. In order to arrive at a definitive conclusion on this subject, it is indispensable to have recourse to the actual solution of the algebraic equation above referred to. This was the course adopted by the illustrious Lagrange in his researches on the secular variations of the planetary orbits. (*Mem. Acad. Berlin*, 1783-4.) Having investigated the values of the masses of the planets, he then determined, by an approximate solution, the values of the several roots of the algebraic equation upon which the* variations of the eccentricities and inclinations of the orbits depended. In this way, he found the limiting values of the eccentricity and inclination for the orbit of each of the principal planets of the system. The results obtained by that great geometer have been mainly confirmed by the recent researches of Le Verrier on the same subject. (*Connaissance des Temps*, 1843.)—*Translator*.

jects, are no luxury of erudition. The memoir in which Laplace communicated his results on the invariability of the mean motions or mean distances, is dated 1773.* It was in 1784 only, that he established the stability of the other elements of the system from the smallness of the planetary masses, the inconsiderable eccentricity of the orbits, and the revolution of the planets in one common direction around the sun.

The discovery of which I have just given an account to the reader excluded at least from the solar system the idea of the Newtonian attraction being a cause of disorder. But might not other forces, by combining with attraction, produce gradually increasing perturbations as Newton and Euler dreaded? Facts of a positive nature seemed to justify these fears.

A comparison of ancient with modern observations revealed the existence of a continual acceleration of the mean motions of the moon and the planet Jupiter, and an

* Laplace was originally led to consider the subject of the perturbations of the mean motions of the planets by his researches on the theory of Jupiter and Saturn. Having computed the numerical value of the secular inequality affecting the mean motion of each of those planets, neglecting the terms of the fourth and higher orders relative to the eccentricities and inclinations, he found it to be so small that it might be regarded as totally insensible. Justly suspecting that this circumstance was not attributable to the particular values of the elements of Jupiter and Saturn, he investigated the expression for the secular perturbation of the mean motion by a general analysis, neglecting, as before, the fourth and higher powers of the eccentricities and inclinations, and he found in this case, that the terms which were retained in the investigation absolutely destroyed each other, so that the expression was reduced to zero. In a memoir which he communicated to the Berlin Academy of Sciences, in 1776, Lagrange first showed that the mean distance (and consequently the mean motion) was not affected by any secular inequalities, no matter what were the eccentricities or inclinations of the disturbing and disturbed planets.— *Translator.*

equally striking diminution of the mean motion of Saturn. These variations led to conclusions of the most singular nature.

In accordance with the presumed cause of these perturbations, to say that the velocity of a body increased from century to century was equivalent to asserting that the body continually approached the centre of motion; on the other hand, when the velocity diminished, the body must be receding from the centre.

Thus, by a strange arrangement of nature, our planetary system seemed destined to lose Saturn, its most mysterious ornament,—to see the planet accompanied by its ring and seven satellites, plunge gradually into unknown regions, whither the eye armed with the most powerful telescopes has never penetrated. Jupiter, on the other hand, the planet compared with which the earth is so insignificant, appeared to be moving in the opposite direction, so as to be ultimately absorbed in the incandescent matter of the sun. Finally, the moon seemed as if it would one day precipitate itself upon the earth.

There was nothing doubtful or speculative in these sinister forebodings. The precise dates of the approaching catastrophes were alone uncertain. It was known, however, that they were very distant. Accordingly, neither the learned dissertations of men of science nor the animated descriptions of certain poets produced any impression upon the public mind.

It was not so with our scientific societies, the members of which regarded with regret the approaching destruction of our planetary system. The Academy of Sciences called the attention of geometers of all countries to these menacing perturbations. Euler and Lagrange descended into the arena. Never did their mathematical genius shine with a brighter lustre. Still, the question remained undecided. The inutility of such efforts seemed to suggest only a feeling of resignation on the subject, when from two disdained corners of the theories of analysis, the author of the *Mécanique Céleste* caused the laws of these great phenomena clearly to emerge. The variations of velocity of Jupiter, Saturn, and the Moon flowed then from evident physical causes, and entered into the category of ordinary periodic perturbations depending upon the principle of attraction. The variations in the dimensions of the orbits which were so much dreaded resolved themselves into simple oscillations included within narrow limits. Finally, by the powerful instrumentality of mathematical analysis, the physical universe was again established on a firm foundation.

I cannot quit this subject without at least alluding to the circumstances in the solar system upon which depend the so long unexplained variations of velocity of the Moon, Jupiter, and Saturn.

The motion of the earth around the sun is mainly effected in an ellipse, the form of which is liable to vary from the effects of planetary perturbation. These alterations of form are periodic; sometimes the curve, without ceasing to be elliptic, approaches the form of a circle, while at other times it deviates more and more from that form. From the epoch of the earliest recorded observations, the eccentricity of the terrestrial orbit has been diminishing from year to year; at some future epoch the orbit, on the contrary, will begin to deviate from the form of a circle, and the eccentricity will increase to the same extent as it previously diminished, and according to the same laws.

Now, Laplace has shown that the mean motion of the

moon around the earth is connected with the form of the
ellipse which the earth describes around the sun ; that a
diminution of the eccentricity of the ellipse inevitably induces an increase in the velocity of our satellite, and *vice
versâ ;* finally, that this cause suffices to explain the numerical value of the acceleration which the mean motion
of the moon has experienced from the earliest ages down
to the present time.*

The origin of the inequalities in the mean motions of
Jupiter and Saturn will be, I hope, as easy to conceive.

Mathematical analysis has not served to represent in
finite terms the values of the derangements which each
planet experiences in its movement from the action of all
the other planets.  In the present state of science, this
value is exhibited in the form of an indefinite series of
terms diminishing rapidly in magnitude.  In calculation,
it is usual to neglect such of those terms as correspond in
the order of magnitude to quantities beneath the errors of
observation.  But there are cases in which the order of
the term in the series does not decide whether it be small

---

* Mr. Adams has recently detected a remarkable oversight committed by Laplace and his successors in the analytical investigation
of the expression for this inequality.  The effect of the rectification
rendered necessary by the researches of Mr. Adams will be to
diminish by about one sixth the coefficient of the principal term of
the secular inequality.  This coefficient has for its multiplier the
square of the number of centuries which have elapsed from a given
epoch; its value was found by Laplace to be $10''\cdot18$.  Mr. Adams has
ascertained that it must be diminished by $1''\cdot66$.  This result has recently been verified by the researches of M. Plana.  Its effect will be
to alter in some degree the calculations of ancient eclipses.  The Astronomer Royal has stated in his last Annual Report, to the Board of
Visitors of the Royal Observatory, (June 7, 1856,) that steps have recently been taken at the Observatory, for calculating the various
circumstances of those phenomena, upon the basis of the more correct data furnished by the researches of Mr. Adams.—*Translator.*

or great. Certain numerical relations between the primitive elements of the disturbing and disturbed planets may impart sensible values to terms which usually admit of being neglected. This case occurs in the perturbations of Saturn produced by Jupiter, and in those of Jupiter produced by Saturn. There exists between the mean motions of these two great planets a simple relation of commensurability, five times the mean motion of Saturn, being, in fact, very nearly equal to twice the mean motion of Jupiter. It happens, in consequence, that certain terms, which would otherwise be very small, acquire from this circumstance considerable values. Hence arise in the movements of these two planets, inequalities of long duration which require more than 900 years for their complete development, and which represent with marvellous accuracy all the irregularities disclosed by observation.

Is it not astonishing to find in the commensurability of the mean motions of two planets, a cause of perturbation of so influential a nature; to discover that the definitive solution of an immense difficulty—which baffled the genius of Euler, and which even led persons to doubt whether the theory of gravitation was capable of accounting for all the phenomena of the heavens—should depend upon the fortuitous circumstance of five times the mean motion of Saturn being equal to twice the mean motion of Jupiter? The beauty of the conception and the ultimate result are here equally worthy of admiration.*

* The origin of this famous inequality may be best understood by reference to the mode in which the disturbing forces operate. Let P Q R, P/ Q/ R/ repsesent the orbits of Jupiter and Saturn, and let us suppose, for the sake of illustration, that they are both situate in the same plane. Let the planets be in conjunction at P, P/, and let them both be revolving around the sun s, in the direction represented by

We have just explained how Laplace demonstrated
that the solar system can experience only small periodic

the arrows. Assuming that the mean motion of Jupiter is to that of
Saturn exactly in the proportion of five to two, it follows that when
Jupiter has completed one revolution, Saturn will have advanced
through two fifths of a revolution. Similarly, when Jupiter has com-

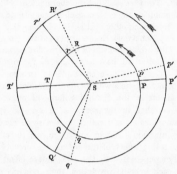

pleted a revolution and a half, Saturn will have effected three fifths of
a revolution. Hence when Jupiter arrives at T, Saturn will be a little
in advance of T′. Let us suppose that the two planets come again
into conjunction at Q, Q′. It is plain that while Jupiter has completed
one revolution, and, advanced through the angle P S Q (measured in
the direction of the arrow), Saturn has simply described around S the
angle P′ S′ Q′. Hence the *excess* of the angle described around S, by
Jupiter, over the angle similarly described by Saturn, will amount to
one complete revolution, or, 360°. But since the mean motions of the
two planets are in the proportion of five to two, the angles described
by them around S in any given time will be in the same proportion,
and therefore the *excess* of the angle described by Jupiter over that
described by Saturn will be to the angle described by Saturn in the
proportion of three to two. But we have just found that the excess of
these two angles in the present case amounts to 360°, and the angle described by Saturn is represented by P′ S′ Q′; consequently 360° is to the
angle P′ S′ Q′ in the proportion of three to two, in other words P′ S′ Q′ is
equal to two thirds of the circumference or 240°. In the same way it
may be shown that the two planets will come into conjunction again
at R, when Saturn has described another arc of 240°. Finally, when
Saturn has advanced through a third arc of 240°, the two planets will

oscillations around a certain mean state. Let us now see in what way he succeeded in determining the absolute dimensions of the orbits.

come into conjunction at P, P′, the points whence they originally set out; and the two succeeding conjunctions will also manifestly occur at Q, Q′ and R, R′. Thus we see, that the conjunctions will always occur in three given points of the orbit of each planet situate at angular distances of 120° from each other. It is also obvious, that during the interval which elapses between the occurrence of two conjunctions in the same points of the orbits, and which includes three synodic revolutions of the planets, Jupiter will have accomplished five revolutions around the sun, and Saturn will have accomplished two revolutions. Now if the orbits of both planets were perfectly circular, the retarding and accelerating effects of the disturbing force of either planet would neutralize each other in the course of a synodic revolution, and therefore both planets would return to the same condition at each successive conjunction. But in consequence of the ellipticity of the orbits, the retarding effect of the disturbing force is manifestly no longer exactly compensated by the accelerative effect, and hence at the close of each synodic revolution, there remains a minute outstanding alteration in the movement of each planet. A similar effect will be produced at each of the three points of conjunction; and as the perturbations which thus ensue do not generally compensate each other, there will remain a minute outstanding perturbation as the result of every three conjunctions. The effect produced being of the same kind (whether tending to accelerate or retard the movement of the planet) for every such triple conjunction, it is plain that the action of the disturbing forces would ultimately lead to a serious derangement of the movements of both planets. All this is founded on the supposition that the mean motions of the two planets are to each other as two to five; but in reality, this relation does not exactly hold. In fact while Jupiter requires 21,663 days to accomplish five revolutions, Saturn effects two revolutions in 21,518 days. Hence when Jupiter, after completing his fifth revolution, arrives at P, Saturn will have advanced a little beyond P′, and the conjunction of the two planets will occur at P, P′ when they have both described around s an additional arc of about 8°. In the same way it may be shown that the two succeeding conjunctions will take place at the points q, q′, r, r′ respectively 8° in advance of Q, Q′, R, R′. Thus we see that the points of conjunction will travel with extreme slowness in the same direction as that in which the planets revolve. Now since the angular

What is the distance of the sun from the earth ? No scientific question has occupied in a greater degree the attention of mankind ; mathematically speaking, nothing is more simple. It suffices, as in common operations of surveying, to draw visual lines from the two extremities of a known base to an inaccessible object. The remainder is a process of elementary calculation. Unfortunately, in the case of the sun, the distance is great and the bases which can be measured upon the earth are comparatively very small. In such a case the slightest

distance between P and R is 120°, and since in a period of three synodic revolutions or 21,758 days, the line of conjunction travels through an arc of 8°, it follows that in 892 years the conjunction of the two planets will have advanced from P, P/ to R, R/. In reality, the time of travelling from P, P/ to R, R/ is somewhat longer from the indirect effects of planetary perturbation, amounting to 920 years. In an equal period of time the conjunction of the two planets will advance from Q, Q/ to R, R/ and from R, R/ to P, P/. During the half of this period the perturbative effect resulting from every triple conjunction will lie constantly in one direction, and during the other half it will lie in the contrary direction; that is to say, during a period of 460 years the mean motion of the disturbed planet will be continually accelerated, and, in like manner, during an equal period it will be continually retarded. In the case of Jupiter disturbed by Saturn, the inequality in longitude amounts at its maximum to 21/; in the converse case of Saturn disturbed by Jupiter, the inequality is more considerable in consequence of the greater mass of the disturbing planet, amounting at its maximum to 49/. In accordance with the mechanical principle of the equality of action and reaction, it happens that while the mean motion of one planet is increasing, that of the other is diminishing, and *vice versâ*. We have supposed that the orbits of both planets are situate in the same plane. In reality, however, they are inclined to each other, and this circumstance will produce an effect exactly analogous to that depending on the eccentricities of the orbits. It is plain that the more nearly the mean motions of the two planets approach a relation of commensurability, the smaller will be the displacement of every third conjunction, and consequently the longer will be the duration, and the greater the ultimate accumulation, of the inequality.— *Translator.*

errors in the direction of the visual lines exercise an enormous influence upon the results.

In the beginning of the last century Halley remarked that certain interpositions of Venus between the earth and the sun, or, to use an expression applied to such conjunctions, that the *transits* of the planet across the sun's disk, would furnish at each observatory an indirect means of fixing the position of the visual ray very superior in accuracy to the most perfect direct methods.*

Such was the object of the scientific expeditions undertaken in 1761 and 1769, on which occasions France, not to speak of stations in Europe, was represented at the Isle of Rodrigo by Pingré, at the Isle of St. Domingo by Fleurin, at California by the Abbé Chappe, at Pondicherry by Legentil. At the same epochs England sent Maskelyne to St. Helena, Wales to Hudson's Bay, Mason to the Cape of Good Hope, Captain Cooke to Otaheite, &c. The observations of the southern hemisphere compared with those of Europe, and especially with the observations made by an Austrian astronomer Father Hell at Wardhus in Lapland, gave for the distance of the sun the result which has since figured in all treatises on astronomy and navigation.

No government hesitated in furnishing Academies with the means, however expensive they might be, of conveniently establishing their observers in the most distant regions. We have already remarked that the determination of the contemplated distance appeared to demand imperiously an extensive base, for small bases would have been totally inadequate to the purpose. Well,

---

* The utility of observations of the transits of the inferior planets for determining the solar parallax, was first pointed out by James Gregory ( *Optica Promota*, 1663).— *Translator*.

Laplace has solved the problem numerically without a base of any kind whatever; he has deduced the distance of the sun from observations of the moon made in one and the same place!

The sun is, with respect to our satellite, the cause of perturbations which evidently depend on the distance of the immense luminous globe from the earth. Who does not see that these perturbations would diminish if the distance increased; that they would increase on the contrary, if the distance diminished; that the distance finally determines the magnitude of the perturbations?

Observation assigns the numerical value of these perturbations; theory, on the other hand, unfolds the general mathematical relation which connects them with the solar parallax, and with other known elements. The determination of the mean radius of the terrestrial orbit then becomes one of the most simple operations of algebra. Such is the happy combination by the aid of which Laplace has solved the great, the celebrated problem of parallax. It is thus that the illustrious geometer found for the mean distance of the sun from the earth, expressed in radii of the terrestrial orbit, a value differing only in a slight degree from that which was the fruit of so many troublesome and expensive voyages. According to the opinion of very competent judges the result of the indirect method might not impossibly merit the preference.*

---

* Mayer, from the principles of gravitation ( *Theoria Lunæ*, 1767), computed the value of the solar parallax to be 7″·8. He remarked that the error of this determination did not amount to one twentieth of the whole, whence it followed that the true value of the parallax could not exceed 8″·2. Laplace, by an analogous process, determined the parallax to be 8″·45. Encke, by a profound discussion of the observations of the transits of Venus in 1761 and 1769, found the value of the same element to be 8″·5776.— *Translator.*

The movements of the moon proved a fertile mine of research to our great geometer. His penetrating intellect discovered in them unknown treasures. He disentangled them from every thing which concealed them from vulgar eyes with an ability and a perseverance equally worthy of admiration. The reader will excuse me for citing another of such examples.

The earth governs the movements of the moon. The earth is flattened, in other words its figure is spheroidal. A spheroidal body does not attract like a sphere. There ought then to exist in the movement, I had almost said in the countenance of the moon, a sort of impression of the spheroidal figure of the earth. Such was the idea as it originally occurred to Laplace.

It still remained to ascertain (and here consisted the chief difficulty), whether the effects attributable to the spheroidal figure of the earth were sufficiently sensible not to be confounded with the errors of observation. It was accordingly necessary to find the general formula of perturbations of this nature, in order to be able, as in the case of the solar parallax, to eliminate the unknown quantity.

The ardour of Laplace, combined with his power of analytical research, surmounted all obstacles. By means of an investigation which demanded the most minute attention, the great geometer discovered in the theory of the moon's movements, two well-defined perturbations depending on the spheroidal figure of the earth. The first affected the resolved element of the motion of our satellite which is chiefly measured with the instrument known in observatories by the name of the transit instrument; the second, which operated in the direction north and south, could only be effected by observations with a second instrument termed the mural circle. These two inequalities of very different magnitudes connected with the cause which produces them by analytical combinations of totally different kinds have, however, both conducted to the same value of the ellipticity. It must be borne in mind, however, that the ellipticity thus deduced from the movements of the moon, is not the ellipticity corresponding to such or such a country, the ellipticity observed in France, in England, in Italy, in Lapland, in North America, in India, or in the region of the Cape of Good Hope, for the earth's materials having, undergone considerable upheavings at different times and in different places, the primitive regularity of its curvature has been sensibly disturbed by this cause. The moon, and it is this circumstance which renders the result of such inestimable value, ought to assign, and has in reality assigned the general ellipticity of the earth ; in other words, it has indicated a sort of mean value of the various determinations obtained at enormous expense, and with infinite labour, as the result of long voyages undertaken by astronomers of all the countries of Europe.

I shall add a few brief remarks, for which I am mainly indebted to the author of the *Mécanique Céleste*. They seem to be eminently adapted for illustrating the profound, the unexpected, and almost paradoxical character of the methods which I have just attempted to sketch.

What are the elements which it has been found necessary to confront with each other in order to arrive at results expressed even to the precision of the smallest decimals?

On the one hand, mathematical formulæ deduced from

15

the principle of universal attraction ; on the other hand,
certain irregularities observed in the returns of the moon
to the meridian.

An observing geometer who, from his infancy, had
never quitted his chamber of study, and who had never
viewed the heavens except through a narrow aperture
directed north and south, in the vertical plane in which
the principal astronomical instruments are made to move,
—to whom nothing had ever been revealed respecting
the bodies revolving above his head, except that they
attract each other according to the Newtonian law of
gravitation,—would, however, be enabled to ascertain
that his narrow abode was situated upon the surface of
a spheroidal body, the equatorial axis of which surpassed
the polar axis by a *three hundred and sixth part;* he
would have also found, in his isolated immovable position, his true distance from the sun.

I have stated at the commencement of this Notice,
that it is to D'Alembert we owe the first satisfactory
mathematical explanation of the phenomenon of the
precession of the equinoxes. But our illustrious countryman, as well as Euler, whose solution appeared subsequently to that of D'Alembert, omitted all consideration
of certain physical circumstances, which, however, did
not seem to be of a nature to be neglected without examination. Laplace has supplied this deficiency. He
has shown that the sea, notwithstanding its fluidity, and
that the atmosphere, notwithstanding its currents, exercise the same influence on the movements of the terrestrial
axis as if they formed solid masses adhering to the terrestrial spheroid.

Do the extremities of the axis around which the earth
performs an entire revolution once in every twenty-four

hours, correspond always to the same material points of
the terrestrial spheroid? In other words, do the poles
of rotation, which from year to year correspond to different stars, undergo also a displacement at the surface
of the earth?

In the case of the affirmative, the equator is movable
as well as the poles; the terrestrial latitudes are variable; no country during the lapse of ages will enjoy,
even on an average, a constant climate; regions the
most different will, in their turn, become circumpolar.
Adopt the contrary supposition, and every thing assumes
the character of an admirable permanence.

The question which I have just suggested, one of the
most important in Astronomy, cannot be solved by the
aid of mere observation on account of the uncertainty of
the early determinations of terrestrial latitude. Laplace
has supplied this defect by analysis. The great geometer has demonstrated that no circumstance depending
on universal gravitation can sensibly displace the poles
of the earth's axis relatively to the surface of the terrestrial spheroid. The sea, far from being an obstacle
to the invariable rotation of the earth upon its axis,
would, on the contrary, reduce the axis to a permanent
condition in consequence of the mobility of the waters
and the resistance which their oscillations experience.

The remarks which I have just made with respect to
the position of the terrestrial axis are equally applicable
to the time of the earth's rotation which is the unit, the
true standard of time. The importance of this element
induced Laplace to examine whether its numerical value
might not be liable to vary from internal causes such
as earthquakes and volcanoes. It is hardly necessary
for me to state that the result obtained was negative.

The admirable memoir of Lagrange upon the libration of the moon seemed to have exhausted the subject. This, however, was not the case.

The motion of revolution of our satellite around the earth is subject to perturbations, technically termed *secular*, which were either unknown to Lagrange or which he neglected. These inequalities eventually place the body, not to speak of entire circumferences, at angular distances of a semi-circle, a circle and a half, &c., from the position which it would otherwise occupy. If the movement of rotation did not participate in such perturbations, the moon in the lapse of ages would present in succession all the parts of its surface to the earth.

This event will not occur. The hemisphere of the moon which is actually invisible, will remain invisible for ever. Laplace, in fact, has shown that the attraction of the earth introduces into the rotatory motion of the lunar spheroid the secular inequalities which exist in the movement of revolution.

Researches of this nature exhibit in full relief the power of mathematical analysis. It would have been very difficult to have discovered by synthesis truths so profoundly enveloped in the complex action of a multitude of forces.

We should be inexcusable if we omitted to notice the high importance of the labours of Laplace on the improvement of the lunar tables. The immediate object of this improvement was, in effect, the promotion of maritime intercourse between distant countries, and, what was indeed far superior to all considerations of mercantile interest, the preservation of the lives of mariners.

Thanks to a sagacity without parallel, to a perseverance which knew no limits, to an ardour always youthful and which communicated itself to able coadjutors, Laplace solved the celebrated problem of the longitude more completely than could have been hoped for in a scientific point of view, with greater precision than the art of navigation in its utmost refinement demanded. The ship, the sport of the winds and tempests, has no occasion, in the present day, to be afraid of losing itself in the immensity of the ocean. An intelligent glance at the starry vault indicates to the pilot, in every place and at every time, his distance from the meridian of Paris. The extreme perfection of the existing tables of the moon entitles Laplace to be ranked among the benefactors of humanity.*

In the beginning of the year 1611, Galileo supposed that he found in the eclipses of Jupiter's satellites a simple and rigorous solution of the famous problem of the longitude, and active negotiations were immediately commenced with the view of introducing the new method on board the numerous vessels of Spain and Holland. These negotiations failed. From the discussion it plainly appeared that the accurate observation of the eclipses of the satellites would require powerful telescopes; but

---

* The theoretical researches of Laplace formed the basis of Burckhardt's Lunar Tables, which are chiefly employed in computing the places of the moon for the Nautical Almanac and other Ephemerides. These tables were defaced by an empiric equation, suggested for the purpose of representing an inequality of long period which seemed to affect the mean longitude of the moon. No satisfactory explanation of the origin of this inequality could be discovered by any geometer, although it formed the subject of much toilsome investigation throughout the present century, until at length M. Hansen found it to arise from a combination of two inequalities due to the disturbing action of Venus. The period of one of these inequalities is 273 years, and that of the other is 239 years. The maximum value of the former is 27''·4, and that of the latter is 23''·2.—*Translator.*

such telescopes could not be employed on board a ship tossed about by the waves.

The method of Galileo seemed, at any rate, to retain all its advantages when applied on land, and to promise immense improvements to geography. These expectations were found to be premature. The movements of the satellites of Jupiter are not by any means so simple as the immortal inventor of the method of longitudes supposed them to be. It was necessary that three gen - erations of astronomers and mathematicians should labour with perseverance in unfolding their most considerable perturbations. It was necessary, in fine, that the tables of those bodies should acquire all desirable and necessary precision, that Laplace should introduce into the midst of them the torch of mathematical analysis.

In the present day, the nautical ephemerides contain, several years in advance, the indication of the times of the eclipses and reappearances of Jupiter's satellites. Calculation does not yield in precision to direct observa- tion. In this group of satellites, considered as an inde- pendent system of bodies, Laplace found a series of perturbations analogous to those which the planets ex- perience. The rapidity of the revolutions unfolds, in a sufficiently short space of time, changes in this system which require centuries for their complete development in the solar system.

Although the satellites exhibit hardly an appreciable diameter even when viewed in the best telescopes, our illustrious countryman was enabled to determine their masses. Finally, he discovered certain simple relations of an extremely remarkable character between the move- ments of those bodies, which have been called *the laws of Laplace*. Posterity will not obliterate this designation; it will acknowledge the propriety of inscribing in the heavens the name of so great an astronomer beside that of Kepler.

Let us cite two or three of the laws of Laplace :—

If we add to the mean longitude of the first satellite twice that of the third, and subtract from the sum three times the mean longitude of the second, the result will be exactly equal to 180°.

Would it not be very extraordinary if the three satellites had been placed originally at the distances from Jupiter, and in the positions, with respect to each other, adapted for constantly and rigorously maintaining the foregoing relation? Laplace has replied to this question by showing that it is not necessary that this relation should have been rigorously true at the origin. The mutual action of the satellites would necessarily have reduced it to its present mathematical condition, if once the distances and the positions satisfied the law approximately.

This first law is equally true when we employ the synodical elements. It hence plainly results, that the first three satellites of Jupiter can never be all eclipsed at the same time. Bearing this in mind, we shall have no difficulty in apprehending the import of a celebrated observation of recent times, during which certain astronomers perceived the planet for a short time without any of his four satellites. This would not by any means authorize us in supposing the satellites to be eclipsed. A satellite disappears when it is projected upon the central part of the luminous disk of Jupiter, and also when it passes behind the opaque body of the planet.

The following is another very simple law to which the mean motions of the same satellites of Jupiter are subject:

If we add to the mean motion of the first satellite twice the mean motion of the third, the sum is exactly equal to three times the mean motion of the second.*

This numerical coincidence, which is perfectly accurate, would be one of the most mysterious phenomena in the system of the universe if Laplace had not proved that the law need only have been approximate at the origin, and that the mutual action of the satellites has sufficed to render it rigorous.

The illustrious geometer, who always pursued his researches to their most remote ramifications, arrived

---

* This law is necessarily included in the law already enunciated by the author relative to the mean longitudes. The following is the most usual mode of expressing these curious relations: 1st, the mean motion of the first satellite, plus twice the mean motion of the third, minus three times the mean motion of the second, is rigorously equal to zero; 2d, the mean longitude of the first satellite, plus twice the mean longitude of the third, minus three times the mean longitude of the second, is equal to 180°. It is plain that if we only consider the mean longitude here to refer to a *given epoch*, the combination of the two laws will assure the existence of an analogous relation between the mean longitudes *for any instant of time whatever*, whether past or future. Laplace has shown, as the author has stated in the text, that if these relations had only been approximately true at the origin, the mutual attraction of the three satellites would have ultimately rendered them rigorously so; under such circumstances, the mean longitude of the first satellite, plus twice the mean longitude of the third, minus three times the mean longitude of the second, would continually oscillate about 180° as a mean value. The three satellites would participate in this libratory movement, the extent of oscillation depending in each case on the mass of the satellite and its distance from the primary, but the period of libration is the same for all the satellites, amounting to 2,270 days 18 hours, or rather more than six years. Observations of the eclipses of the satellites have not afforded any indications of the actual existence of such a libratory motion, so that the relations between the mean motions and mean longitudes may be presumed to be always rigorously true.— *Translator.*

at the following result : The action of Jupiter regulates the movements of rotation of the satellites so that, without taking into account the secular perturbations, the time of rotation of the first satellite plus twice the time of rotation of the third, forms a sum which is constantly equal to three times the time of rotation of the second.

Influenced by a deference, a modesty, a timidity, without any plausible motive, our artists in the last century surrendered to the English the exclusive privilege of constructing instruments of astronomy. Thus, let us frankly acknowledge the fact, at the time when Herschel was prosecuting his beautiful observations on the other side of the Channel, there existed in France no instruments adapted for developing them ; we had not even the means of verifying them. Fortunately for the scientific honour of our country, mathematical analysis is also a powerful instrument. Laplace gave ample proof of this on a memorable occasion when from the retirement of his chamber he predicted, he minutely announced, what the excellent astronomer of Windsor would see with the largest telescopes which were ever constructed by the hand of man.

When Galileo, in the beginning of the year 1610, directed towards Saturn a telescope of very low power which he had just executed with his own hands, he perceived that the planet was not an ordinary globe, without however being able to ascertain its real form. The expression *tri-corporate*, by which the illustrious Florentine designated the appearance of the planet, implied even a totally erroneous idea of its structure. Our countryman Roberval entertained much sounder views on the subject, but from not having instituted a detailed comparison between his hypothesis and the results of

15*

observation, he abandoned to Huyghens the honour of being regarded as the author of the true theory of the phenomena presented by the wonderful planet.

Every person knows, in the present day, that Saturn consists of a globe about 900 times greater than the earth, and a ring. This ring does not touch the ball of the planet, being everywhere removed from it at a distance of 20,000 (English) miles. Observation indicates the breadth of the ring to be 54,000 miles. The thickness certainly does not exceed 250 miles. With the exception of a black streak which divides the ring throughout its whole contour into two parts of unequal breadth and of different brightness, this strange colossal bridge without piles had never offered to the most experienced or skilful observers either spot or protuberance adapted for deciding whether it was immovable or endued with a movement of rotation.

Laplace considered it to be very improbable, if the ring was immovable, that its constituent parts should be capable of resisting by their mere cohesion the continual attraction of the planet. A movement of rotation occurred to his mind as constituting the principle of stability, and he hence deduced the necessary velocity. The velocity thus found was exactly equal to that which Herschel subsequently deduced from a course of extremely delicate observations.

The two parts of the ring being placed at different distances from the planet, could not fail to experience from the action of the sun, different movements of rotation. It would hence seem that the planes of both rings ought to be generally inclined towards each other, whereas they appear from observation always to coincide. It was necessary then that some physical cause should exist which would be capable of neutralizing the action of the sun. In a memoir published in February, 1789, Laplace found that this cause must reside in the ellipticity of Saturn produced by a rapid movement of rotation of the planet, a movement the existence of which Herschel announced in November, 1789.

The reader cannot fail to remark how, on certain occasions, the eyes of the mind can supply the want of the most powerful telescopes, and lead to astronomical discoveries of the highest importance.

Let us descend from the heavens upon the earth. The discoveries of Laplace will appear not less important, not less worthy of his genius.

The phenomena of the tides, which an ancient philosopher designated in despair as *the tomb of human curiosity*, were connected by Laplace with an analytical theory in which the physical conditions of the question figure for the first time. Accordingly calculators, to the immense advantage of the navigation of our maritime coasts, venture in the present day to predict several years in advance the details of the time and height of the full tides without more anxiety respecting the result than if the question related to the phases of an eclipse.

There exists between the different phenomena of the ebb and flow of the tides and the attractive forces which the sun and moon exercise upon the fluid sheet which covers three fourths of the globe, an intimate and necessary connection from which Laplace, by the aid of a series of twenty years of observations executed at Brest, deduced the value of the mass of our satellite. Science knows in the present day that seventy-five moons would be necessary to form a weight equivalent to that of the terrestrial globe, and it is indebted for this result to an attentive and minute study of the oscillations of the ocean. We know only one means of enhancing the admiration which every thoughtful mind will entertain for theories capable of leading to such conclusions. An historical statement will supply it. In the year 1631, the illustrious Galileo, as appears from his *Dialogues*, was so far from perceiving the mathematical relations from which Laplace deduced results so beautiful, so unequivocal, and so useful, that he taxed with frivolousness the vague idea which Kepler entertained of attributing to the moon's attraction a certain share in the production of the diurnal and periodical movements of the waters of the ocean.

Laplace did not confine himself to extending so considerably, and improving so essentially, the mathematical theory of the tides; he considered the phenomenon from an entirely new point of view; it was he who first treated of the stability of the ocean. Systems of bodies, whether solid or fluid, are subject to two kinds of equilibrium, which we must carefully distinguish from each other. In the case of stable equilibrium the system, when slightly disturbed, tends always to return to its original condition. On the other hand, when the system is in unstable equilibrium, a very insignificant derangement might occasion an enormous dislocation in the relative positions of its constituent parts.

If the equilibrium of waves is of the latter kind, the waves engendered by the action of winds, by earthquakes, and by sudden movements from the bottom of the ocean, have perhaps risen in past times and may rise in the future to the height of the highest mountains. The geologist will have the satisfaction of deducing from these prodigious oscillations a rational explanation of a

great multitude of phenomena, but the public will thereby
be exposed to new and terrible catastrophes.

Mankind may rest assured: Laplace has proved that
the equilibrium of the ocean is stable, but upon the express condition (which, however, has been amply verified by established facts), that the mean density of the
fluid mass is less than the mean density of the earth.
Every thing else remaining the same, let us substitute
an ocean of mercury for the actual ocean, and the stability will disappear, and the fluid will frequently surpass its boundaries, to ravage continents even to the
height of the snowy regions which lose themselves in
the clouds.

Does not the reader remark how each of the analytical investigations of Laplace serves to disclose the harmony and duration of the universe and of our globe !

It was impossible that the great geometer, who had
succeeded so well in the study of the tides of the ocean,
should not have occupied his attention with the tides of
the atmosphere ; that he should not have submitted to
the delicate and definitive tests of a rigorous calculus,
the generally diffused opinions respecting the influence
of the moon upon the height of the barometer and other
meteorological phenomena.

Laplace, in effect, has devoted a chapter of his splendid
work to an examination of the oscillations which the
attractive force of the moon is capable of producing in
our atmosphere. It results from these researches, that,
at Paris, the lunar tide produces no sensible effect upon
the barometer. The height of the tide, obtained by the
discussion of a long series of observations, has not exceeded two-hundredths of a millimètre, a quantity which,
in the present state of meteorological science, is less than
the probable error of observation.

The calculation to which I have just alluded, may be cited in support of considerations to which I had recourse when I wished to establish, that if the moon alters more or less the height of the barometer, according to its different phases, the effect is not -attributable to attraction.

No person was more sagacious than Laplace in discovering intimate relations between phenomena apparently very dissimilar; no person showed himself more skilful in deducing important conclusions from those unexpected affinities.

Towards the close of his days, for example, he overthrew with a stroke of the pen, by the aid of certain observations of the moon, the cosmogonic theories of Buffon and Bailly, which were so long in favour.

According to these theories, the earth was inevitably advancing to a state of congelation which was close at hand. Laplace, who never contented himself with a vague statement, sought to determine in numbers the rapid cooling of our globe which Buffon had so eloquently but so gratuitously announced. Nothing could be more simple, better connected, or more demonstrative, than the chain of deductions of the celebrated geometer.

A body diminishes in volume when it cools. According to the most elementary principles of mechanics, a rotating body which contracts in dimensions ought inevitably to turn upon its axis with greater and greater rapidity. The length of the day has been determined in all ages by the time of the earth's rotation; if the earth is cooling, the length of the day must be continually shortening. Now there exists a means of ascertaining whether the length of the day has undergone any variation; this consists in examining, for each century, the

arc of the celestial sphere described by the moon during
the interval of time which the astronomers of the existing epoch called a day,—in other words, the time required by the earth to effect a complete rotation on its
axis, the velocity of the moon being in fact independent
of the time of the earth's rotation.

Let us now, after the example of Laplace, take from
the standard tables the least considerable values, if you
choose, of the expansions or contractions which solid
bodies experience from changes of temperature; search
then the annals of Grecian, Arabian, and modern astronomy for the purpose of finding in them the angular
velocity of the moon, and the great geometer will prove,
by incontrovertible evidence founded upon these data,
that during a period of two thousand years the mean
temperature of the earth has not varied to the extent of
the hundredth part of a degree of the centigrade thermometer. No eloquent declamation is capable of resisting such a process of reasoning, or withstanding the force
of such numbers. The mathematics have been in all
ages the implacable adversaries of scientific romances.

The fall of bodies, if it was not a phenomenon of perpetual occurrence, would justly excite in the highest
degree the astonishment of mankind. What, in effect, is
more extraordinary than to see an inert mass, that is to
say, a mass deprived of will, a mass which ought not to
have any propensity to advance in one direction more
than in another, precipitate itself towards the earth as
soon as it ceased to be supported !

Nature engenders the gravity of bodies by a process
so recondite, so completely beyond the reach of our
senses and the ordinary resources of human intelligence,
that the philosophers of antiquity, who supposed that

they could explain every thing mechanically according to the simple evolutions of atoms, excepted gravity from their speculations.

Descartes attempted what Leucippus, Democritus, Epicurus, and their followers thought to be impossible.

He made the fall of terrestrial bodies depend upon the action of a vortex of very subtle matter circulating around the earth. The real improvements which the illustrious Huyghens applied to the ingenious conception of our countryman were far, however, from imparting to it clearness and precision, those characteristic attributes of truth.

Those persons form a very imperfect estimate of the meaning of one of the greatest questions which has occupied the attention of modern inquirers, who regard Newton as having issued victorious from a struggle in which his two immortal predecessors had failed. Newton did not discover the cause of gravity any more than Galileo did. Two bodies placed in juxtaposition approach each other. Newton does not inquire into the nature of the force which produces this effect. The force exists, he designates it by the term attraction; but, at the same time, he warns the reader that the term as thus used by him does not imply any definite idea of the physical process by which gravity is brought into existence and operates.

The force of attraction being once admitted as a fact, Newton studies it in all terrestrial phenomena, in the revolutions of the moon, the planets, satellites, and comets; and, as we have already stated, he deduced from this incomparable study the simple, universal, mathematical characteristics of the forces which preside over the movements of all the bodies of which our solar system is composed.

The applause of the scientific world did not prevent the immortal author of the *Principia* from hearing some persons refer the principle of gravitation to the class of occult qualities. This circumstance induced Newton and his most devoted followers to abandon the reserve which they had hitherto considered it their duty to maintain. Those persons were then charged with ignorance who regarded attraction as an essential property of matter, as the mysterious indication of a sort of charm; who supposed that two bodies may act upon each other without the intervention of a third body. This force was then either the result of the tendency of an ethereal fluid to move from the free regions of space, where its density is a maximum, towards the planetary bodies around which there exists a greater degree of rarefaction, or the consequence of the impulsive force of some fluid medium.

Newton never expressed a definitive opinion respecting the origin of the impulse which occasioned the attractive force of matter, at least in our solar system. But we have strong reasons for supposing, in the present day, that in using the word *impulse*, the great geometer was thinking of the systematic ideas of Varignon and Fatio de Duillier, subsequently reinvented and perfected by Lesage: these ideas, in effect, had been communicated to him before they were published to the world.

According to Lesage, there are, in the regions of space, bodies moving in every possible direction, and with excessive rapidity. The author applied to these the name of ultra-mundane corpuscles. Their totality constituted the gravitative fluid, if indeed, the designation of a fluid be applicable to an assemblage of particles having no mutual connexion.

A single body placed in the midst of such an ocean of

movable particles, would remain at rest although it were impelled equally in every direction. On the other hand, two bodies ought to advance towards each other, since they would serve the purpose of mutual screens, since the surfaces facing each other would no longer be hit in the direction of their line of junction by the ultra-mundane particles, since there would then exist currents, the effect of which would no longer be neutralized by opposite currents. It will be easily seen, besides, that two bodies plunged into the gravitative fluid, would tend to approach each other with an intensity which would vary in the inverse proportion of the square of the distance.

If attraction is the result of the impulse of a fluid, its action ought to employ a finite time in traversing the immense spaces which separate the celestial bodies. If the sun, then, were suddenly extinguished, the earth after the catastrophe would, mathematically speaking, still continue for some time to experience its attractive influence. The contrary would happen on the occasion of the sudden birth of a planet; a certain time would elapse before the attractive force of the new body would make itself felt on the earth.

Several geometers of the last century were of opinion that the force of attraction is not transmitted instantaneously from one body to another; they even assigned to it a comparatively inconsiderable velocity of propagation. Daniel Bernoulli, for example, in attempting to explain how the spring tide arrives upon our coasts a day and a half after the sizygees, that is to say, a day and a half after the epochs when the sun and moon are most favourably situated for the production of this magnificent phenomenon, assumed that the disturbing force required all this time (a day and a half) for its propaga-

tion from the moon to the ocean.   So feeble a velocity
was inconsistent with the mechanical explanation of attraction of which we have just spoken.   The explanation, in effect, necessarily supposes that the proper
motions of the celestial bodies are insensible compared
with the motion of the gravitative fluid.

After having discovered that the diminution of the
eccentricity of the terrestrial orbit is the real cause of
the observed acceleration of the motion of the moon,
Laplace, on his part, endeavoured to ascertain whether
this mysterious acceleration did not depend on the
gradual propagation of attraction.

The result of calculation was at first favourable to the
plausibility of the hypothesis.   It showed that the gradual
propagation of the attractive force would introduce into
the movement of our satellite a perturbation proportional
to the square of the time which elapsed from the commencement of any epoch; that in order to represent
numerically the results of astronomical observations it
would not be necessary to assign a feeble velocity to
attraction; that a propagation eight millions of times
more rapid than that of light would satisfy all the phenomena.

Although the true cause of the acceleration of the
moon is now well known, the ingenious calculation of
which I have just spoken does not the less on that account maintain its place in science.   In a mathematical
point of view, the perturbation depending on the gradual
propagation of the attractive force which this calculation
indicates has a certain existence.   The connexion between the velocity of perturbation and the resulting inequality is such that one of the two quantities leads to a
knowledge of the numerical value of the other.   Now,

upon assigning to the inequality the greatest value which is consistent with the observations after they have been corrected for the effect due to the variation of the eccentricity of the terrestrial orbit, we find the velocity of the attractive force to be fifty millions of times the velocity of light!

If it be borne in mind, that this number is an inferior limit, and that the velocity of the rays of light amounts to 77,000 leagues (192,000 English miles) per second, the philosophers who profess to explain the force of attraction by the impulsive energy of a fluid, will see what prodigious velocities they must satisfy.

The reader cannot fail again to remark the sagacity with which Laplace singled out the phenomena which were best adapted for throwing light upon the most obscure points of celestial physics; nor the success with which he explored their various parts, and deduced from them numerical conclusions in presence of which the mind remains confounded.

The author of the *Mécanique Céleste* supposed, like Newton, that light consists of material molecules of excessive tenuity and endued in empty space with a velocity of 77,000 leagues in a second. However, it is right to warn those who would be inclined to avail themselves of this imposing authority, that the principal argument of Laplace, in favour of the system of emission, consisted in the advantage which it afforded of submitting every question to a process of simple and rigorous calculation; whereas, on the other hand, the theory of undulations has always offered immense difficulties to analysts. It was natural that a geometer who had so elegantly connected the laws of simple refraction which light undergoes in its passage through the atmosphere, and the laws

of double refraction which it is subject to in the course
of its passage through certain crystals, with the action of
attractive and repulsive forces, should not have abandoned this route, before he recognized the impossibility
of arriving by the same path, at plausible explanations
of the phenomena of diffraction and polarization. In
other respects, the care which Laplace always employed
in pursuing his researches, as far as possible, to their
numerical results, will enable those who are disposed to
institute a complete comparison between the two rival
theories of light, to derive from the *Mécanique Céleste*
the materials of several interesting relations.

Is light an emanation from the sun? Does this body
launch out incessantly in every direction a part of its
own substance? Is it gradually diminishing in volume
and mass? The attraction exercised by the sun upon
the earth will, in that case, gradually become less and
less considerable. The radius of the terrestrial orbit, on
the other hand, cannot fail to increase, and a corresponding effect will be produced on the length of the year.

This is the conclusion which suggests itself to every
person upon a first glance at the subject. By applying
analysis to the question, and then proceeding to numerical computations, founded upon the most trustworthy
results of observation relative to the length of the year
in different ages, Laplace has proved that an incessant
emission of light, going on for a period of two thousand
years, has not diminished the mass of the sun by the
two-millionth part of its original value.

Our illustrious countryman never proposed to himself
any thing vague or indefinite. His constant object was
the explanation of the great phenomena of nature, according to the inflexible principles of mathematical

analysis. No philosopher, no mathematician, could have maintained himself more cautiously on his guard against a propensity to hasty speculation. No person dreaded more the scientific errors which the imagination gives birth to, when it ceases to remain within the limits of facts, of calculation, and of analogy. Once, and once only, did Laplace launch forward, like Kepler, like Descartes, like Leibnitz, like Buffon, into the region of conjectures. His conception was not then less than a cosmogony.

All the planets revolve around the sun, from west to east, and in planes which include angles of inconsiderable magnitude.

The satellites revolve around their respective primaries in the same direction as that in which the planets revolve around the sun, that is to say, from west to east.

The planets and satellites which have been found to have a rotatory motion, turn also upon their axes from west to east. Finally, the rotation of the sun is directed from west to east. We have here then an assemblage of forty-three movements, all operating in the same direction. By the calculus of probabilities, the odds are four thousand millions to one, that this coincidence in the direction of so many movements is not the effect of accident.

It was Buffon, I think, who first attempted to explain this singular feature of our solar system. Having wished, in the explanation of phenomena, to avoid all recourse to causes which were not warranted by nature, the celebrated academician investigated a physical origin of the system in what was common to the movements of so many bodies differing in magnitude, in form, and in distance from the principal centre of attraction. He imagined that he discovered such an origin by making this triple supposition: a comet fell obliquely upon the sun; it pushed before it a torrent of fluid matter; this substance transported to a greater or less distance from the sun according to its mass formed by concentration all the known planets.

The bold hypothesis of Buffon is liable to insurmountable difficulties. I proceed to indicate, in a few words, the cosmogonic system which Laplace substituted for that of the illustrious author of the *Histoire Naturelle*.

According to Laplace, the sun was at a remote epoch the central nucleus of an immense nebula, which possessed a very high temperature, and extended far beyond the region in which Uranus revolves in the present day. No planet was then in existence.

The solar nebula was endued with a general movement of revolution directed from west to east. As it cooled it could not fail to experience a gradual condensation, and, in consequence, to rotate with greater and greater rapidity. If the nebulous matter extended originally in the plane of the equator as far as the limit at which the centrifugal force exactly counterbalanced the attraction of the nucleus, the molecules situate at this limit ought, during the process of condensation, to separate from the rest of the atmospheric matter and form an equatorial zone, a ring revolving separately and with its primitive velocity. We may conceive that analogous separations were effected in the higher strata of the nebula at different epochs, that is to say, at different distances from the nucleus, and that they give rise to a succession of distinct rings, included almost in the same plane and endued with different velocities.

This being once admitted, it is easy to see that the

indefinite stability of the rings would have required a
regularity of structure throughout their whole contour,
which is very improbable. Each of them accordingly
broke in its turn into several masses, which were plainly
endued with a movement of rotation, coinciding in direction with the common movement of revolution, and
which in consequence of their fluidity assumed spheroidal forms.

In order, then, that one of those spheroids might ab-
sorb all the others belonging to the same ring, it will be
sufficient to assign to it a mass greater than that of any
other spheroid.

Each of the planets, while in the vaporous condition to
which we have just alluded, would manifestly have a central nucleus gradually increasing in magnitude and mass,
and an atmosphere offering, at its successive limits, phenomena entirely similar to those which the solar atmosphere, properly so called, had exhibited. We here
witness the birth of satellites, and that of the ring of
Saturn.

The system, of which I have just given an imperfect
sketch, has for its object to show how a nebula endued
with a general movement of rotation must eventually
transform itself into a very luminous central nucleus
(a sun) and into a series of distinct spheroidal planets,
situate at considerable distances from each other, revolving all around the central sun in the direction of the original movement of the nebula; how these planets ought
also to have movements of rotation operating in similar
directions; how, finally, the satellites, when any of such
are formed, cannot fail to revolve upon their axes and
around their respective primaries, in the direction of rotation of the planets and of their movement of revolution
around the sun.

We have just found, conformably to the principles of mechanics, the forces with which the particles of the nebula were originally endued, in the movements of rotation and revolution of the compact and distinct masses which these particles have brought into existence by their condensation. But we have thereby achieved only a single step. The primitive movement of rotation of the nebula is not connected with the simple attraction of the particles. This movement seems to imply the action of a primordial impulsive force.

Laplace is far from adopting, in this respect, the almost universal opinion of philosophers and mathematicians. He does not suppose that the mutual attractions of originally immovable bodies must ultimately reduce all the bodies to a state of rest around their common centre of gravity. He maintains, on the contrary, that three bodies, in a state of rest, two of which have a much greater mass than the third, would concentrate into a single mass only in certain exceptional cases. In general, the two most considerable bodies would unite together, while the third would revolve around their common centre of gravity. Attraction would thus become the cause of a sort of movement which would seem to be explicable solely by an impulsive force.

It might be supposed, indeed, that in explaining this part of his system Laplace had before his eyes the words which Rousseau has placed in the mouth of the vicar of Savoy, and that he wished to refute them : "Newton has discovered the law of attraction," says the author of *Emile*, "but attraction alone would soon reduce the universe to an immovable mass : with this law we must combine a projectile force in order to make the celestial bodies describe curve lines. Let Descartes reveal to us

16

the physical law which causes his vortices to revolve ; and let Newton show us the hand which launched the planets along the tangents of their orbits."

According to the cosmogonic ideas of Laplace, comets did not originally form part of the solar system ; they are not formed at the expense of the matter of the immense solar nebula ; we must consider them as small wandering nebulæ which the attractive force of the sun has caused to deviate from their original route. Such of those comets as penetrated into the great nebula at the epoch of condensation and of the formation of planets fell into the sun, describing spiral curves, and must by their action have caused the planetary orbits to deviate more or less from the plane of the solar equator, with which they would otherwise have exactly coincided.

With respect to the zodiacal light, that rock against which so many reveries have been wrecked, it consists of the most volatile parts of the primitive nebula. These molecules not having united with the equatorial zones successively abandoned in the plane of the solar equator, continued to revolve at their original distances, and with their original velocities. The circumstance of this extremely rare substance being included wholly within the earth's orbit, and even within that of Venus, seemed irreconcilable with the principles of mechanics ; but this difficulty occurred only when the zodiacal substance being conceived to be in a state of direct and intimate dependence on the solar photosphere properly so called, an angular movement of rotation was impressed on it equal to that of the photosphere, a movement in virtue of which it effected an entire revolution in twenty-five days and a half. Laplace presented his conjectures on the formation of the solar system with the diffidence inspired by a re-

sult which was not founded upon calculation and observation.* Perhaps it is to be regretted that they did not
receive a more complete development, especially in so far
as concerns the division of the matter into distinct rings ;
perhaps it would have been desirable if the illustrious
author had expressed himself more fully respecting the
primitive physical condition, the molecular condition of
the nebula at the expense of which the sun, planets, and
satellites, of our system were formed. It is perhaps
especially to be regretted that Laplace should have only
briefly alluded to what he considered the obvious possibility of movements of revolution having their origin in
the action of simple attractive forces, and to other questions of a similar nature.

Notwithstanding these defects, the ideas of the author
of the *Mécanique Céleste* are still the only speculations of
the kind which, by their magnitude, their coherence, and
their mathematical character, may be justly considered as
forming a physical cosmogony ; those alone which in the
present day derive a powerful support from the results
of the recent researches of astronomers on the nebulæ of
every form and magnitude, which are scattered throughout the celestial vault.

In this analysis, we have deemed it right to concentrate
all our attention upon the *Mécanique Céleste*. The *Système du Monde* and the *Théorie Analytique des Probabilités* would also require detailed notices.

The *Exposition du Système du Monde* is the *Mécanique
Céleste* divested of the great apparatus of analytical formulæ which ought to be attentively perused by every
astronomer who, to use an expression of Plato, is desir-

* Laplace has explained this theory in his *Exposition du Système du
Monde* (liv. iv. note vii.).—*Translator.*

ous of knowing the numbers which govern the physical universe. It is in the *Exposition du Systéme du Monde* that persons unacquainted with mathematical studies will obtain an exact and competent knowledge of the methods to which physical astronomy is indebted for its astonishing progress. This work, written with a noble simplicity of style, an exquisite propriety of expression, and a scrupulous accuracy, is terminated by a sketch of the history of astronomy, universally ranked in the present day among the finest monuments of the French language.

A regret has been often expressed, that Cæsar, in his immortal *Commentaries*, should have confined himself to a narration of his own campaigns : the astronomical commentaries of Laplace ascend to the origin of communities. The labours undertaken in all ages for the purpose of extracting new truths from the heavens, are there justly, clearly, and profoundly analyzed ; it is genius presiding as the impartial judge of genius. Laplace has always remained at the height of his great mission ; his work will be read with respect so long as the torch of science shall continue to throw any light.

The calculus of probabilities, when confined within just limits, ought to interest, in an equal degree, the mathematician, the experimentalist, and the statesman. From the time when Pascal and Fermat established its first principles, it has rendered and continues daily to render services of the most eminent kind. It is the calculus of probabilities, which, after having suggested the best arrangements of the tables of population and mortality, teaches us to deduce from those numbers, in general so erroneously interpreted, conclusions of a precise and useful character: it is the calculus of probabilities which alone can regulate justly the premiums to be paid for assurances ; the reserve funds for the disbursement of pensions, annuities, discounts, &c.: it is under its influence that lotteries, and other shameful snares cunningly laid for avarice and ignorance, have definitively disappeared. Laplace has treated these questions, and others of a much more complicated nature, with his accustomed superiority. In short, the *Théorie Analytique des Probabilités* is worthy of the author of the *Mécanique Céleste*.

A philosopher, whose name is associated with immortal discoveries, said to his audience who had allowed themselves to be influenced by ancient and consecrated authorities, " Bear in mind, Gentlemen, that in questions of science the authority of a thousand is not worth the humble reasoning of a single individual." Two centuries have passed over these words of Galileo without depreciating their value, or obliterating their truthful character. Thus, instead of displaying a long list of illustrious admirers of the three beautiful works of Laplace, we have preferred glancing briefly at some of the sublime truths which geometry has there deposited. Let us not, however, apply this principle in its utmost rigour, and since chance has put into our hands some unpublished letters of one of those men of genius, whom nature has endowed with the rare faculty of seizing at a glance the salient points of an object, we may be permitted to extract from them two or three brief and characteristic appreciations of the *Mécanique Céleste* and the *Traité des Probabilités*.

On the 27th Vendemiaire in the year X., General Bonaparte, after having received a volume of the *Mécanique Céleste*, wrote to Laplace in the following terms :—
" The first *six months* which I shall have at my disposal

will be employed in reading your beautiful work." It would appear that the words, the first *six months,* deprive the phrase of the character of a common-place expression of thanks, and convey a just appreciation of the importance and difficulty of the subject-matter.

On the 5th Frimaire in the year XI., the reading of some chapters of the volume, which Laplace had dedicated to him, was to the general "a new occasion for regretting, that the force of circumstances had directed him into a career which removed him from the pursuit of science."

"At all events," added he, "I have a strong desire that future generations, upon reading the *Mécanique Céleste,* shall not forget the esteem and friendship which I have entertained towards its author."

On the 17th Prairial in the year XIII., the general, now become emperor, wrote from Milan : " The *Mécanique Céleste* appears to me destined to shed new lustre on the age in which we live."

Finally, on the 12th of August, 1812, Napoleon, who had just received the *Traité du Calcul des Probabilités,* wrote from Witepsk the letter which we transcribe textually :—

" There was a time when I would have read with interest your *Traité du Calcul des Probabilités.* For the present I must confine myself to expressing to you the satisfaction which I experience every time that I see you give to the world new works which serve to improve and extend the most important of the sciences, and contribute to the glory of the nation. The advancement and the improvement of mathematical science are connected with the prosperity of the state."

I have now arrived at the conclusion of the task

which I had imposed upon myself.  I shall be pardoned for having given so detailed an exposition of the principal discoveries for which philosophy, astronomy, and navigation are indebted to our geometers.

It has appeared to me that in thus tracing the glorious past I have shown our contemporaries the full extent of their duty towards the country.   In fact, it is for nations especially to bear in remembrance the ancient adage : *noblesse obligé !*

# APPENDIX.

## (A.)

THE FOLLOWING IS A BRIEF NOTICE OF SOME OTHER
INTERESTING RESULTS OF THE RESEARCHES OF LA-
PLACE WHICH HAVE NOT BEEN MENTIONED IN THE
TEXT.

*Method for determining the orbits of comets.*—Since comets
are generally visible only during a few days or weeks at the
utmost, the determination of their orbits is attended with
peculiar difficulties. The method devised by Newton for
effecting this object was in every respect worthy of his
genius. Its practical value was illustrated by the brilliant
researches of Halley on cometary orbits. It necessitated,
however, a long train of tedious calculations, and, in consequence, was not much used, astronomers generally preferring
to attain the same end by a tentative process. In the year
1780, Laplace communicated to the Academy of Sciences an
analytical method for determining the elements of a comet's
orbit. This method has been extensively employed in France.
Indeed, previously to the appearance of Olber's method, about
the close of the last century, it furnished the easiest and most
expeditious process hitherto devised, for calculating the parabolic elements of a comet's orbit.

*Invariable plane of the solar system.*—In consequence of
the mutual perturbations of the different bodies of the planetary system, the planes of the orbits in which they revolve

are perpetually varying in position. It becomes therefore desirable to ascertain some fixed plane to which the movements of the planets in all ages may be referred, so that the observations of one epoch might be rendered readily comparable with those of another. This object was accomplished by Laplace, who discovered that notwithstanding the perpetual fluctuations of the planetary orbits, there exists a fixed plane, to which the positions of the various bodies may at any instant be easily referred. This plane passes through the centre of gravity of the solar system, and its position is such, that if the movements of the planets be projected upon it, and if the mass of each planet be multiplied by the area which it describes in a given time, the sum of such products will be a maximum. The position of the plane for the year 1750 has been calculated by referring it to the ecliptic of that year. In this way it has been found that the inclination of the plane is 1° 35′ 31″, and that the longitude of the ascending node is 102° 57′ 30″. The position of the plane when calculated for the year 1950, with respect to the ecliptic of 1750, gives 1° 35′ 31″ for the inclination, and 102° 57′ 15″ for the longitude of the ascending node. It will be seen that a very satisfactory accordance exists between the elements of the position of the invariable plane for the two epochs.

*Diminution of the obliquity of the ecliptic.*—The astronomers of the eighteenth century had found, by a comparison of ancient with modern observations, that the obliquity of the ecliptic is slowly diminishing from century to century. The researches of geometers on the theory of gravitation had shown that an effect of this kind must be produced by the disturbing action of the planets on the earth. Laplace determined the secular displacement of the plane of the earth's orbit due to each of the planets, and in this way ascertained the whole effect of perturbation upon the obliquity of the ecliptic. A comparison which he instituted between the results of his formula and an ancient observation recorded in the Chinese Annals exhibited a most satisfactory accordance. The observation in question indicated the obliquity of the

16 *

ecliptic for the year 1100 before the Christian era, to be 23° 54′ 2″.5. According to the principles of the theory of gravitation, the obliquity for the same epoch would be 23° 51′ 30″.

*Limits of the obliquity of the ecliptic modified by the action of the sun and moon upon the terrestrial spheroid.*—The ecliptic will not continue indefinitely to approach the equator. After attaining a certain limit it will then vary in the opposite direction, and the obliquity will continually increase in like manner as it previously diminished. Finally, the inclination of the equator and the ecliptic will attain a certain maximum value, and then the obliquity will again diminish. Thus the angle contained between the two planes will perpetually oscillate within certain limits. The extent of variation is inconsiderable. Laplace found that, in consequence of the spheroidal figure of the earth, it is even less than it would otherwise have been. This will be readily understood, when we state that the disturbing action of the sun and moon upon the terrestrial spheroid produces an oscillation of the earth's axis which occasions a periodic variation of the obliquity of the ecliptic. Now, as the plane of the ecliptic approaches the equator, the mean disturbing action of the sun and moon upon the redundant matter accumulated around the latter will undergo a corresponding variation, and hence will arise an inconceivably slow movement of the plane of the equator, which will necessarily affect the obliquity of the ecliptic. Laplace found that if it were not for this cause, the obliquity of the ecliptic would oscillate to the extent of 4° 53′ 33″ on each side of a mean value, but that when the movements of both planes are taken into account, the extent of oscillation is reduced to 1° 33′ 45″.

*Variation of the length of the tropical year.*—The disturbing action of the sun and moon upon the terrestrial spheroid occasions a continual *regression* of the equinoctial points, and hence arises the distinction between the sidereal and tropical year. The effect is modified in a small degree by the variation of the plane of the ecliptic, which tends to produce a *progression* of the equinoxes. If the movement of the equinoctial points arising from these combined causes was uniform, the length of the tropical year would be manifestly invariable. Theory, however, indicates that for ages past the rate of regression has been slowly increasing, and, consequently, the length of the tropical year has been gradually diminishing. The rate of diminution is exceedingly small. Laplace found that it amounts to somewhat less than half a second in a century. Consequently, the length of the tropical year is now about ten seconds less than it was in the time of Hipparchus.

*Limits of variation of the tropical year modified by the disturbing action of the sun and moon upon the terrestrial spheroid.*—The tropical year will not continue indefinitely to diminish in length. When it has once attained a certain minimum value, it will then increase until finally having attained an extreme value in the opposite direction, it will again begin to diminish, and thus it will perpetually oscillate between certain fixed limits. Laplace found that the extent to which the tropical year is liable to vary from this cause, amounts to thirty-eight seconds. If it were not for the effect produced upon the inclination of the equator to the ecliptic by the mean disturbing action of the sun and moon upon the terrestrial spheroid, the extent of variation would amount to 162 seconds.

*Motion of the perihelion of the terrestrial orbit.*—The major axis of the orbit of each planet is in a state of continual movement from the disturbing action of the other planets. In some cases, it makes the complete tour of the heavens; in others, it merely oscillates around a mean position. In the case of the earth's orbit, the perihelion is slowly advancing in the same direction as that in which all the planets are revolving around the sun. The alteration of its position with respect to the stars amounts to about 11″ in a year, but since the equinox is regressing in the opposite direction at the rate of 50″ in a year, the whole annual variation of the longitude of the terrestrial perihelion amounts to 61″. Laplace has considered two remarkable epochs in connection with this fact; viz : the epoch at which the major axis of the earth's orbit coincided with the line of the equinoxes, and the epoch at which it stood perpendicular to that line. By calculation, he found the former of these epochs to be referable to the year 4107, B.C., and the latter to the year 1245, A.D. He accordingly suggested that the latter should be used as a universal epoch for the regulation of chronological occurrences.

## (B.)

The *Mécanique Céleste*.—This stupendous monument of intellectual research consists, as stated by the author, of five quarto volumes. The subject-matter is divided into sixteen books, and each book again is subdivided into several chapters. Vol. I. contains the first and second books of the work; Vol. II. contains the third, fourth, and fifth books; Vol. III. contains the sixth and seventh books; Vol. IV. contains the eighth, ninth, and tenth books; and, finally, Vol. V. contains the remaining six books. In the first book the author treats of the general laws of equilibrium and motion. In the second book he treats of the law of gravitation, and the movements of the centres of gravity of the celestial bodies. In the third book he investigates the subject of the figures of the celestial bodies. In the fourth book he considers the oscillations of the ocean and the atmosphere, arising from the disturbing action of the celestial bodies. The fifth book is devoted to the investigation of the movements of the celestial bodies around their centres of gravity. In this book the author gives a solution of the great problems of the precession of the equinoxes and the libration of the moon, and determines the conditions upon which the stability of Saturn's ring depends. The sixth book is devoted to the theory of the planetary movements; the seventh, to the lunar theory; the eighth, to the theory of the satellites of Jupiter, Saturn, and Uranus; and the ninth, to the theory of comets. In the tenth book the author investigates various subjects relating to the system of the universe. Among these may be mentioned the theory of astronomical refractions; the determination of heights by the barometer; the investigation of the effects produced on the movements of the planets and comets by a resisting medium; and the determination of the values of the masses of the planets and satellites. In the six books forming the fifth volume of the work, the author, besides presenting his readers with an historical exposition of the labours of Newton and his successors on the theory of gravitation, gives an account of various researches relative to the system of the universe, which had occupied his attention subsequently to the publication of the previous volumes. In the eleventh book he considers the subjects of the figure and rotation of the earth. In the twelfth book he investigates the attraction and repulsion of spheres, and the laws of equilibrium and motion of elastic fluids. The thirteenth book is devoted to researches on the oscillations of the fluids which cover the surfaces of the planets; the fourteenth, to the subject of the movements of the celestial bodies around their centres of gravity; the fifteenth, to the movements of the planets and comets; and the sixteenth, to the movements of the satellites. The author published a supplement to the third volume, containing the results of certain researches on the planetary theory, and a supplement to the tenth book, in which he investigates very fully the theory of capillary attraction. There was also published a posthumous supplement to the fifth volume, the manuscript of which was found among his papers after his death.

# JOSEPH FOURIER.

BIOGRAPHY READ AT A PUBLIC ASSEMBLY OF THE ACADEMY OF
SCIENCES, ON THE 18TH OF NOVEMBER, 1833.

Gentlemen,—In former times one academician differed from another only in the number, the nature, and the brilliancy of his discoveries. Their lives, thrown in some respects into the same mould, consisted of events little worthy of remark. A boyhood more or less studious; progress sometimes slow, sometimes rapid; inclinations thwarted by capricious or shortsighted parents; inadequacy of means, the privations which it introduces in its train; thirty years of a laborious professorship and difficult studies,—such were the elements from which the admirable talents of the early secretaries of the Academy were enabled to execute those portraits, so piquant, so lively, and so varied, which form one of the principal ornaments of your learned collections.

In the present day, biographies are less confined in their object. The convulsions which France has experienced in emancipating herself from the swaddling-clothes of routine, of superstition and of privilege, have cast into the storms of political life citizens of all ages, of all conditions, and of all characters. Thus has the Academy of Sciences figured during forty years in the

devouring arena, wherein might and right have alternately seized the supreme power by a glorious sacrifice
of combatants and victims !

Recall to mind, for example, the immortal National
Assembly. You will find at its head a modest academician, a patern of all the private virtues, the unfortunate
Bailly, who, in the different phases of his political life,
knew how to reconcile a passionate affection for his
country with a moderation which his most cruel enemies
themselves have been compelled to admire.

When, at a later period, coalesced Europe launched
against France a million of soldiers; when it became
necessary to organize for the crisis fourteen armies, it
was the ingenious author of the *Essai sur les Machines*
and of the *Géométrie des Positions* who directed this
gigantic operation. It was, again, Carnot, our honourable colleague, who presided over the incomparable campaign of seventeen months, during which French troops,
novices in the profession of arms, gained eight pitched
battles, were victorious in one hundred and forty com-
bats, occupied one hundred and sixteen fortified places
and two hundred and thirty forts or redoubts, enriched
our arsenals with four thousand cannon and seventy
thousand muskets, took a hundred thousand prisoners,
and adorned the dome of the Invalides with ninety flags.
During the same time the Chaptals, the Fourcroys, the
Monges, the Berthollets rushed also to the defence of
French independence, some of them extracting from our
soil, by .prodigies of industry, the very last atoms of salt-
petre which it contained; others transforming, by the
aid of new and rapid methods, the bells of the towns,
villages, and smallest hamlets into a formidable artillery,
which our enemies supposed, as indeed they had a right

to suppose, we were deprived of. At the voice of his country in danger, another academician, the young and learned Meunier, readily renounced the seductive pursuits of the laboratory; he went to distinguish himself upon the ramparts of Königstein, to contribute as a hero to the long defence of Mayence, and met his death, at the age of forty years only, after having attained the highest position in a garrison wherein shone the Aubert-Dubayets, the Beaupuys, the Haxos, the Klebers.

How could I forget here the last secretary of the original Academy? Follow him into a celebrated Assembly, into that Convention, the sanguinary delirium of which we might almost be inclined to pardon, when we call to mind how gloriously terrible it was to the enemies of our independence, and you will always see the illustrious Condorcet occupied exclusively with the great interests of reason and humanity. You will hear him denounce the shameful brigandage which for two centuries laid waste the African continent by a system of corruption; demand in a tone of profound conviction that the Code be purified of the frightful stain of capital punishment, which renders the error of the judge for ever irreparable. He is the official organ of the Assembly on every occasion when it is necessary to address soldiers, citizens, political parties, or foreign nations in language worthy of France; he is not the tactician of any party, he incessantly entreats all of them to occupy their attention less with their own interests and a little more with public matters; he replies, finally, to unjust reproaches of weakness by acts which leave him the only alternative of the poison cup or the scaffold.

The French Revolution thus threw the learned geometer, whose discoveries I am about to celebrate, far away from the route which destiny appeared to have traced out for him.  In ordinary times it would be about Dom* Joseph Fourier that the secretary of the Academy would have deemed it his duty to have occupied your attention.  It would be the tranquil, the retired life of a Benedictine which he would have unfolded to you.  The life of our colleague, on the contrary, will be agitated and full of perils ; it will pass into the fierce contentions of the forum and amid the hazards of war; it will be a prey to all the anxieties which accompany a difficult administration.  We shall find this life intimately associated with the great events of our age.  Let us hasten to add, that it will be always worthy and honourable, and that the personal qualities of the man of science will enhance the brilliancy of his discoveries.

## BIRTH OF FOURIER.—HIS YOUTH.

Fourier was born at Auxerre on the 21st of March, 1768.  His father, like that of the illustrious geometer Lambert, was a tailor.  This circumstance would formerly have occupied a large place in the *éloge* of our learned colleague; thanks to the progress of enlightened ideas, I may mention the circumstance as a fact of no importance: nobody, in effect, thinks in the present day, nobody even pretends to think, that genius is the privilege of rank or fortune.

Fourier became an orphan at the age of eight years. A lady who had remarked the amiability of his manners and his precocious natural abilities, recommended him to the Bishop of Auxerre.  Through the influence of this prelate, Fourier was admitted into the military school

---

* An abbreviation of Dominus, equivalent to the English prefix Reverend.— *Translator.*

which was conducted at that time by the Benedictines of the Convent of St. Mark. There he prosecuted his literary studies with surprising rapidity and success. Many sermons very much applauded at Paris in the mouth of high dignitaries of the Church were emanations from the pen of the schoolboy of twelve years of age. It would be impossible in the present day to trace those first compositions of the youth Fourier, since, while divulging the plagiarism, he had the discretion never to name those who profited by it.

At thirteen years Fourier had the petulance, the noisy vivacity of most young people of the same age ; but his character changed all at once, and as if by enchantment, as soon as he was initiated in the first principles of mathematics, that is to say, as soon as he became sensible of his real vocation. The hours prescribed for study no longer sufficed to gratify his insatiable curiosity. Ends of candles carefully collected in the kitchen, the corridors and the refectory of the college, and placed on a hearth concealed by a screen, served during the night to illuminate the solitary studies by which Fourier prepared himself for those labours which were destined, a few years afterwards, to adorn his name and his country.

In a military school directed by monks, the minds of the pupils necessarily waver only between two careers in life—the church and the sword. Like Descartes, Fourier wished to be a soldier ; like that philosopher, he would doubtless have found the life of a garrison very wearisome. But he was not permitted to make the experiment. His demand to undergo the examination for the artillery, although strongly supported by our illustrious colleague Legendre, was rejected with a severity of expression of which you may judge yourselves: " Fourier," replied the minister, " not being noble, could not enter the artillery, although he were a second Newton."

Gentlemen, there is in the strict enforcement of regulations, even when they are most absurd, something respectable which I have a pleasure in recognizing; in the present instance nothing could soften the odious character of the minister's words. It is not true in reality that no one could formerly enter into the artillery who did not possess a title of nobility; a certain fortune frequently supplied the want of parchments. Thus it was not a something undefinable, which, by the way, our ancestors the Franks had not yet invented, that was wanting to young Fourier, but rather an income of a few hundred livres, which the men who were then placed at the head of the country would have refused to acknowledge the genius of Newton as a just equivalent for! Treasure up these facts, Gentlemen; they form an admirable illustration of the immense advances which France has made during the last forty years. Posterity, moreover, will see in this, not the excuse, but the explanation of some of those sanguinary dissensions which stained our first revolution.

Fourier not having been enabled to gird on the sword, assumed the habit of a Benedictine, and repaired to the Abbey of St. Benoît-sur-Loire, where he intended to pass the period of his noviciate. He had not yet taken any vows when, in 1789, every mind was captivated with beautifully seductive ideas relative to the social regeneration of France. Fourier now renounced the profession of the Church; but this circumstance did not prevent his former masters from appointing him to the principal chair of mathematics in the Military School of

Auxerre, and bestowing upon him numerous tokens of a lively and sincere affection. I venture to assert that no event in the life of our colleague affords a more striking proof of the goodness of his natural disposition and the amiability of his manners. It would be necessary not to know the human heart to suppose that the monks of St. Benoît did not feel some chagrin upon finding themselves so abruptly abandoned, to imagine especially that they should give up without lively regret the glory which the order might have expected from the ingenious colleague who had just escaped from them.

Fourier responded worthily to the confidence of which he had just become the object. When his colleagues were indisposed, the titular professor of mathematics occupied in turns the chairs of rhetoric, of history, and of philosophy; and whatever might be the subject of his lectures, he diffused among an audience which listened to him with delight, the treasures of a varied and profound erudition, adorned with all the brilliancy which the most elegant diction could impart to them.

## MEMOIR ON THE RESOLUTION OF NUMERICAL EQUATIONS.

About the close of the year 1789 Fourier repaired to Paris and read before the Academy of Sciences a memoir on the resolution of numerical equations of all degrees. This work of his early youth our colleague, so to speak, never lost sight of. He explained it at Paris to the pupils of the Polytechnic School; he developed it upon the banks of the Nile in presence of the Institute of Egypt; at Grenoble, from the year 1802, it was his favourite subject of conversation with the Professors of the Central School and of the Faculty of Sciences; this finally, contained the elements of the work which Fourier was engaged in seeing through the press when death put an end to his career.

A scientific subject does not occupy so much space in the life of a man of science of the first rank without being important and difficult. The subject of algebraic analysis above mentioned, which Fourier had studied with a perseverance so remarkable, is not an exception to this rule. It offers itself in a great number of applications of calculation to the movements of the heavenly bodies, or to the physics of terrestrial bodies, and in general in the problems which lead to equations of a high degree. As soon as he wishes to quit the domain of abstract relations, the calculator has occasion to employ the roots of these equations; thus the art of discovering them by the aid of an uniform method, either exactly or by approximation, did not fail at an early period to excite the attention of geometers.

An observant eye perceives already some traces of their efforts in the writings of the mathematicians of the Alexandrian School. These traces, it must be *acknowledged*, are so slight and so imperfect, that we should truly be justified in referring the origin of this branch of analysis only to the excellent labours of our countryman Vieta. Descartes, to whom we render very imperfect justice when we content ourselves with saying that he taught us much when he taught us to doubt, occupied his attention also for a short time with this problem, and left upon it the indelible impress of his powerful mind. Hudde gave for a particular but very important case rules to which nothing has since been added; Rolle, of the Academy of Sciences, devoted to this one subject his entire life. Among our neighbours on the other side of the channel, Harriot, Newton, Maclaurin, Stirling, Waring, I may say all the illustrious geometers which England produced in the last century, made it also the subject of their researches. Some years afterwards the names of Daniel Barnoulli, of Euler, and of Fontaine came to be added to so many great names. Finally, Lagrange in his turn embarked in the same career, and at the very commencement of his researches he succeeded in substituting for the imperfect, although very ingenious, essays of his predecessors, a complete method which was free from every objection. From that instant the dignity of science was satisfied; but in such a case it would not be permitted to say with the poet:

" Le temps ne fait rien à l'affaire."

Now although the processes invented by Lagrange, simple in principle and applicable to every case, have theoretically the merit of leading to the result with certainty, still, on the other hand, they demand calculations of a most repulsive length. It remained then to perfect the practical part of the question; it was necessary to devise the means of shortening the route without depriving it in any degree of its certainty. Such was the principal object of the researches of Fourier, and this he has attained to a great extent.

Descartes had already found, in the order according to which the signs of the different terms of any numerical equation whatever succeed each other, the means of deciding, for example, how many real positive roots this equation may have. Fourier advanced a step further; he disćovered a method for determining what number of the equally positive roots of every equation may be found included between two given quantities. Here certain calculations become necessary, but they are very simple, and whatever be the precision desired, they lead without any trouble to the solutions sought for.

I doubt whether it were possible to cite a single scientific discovery of any importance which has not excited discussions of priority. The new method of Fourier for solving numerical equations is in this respect amply comprised within the common law. We ought, however, to acknowledge that the theorem which serves as the basis of this method, was first published by M. Budan ; that according to a rule which the principal Academies of Europe have solemnly sanctioned, and from which the historian of the sciences dares not deviate without falling into arbitrary assumptions and confusion, M. Budan ought to be considered as the inventor. I will assert with equal assurance that it would be impossible to refuse to Fourier the merit of having attained the same object by his own efforts. I even regret that, in order to establish rights which nobody has contested, he deemed it necessary to have recourse to the certificates of early pupils of the Polytechnic School, or Professors of the University. Since our colleague had the modesty to suppose that his simple declaration would not be sufficient, why (and the argument would have had much weight) did he not remark in what respect his demonstration differed from that of his competitor ?—an admirable demonstration, in effect, and one so impregnated with the elements of the question, that a young geometer, M. Sturm, has just employed it to establish the truth of the beautiful theorem by the aid of which he determines not the simple limits, but the exact number of roots of any equation whatever which are comprised between two given quantities.

PART PLAYED BY FOURIER IN OUR REVOLUTION.—
HIS ENTRANCE INTO THE CORPS OF PROFESSORS
OF THE NORMAL SCHOOL AND THE POLYTECHNIC
SCHOOL.—EXPEDITION TO EGYPT.

We had just left Fourier at Paris, submitting to the
Academy of Sciences the analytical memoir of which I
have just given a general view.   Upon his return to
Auxerre, the young geometer found the town, the surrounding country, and even the school to which he belonged, occupied intensely with the great questions relative to the dignity of human nature, philosophy, and
politics, which were then discussed by the orators of the
different parties of the National Assembly.   Fourier
abandoned himself also to this movement of the human
mind.   He embraced with enthusiasm the principles of
the Revolution, and he ardently associated himself with
every thing grand, just, and generous which the popular
impulse offered.   His patriotism made him accept the
most difficult missions.   We may assert, that never, even
when his life was at stake, did he truckle to the base,
covetous, and sanguinary passions which displayed themselves on all sides.

A member of the popular society of Auxerre, Fourier
exercised there an almost irresistible ascendency.   One
day—all Burgundy has preserved the remembrance of
it—on the occasion of a levy of three hundred thousand
men, he made the words honour, country, glory, ring so
eloquently, he induced so many voluntary enrolments,
that the ballot was not deemed necessary.   At the command of the orator the contingent assigned to the chief
town of the Yonne formed in order, assembled together
within the very enclosure of the Assembly, and marched

forthwith to the frontier. Unfortunately these struggles of the forum, in which so many noble lives then exercised themselves, were far from having always a real importance. Ridiculous, absurd, and burlesque motions injured incessantly the inspirations of a pure, sincere, and enlightened patriotism. The popular society of Auxerre would furnish us, in case of necessity, with more than one example of those lamentable contrasts. Thus I might say that in the very same apartment wherein Fourier knew how to excite the honourable sentiments which I have with pleasure recalled to mind, he had on another occasion to contend with a certain orator, perhaps of good intentions, but assuredly a bad astronomer, who, wishing to escape, said he, from *the good pleasure* of municipal rulers, proposed that the names of the north, east, south, and west quarters should be assigned by lot to the different parts of the town of Auxerre.

Literature, the fine arts, and the sciences appeared for a moment to flourish under the auspicious influence of the French Revolution. Observe, for example, with what grandeur of conception the reformation of weights and measures was planned ; what geometers, what astronomers, what eminent philosophers presided over every department of this noble undertaking ! Alas ! frightful revolutions in the interior of the country soon saddened this magnificent spectacle. The sciences could not prosper in the midst of the desperate contest of factions. They would have blushed to owe any obligations to the men of blood, whose blind passions immolated a Saron, a Bailly, and a Lavoisière.

A few months after the 9th Thermidor, the Convention being desirous of diffusing throughout the country

17

ideas of order, civilization, and internal prosperity, resolved upon organizing a system of public instruction,
but a difficulty arose in finding professors. The members of the corps of instruction had become officers of
artillery, of engineering, or of the staff, and were com-
bating the enemies of France at the frontiers. Fortunately at this epoch of intellectual exaltation, nothing
seemed impossible. Professors were wanting; it was
resolved without delay to create some, and the Normal
School sprung into existence. Fifteen hundred citizens
of all ages, despatched from the principal district towns,
assembled together, not to study in all their ramifications
the different branches of human knowledge, but in order
to learn the art of teaching under the greatest masters.

Fourier was one of these fifteen hundred pupils. It
will, no doubt, excite some surprise that he was elected
at St. Florentine, and that Auxerre appeared insensible
to the honour of being represented at Paris by the most
illustrious of her children. But this indifference will be
readily understood. The elaborate scaffolding of calumny
which it has served to support will fall to the ground as
soon as I recall to mind, that after the 9th Thermidor
the capital, and especially the provinces, became a prey
to a blind and disorderly reaction, as all political reactions
invariably are; that crime (the crime of having changed
opinions—it was nothing less hideous) usurped the place
of justice; that excellent citizens, that pure, moderate,
and conscientious patriots were daily massacred by hired
bands of assassins in presence of whom the inhabitants
remained mute with fear. Such are, Gentlemen, the
formidable influences which for a moment deprived
Fourier of the suffrages of his countrymen; and carica-
tured, as a partisan of Robespierre, the individual whom

St. Just, making allusion to his sweet and persuasive eloquence, styled a *patriot in music;* who was so often thrown into prison by the decemvirs; who, at the very height of the Reign of Terror, offered before the Revolutionary Tribunal the assistance of his admirable talents to the mother of Marshal Davoust, accused of the crime of having at that unrelenting epoch sent some money to the emigrants; who had the incredible boldness to shut up at the inn of Tonnerre an agent of the Committee of Public Safety, into the secret of whose mission he penetrated, and thus obtained time to warn an honourable citizen that he was about to be arrested; who, finally, attaching himself personally to the sanguinary proconsul before whom every one trembled in Yonne, made him pass for a madman, and obtained his recall! You see, Gentlemen, some of the acts of patriotism, of devotion, and of humanity which signalized the early years of Fourier. They were, you have seen, repaid with ingratitude. But ought we in reality to be astonished at it? To expect gratitude from the man who cannot make an avowal of his feelings without danger, would be to shut one's eyes to the frailty of human nature, and to expose one's self to frequent disappointments.

In the Normal School of the Convention, discussion from time to time succeeded ordinary lectures. On those days an interchange of characters was effected; the pupils interrogated the professors. Some words pronounced by Fourier at one of those curious and useful meetings sufficed to attract attention towards him. Accordingly, as soon as a necessity was felt to create Masters of Conference, all eyes were turned towards the pupil of St. Florentine. The precision, the clearness, and the elegance of his lectures soon procured for him the unanimous applause of the fastidious and numerous audience which was confided to him.

When he attained the height of his scientific and lite-rary glory, Fourier used to look back with pleasure upon the year 1794, and upon the sublime efforts which the French nation then made for the purpose of organiz-ing a Corps of Public Instruction. If he had ventured, the title of Pupil of the original Normal School would have been beyond doubt that which he would have assumed by way of preference. Gentlemen, that school perished of cold, of wretchedness, and of hunger, and not, whatever people may say, from certain defects of organization which time and reflection would have easily rectified. Notwithstanding its short existence, it im-parted to scientific studies quite a new direction which has been productive of the most important results. In supporting this opinion at some length, I shall acquit myself of a task which Fourier would certainly have imposed upon me, if he could have suspected, that with just and eloquent eulogiums of his character and his labours there should mingle within the walls of this apartment, and even emanate from the mouth of one of his successors, sharp critiques of his beloved Normal School.

It is to the Normal School that we must inevitably ascend if we would desire to ascertain the earliest public teaching of *descriptive Geometry*, that fine creation of the genius of Monge. It is from this source that it has passed almost without modification to the Polytechnic School, to foundries, to manufactories, and the most hum-ble workshops.

The establishment of the Normal School accordingly

indicates the commencement of a veritable revolution in
the study of pure mathematics; with it demonstrations,
methods, and important theories, buried in academical
collections, appeared for the first time before the pupils,
and encouraged them to recast upon new bases the works
destined for instruction.

With some rare exeeptions, the philosophers engaged
in the cultivation of science constituted formerly in
France a class totally distinct from that of the professors.
By appointing the first geometers, the first philosophers,
and the first naturalists of the world to be professors,
the Convention threw new lustre upon the profession of
teaching, the advantageous influence of which is felt in
the present day.   In the opinion of the public at large
a title which a Lagrange, a Laplace, a Monge, a Berthollet, had borne, became a proper match to the finest
titles.   If under the empire, the Polytechnic School
counted among its active professors councillors of state,
ministers, and the president of the senate, you must look
for the explanation of this fact in the impulse given by
the Normal School.

You see in the ancient great colleges, professors concealed in some degree behind their portfolios, reading as
from a pulpit, amid the indifference and inattention of
their pupils, discourses prepared beforehand with great
labour, and which reappear every year in the same form.
Nothing of this kind existed at the Normal School; oral
lessons alone were there permitted.   The authorities
even went so far as to require of the illustrious savans
appointed to the task of instruction the formal promise
never to recite any lectures which they might have
learned by heart.   From that time the chair has become
a tribune where the professor, identified, so to speak,

with his audience, sees in their looks, in their gestures, in their countenance, sometimes the necessity for proceeding at greater speed, sometimes, on the contrary, the necessity of retracing his steps, of awakening the attention by some incidental observations, of clothing in a new form the thought which, when first expressed, had left some doubts in the minds of his audience. And do not suppose that the beautiful impromptu lectures with which the amphitheatre of the Normal School resounded, remained unknown to the public. Short-hand writers paid by the State reported them. The sheets, after being revised by the professors, were sent to the fifteen hundred pupils, to the members of Convention, to the consuls and agents of the Republic in foreign countries, to all governors of districts. There was in this something certainly of profusion compared with the parsimonious and mean habits of our time. Nobody, however, would concur in this reproach, however slight it may appear, if I were permitted to point out in this very apartment an illustrious Academician, whose mathematical genius was awakened by the lectures of the Normal School in an obscure district town!

The necessity of demonstrating the important services, ignored in the present day, for which the dissemination of the sciences is indebted to the first Normal School, has induced me to dwell at greater length on the subject than I intended. I hope to be pardoned; the example in any case will not be contagious. Eulogiums of the past, you know, Gentlemen, are no longer fashionable. Every thing which is said, every thing which is printed, induces us to suppose that the world is the creation of yesterday. This opinion, which allows to each a part more or less brilliant in the cosmogonic drama, is under the safeguard of too many vanities to have any thing to fear from the efforts of logic.

I have already stated that the brilliant success of Fourier at the Normal School assigned to him a distinguished place among the persons whom nature has endowed in the highest degree with the talent of public tuition. Accordingly, he was not forgotten by the founders of the Polytechnic School. Attached to that celebrated establishment, first with the title of Superintendent of Lectures on Fortification, afterwards appointed to deliver a course of lectures on Analysis, Fourier has left there a venerated name, and the reputation of a professor distinguished by clearness, method, and erudition; I shall add even the reputation of a professor full of grace, for our colleague has proved that this kind of merit may not be foreign to the teaching of mathematics.

The lectures of Fourier have not been collected together. The Journal of the Polytechnic School contains only one paper by him, a memoir upon the "principle of virtual velocities." This memoir, which probably had served for the text of a lecture, shows that the secret of our celebrated professor's great success consisted in the combination of abstract truths, of interesting applications, and of historical details little known, and derived, a thing so rare in our days, from original sources.

We have now arrived at the epoch when the peace of Leoben brought back to the metropolis the principal ornaments of our armies. Then the professors and the pupils of the Polytechnic School had sometimes the distinguished honour of sitting in their amphitheatres beside Generals Desaix and Bonaparte. Every thing indicated to them then an active participation in the events which each foresaw, and which in fact were not long of occurring.

Notwithstanding the precarious condition of Europe, the Directory decided upon denuding the country of its best troops, and launching them upon an adventurous expedition. The five chiefs of the Republic were then desirous of removing from Paris the conqueror of Italy, of thereby putting an end to the popular demonstrations of which he everywhere formed the object, and which sooner or later would become a real danger.

On the other hand, the illustrious general did not dream merely of the momentary conquest of Egypt; he wished to restore to that country its ancient splendour; he wished to extend its cultivation, to improve its system of irrigation, to create new branches of industry, to open to commerce numerous outlets, to stretch out a helping hand to the unfortunate inhabitants, to rescue them from the galling yoke under which they had groaned for ages, in a word, to bestow upon them without delay all the benefits of European civilization. Designs of such magnitude could not have been accomplished with the mere *personnel* of an ordinary army. It was necessary to appeal to science, to literature, and to the fine arts; it was necessary to ask the coöperation of several men of judgment and of experience. Monge and Berthollet, both members of the Institute and Professors in the Polytechnic School, became, with a view to this object, the principal recruiting aids to the chief of the expedition. Were our colleagues really acquainted with the object of this expedition? I dare not reply in the affirmative; but I know at all events that they were not permitted to divulge it. We are going to a distant country; we shall embark at Toulon; we shall be constantly with you; General Bonaparte will command the army, such was in form and substance the limited amount of confidential information which had been imperiously traced out to them.  Upon the faith of words so vague, with the chances of a naval battle, with the English hulks in perspective, go in the present day and endeavour to enroll a father of a family, a savant already known by useful labours and placed in some honourable position, an artist in possession of the esteem and confidence of the public, and I am much mistaken if you obtain any thing else than refusals; but in 1798, France had hardly emerged from a terrible crisis, during which her very existence was frequently at stake.  Who, besides, had not encountered imminent personal danger?  Who had not seen with his own eyes enterprises of a truly desperate nature brought to a fortunate issue?  Is any thing more wanted to explain that adventurous character, that absence of all care for the morrow, which appears to have been one of the most distinguishing features of the epoch of the Directory.  Fourier accepted then without hesitation the proposals which his colleagues brought to him in the name of the Commander-in-Chief; he quitted the agreeable duties of a professor of the Polytechnic School, to go— he knew not where, to do—he knew not what.

Chance placed Fourier during the voyage in the vessel in which Kléber sailed.  The friendship which the philosopher and the warrior vowed to each other from that moment was not without some influence upon the events of which Egypt was the theatre after the departure of Napoleon.

He who signed his orders of the day, the *Member of the Institute, Commander-in-Chief of the Army in the East*, could not fail to place an Academy among the means of regenerating the ancient kingdom of the Pharaohs.  The valiant army which he commanded had barely

17 *

conquered at Cairo, on the occasion of the memorable
battle of the Pyramids, when the Institute of Egypt
sprung into existence.  It consisted of forty-eight members, divided into four sections.  Monge had the honour
of being the first president.  As at Paris, Bonaparte
belonged to the section of Mathematics.  The situation
of perpetual secretary, the filling up of which was left to
the free choice of the Society, was unanimously assigned
to Fourier.

You have seen the celebrated geometer discharge the
same duty at the Academy of Sciences ; you have appreciated his liberality of mind, his enlightened benevolence,
his unvarying affability, his straightforward and concili-
atory disposition : add in imagination to so many rare
qualities the activity which youth, which health can alone
give, and you will have again conjured into existence the
Secretary of the Institute of Egypt; and yet the portrait
which I have attempted to draw of him would grow pale
beside the original.

Upon the banks of the Nile, Fourier devoted himself
to assiduous researches on almost every branch of knowledge which the vast plan of the Institute embraced.  The
*Decade* and the *Courier of Egypt* will acquaint the reader
with the titles of his different labours.  I find in these
journals a memoir upon the general solution of algebraic
equations ; researches on the methods of elimination ; the
demonstration of a new theorem of algebra ; a memoir
upon the indeterminate analysis ; studies on general
mechanics ; a technical and historical work upon the
aqueduct which conveys the waters of the Nile to the
Castle of Cairo ; reflections upon the Oases ; the plan
of statistical researches to be undertaken with respect to
the state of Egypt ; programme of an intended explora-

tion of the site of the ancient Memphis, and of the whole extent of burying-places ; a descriptive account of the revolutions and manners of Egypt, from the time of its conquest by Selim.

I find also in the Egyptian *Decade*, that, on the first complementary day of the year VI., Fourier communicated to the Institute the description of a machine designed to promote irrigation, and which was to be driven by the power of wind.

This work, so far removed from the ordinary current of the ideas of our colleague, has not been printed. It would very naturally find a place in a work of which the Expedition to Egypt might again furnish the subject, notwithstanding the many beautiful publications which it has already called into existence. It would be a description of the manufactories of steel, of arms, of powder, of cloth, of machines, and of instruments of every kind which our army had to prepare for the occasion. If, during our infancy, the expedients which Robinson Crusoe practised in order to escape from the romantic dangers which he had incessantly to encounter, excite our interest in a lively degree, how, in mature age, could we regard with indifference a handful of Frenchmen thrown upon the inhospitable shores of Africa, without any possible communication with the mother country, obliged to contend at once with the elements and with formidable armies, destitute of food, of clothing, of arms, and of ammunition, and yet supplying every want by the force of genius !

The long route which I have yet to traverse, will hardly allow me to add a few words relative to the administrative services of the illustrious geometer. Appointed French Commissioner at the Divan of Cairo, he became the official medium between the General-in-Chief and every Egyptian who might have to complain of an attack against his person, his property, his morals, his habits, or his creed.   An invariable sauvity of manner, a scrupulous regard for prejudices to oppose which directly would have been vain, an inflexible sentiment of justice, had given him an ascendency over the Mussulman population, which the precepts of the Koran could not lead any one to hope for, and which powerfully contributed to the maintenance of friendly relations between the inhabitants of Cairo and the French soldiers.   Fourier was especially held in veneration by the Cheiks and the Ulémas.   A single anecdote will serve to show that this sentiment was the offspring of genuine gratitude.

The Emir Hadgey, or Prince of the Caravan, who had been nominated by General Bonaparte upon his arrival in Cairo, escaped during the campaign of Syria. There existed strong grounds at the time for supposing that four *Cheiks Ulémas* had rendered themselves accomplices of the treason..   Upon his return to Egypt, Bonaparte confided the investigation of this grave affair to Fourier.   "Do not," said he, "submit half measures to me. You have to pronounce judgment upon high personages : we must either cut off their heads or invite them to dinner."   On the day following that on which this conversation took place, the four Cheiks dined with the General-in-Chief.   By obeying the inspirations of his heart, Fourier did not perform merely an act of humanity ; it was moreover one of excellent policy.   Our learned colleague, M. Geoffroy Saint-Hilaire, to whom I am indebted for this anecdote, has stated in fact that Soleyman and Fayoumi, the principal of the Egyptian chiefs, whose punishment, thanks to our colleague, was so happily

transformed into a banquet, seized every occasion of ex-
tolling among their countrymen the generosity of the
French.

Fourier did not display less ability when our generals confided diplomatic missions to him.   It is to his
tact and urbanity that our army is indebted for an offen-
sive and defensive treaty of alliance with Mourad Bey.
Justly proud of this result, Fourier omitted to make
known the details of the negotiation.   This is deeply to
be regretted, for the plenipotentiary of Mourad was a
woman, the same Sitty Nefiçah whom Kléber has immortalized by proclaiming her *beneficence, her noble character*, in the bulletin of Heliopolis, and who moreover was
already celebrated from one extremity of Asia to the
other, in consequence of the bloody revolutions which
her unparalleled beauty had excited among the Mamelukes.

The incomparable victory which Kléber gained over
the army of the Grand Vizier did not damp the energy
of the Janissaries, who had seized upon Cairo while the
war was raging at Heliopolis.   They defended themselves from house to house with heroic courage.   The
besieged had to choose between the entire destruction
of the city and an honourable capitulation.   The latter
alternative was adopted.   Fourier, charged, as usual,
with the negotiations, conducted them to a favourable
issue ; but on this occasion the treaty was not discussed,
agreed to, and signed within the mysterious precincts of
a harem, upon downy couches, under the shade of balmy
groves.   The preliminary discussions were held in a
house half ruined by bullets and grape-shot ; in the centre of the quarter of which the insurgents valiantly disputed the possession with our soldiers ; before even it

would have been possible to agree to the basis of a treaty of a few hours. Accordingly, when Fourier was preparing to celebrate the welcome of the Turkish commissioner conformably to oriental usages, a great number of musket-shots were fired from the house in front, and a ball passed through the coffee-pot which he was holding in his hand. Without calling in question the bravery of any person, do you not think, Gentlemen, that if diplomatists were usually placed in equally perilous positions, the public would have less reason to complain of their proverbial slowness ?

In order to exhibit, under one point of view, the various administrative duties of our indefatigable colleague, I should have to show him to you on board the English fleet, at the instant of the capitulation of Menou, stipulating for certain guarantees in favour of the members of the Institute of Egypt; but services of no less importance and of a different nature demand also our attention. They will even compel us to retrace our steps, to ascend even to the epoch of glorious memory when Desaix achieved the conquest of Upper Egypt, as much by the sagacity, the moderation, and the inflexible justice of all his acts, as by the rapidity and boldness of his military operations. Bonaparte then appointed two numerous commissions to proceed to explore in those remote regions, a multitude of monuments of which the moderns hardly suspected the existence. Fourier and Costas were the commandants of these commissions ; I say the commandants, for a sufficiently imposing military force had been assigned to them ; since it was frequently after a combat with the wandering tribes of Arabs that the astronomer found in the movements of the heavenly bodies the elements of a future geographical map ; that

the naturalist collected unknown plants, determined the
geological constitution of the soil, occupied himself with
troublesome dissections; that the antiquary measured
the dimensions of edifices, that he attempted to take a
faithful sketch of the fantastic images with which every
thing was covered in that singular country,—from the
smallest pieces of furniture, from the simple toys of children, to those prodigious palaces, to those immense façades, beside which the vastest of modern constructions
would hardly attract a look.

The two learned commissions studied with scrupulous
care the magnificent temple of the ancient Tentyris, and
especially the series of astronomical signs which have
excited in our days such lively discussions; the remarkable monuments of the mysterious and sacred Isle of
Elephantine; the ruins of Thebes, with her hundred
gates, before which (and yet they are nothing but ruins)
our whole army halted, in a state of astonishment, to
applaud.

Fourier also presided in Upper Egypt over these
memorable works, when the Commander-in-Chief suddenly quitted Alexandria and returned to France with
his principal friends.  Those persons then were very
much mistaken who, upon not finding our colleague on
board the frigate *Muiron* beside Monge and Berthollet,
imagined that Bonaparte did not appreciate his eminent
qualities.  If Fourier was not a passenger, this arose
from the circumstance of his having been a hundred
leagues from the Mediterranean when the *Muiron* set
sail.  The explanation contains nothing striking, but it
is true.  In any case, the friendly feeling of Kléber towards the Secretary of the Institute of Egypt, the influence which he justly granted to him on a multitude of

delicate occasions, amply compensated him for an unjust omission.

I arrive, Gentlemen, at the epoch so suggestive of painful recollections, when the *Agas* of the Janissaries who had fled into Syria, having despaired of vanquishing our troops so admirably commanded, by the honourable arms of the soldier, had recourse to the dagger of the assassin. You are aware that a young fanatic, whose imagination had been wrought up to a high state of excitement in the mosques by a month of prayers and abstinence, aimed a mortal blow at the hero of Heliopolis at the instant when he was listening, without suspicion, and with his usual kindness, to a recital of pretended grievances, and was promising redress.

This sad misfortune plunged our colony into profound grief. The Egyptians themselves mingled their tears with those of the French soldiers. By a delicacy of feeling which we should be wrong in supposing the Mahometans not to be capable of, they did not then omit, they have not since omitted, to remark, that the assassin and his three accomplices were not born on the banks of the Nile.

The army, to mitigate its grief, desired that the funeral of Kléber should be celebrated with great pomp. It wished, also, that on that solemn day, some person should recount the long series of brilliant actions which will transmit the name of the illustrious general to the remotest posterity. By unanimous consent this honourable and perilous mission was confided to Fourier.

There are very few individuals, Gentlemen, who have not seen the brilliant dreams of their youth wrecked one after the other against the sad realities of mature age. Fourier was one of those few exceptions.

In effect, transport yourselves mentally back to the year 1789, and consider what would be the future prospects of the humble convert of St. Benoît-sur-Loire. No doubt a small share of literary glory; the favour of being heard occasionally in the churches of the metropolis; the satisfaction of being appointed to eulogize such or such a public personage. Well! nine years have hardly passed and you find him at the head of the Institute of Egypt, and he is the oracle, the idol of a society which counted among its members Bonaparte, Berthollet, Monge, Malus, Geoffroy Saint Hilaire, Conté, &c.; and the generals rely upon him for overcoming apparently insurmountable difficulties, and the army of the East, itself so rich in adornments of all kinds, would desire no other interpreter when it is necessary to recount the lofty deeds of the hero which it had just lost.

It was upon the breach of a bastion which our troops had recently taken by assault, in sight of the most majestic of rivers, of the magnificent valley which it fertilizes, of the frightful desert of Lybia, of the colossal pyramids of Gizeh; it was in presence of twenty populations of different origins which Cairo unites together in its vast basin; in presence of the most valiant soldiers that had ever set foot on a land, wherein, however, the names of Alexander and of Cæsar still resound; it was in the midst of every thing which could move the heart, excite the ideas, or exalt the imagination, that Fourier unfolded the noble life of Kléber. The orator was listened to with religious silence; but soon, addressing himself with a gesture of his hand to the soldiers ranged in battle array before him, he exclaims: " Ah! how many of you would have aspired to the honour of throwing yourselves between Kléber and his assassin!

I call you to witness, intrepid cavalry, who rushed to save him upon the heights of Koraïm, and dispelled in an instant the multitude of enemies who had surrounded him!" At these words an electric tremor thrills throughout the whole army, the colours droop, the ranks close, the arms come into collision, a deep sigh escapes from some ten thousand breasts torn by the sabre and the bullet, and the voice of the orator is drowned amid sobs.

A few months after, upon the same bastion, before the same soldiers, Fourier celebrated with no less eloquence the exploits, the virtues of the general whom the people conquered in Africa saluted with the name so flattering of *Just Sultan;* and who sacrificed his life at Marengo to secure the triumph of the French arms.

Fourier quitted Egypt only with the last wreck of the army, in virtue of the capitulation signed by Menou. On his return to France, the object of his most constant solicitude was to illustrate the memorable expedition of which he had been one of the most active and most useful members. The idea of collecting together the varied labours of all his colleagues incontestibly belongs to him. I find the proof of this in a letter, still unpublished, which he wrote to Kléber from Thebes, on the 20th Vendémiaire, in the year VII. No public act, in which mention is made of this great literary monument, is of an earlier date. The Institute of Cairo having adopted the project of a *work upon Egypt* as early as the month of Frimaire, in the year VIII., confided to Fourier the task of uniting together the scattered elements of it, of making them consistent with each other, and drawing up the general introduction.

This introduction was published under the title of *Historical Preface:* Fontanes saw in it the graces of

Athens and the wisdom of Egypt united together. What could I add to such an eulogium ? I shall say only that there are to be found there, in a few pages, the principal features of the government of the Pharaohs, and the results of the subjection of ancient Egypt by the kings of Persia, the Ptolemies, the successors of Augustus, the emperors of Byzantium, the first Caliphs, the celebrated Saladin, the Mamelukes and the Ottoman princes. The different phases of our adventurous expedition are there characterized with the greatest care. Fourier carries his scruples to so great a length as *to attempt* to prove that it was just. I have said only so far as *to attempt,* for in that case there might have been something to deduct from the second part of the eulogium of Fontanes. If, in 1797, our countryman experienced at Cairo, or at Alexandria, outrages and extortions which the Grand Seignior either would not or could not repress, one may in all rigour admit that France ought to have exacted justice to herself; that she had the right to send a powerful army to bring the Turkish Custom-house officers to reason. But this is far from maintaining that the divan of Constantinople ought to have favoured the French expedition ; that our conquest was about to restore to him, *in some sort,* Egypt and Syria; that the capture of Alexandria and the battle of the *Pyramids would enhance the lustre of the Ottoman name !* However, the pnblic hastened to acquit Fourier of what appears hazarded in this small part of his beautiful work. The origin of it has been sought for in political exigencies. Let us be brief; behind certain sophisms the hand of the original Commander-in-Chief of the army of the East was suspected to be seen !

Napoleon, then, would appear to have participated by

his instructions, by his counsels, or, if we choose, by his imperative orders, in the composition of the essay of Fourier. What was not long ago nothing more than a plausible conjecture, has now become an incontestable fact. Thanks to the courtesy of M. Champollion-Figeac, I held in my hands, within the last few days, some parts of the first *proof sheets* of the historical preface. These proofs were sent to the Emperor, who wished to make himself acquainted with them at leisure before reading them with Fourier. They are covered with marginal notes, and the additions which they have occasioned amount to almost a third of the original discourse. Upon these pages, as in the definitive work given to the public,- one remarks a complete absence of proper names; the only exception is in the case of the three Generals-in-Chief. Thus Fourier had imposed upon himself the reserve which certain vanities have blamed so severely. I shall add that nowhere throughout the precious proof sheets of M. Champollion do we perceive traces of the miserable feelings of jealousy which have been attributed to Napoleon. It is true that upon pointing out with his finger the word illustrious applied to Kléber, the Emperor said to our colleague: " SOME ONE has directed my attention to THIS EPITHET; " but, after a short pause, he added, " it is desirable that you should leave it, for it is just and well deserved." These words, Gentlemen, honoured the monarch still less than they branded with disgrace the *some one* whom I regret not being able to designate in more definite terms,—one of those vile courtiers whose whole life is occupied in spying out the frailties, the evil passions of their masters, in order to make them subservient in conducting themselves to honours and fortune !

## FOURIER PREFECT OF L'ISÈRE.

Fourier had no sooner returned to Europe, than he was named (January 2, 1802) Prefect of the Department of l'Isère. The Ancient Dauphiny was then a prey to ardent political dissensions. The republicans, the partisans of the emigrants, those who had ranged themselves under the banners of the consular government, formed so many distinct castes, between whom all reconciliation appeared impossible. Well, Gentlemen, this impossibility Fourier achieved. His first care was to cause the Hôtel of the Prefecture to be considered as a neutral ground, where each might show himself without even the appearance of a concession. Curiosity alone at first brought the people there, but the people returned; for in France they seldom desert the saloons wherein are to be found a polished and benevolent host, witty without being ridiculous, and learned without being pedantic. What had been divulged of the opinions of our colleague, respecting the anti-biblican antiquity of the Egyptian monuments, inspired the religious classes especially with lively apprehensions; they were very adroitly informed that the new prefect counted a *Saint* in his family ; that the *blessed* Pierre Fourier, who established the religious sisters of the congregation of Notre-Dame, was his grand uncle, and this circumstance effected a reconciliation which the unalterable respect of the first magistrate of Grenoble for all conscientious opinions cemented every day more and more.

As soon as he was assured of a truce with the political and religious parties, Fourier was enabled to devote himself exclusively to the duties of his office. These duties did not consist with him in heaping up old papers to no advantage. He took personal cognizance of the projects which were submitted to him ; he was the indefatigable promoter of all those which narrow-minded persons sought to stifle in their birth ; we may include in this last class, the superb road from Grenoble to Turin by Mount Genèvre, which the events of 1814 have so unfortunately interrupted, and especially the drainage of the marshes of Bourgoin.

These marshes, which Louis XIV. had given to Marshal Turenne, were a focus of infection to the thirty-seven communes, the lands of which were partially covered by them. Fourier directed personally the topographic operations which established the possibility of drainage. With these documents in his hand he went from village to village, I might almost say from house to house, to fix the sacrifice which each family ought to impose upon itself for the general interest. By tact and perseverance, taking "the *ear of corn always in the right direction*, thirty-seven municipal councils were induced to contribute to a common fund, without which the projected operation would not even have been commenced. Success crowned this rare perseverance. Rich harvests, fat pastures, numerous flocks, a robust and happy population now covered an immense territory, where formerly the traveller dared not remain more than a few hours.

One of the predecessors of Fourier, in the situation of perpetual secretary of the Academy of Sciences, deemed it his duty, on one occasion, to beg an excuse for having given a detailed account of certain researches of Leibnitz, which had not required great efforts of the intellect: "We ought," says he, "to be very much obliged to a man such as he is, when he condescends, for the public good, to do something which does not partake of genius!"

I cannot conceive the ground of such scruples; in the present day, the sciences are regarded from too high a point of view, that we should hesitate in placing in the first rank of the labours with which they are adorned, those which diffuse comfort, health, and happiness amidst the working population.

In presence of a part of the Academy of Inscriptions, in an apartment wherein the name of hieroglyph has so often resounded, I cannot refrain from alluding to the service which Fourier rendered to science by retaining Champollion. The young professor of history of the Faculty of Letters of Grenoble had just attained the twentieth year of his age. Fate calls him to shoulder the musket. Fourier exempts him by investing him with the title of pupil of the School of Oriental Languages which he had borne at Paris. The Minister of War learns that the pupil formerly gave in his resignation; he denounces the fraud, and dispatches a peremptory order for his departure, which seems even to exclude all idea of remonstrance. Fourier, however, is not discouraged; his intercessions are skilful and of a pressing nature; finally, he draws so animated a portrait of the precocious talent of *his young friend,* that he succeeds in wringing from the government an order of special exemption. It was not easy, Gentlemen, to obtain such success. At the same time, a conscript, a *member of our Academy,* succeeded in obtaining a revocation of his order for departure only by declaring that he would follow on foot, in the costume of the Institute, the contingent of the arrondissement of Paris in which he was classed.

## MATHEMATICAL THEORY OF HEAT.

The administrative duties of the prefect of l'Isère hardly interrupted the labours of the geometer and the man of letters. It is from Grenoble that the principal writings of Fourier are dated; it was at Grenoble that he composed the *Théorie Mathématique de la Chaleur*, which forms his principal title to the gratitude of the scientific world.

I am far from being unconscious of the difficulty of analyzing that admirable work, and yet I shall attempt to point out the successive steps which he has achieved in the advancement of science. You will listen to me, Gentlemen, with indulgence, notwithstanding several minute details which I shall have to recount, since I thereby fulfil the mission with which you have honoured me.

The ancients had a taste, let us say rather a passion, for the marvellous, which caused them to forget even the sacred duties of gratitude. Observe them, for example, grouping together the lofty deeds of a great number of heroes, whose names they have not even deigned to preserve, and investing the single personage of Hercules with them. The lapse of ages has not rendered us wiser in this respect. In our own time the public delight in blending fable with history. . In every career of life, in the pursuit of science especially, they enjoy a pleasure in creating Herculeses. According to vulgar opinion, there is no astronomical discovery which is not due to Herschel. The theory of the planetary movements is identified with the name of Laplace; hardly is a passing allusion made to the eminent labours of D'Alembert, of Clairaut, of Euler, of Lagrange. Watt is the sole inventor of the steam-engine.  Chaptal has enriched the arts of Chemistry with the totality of the fertile and ingenious processes which constitute their prosperity.  Even within this apartment has not an eloquent voice lately asserted, that before Fourier the phenomenon of heat was hardly studied; that the celebrated geometer had alone made more observations than all his predecessors put together; that he had with almost a single effort invented a new science.

Although he runs the risk of being less lively, the organ of the Academy of Sciences cannot permit himself such bursts of enthusiasm.  He ought to bear in mind, that the object of these solemnities is not merely to celebrate the discoveries of academicians; that they are also designed to encourage modest merit; that an observer forgotten by his contemporaries, is frequently supported in his laborious researches by the thought that he will obtain a benevolent look from posterity.  Let us act, so far as it depends upon us, in such a manner that a hope so just, so natural, may not be frustrated.  Let us award a just, a brilliant homage to those rare men whom nature has endowed with the precious privilege of arranging a thousand isolated facts, of making seductive theories spring from them; but let us not forget to state, that the scythe of the reaper had cut the stalks before one had thought of uniting them into sheaves!

Heat presents itself in natural phenomena, and in those which are the products of art under two entirely distinct forms, which Fourier has separately considered. I shall adopt the same division, commencing however with radiant heat, the historical analysis which I am about to submit to you.

Nobody doubts that there is a physical distinction

which is eminently worthy of being studied between the ball of iron at the ordinary temperature which may be handled at pleasure, and the ball of iron of the same dimensions which the flame of a furnace has very much heated, and which we cannot touch without burning ourselves. This distinction, according to the majority of physical inquirers, arises from a certain quantity of an elastic imponderable fluid, or at least a fluid which has not been weighed, with which the second ball has combined during the process of heating. The fluid which, upon combining with cold bodies renders them hot, has been designated by the name of *heat* or *caloric*.

Bodies unequally heated act upon each other *even at great distances, even through empty space,* for the colder becomes more hot, and the hotter becomes more cold ; for after a certain time they indicate the same degree of the thermometer, whatever may have been the difference of their original temperatures. According to the hypotheses above explained, there is but one way of conceiving this action at a distance ; this is to suppose that it operates by the aid of certain effluvia which traverse space by passing from the hot body to the cold body ; that is, to admit that a hot body emits in every direction rays of heat, as luminous bodies emit rays of light.

The effluvia, the radiating emanations by the aid of which two distant bodies form a calorific communication with each other, have been very appropriately designated by the name of *radiating caloric*.

Whatever may be said to the contrary, radiating heat had already been the object of important experiments before Fourier undertook his labours. The celebrated academicians of the *Cimento* found, nearly two centuries ago, that this heat is reflected like light ; that, as in the case of light, a concave mirror concentrates it at the focus. Upon substituting balls of snow for heated bodies, they even went so far as to prove that frigorific foci may be formed by way of reflection. Some years afterwards Mariotte, a member of this Academy, discovered that there exist different kinds of radiating heat; that the heat with which rays of light are accompanied traverses all transparent media as easily as light does; while, again, the caloric which emanates from a strongly heated, but opaque substance, while the rays of heat, which are found mingled with the luminous rays of a body moderately incandescent, are almost entirely arrested in their passage through the most transparent plate of glass!

This striking discovery, let us remark in passing, will show, notwithstanding the ridicule of pretended savans, how happily inspired were the workmen in founderies, who looked at the incandescent matter of their furnaces, only through a plate of ordinary glass, thinking by the aid of this artifice to arrest the heat which would have burned their eyes.

In the experimental sciences, the epochs of the most brilliant progress are almost always separated by long intervals of almost absolute repose. Thus, after Mariotte, there elapsed more than a century without history having to record any new property of radiating heat. Then, in close succession, we find in the solar light obscure calorific rays, the existence of which could admit of being established only with the thermometer, and which may be completely separated from luminous rays by the aid of the prism; we discover, by the aid of terrestrial bodies, that the emission of caloric rays, and consequently the cooling of those bodies, is considerably retarded by the polish of the surfaces; that the colour, the nature, and the thickness of the outer coating of these same surfaces, exercise also a manifest influence upon their emissive power. Experience, finally, rectifying the vague predictions to which the most enlightened minds abandon themselves with so little reserve, shows that the calorific rays which emanate from the plane surface of a heated body have not the same force, the same intensity in all directions ; that the *maximum* corresponds to the perpendicular emission, and the *minimum* to the emissions parallel to the surface.

Between these two extreme positions, how does the diminution of the emissive power operate ? Leslie first sought the solution of this important question. His observations seem to show that the intensities of the radiating rays are proportional (it is necessary, Gentlemen, that I employ the scientific expression) to the sines of the angles which these rays form with the heated surface. But the quantities upon which the experimenter had to operate were too feeble; the uncertainties of the thermometric estimations compared with the total effect were, on the contrary, too great not to inspire a strong degree of distrust : well, Gentlemen, a problem before which all the processes, all the instruments of modern physics have remained powerless, Fourier has completely solved without the necessity of having recourse to any new experiment. He has traced the law of the emission of caloric sought for, with a perspicuity which one cannot sufficiently admire, in the most ordinary phenomena of temperature, in the phenomena which at first sight appeared to be entirely independent of it.

Such is the privilege of genius ; it perceives, it seizes relations where vulgar eyes see only isolated facts.

Nobody doubts, and besides experiment has confirmed

the fact, that in all the points of a space terminated by any envelop maintained at a constant temperature, we ought also to experience a constant temperature, and precisely that of the envelop.   Now Fourier has established, that if the calorific rays emitted were equally intense in all directions, if the intensity did not vary proportionally to the sine of the angle of emission, the temperature of a body situated in the enclosure would depend on the place which it would occupy there: *that the temperature of boiling water or of melting iron, for example, would exist in certain points of a hollow envelop of glass!*   In all the vast domain of the physical sciences, we should be unable to find a more striking application of the celebrated method of the *reductio ad absurdum* of which the ancient mathematicians made use, in order to demonstrate the abstract truths of geometry.

I shall not quit this first part of the labours of Fourier without adding, that he has not contented himself with demonstrating with so much felicity the remarkable law which connects the comparative intensities of the calorific rays, emanating under all angles from heated bodies; he has sought, moreover, the physical cause of this law, and he has found it in a circumstance which his predecessors had entirely neglected.   Let us suppose, says he, that bodies emit heat not only from the molecules of their surfaces, but also from the particles in the interior.   Let us suppose, moreover, that the heat of these latter particles cannot arrive at the surface by traversing a certain thickness of matter without undergoing some degree of absorption.   Fourier has reduced these two hypotheses to calculation, and he has hence deduced mathematically the experimental law of the sines.   After having resisted so radical a test, the two hypotheses were found to be completely verified, they have become laws of nature; they point out latent properties of caloric which could only be discerned by the eye of the intellect.

In the second question treated by Fourier, heat presents itself under a new form. There is more difficulty in following its movements; but the conclusions deducible from the theory are also more general and more important.

Heat excited, concentrated into a certain point of a solid body, communicates itself by way of conduction, first to the particles nearest the heated point, then gradually to all the regions of the body. Whence the problem of which the following is the enunciation.

By what routes, and with what velocities, is the propagation of heat effected in bodies of different forms and different natures subjected to certain initial conditions?

Fundamentally, the Academy of Sciences had already proposed this problem as the subject of a prize as early as the year 1736. Then the terms heat and caloric were not in use; it demanded *the study of nature, and the propagation* OF FIRE! The word *fire*, thrown thus into the programme without any other explanation, gave rise to a mistake of the most singular kind. The majority of philosophers imagined that the question was to explain in what way *burning* communicates itself, and increases in a mass of combustible matter. Fifteen competitors presented themselves; *three* were crowned.

This competition was productive of very meagre results. However, a singular combination of circumstances and of proper names will render the recollection of it lasting.

Has not the public a right to be surprised upon reading this Academic declaration: "the question affords no

handle to geometry !" In matter of inventions, to attempt
to dive into the future, is to prepare for one's self striking mistakes. One of the competitors, the great Euler,
took these words in their literal sense ; the reveries with
which his memoir abounds, are not compensated in this
instance by any of those brilliant discoveries in analysis,
I had almost said of those sublime inspirations, which
were so familiar to him. Fortunately Euler appended
to his memoir a supplement truly worthy of his genius.
Father Lozeran de Fiesc and the Count of Créqui were
rewarded with the high honour of seeing their names inscribed beside that of the illustrious geometer, although
it would be impossible in the present day to discern in
their memoirs any kind of merit, not even that of politeness, for the courtier said rudely to the Academy : " the
question, which you have raised, interests only the curiosity of mankind."

Among the competitors less favourably treated, we
perceive one of the greatest writers whom France has
produced ; the author of the *Henriade*. The memoir of
Voltaire was, no doubt, far from solving the problem
proposed ; but it was at least distinguished by elegance,
clearness, and precision of language ; I shall add, by a
severe style of argument ; for if the author occasionally
arrives at questionable results, it is only when he bor-
rows false data from the chemistry and physics of the
epoch,—sciences which had just sprung into existence.
Moreover, the anti-Cartesian colour of some of the parts
of the memoir of Voltaire was calculated to find little
favour in a society, where Cartesianism, with its incom-
prehensible vortices, was everywhere held in high estimation.

We should have more difficulty in discovering the

causes of the failure of a fourth competitor, Madame the Marchioness du Châtelet, for she also entered into the contest instituted by the Academy. The work of Emilia was not only an elegant portrait of all the properties of heat, known then to physical inquirers, there were remarked moreover in it, different projects of experiments, among the rest one which Herschel has since developed, and from which he has derived one of the principal flowers of his brilliant scientific crown.

While such great names were occupied in discussing this question, physical inquirers of a less ambitious stamp laid experimentally the solid basis of a future mathematical theory of heat. Some established, that the same quantity of caloric does not elevate by the same number of degrees equal weights of different substances, and thereby introduced into the science the important notion of *capacity*. Others, by the aid of observations no less certain, proved that heat, applied at the extremity of a bar, is transmitted to the extreme parts with greater or less velocity or intensity, according to the nature of the substance of which the bar is composed; thus they suggested the original idea of *conductibility*. The same epoch, if I were not precluded from entering into too minute details, would present to us interesting experiments. We should find that it is not true that, at all degrees of the thermometer, the loss of heat of a body is proportional to the excess of its temperature above that of the medium in which it is plunged; but I have been desirous of showing you geometry penetrating, timidly at first, into questions of the propagation of heat, and depositing there the first germs of its fertile methods.

It is to Lambert of Mulhouse, that we owe this first step. This ingenious geometer had proposed a very simple problem which any person may comprehend. A slender metallic bar is exposed at one of its extremities to the constant action of a certain focus of heat. The parts nearest the focus are heated first. Gradually the heat communicates itself to the more distant parts, and, after a short time, each point acquires the maximum temperature which it can ever attain. Although the experiment were to last a hundred years, the thermometric state of the bar would not undergo any modification.

As might be reasonably expected, this maximum of heat is so much less considerable as we recede from the focus. Is there any relation between the final temperatures and the distances of the different particles of the bar from the extremity directly heated? Such a relation exists. It is very simple. Lambert investigated it by calculation, and experience confirmed the results of theory.

In addition to the somewhat elementary question of the *longitudinal* propagation of heat, there offered itself the more general but much more difficult problem of the propagation of heat in a body of three dimensions terminated by any surface whatever. This problem demanded the aid of the higher analysis. It was Fourier who first assigned the equations. It is to Fourier, also, that we owe certain theorems, by means of which we may ascend from the differential equations to the integrals, and push the solutions in the majority of cases to the final numerical applications.

The first memoir of Fourier on the theory of heat dates from the year 1807. The Academy, to which it was communicated, being desirous of inducing the author to extend and improve his researches, made the question

18 *

of the propagation of heat the subject of the great mathematical prize which was to be awarded in the beginning of the year 1812. Fourier did, in effect, compete, and his memoir was crowned. But, alas! as Fontenelle said: "In the country even of demonstrations, there are to be found causes of dissension." Some restrictions mingled with the favourable judgment. The illustrious commissioners of the prize, Laplace, Lagrange, and Legendre, while acknowledging the novelty and importance of the subject, while declaring that the real differential equations of the propagation of heat were finally found, asserted that they perceived difficulties in the way in which the author arrived at them. They added, that his processes of integration left something to be desired, even on the score of rigour. They did not, however, support their opinion by any arguments.

Fourier never admitted the validity of this decision. Even at the close of his life he gave unmistakable evidence that he thought it unjust, by causing his memoir to be printed in our volumes without changing a single word. Still, the doubts expressed by the Commissioners of the Academy reverted incessantly to his recollection. From the very beginning they had poisoned the pleasure of his triumph. These first impressions, added to a high susceptibility, explain how Fourier ended by regarding with a certain degree of displeasure the efforts of those geometers who endeavoured to improve his theory. This, Gentlemen, was a very strange aberration of a mind of so elevated an order! Our colleague had almost forgotten that it is not allotted to any person to conduct a scientific question to a definitive termination, and that the important labours of D'Alembert, Clairaut, Euler, Lagrange, and Laplace, while immortalizing their authors, have continually added new lustre to the imperishable glory of Newton. Let us act so that this example may not be lost. While the civil law imposes upon the tribunes the obligation to assign the motives of *their judgments*, the academies, which are the tribunes of science, cannot have even a pretext to escape from this obligation. Corporate bodies, as well as individuals, act wisely when they reckon in every instance only upon the authority of reason.

### CENTRAL HEAT OF THE TERRESTRIAL GLOBE.

At any time the *Théorie Mathématique de la Chaleur* would have excited a lively interest among men of reflection, since, upon the supposition of its being complete, it threw light upon the most minute processes of the arts. In our time the numerous points of affinity existing between it and the curious discoveries of the geologists, have made it, if I may use the expression, a work for the occasion. To point out the intimate relation which exists between these two kinds of researches would be to present the most important part of the discoveries of Fourier, and to show how happily our colleague, by one of those inspirations reserved for genius, had chosen the subject of his researches.

The parts of the earth's crust, which the geologists call the sedimentary formations, were not formed all at once. The waters of the ocean, on several former occasions, covered regions which are situated in the present day in the centre of the continent. There they deposited, in thin horizontal strata, a series of rocks of different kinds. These rocks, although superposed like the layers of stones of a wall, must not be confounded together; their dissimilarities are palpable to the least practised eye. It is necessary also to note this capital fact, that each stratum has a well-defined limit; that no process of transition connects it with the stratum which it supports. The ocean, the original source of all these deposits, underwent then formerly enormous changes in its chemical composition to which it is no longer subject.

With some rare exceptions, resulting from local convulsions the effects of which are otherwise manifest, the order of antiquity of the successive strata of rocks which form the exterior crust of the globe ought to be that of their superposition. The deepest have been formed at the most remote epochs. The attentive study of these different envelops may aid us in ascending the stream of time, even beyond the most remote epochs, and enlightening us with respect to those stupendous revolutions which periodically overwhelmed continents beneath the waters of the ocean, or again restored them to their former condition. Crystalline rocks of granite upon which the sea has effected its original deposits have never exhibited any remains of life. Traces of such are to be found only in the sedimentary strata.

Life appears to have first exhibited itself on the earth in the form of vegetables. The remains of vegetables are all that we meet with in the most ancient strata deposited by the waters; still, they belong to plants of the simplest structure,—to ferns, to species of rushes, to lycopodes.

As we ascend into the upper strata, vegetation becomes more and more complex. Finally, near the surface, it resembles the vegetation actually existing on the earth, with this characteristic circumstance, however, which is well deserving attention, that certain vegetables which grow only in southern climates, that the large palm-trees, for example, are found in their fossil state in all latitudes, and even in the centre of the frozen regions of Siberia. -

In the primitive world, these northern regions enjoyed then, in winter, a temperature at least equal to that which is experienced in the present day under the parallels where the great palms commence to appear: at Tobolsk, the inhabitants enjoyed the climate of Alicante or Algiers !

We shall deduce new proofs of this mysterious result from an attentive examination of the size of plants.

There exist, in the present day, willow grass or marshy rushes, ferns, and lycopodes, in Europe as well as in the tropical regions ; but they are not met with in large dimensions, except in warm countries.  Thus, to compare together the dimensions of the same plants is, in reality, to compare, in respect to temperature, the regions where they are produced.   Well, place beside the fossil plants of our coal mines, I will not say the analogous plants of Europe, but those which grow in the countries of South America, and which are most celebrated for the richness of their vegetation, and you will find the former to be of incomparably greater dimensions than the latter.

The *fossil flora* of France, England, Germany, and Scandinavia offer, for example, ferns ninety feet high, the stalks being six feet in diameter, or eighteen feet in circumference.

The *lycopodes* which, in the present day, whether in cold or temperate climates, are creeping-plants rising hardly to the height of a decimètre above the soil ; which even at the equator, under the most favourable circumstances, do not attain a height of more than *one* mètre, had in Europe, in the primitive world, an altitude of twenty-five mètres.

One must be blind to all reason not to find, in these enormous dimensions, a new proof of the high temperature enjoyed by our country before the last irruptions of the ocean !

The study of *fossil animals* is no less fertile in results. I should digress from my subject if I were to examine here how the organization of animals is developed upon the earth; what modifications, or more strictly speaking, what complications it has undergone after each cataclysm, or if I even stopped to describe one of those ancient epochs during which the earth, the sea, and the atmosphere had for inhabitants cold-blooded reptiles of enormous dimensions ; tortoises with shells three feet in diameter ; lizards seventeen mètres long; pterodactyles, veritable flying dragons of such strange forms, that they might be classed on good grounds either among reptiles, among mammiferous animals, or among birds.   The object, which I have proposed, does not require that I should enter into such details; a single remark will suffice.

Among the bones contained in the strata nearest the present surface of the earth, are those of the hippopotamus, the rhinoceros, and the elephant.   These remains of animals of warm countries are to be found in all latitudes.   Travellers have discovered specimens of them even at Melville Island, where the temperature descends, in the present day, 50° beneath zero.   In Siberia they are found in such abundance as to have become an article of commerce.   Finally, upon the rocky shores of the Arctic Ocean, there are to be found not merely fragments of skeletons, but whole elephants still covered with their flesh and skin.

I should deceive myself very much, Gentlemen, if I

were to suppose that each of you had not deduced from these remarkable facts a conclusion no less remarkable, to which indeed the fossil flora had already habituated us ; namely, that as they have grown older, the polar regions of the earth have cooled down to a prodigious extent.

In the explanation of so curious a phenomenon, cosmologists have not taken into account the existence of possible variations of the intensity of the solar heat ; and yet the stars, those distant suns, have not the constant brightness which the common people attribute to them. Nay, some of them have been observed to diminish in a sufficiently short space of time to the hundredth part of their original brightness ; and several have even totally disappeared. They have preferred to attribute every thing to an internal or primitive heat with which the earth was at some former epoch impregnated, and which is gradually being dissipated in space.

Upon this hypothesis the inhabitants of the polar regions, although deprived of the sight of the sun for whole months together, must have evidently enjoyed, at very ancient epochs, a temperature equal to that of the tropical regions, wherein exist elephants in the present day.

It is not, however, as an explanation of the existence of elephants in Siberia, that the idea of the intrinsic heat of the globe has entered for the first time into science. Some savans had adopted it before the discovery of those fossil animals. Thus, Descartes was of opinion that originally (I cite his own words,) *the earth did not differ from the sun in any other respect than in being smaller.* Upon this hypothesis, then, it ought to be considered as an extinct sun.

Leibnitz conferred upon this hypothesis the honour of appropriating it to himself. He attempted to deduce from it the mode of formation of the different solid envelopes of which the earth consists. Buffon, also, imparted to it the weight of his eloquent authority. According to that great naturalist, the planets of our system are merely portions of the sun, which the shock of a comet had detached from it some tens of thousands of years ago.

In support of this igneous origin of the earth, Mairan and Buffon cited already the high temperature of deep mines, and, among others, those of the mines of Giromagny. It appears evident that if the earth was formerly incandescent, we should not fail to meet in the interior strata, that is to say, in those which ought to have cooled last, traces of their primitive temperature. The observer who, upon penetrating into the interior of the earth, did not find an increasing heat, might then consider himself amply authorized to reject the hypothetical conceptions of Descartes, of Mairan, of Leibnitz, and of Buffon. But has the converse proposition the same certainty? Would not the torrents of heat, which the sun has continued incessantly to launch for so many ages, have diffused themselves into the mass of the earth, so as to produce there a temperature increasing with the depth? This a question of high importance. Certain easily satisfied minds conscientiously supposed that they had solved it, when they stated that the idea of a constant temperature was by far the *most natural ;* but woe to the sciences if they thus included vague considerations which escape all criticism, among the motives for admitting and rejecting facts and theories! Fontenelle, Gentlemen, would have traced their horoscope in these words, so well adapted for humbling our pride, and the truth of which the history of discoveries reveals in a thousand places : " When a thing may be in two different ways, it is almost always that which appears at first the least natural."

Whatever importance these reflections may possess, I hasten to add that, instead of the arguments of his predecessors, which have no real value, Fourier has substituted proofs, demonstrations; and we know what meaning such terms convey to the Academy of Sciences.

In all places of the earth, as soon as we descend to a certain depth, the thermometer no longer experiences either diurnal or annual variation. It marks the same degree, and the same fraction of a degree, from day to day, and from year to year. Such is the fact : what says theory ?

Let us suppose, for a moment, that the earth has constantly received all its heat from the sun. Descend into its mass to a sufficient depth, and you will find, with Fourier, by the aid of calculation, a constant temperature for each day of the year. You will recognize further, that this solar temperature of the inferior strata varies from one climate to another; that in each country, finally, it ought to be always the same, so long as we do not descend to depths which are too great relatively to the earth's radius.

Well, the phenomena of nature stand in manifest contradiction to this result. The observations made in a multitude of mines, observations of the temperature of hot springs coming from different depths, have all given an increase of one degree of the centigrade for every twenty or thirty mètres of depth. Thus, there was some inaccuracy in the hypothesis which we were discussing upon the footsteps of our colleague. It is not true that the temperature of the terrestrial strata may be attributed solely to the action of the solar rays.

This being established, the increase of heat which is observed in all climates when we penetrate into the interior of the globe, is the manifest indication of an intrinsic heat. The earth, as Descartes and Leibnitz maintained it to be, but without being able to support their assertions by any demonstrative reasoning,—thanks to a combination of the observations of physical inquirers with the analytical calculations of Fourier,—is *an encrusted sun*, the high temperature of which may be boldly invoked every time that the explanation of ancient geological phenomena will require it.

After having established that there is in our earth an inherent heat,—a heat the source of which is not the sun, and which, if we may judge of it by the rapid increase which observation indicates, ought to be already sufficiently intense at the depth of only seven or eight leagues to hold in fusion all known substances,—there arises the question, what is its precise value at the surface of the earth ; what weight are we to attach to it in the determination of terrestrial temperatures ; what part does it play in the phenomena of life ?

According to Mairan, Buffon, and Bailly, this part is immense. For France, they estimate the heat which escapes from the interior of the earth, at twenty-nine times in summer, and four hundred times in winter, the heat which comes to us from the sun. Thus, contrary to general opinion, the heat of the body which illuminates us would form only a very small part of that whose propitious influence we feel.

This idea was developed with ability and great eloquence in the *Memoirs of the Academy*, in the *Epoques sur la Nature* of Buffon, in the letters from Bailly to Voltaire *upon the Origin of the Sciences and upon the Atlantide.* But the ingenious romance to which it has served as a base, has vanished like a shadow before the torch of mathematical science.

Fourier having discovered that the excess of the aggregate temperature of the earth's surface above that which would result from the sole action of the solar rays, has a determinate relation to the increase of temperature at different depths, succeeded in deducing from the experimental value of this increase a numerical determination of the excess in question. This excess is the thermometric effect which the solar heat produces at the surface; now, instead of the large numbers adopted by Mairan, Bailly, and Buffon, what has our colleague found? *A thirtieth* of a degree, not more.

The surface of the earth, which originally was perhaps incandescent, has cooled then in the course of ages, so as hardly to preserve any sensible trace of its primitive heat. However, at great depths, the original heat is still enormous. Time will alter sensibly the internal temperature; but at the surface (and the phenomena of the surface can alone modify or compromise the existence of living beings), all the changes are almost accomplished. The frightful freezing of the earth, the epoch of which Buffon fixed at the instant when the central heat would be totally dissipated, is then a pure dream. At the surface, the earth is no longer impregnated except by the solar heat. So long as the sun shall continue to preserve the same brightness, mankind will find, from pole to pole, under each latitude, the climates which have permitted them to live and to establish their residence. These, Gentlemen, are great, magnificent results. While recording them in the annals of science, historians will not neglect to draw attention to this singular peculiarity : that the geometer to whom we owe the first certain demonstration of the existence of a heat independent of a solar influence in the interior of the earth, has annihilated the immense part which this primitive heat was made to play in the explanation of the phenomena of terrestrial temperature.

Besides divesting the theory of climates of an error which occupied a prominent place in science, supported as it was by the imposing authority of Mairan, of Bailly, and of Buffon, Fourier is entitled to the merit of a still more striking achievement : he has introduced into this theory a consideration which hitherto had been totally neglected ; he has pointed out the influence exercised by the *temperature of the celestial regions*, amid which the hearth describes its immense orb around the sun.

When we perceive, even under the equator, certain mountains covered with eternal snow, upon observing the rapid diminution of temperature which the strata of the atmosphere undergo during ascents in balloons, meteorologists have supposed, that in the regions wherein the extreme rarity of the air will always exclude the presence of mankind, and that especially beyond the limits of the atmosphere, there ought to prevail a prodigious intensity of cold. It was not merely by hundreds, it was by thousands of degrees, that they had arbitrarily measured it. But, as usual, the imagination (*cette folie de la maison*) had exceeded all reasonable limits. The hundreds, the tens of thousands of degrees, have dwindled down, after the rigorous researches of Fourier, to fifty or sixty degrees only. Fifty or sixty degrees *beneath zero*, such is the temperature which the radiation of heat from the stars has established in the regions furrowed indefinitely by the planets of our system.

You recollect, Gentlemen, with what delight Fourier used to converse on this subject. You know well that he thought himself sure of having assigned the temperature of space within eight or ten degrees. By what fatality has it happened that the memoir, wherein no doubt our colleague had recorded all the elements of that important determination, is not to be found? May that irreparable loss prove at least to so many observers, that instead of pursuing obstinately an ideal perfection, which it is not allotted to man to attain, they will act wisely in placing the public, as soon as possible, in the confidence of their labours.

I should have yet a long course to pursue, if, after having pointed out some of those problems of which the condition of science enabled our learned colleague to give numerical solutions, I were to analyze all those which, still enveloped in general formulæ, await merely the data of experience to assume a place among the most curious acquisitions of modern physics. Time, which is not at my disposal, precludes me from dwelling upon such developments. I should be guilty, however, of an unpardonable omission, if I did not state that, among the formulæ of Fourier, there is one which serves to assign the value of the secular cooling of the earth, and in which there is involved the number of centuries which have elapsed since the origin of this cooling. The question of the antiquity of the earth, including even the period of incandescence, which has been so keenly discussed, is thus reduced to a thermometric determination. Unfortunately this point of theory is subject to serious difficulties. Besides, the thermometric determination, in consequence of its excessive smallness, must be reserved for future ages.

RETURN OF NAPOLEON FROM ELBA.—FOURIER PRE-
FECT OF THE RHONE.—HIS NOMINATION TO THE
OFFICE OF DIRECTOR OF THE BOARD OF STATIS-
TICS OF THE SEINE.

I have just exhibited to you the scientific fruits of the
leisure hours of the Prefect of l'Isère. Fourier still occupied this situation when Napoleon arrived at Cannes.
His conduct during this grave conjuncture has been
the object of a hundred false rumours. I shall then discharge a duty by establishing the facts in all their truth,
according to what I have heard from our colleague's own
mouth.

Upon the news of the Emperor having disembarked,
the principal authorities of Grenoble assembled at the
residence of the Prefect. There each individual explained ably, but especially, said Fourier, with much
detail, the difficulties which he perceived. As regards
the means of vanquishing them, the authorities seemed
to be much less inventive. Confidence in administrative
eloquence was not yet worn out at that epoch; it was
resolved accordingly to have recourse to proclamations.
The commanding officer and the Prefect presented each
a project. The assembly was discussing minutely the
terms of them, when an officer of the gendarmes, an old
soldier of the Imperial armies, exclaimed rudely, " Gentlemen, be quick, otherwise all deliberation will become
useless. Believe me, I speak from experience; Napoleon always follows very closely the couriers who announce his arrival." Napoleon was in fact close at hand.
After a short moment of hesitation, two companies of
sappers which had been dispatched to cut down a bridge,
joined their former commander. A battalion of infantry
soon followed their example. Finally, upon the very

glacis of the fortress, in presence of the numerous population which crowned the ramparts, the fifth regiment of the line to a man assumed the tricolour cockade, substituted for the white flag the eagle,—witness of twenty battles,—which it had preserved, and departed with shouts of *Vive l'Empereur!* After such a commencement, to attempt to hold the country would have been an act of folly. General Marchand caused accordingly the gates of the city to be shut. He still hoped, notwithstanding the evidently hostile disposition of the inhabitants, to sustain a siege with the sole assistance of the third regiment of engineers, the fourth regiment of artillery, and some weak detachments of infantry, which had not abandoned him.

From that moment, the civil authority had disappeared. Fourier thought then that he might quit Grenoble, and repair to Lyons, where the princes had assembled together. At the second restoration, this departure was imputed to him as a crime. He was very near being brought before a court of assizes, or even a provost's court. Certain personages pretended that the presence of the Prefect of the chief place of l'Isère might have conjured the storm; that the resistance might have been more animated, better arranged. People forgot that nowhere, and at Grenoble even less than anywhere else, was it possible to organize even a pretext of resistance. Let us see then, finally, how this martial city, —the fall of which Fourier might have prevented by his mere presence,—let us see how it was taken. It is eight o'clock in the evening. The inhabitants and the soldiers garrison the ramparts. Napoleon precedes his little troop by some steps; he advances even to the gate; he knocks (be not alarmed, Gentlemen, it is not a battle which I am about to describe,) *he knocks with his snuff-box!* " Who is there ? " cried the officer of the guard. " It is the Emperor ! Open ! "—" Sire, my duty forbids me."—" Open—I tell you ; I have no time to lose."— " But, sire, even though I should open to you, I could not. The keys are in the possession of General Marchand."—" Go, then, and fetch them."—" I am certain that he will refuse them to me."—" If the General refuse them, *tell him that I will dismiss him.*"

These words petrified the soldiers. During the previous two days, hundreds of proclamations designated Bonaparte as a wild beast which it was necessary to seize without scruple ; they ordered everybody to run away from him, and yet this man threatened the general with deprivation of his command ! The single word *dismissal,* effaced the faint line of demarcation which separated for an instant the old soldiers from the young recruits ; one word established the whole garrison in the interest of the emperor.

The circumstances of the capture of Grenoble were not yet known when Fourier arrived at Lyons. He brought thither the news of the rapid advance of Napoleon ; that of the revolt of two companies of sappers, of a regiment of infantry, and of the regiment commanded by Labédoyère. Moreover, he was a witness of the lively sympathy which the country people along the whole route displayed in favour of the proscribed exile of Elba.

The Count d'Artois gave a very cold reception to the Prefect and his communications. He declared that the arrival of Napoleon at Grenoble was impossible ; that no alarm need be apprehended respecting the disposition of the country people. " As regards the facts," said he to Fourier, " which would seem to have occurred in your presence at the very gates of the city, with respect to the tricoloured cockades substituted for the cockade of Henry IV., with respect to the eagles which you say have replaced the white flag, I do not suspect your good faith, but the uneasy state of your mind must have dazzled your eyes. Prefect, return then without delay to Grenoble ; you will answer for the city with your head."

You see, Gentlemen, after having so long proclaimed the necessity of telling the truth to princes, moralists will act wisely by inviting princes to be good enough to listen to its language.

Fourier obeyed the order which had just been given him. The wheels of his carriage had made only a few revolutions in the direction of Grenoble, when he was arrested by hussars, and conducted to the head-quarters at Bourgoin. The Emperor, who was engaged in examining a large chart with a pair of compasses, said, upon seeing him enter: " Well, Prefect, you also have declared war against me?"—" Sire, my oath of allegiance made it my duty to do so !"—" A duty you say? and do you not see that in Dauphiny nobody is of the same mind ? Do not imagine, however, that your plan of the campaign will frighten me much. It only grieved me to see among my enemies an *Egyptian*, a man who had eaten along with me the bread of the bivouac, an old friend ! "

It is painful to add that to those kind words succeeded these also: "How, moreover, could you have forgotten, Monsieur Fourier, that I have made you what you are ? "

You will regret with me, Gentlemen, that a timidity, which circumstances would otherwise easily explain, should have prevented our colleague from at once em-

19

phatically protesting against this confusion, which the powerful of the earth are constantly endeavouring to establish between the perishable bounties of which they are the dispensers, and the noble fruits of thought. Fourier was Prefect and Baron by the favour of the Emperor; he was one of the glories of France by his own genius!

On the 9th of March, Napoleon, in a moment of anger, ordered Fourier, by a mandate, dated from Grenoble, *to quit the territory of the seventh military division within five days, under pain of being arrested and treated as an enemy of the country!* On the following day, our colleague departed from the Conference of Bourgoin, with the appointment of Prefect of the Rhone and the title of *Count,* for the Emperor after his return from Elba was again at his old practices.

These unexpected proofs of favour and confidence afforded little pleasure to our colleague, but he dared not refuse them, although he perceived very distinctly the immense gravity of the events in which he was led by the vicissitude of fortune to play a part.

" What do you think of my enterprise? " said the Emperor to him on the day of his departure from Lyons. " Sire," replied Fourier, " I am of opinion that you will fail. Let but a fanatic meet you on your way, and all is at an end."—" Bah!" exclaimed Napoleon, " the Bourbons have nobody on their side, not even a fanatic. In connection with this circumstance, you have read in the journals that they have excluded me from the protection of the law. I shall be more indulgent on my part; I shall content myself with excluding them from the Tuileries."

Fourier held the appointment of Prefect of the Rhone

only till the 1st of May. It has been alleged that he
was recalled, because he refused to be accessory to the
deeds of terrorism which the minister of the hundred
days enjoined him to execute. The Academy will always be pleased when I collect together, and place on
record, actions which, while honouring its members,
throw new lustre around the entire body. I even feel
that, in such a case, I may be disposed to be somewhat
credulous. On the present occasion, it was imperatively
necessary to institute a most rigorous examination. If
Fourier honoured himself by refusing to obey certain
orders, what are we to think of the minister of the interior from whom those orders emanated? Now this minister, it must not be forgotten, was also an academician,
illustrious by his military services, distinguished by his
mathematical works, esteemed and cherished by all his
colleagues. Well! I declare, Gentlemen, with a satisfaction which you will all share, that a most scrupulous
investigation of all the acts of the hundred days has not
disclosed a trace of anything which might detract from
the feelings of admiration with which the memory of
Carnot is associated in your minds.

Upon quitting the Prefecture of the Rhone, Fourier
repaired to Paris. The Emperor, who was then upon
the eve of setting out to join the army, perceiving him
amid the crowd at the Tuileries, accosted him in a
friendly manner, informed him that Carnot would ex-
plan to him why his displacement at Lyons had become
indispensable, and promised to attend to his interest as
soon as military affairs would allow him some leisure
time. The second restoration found Fourier in the capital without employment, and justly anxious with respect
to the future. He, who, during a period of fifteen years,
administered the affairs of a great department; who

directed works of such an expensive nature ; who, in the affair of the marshes of Bourgoin, had to contract engagements for so many millions, with private individuals, with the communes and with public companies, had not *twenty thousand francs* in his possession.  This honourable poverty, as well as the recollection of glorious and important services, was little calculated to make an impression upon ministers influenced by political passion, and subject to the capricious interference of foreigners. A demand for a pension was accordingly repelled with rudeness.  Be reassured, however, France will not have to blush for having left in poverty one of her principal ornaments.  The Prefect of Paris,—I have committed a mistake, Gentlemen, a proper name will not be out of place here,—M. Chabrol, learns that his old professor at the Polytechnic School, that the Perpetual Secretary of the Institute of Egypt, that the author of the *Théorie Analytique de la Chaleur*, was reduced, in order to obtain the means of living, to give private lessons at the residences of his pupils.  The idea of this revolts him.  He accordingly shows himself deaf to the clamours of party, and Fourier receives from him the superior direction of the *Bureau de la Statistique* of the Seine, with a salary of 6,000 francs.  It has appeared to me, Gentlemen, that I ought not to suppress these details.  Science may show herself grateful towards all those who give her support and protection, when there is some danger in doing so, without fearing that the burden should ever become too heavy.

Fourier responded worthily to the confidence reposed in him by M. de Chabrol.  The memoirs with which he enriched the interesting volumes published by the Prefecture of the Seine, will serve henceforth as a guide to all those who have the good sense to see in statistics,

something else than an indigestible mass of figures and
tables.

## ENTRANCE OF FOURIER INTO THE ACADEMY OF SCIENCES.—HIS ELECTION TO THE OFFICE OF PERPETUAL SECRETARY.—HIS ADMISSION TO THE FRENCH ACADEMY.

The Academy of Sciences seized the first occasion
which offered itself to attach Fourier to its interests.
On the 27th of May, 1816, he was nominated a free
academician. This election was not confirmed. The
solicitations and influence of the Dauphin whom circumstances detained at Paris, had almost disarmed the authorities, when a courtier exclaimed that an amnesty was
to be granted to *the civil Labédoyère!* * This word,—
for during many ages past the poor human race has been
governed by words,—decided the fate of our colleague.
Thanks to political intrigue, the ministers of Louis
XVIII. decided that one of the most learned men of
France should not belong to the Academy; that a citizen
who enjoyed the friendship of all the most distinguished
persons in the metropolis, should be publicly stricken with
disapprobation!

In our country, the reign of absurdity does not last
long. Accordingly in 1817, when the Academy, without
being discouraged by the ill success of its first attempt,
unanimously nominated Fourier to the place which had
just been vacant in the section of physics, the royal con-
firmation was accorded without difficulty. I ought to
add that soon afterwards, the ruling authorities whose
repugnances were entirely dissipated, frankly and unre-

---

* In allusion to the *military* traitor Colonel Labédoyère, who was
condemned to death for espousing the cause of Napoleon.— *Translator.*

19 *

servedly applauded the happy choice which you made of the learned geometer to replace Delambre as perpetual secretary. They even went so far as to offer him the Directorship of the Fine Arts; but our colleague had the good sense to refuse the appointment.

Upon the death of Lémontey, the French Academy, where Laplace and Cuvier already represented the sciences, called also Fourier into its bosom. The literary titles of the most eloquent of the writers connected with the work on Egypt were incontestable; they even were not contested, and still this nomination excited violent discussions in the journals, which profoundly grieved our colleague. And yet after all, was it not a fit subject for discussion, whether, these double nominations are of any real utility? Might it not be maintained, without incurring the reproach of paradox, that it extinguishes in youth an emulation which we are bound by every consideration to encourage? Besides, with double, triple, and quadruple academicians, what would eventually become of the justly boasted unity of the Institute? Without insisting further on these remarks, the justness of which you will admit if I mistake not, I hasten to repeat that the academic titles of Fourier did not form even the subject of a doubt. The applause which was lavished upon the eloquent éloges of Delambre, of Bréguet, of Charles, and of Herschel, would sufficiently evince that, if their author had not been already one of the most distinguished members of the Academy of Sciences, the public would have invited him to assume a place among the judges of French literature.

### CHARACTER OF FOURIER.—HIS DEATH.

Restored at length, after so many vicissitudes, to his favourite pursuits, Fourier passed the last years of his life in retirement and in the discharge of academic duties. *To converse* had become the half of his existence. Those who have been disposed to consider this the subject of just reproach, have no doubt forgotten that constant reflection is no less imperiously forbidden to man than the abuse of physical powers. Repose, in every thing, recruits our frail machine ; but, Gentlemen, he who desires repose may not obtain it. Interrogate your own recollections and say, if, when you are pursuing a new truth, a walk, the intercourse of society, or even sleep, have the privilege of distracting you from the object of your thoughts ? The extremely shattered state of Fourier's health enjoined the most careful attention. After many attempts, he only found one means of escaping from the contentions of mind which exhausted him : this consisted in speaking aloud upon the events of his life ; upon his scientific labours, which were either in course of being planned, or which were already terminated ; upon the acts of injustice of which he had reason to complain. Every person must have remarked, how insignificant was the state which our gifted colleague assigned to those who were in the habit of conversing with him ; we are now acquainted with the cause of this.

Fourier had preserved, in old age, the grace, the urbanity, the varied knowledge which, a quarter of a century previously, had imparted so great a charm to his lectures at the Polytechnic School. There was a pleasure in hearing him relate the anecdote which the listener already knew by heart, even the events in which the individual had taken a direct part. I happened to be a witness of the kind of *fascination* which he exercised upon his audience, in connection with an incident which deserves to be known, for it will prove that the word which I have just employed is not in anywise exaggerated.

We found ourselves seated at the same table. The guest from whom I separated him was an old officer. Our colleague was informed of this, and the question, " Have you been in Egypt ? " served as the commencement of a conversation between them. The reply was in the affirmative. Fourier hastened to add: "As regards myself, I remained in that magnificent country until the period of its complete evacuation. Although foreign to the profession of arms, I have, in the midst of our soldiers, fired against the insurgents of Cairo; I have had the honour of hearing the cannon of Heliopolis." Hence to give an account of the battle was but a step. This step was soon made, and we were presented with four battalions drawn up in squares in the plain of Quoubbéh, and manœuvring, with admirable precision, conformably to the orders of the illustrious geometer. My neighbour, with attentive ear, with immovable eyes, and with outstretched neck, listened to this recital with the liveliest interest. He did not lose a single syllable of it : one would have sworn that he had for the first time heard of those memorable events. Gentlemen, it is so delightful a task to please ! After having remarked the effect which he produced, Fourier reverted, with still greater detail, to the principal fight of those great days : to the capture of the fortified village of Mattaryeh, to the passage of two feeble columns of French grenadiers across ditches heaped up with the dead and wounded of the Ottoman army. " Generals ancient and modern, have sometimes spoken of similar deeds of prowess," exclaimed our colleague, " but it was in the hyperbolic style of the bulletin : here the fact is materially true,—it is true like geometry. I feel conscious, however," added he, " that in order to induce your belief in it, all my assurances will not be more than sufficient."

" Do not be anxious upon this point," replied the officer, who at that moment seemed to awaken from a long dream. " In case of necessity, I might guarantee the accuracy of your statement. It was I who, at the head of the grenadiers of the 13th and 85th semi-brigades, forced the entrenchments of Mattaryeh, by passing over the dead bodies of the Janissaries ! "

My neighbour was General Tarayre : you may imagine much better than I can express, the effect of the few words which had just escaped from him. Fourier made a thousand excuses, while I reflected upon the seductive influence, upon the power of language, which for more than half an hour had robbed the celebrated general even of the recollection of the part which he had played in the battle of giants he was listening to.

The more our secretary had occasion to converse, the greater repugnance he experienced to verbal discussions. Fourier cut short every debate as soon as there presented itself a somewhat marked difference of opinion, only to resume afterwards the same subject upon the modest pretext of making a small step in advance each time. Some one asked Fontaine, a celebrated geometer of this Academy, how he occupied his thoughts in society, wherein he maintained an almost absolute silence : " I observe," he replied, " the vanity of mankind, to wound it as occasion offers." If, like his predecessor, Fourier also studied the baser passions which contend for honours, riches, and power, it was not in order to engage in hostilities with them : resolved never to compromise matters with them, he yet so calculated his movements beforehand, as not to find himself in their way. We perceive a wide difference between this disposition and the ardent impetuous character of the young orator of the popular society of Auxerre. But what purpose would philosophy serve, if it did not teach us to conquer our passions? It is not that occasionally the natural disposition of Fourier did not display itself in full relief. "It is strange," said one day a certain very influential personage of the court of Charles X., whom Fourier's servant would not allow to pass beyond the antechamber of our colleague,—"it is truly strange that your master should be more difficult of access than a minister!" Fourier heard the conversation, leaped out of his bed to which he was confined by indisposition, opened the door of the chamber, and exclaimed, face to face with the courtier: "Joseph, tell Monsieur, that if I was minister, I should receive everybody, because it would be my duty to do so; but, being a private individual, I receive whomsoever I please, and at what hour soever I please!" Disconcerted by the liveliness of the retort, the great seignior did not utter one word in reply. We must even believe that from that moment he resolved not to visit any but ministers, for the plain man of science heard nothing more of him.

Fourier was endowed with a constitution which held forth a promise of long life; but what can natural advantages avail against the anti-hygienic habits which men arbitrarily acquire! In order to guard against slight attacks of rheumatism, our colleague was in the habit of clothing himself, even in the hottest season of the year, after a fashion which is not practised even by travellers condemned to spend the winter amid the snows of the polar regions. "One would suppose me to be corpulent," he used to say occasionally with a smile; " be assured, however, that there is much to deduct from this opinion. If, after the example of the Egyptian mummies, I was subjected to the operation of disembowelment,—from which heaven preserve me,—the residue would be found to be a very slender body." I might

HIS ANTI-HYGIENIC HABITS.

add, selecting also my comparison from the banks of the
Nile, that in the apartments of Fourier, which were
always of small extent, and intensely heated even in
summer, the currents of air to which one was exposed,
resembled sometimes the terrible simoon, that burning
wind of the desert, which the caravans dread as much as
the plague.

The prescriptions of medicine which, in the mouth of
M. Larrey, were blended with the anxieties of a long
and constant friendship, failed to induce a modification of
this mortal régime.   Fourier had already experienced,
in Egypt and Grenoble, some attacks of aneurism of the
heart.   At Paris, it was impossible to be mistaken with
respect to the primary cause of the frequent suffocations
which he experienced.   A fall, however, which he sustained on the 4th of May, 1830, while descending a flight
of stairs, aggravated the malady to an extent beyond
what could have been ever feared.   Our colleague, notwithstanding pressing solicitations, persisted in refusing
to combat the most threatening symptoms, except by the
aid of patience and a high temperature.   On the 16th of
May, 1830, about four o'clock in the evening, Fourier
experienced in his study a violent crisis the serious
nature of which he was far from being sensible of; for,
having thrown himself completely dressed upon his bed,
he requested M. Petit, a young doctor of his acquaintance who carefully attended him, not to go far away, in
order, said he, that we may presently converse together.
But to these words succeeded soon the cries, " Quick,
quick! some vinegar! I am fainting!" and one of the
men of science who has shed the brightest lustre upon
the Academy had ceased to live.

Gentlemen, this cruel event is too recent, that I should

recall here the grief which the Institute experienced
upon losing one of its most important members ; and
those obsequies, on the occasion of which so many persons, usually divided by interests and opinions, united
together, in one common feeling of admiration and regret,
around the mortal remains of Fourier ; and the Polytechnic School swelling in a mass the cortége, in order
to render homage to one of its earliest, of its most celebrated professors ; and the words which, on the brink of
the tomb, depicted so eloquently the profound mathematician, the elegant writer, the upright administrator,
the good citizen, the devoted friend.  We shall merely
state that Fourier belonged to all the great learned societies of the world, that they united with the most touching unanimity in the mourning of the Academy, in the
mourning of all France : a striking testimony that the
republic of letters is no longer, in the present day, merely
a vain name !  What, then, was wanting to the memory
of our colleague ?  A more able successor than I have
been to exhibit in full relief the different phases of a life
so varied, so laborious, so gloriously interlaced with the
greatest events of the most memorable epochs of our
history.  Fortunately, the scientific discoveries of the
illustrious secretary had nothing to dread from the in-
competency of the panegyrist.  My object will have been
completely attained if, notwithstanding the imperfection
of my sketches, each of you will have learned that the
progress of general physics, of terrestrial physics, and of
geology, will daily multiply the fertile applications of the
*Théorie Analytique de la Chaleur*, and that this work
will transmit the name of Fourier down to the remotest
posterity.

THE END.